This House We Build

This House We Build

Lessons for Healthy Synagogues and the People Who Dwell There

Terry Bookman and William Kahn

THE
ALBAN
INSTITUTE

Herndon, Virginia
www.alban.org

The Alban Institute
2121 Cooperative Way, Suite 100
Herndon, VA 20171

The case studies in this book are based on real situations, but both the names and places have been changed to protect the privacy of those involved.

Cover Stained Glass Window Design by Curtis R Doll Jr., www.curtisgraphics. com.

Library of Congress Cataloging-in-Publication Data

Bookman, Terry.
  This house we build : lessons for healthy synagogues and the people who dwell there / Terry Bookman and WilliamKahn.
      p. cm.
  ISBN-13: 978-1-56699-333-3
  ISBN-10: 1-56699-333-4
  1. Synagogues—Organization and administration. I. Kahn, William. II. Title.
  BM653.B66 2006
  296.6'5—dc22

                              2006036120

        11 10 09 08 07   VG   1 2 3 4 5

To my wife Karen
and our sons Ariel, Jonah, Micah and Jesse
who shared with me
every step,
all the joys
and all the struggles
of synagogue life
And
To the members and leaders
of Temple Sinai in Milwaukee
and Temple Beth Am in Miami
with whom I was privileged to build
two separate houses
of community caring and holiness

Terry Bookman

To my wife, Dana, and our children, Noam, Eliana and Zach-
ary. Each of you—and all of us together—constantly create the
house in which we dwell, and fill it with your heart, laughter,
and all the love that we need. I am forever grateful
for your presence in my life.

William Kahn

In This House
Beth Schafer

Chorus:
In this house, in this house, it all comes together in this house
In this house, in this house, it all comes together in this house, of God

Verse 1:
In this house beats the heart of a family
In this house is the center of a community
We study and we pray, find meaning in each day
In this house, in this house, in this house

Chorus

Verse 2:
In this house is a spark of God's creation
In this house there is joy and celebration
By song or by word your prayers will be heard
In this house, in this house, in this house

Chorus

Verse 3:
In this house we can shelter we can clothe and feed
In this house there is always help for those in need
A stranger makes a friend, becomes inspired again
In this house, in this house, in this house

Chorus

Bridge:
A house of study (in this house), a house of prayer (in this house)
A house of gathering (in this house), from everywhere
How lovely is your dwelling place (in this house), oh Jacob (in this house)
Blessing upon blessing built these walls (in this house…)

CONTENTS

Part 4   Healthy Relationships

ACKNOWLEDGMENTS

For decades, the Alban Institute has been a lifeline for leaders (both professional and lay) of houses of worship. Therefore, their support of this book project should have come as no surprise. Nevertheless, we are enormously grateful for their immediate and continued embrace. While they might have seen *This House We Build* as "competition," the opposite was true. That is a tribute to Alban and its leadership. Special thanks to Kristy Pullen who took over the editing and saw it to completion. Her special touch made that process a most positive experience. Thanks also to Laura Weller, our copy editor, for her clarity and encouragement.

Beth Schafer is a gift to the Jewish community. When we first heard, "In This House" we knew she had expressed in one song what took us an entire book to write. We thank her for allowing us to share her words with all of you. Listen to the music!

Thanks to Lisa Maloney for her help with the many versions of this manuscript. Her dedication to our work is truly unique and deeply appreciated.

And we would like to acknowledge the gift it was to work collaboratively on this book. The struggle to find balance, a voice, and a schedule that worked for both of us, and to meld our different perspectives on synagogues and organizational life, was occasionally difficult, usually exhilarating, and always worthwhile. We have grown from the process as we have from our work at Eitzah. We are, of course, indebted to the many rabbis and synagogues with whom we have worked. Their stories (but not their names) appear in these pages, albeit fictionalized to fit the particular lessons we hope to teach. It is both a blessing and a privilege to work on behalf of the Jewish community.

Terry Bookman
William Kahn

FOREWORD

Did you hear the one about the rabbi and the psychologist. . . ? While this sounds like the beginning of a tall tale, Terry Bookman (rabbi) and Dr. Bill Kahn (psychologist), treat synagogue life seriously in *This House We Build: Lessons for Healthy Synagogues and the People Who Dwell There.* Synagogues, even with their limitations, are the places in which more Jews and non-Jews interact than any other formal Jewish institution. In times of personal crisis and celebration, in times of national or global distress, during holidays, and for Jewish educational programs, synagogues play a vital role as a center of Jewish life. Synagogues are also the place where Judaism is presented publicly. As such, impressions that visitors from all walks of life form from their experiences with synagogues often develop into lasting judgments about the overall value of Jewish life.

According to the last census of synagogues conducted in 2001, there are an estimated 3,727 synagogues in the United States. While no recent, clear records exist on the human and financial capital that this number represents, it is no exaggeration to suggest that the figure is probably in the billions of dollars. Synagogues, then, clearly represent a significant investment of infrastructure and professional and volunteer talent on the part of the American Jewish community. Currently the American Jewish community is poised either to enjoy a renaissance or is at risk to suffer serious decline because of changed demographics. If synagogues can assume a more prominent communal role, and if they can become more vibrant, relevant institutions, they have the potential to tip the scales in favor of renaissance.

For these reasons and more, synagogues require the kind of supportive attention that this groundbreaking book provides. Rabbi Terry Bookman, a gifted rabbi with longevity in the congregation, and Dr. Bill Kahn, an award-winning organizational psychologist, provide readers with an unusual team that combines real-world experience with reflection and insight about how synagogues work and the healthy and unhealthy motivations that move people to involvement in them.

The authors' premise is that congregations can become and remain healthy institutions. Based on their experience, clergy, synagogue staff, and lay leaders may be somewhat doubtful about this belief. The authors are not naive about the politics and behaviors that can make synagogue involvement unfulfilling. Yet they provide a welcome and preferable picture of healthy synagogues as an alternative to the dysfunctional one that often characterizes synagogues.

In this model, conflict and differences, as well as celebrations and achievements, are treated as normal features of synagogue life, just as they characterize other parts of our lives. Denial, avoidance, or abuses of power are often the strategies used in dealing with conflict. Bookman and Kahn instead provide alternative, constructive approaches for engaging with these often painful parts of congregational life. They give us a vision of what is preferable in congregational life and practical wisdom to make that vision possible.

A major contribution of this book is to place congregational life in the framework of organizational systems theory. Professional staff (especially the rabbi), lay leadership, and congregational members comprise this system. This book examines each of the separate pieces of the system and how they can create an interlocking, dynamic whole.

The authors have given us another gift. Finally, we now have a book that incorporates and unites Jewish values with management concepts. Often, rabbis express concerns about the invasion of business "talk" into the synagogue. It is not language that they are accustomed to from their training and often causes lingering discomfort. After all, isn't the synagogue more than a business? Yet lay leaders and members, who more naturally speak this language today, often lack the access to Jewish values and concepts that can guide the business aspects of the synagogue. In fact, when clergy speak about Jewish values during board meetings, some of their lay leaders may not perceive their relevance for the management of the synagogue. Nonprofit management resources, with adaptation, can be very helpful in closing this language gap. But they still require "translation" to a synagogue context. *This House We Build* closes the chasm between the business/nonprofit world and the world of Jewish values.

This volume is useful for synagogues of all denominations and for an increasing number of emerging nondenominational synagogues, for one thing that synagogues share in common is the challenge of creating, sustaining, and renewing themselves spiritually and organizationally. While denominational orientation may color the specifics of how these issues manifest themselves, they transcend denominational boundaries. The case study method of elucidating congregational dynamics gives real life experience to these issues. After reading them, readers may find themselves asking, "How do the authors know my congregation so well?" The answer is that the authors have worked with rabbis, congregations, and seminaries of all kinds for many years and have gleaned and imparted wisdom from these experiences.

This House We Build speaks wisely to multiple readerships. It should be a gift given to every person who serves on a congregational board and to professional staff members, especially clergy. Why? Because one of the weakest links in the synagogue system is board leadership development. There are few high-quality, sophisticated leadership training opportunities available for board members who form the backbone of the congregation. Without a high-functioning board, a synagogue will be only a moderately effective institution at best. *This House We Build* should be required study material for all synagogue board members and can be used effectively within the national and regional congregational arms of denominational Judaism.

This volume will also naturally become required reading for synagogue professionals—especially rabbis, cantors, and executive directors. Those who educate synagogue clergy, whether through seminary training or through continuing education programs, will be sure to want to digest this volume carefully. Hopefully, those who fund synagogues and training programs for synagogue professionals and staff will also want to familiarize themselves with some of its chapters.

There is currently no book like *This House We Build* available. However, just because authors identify a niche first, it does not mean what they write will last. The wisdom and warmth of Rabbi Bookman and Dr. Kahn will likely make their book a classic. While they deserve recognition for their pioneering volume, they also deserve our gratitude for setting a high standard in the emerging field of congregational studies.

Rabbi Hayim Herring, Ph.D.
Executive Director
Synagogues: Transformation and Renewal (STAR)

Part 1

Healthy Houses

1

MISSION, NOT MARKET

K'doshim t'hiyu
You shall be holy.
(Leviticus 19:1)

"What do you exist to be?" This is a question we often ask synagogue leaders when we begin our work with them. In healthy synagogues, the leaders know the answer, and so do most congregants. The answer may have been the impetus for the creation of the synagogue in the first place. It may, in fact, be what continues to draw people to become members. It is the synagogue's mission. A mission statement is a destination. It is not just words that appear on the temple's brochure or Web site. Rather, a mission statement tells everyone where they as a community are headed. It answers the question, "What is this institution meant to do in the world?" In synagogues, missions provide a common ground for congregants, lay leaders, staff, and clergy—that serve to anchor us. And, of course, in synagogues missions ought to grow out of Jewish values and traditions.

"*K'doshim t'hiyu*/You shall be holy" (Leviticus 19:1) is the original mission statement of the Jewish people. It tells us what the Jewish people exist to be—a holy people, a nation of *kohanim*/priests. We are to be unique, a nation set apart from all others. Our behavior, guided by commandments, needs to reflect that principle—holiness—not what is popular, not what is easy or expedient, and not even necessarily what we want. The individual Jew is able to make decisions in his or her life based on this mission. "Does it lead to holiness in my life?" Yes? Do it. No? Stay away.

Similarly, the mission statement of the synagogue ought to shape the choices it will make in terms of staff, programming, finances, and religious practices. Much like the Torah itself, compelling missions serve as touchstones to which congregants and leaders may return, reaffirming them, even changing them from time to time as they struggle with the difficult decisions and choices that confront their synagogues. In healthy synagogues members struggle well together. They return, time and again, to the specific missions that hold them together, serving as a collective source of meaning and purpose. The particular answers to the question, "What do we exist to be?" matter less than that synagogues *have* answers to the question, and that the answers make sense as well as matter to congregants, clergy, and staff. When synagogues are able to develop compelling answers, common ground is created for congregants and staff alike, and that leads to common goals and direction.

A Brief History of the Synagogue

No one is really certain when the first synagogues were formed. Were they in existence before the destruction of the Second Temple in Jerusalem in 70 C.E.? Did they develop afterward as a substitute for that central institution in the life of the people and the nation? Or do they have their roots in the Babylonian exile, long before the Common Era, as a place where Jews gathered to remember and recall all they had lost? What we do know is that from their earliest days, synagogues served three purposes: a house of assembly/*bet k'nesset,* a house of study/*bet midrash,* and a house of prayer/*bet t'fillah.*

As a *house of assembly,* the synagogue was a place where Jews gathered to discuss the issues of the day. Opinions were expressed, arguments took place, decisions were reached. The synagogue was also the place where the cycle of life was marked—babies were welcomed into the covenant, adolescent boys (and later adolescent girls) demonstrated that they had reached the age of maturity by becoming bar or bat mitzvah, weddings were consecrated, and funeral talks were delivered. In this regard, the synagogue served to bind its community members together.

As a *house of study,* people came to hear and discuss the scrolls of the law and lore as they were read. Young children were also educated as the community followed the commandment, "You shall teach your children." But learning was considered a lifelong commitment, so ideally everyone was a student, and rabbis focused on their role as our teachers.

As a *house of prayer,* synagogues were the place where worship was instituted to reflect on the sacrificial offerings that could no longer be made in the Temple. Thus, three distinct worship times were observed—

morning/*shacharit,* midday/*mincha,* and evening/*ma'ariv,* as well as Shabbat
and holy days. At first the liturgy was minimal, but over time it grew and
ultimately was arranged as a *siddur,* or prayer book. These services were
led by someone versed in the liturgy, someone with a pleasing voice.

As the Diaspora grew, Jews took the institution of the synagogue
with them. Often, the first public building a community would create
was the synagogue. It has nurtured and sustained our people in all four
corners of the world, reflecting the art, architecture, and aesthetics of the
community's locale, all the while maintaining its allegiance to its trifold
mission. And we are certain, if travel in space ever becomes a reality, Jews
will create synagogues on each of the planets. In fact, a story is told to
illustrate the mission of establishing synagogues in all kinds of places.
The story goes like this:

> A guy was shipwrecked on a desert island. After many years, a boat
> came to rescue him. But before he would leave, he insisted on taking
> his rescuers on a tour of what he had built there. "Sure," they agreed.
> They walked with him to what appeared to be a small village.
>
> "There is my restaurant where I would take my meals. Over there
> is my bakery. That building is the Federation of Jewish Philanthropies,
> just in case someone came along who was in need."
>
> "What are those two buildings directly opposite from one another?"
> one of his rescuers asked. "They look a lot alike."
>
> "Oh, those are the two synagogues."
>
> "Two synagogues? But you are only one person. Why does one
> person need two synagogues?"
>
> "Well, that is the one I go to each day, to *daven.* And that one I
> wouldn't be caught dead in!"

As Jews, we laugh at this joke. It reminds us of just how contentious
synagogue life can be at times. But underneath it, there is a serious truism
—we need synagogues to sustain Jewish life.

To this day, synagogues must translate these three general purposes—
assembly, study, and prayer—into specific terms and actual practices that
have meaning for them and their communities. A community's understanding of its mission, and even what it means to be a member, is partly
a matter of denomination, history, and location. But it is also a matter of

how synagogue leaders and members define their own specific purposes as a community of Jews. Congregations can make many choices about how they wish to live their religious and spiritual lives, how they wish to take up the practices of prayer, study, ritual, and gathering. These choices answer the question, "What are we meant to do in this world?" The answers must make sense to those who call their synagogue "home."

Choices, Choices

Congregation Sinai (Reform) was formed when thirty households got together because they did not like the direction the synagogue in which they grew up was taking. They desired a more classical approach to prayer with more English and singing led by a choir. They also wanted a small, intimate congregation in which everyone could know the rabbi. They built a building that would be difficult to expand and limited membership to three hundred households.

Bais Yisroel (Orthodox) believes that understanding and knowledge must come before observance. In accordance with this core principle, the congregation endeavors to increase Torah knowledge at every opportunity. As a result, diverse learning opportunities abound at the shul.

Temple Adath Israel (Reform) had its origins in the early part of the twentieth century. A handful of Jewish pioneers came together for the purpose of religious services, a Sabbath school, and other matters pertaining to the moral elevation among the Jewish people of Lexington and Central Kentucky. Its first charter identifies its purpose as "conducting and maintaining religious institutions and religious worship, teaching and training according to the customs of American Israelites."

Shalom Rav (Reconstructionist) is an inclusive community that emphasizes innovation in prayer and ritual, as well as learning for adults and children. It chose its name (which means "abundant peace") in the hope that what it does contributes to establishing peace in the world.

When other synagogues were moving to the suburbs, Temple B'nai Emunah (Reform) decided to stay in the inner core of a large metropolitan city. It operates a homeless men's shelter and partners with area churches on many social action projects. It is not uncommon to see ministers from various city churches preaching from their *bimah* or mixed choirs helping to lead the worship services.

Temple Shalom (Conservative-Reform) is the result of many years of a small community trying to work together to provide for all the needs of its small but growing Jewish population. It represents a merger of a Conservative and a Reform synagogue and holds separate worship services—Reform on Friday evening, Conservative on Saturday morning—to meet the diverse spiritual needs of its members. There is, however, only one religious school, which all the children attend. Temple Shalom is affiliated with both the United Synagogue of Conservative Judaism and the Union of Reform Judaism. Unity of the community has been its guiding principle.

Missions as Anchors

As we can see from the above examples, a variety of factors influence the nature and culture of a synagogue. Like people, no two are exactly alike. Thus, synagogues, in order to be true to their calling, must be mission-based organizations, grounded in Jewish traditions that are given particular meaning in the modern world. Of course they must also come to terms with the realities of organizational survival, expressed in a language that is at once foreign to the idea of spirituality but quite familiar to congregants in their "real-world" lives. This is the language of the marketplace—revenue streams, profit and loss statements, balanced books, budgets, audience, marketability, and the like.

Compelling missions anchor people as they struggle with these more practical issues of financial viability and attracting and expending resources. As stated above, missions serve as touchstones. Congregants and leaders may keep returning to them, reaffirming them, even changing them as they struggle with difficult decisions and choices. There may be a naive illusion that good synagogues should never have problems or crises. In "those" synagogues everyone does their appropriate work, and no one ever complains. In fact, healthy synagogues are resilient. They will naturally face difficult situations and defining moments in time—shifting demographics and declining membership, leadership transitions, loss of significant congregants, scandals. But they will do so cleanly, for their members have learned to struggle well together. They do so because they return, time and again, to the specific missions that hold them together, that serve as a collective source of meaning and purpose.

Mission Statements

When we began to conceive of our organization, which we call Eitzah, the first task we set for ourselves was enunciating our goals for doing so. Did the world need such an organization? Did the Jewish community? What did we hope to bring to and gain from such an enterprise? What would be the purpose of our existence? It was not until we answered these questions and developed our mission statement from our responses that we began to enumerate the programs and services we would hope to provide. And it was only then that we began to network, advertise, and look for potential clients.

Synagogues need to do much the same. They must develop a compelling mission—a reason for being in the world—that takes their members on a journey that matters to them. This is what missions do: they gather people's energies, point them in some direction, and send them on their way. They instruct, guide, and lead people toward or away from certain acts. Indeed, compelling missions help people attain focus and make choices. The world of the synagogue is filled with choices: how to deploy people, time, and money, each of which is a finite resource; how to worship; how to educate children; how to become involved in the community. Statements of the synagogue's mission, succinct and clear, clarify those choices and anchor leaders as they identify paths that are most in line with the synagogue's purposes. Mission statements, when used well, identify what is pursued from what is not.

Mission statements that compel synagogue leaders and members are simply put and therefore immediately graspable. They contain only a few ideas and purposes. They represent consensus rather than compromise, the result of synagogue members laboring to articulate the essential nature of what keeps them together. Mission statements that represent compromise are often large and unwieldy. In an effort to make sure that all people and all purposes are represented, these statements create boundaries that are too vague. There is no particular, special mission that people can sign on to that will engage them fully, that will both orient and limit their work in the world in useful ways. This is what we are after: simple statements that hold people together, represent what they most wish to do in the world through the instrument of their synagogue, and create boundaries between what they will do and what they will not. In the absence of mission statements that ground members in a specific set of values, purposes, and rules for making choices, people often work at cross-purposes and maneuver against one another for scarce resources.

Fortunately, many synagogues create such mission statements. They look like the following:

- The purpose of Temple Beth Am shall be to maintain a Reform religious institution that will meet the spiritual, educational, social and cultural needs of its members and to be a positive contributor to the community in which its members live. (www.tbam.org)
- To promote a spiritually centered community that inspires Jewish values, life, and learning. (www.templeshalom.com)
- We work together to create an integrated and meaningful Jewish life through participatory learning and prayer and acts of caring for each other. (www.re.org/houstntx)
- As members of Congregation Shalom Rav, we connect ourselves to a 4,000 year old worldwide community of Jews, and commit to maintaining the stability, strength, and caring of our congregation and of the Jewish people as a whole. (www.main.org/shalomrav)
- We are a moral force which encourages the age-old quest for justice and righteousness, peace and freedom. (www.bhcong.org)
- Congregation Rodef Shalom, a participatory and egalitarian Conservative synagogue envisions itself as an extended Jewish *mishpucha/family* caring for all its members. (www.rodef-shalom.org)
- We believe that men and women should have equal rights and that the past has a vote, but not a veto. We believe that this allows our warm and friendly congregation to embrace the wonderful past traditions of Judaism while considering our ever changing culture. (www.jrf.org/cjc)

- Our vision is to do its part in ensuring the future of our national community of *chesed*. Youth and Israel are its primary investment: meaningful prayer and Torah study are its personal challenges. (www.yinbh.org)
- Ohav Shalom is an egalitarian Conservative synagogue that is committed to the enhancement of Jewish life through worship, religious education, *mitzvot,* communal outreach, and social action. (www.ohavshalom.com)

These statements of mission are foundations upon which to build. They convey values and beliefs. They are circumscribed: they contain some purposes and not others. They are the products of choices that synagogue members and leaders have made about who they are and wish to be, what they wish to do, and the nature of the conversations and relationships in which they wish to engage.

What people actually do with these mission statements will determine the extent to which they are, in practice, vibrant and compelling. Some mission statements are fully lived; they consistently orient people, compelling them to move toward certain practices and programs and away from others. Others are only symbolic. They may be displayed in synagogue buildings and on Web sites and brochures, but they are removed from what people actually do. Mission statements are thus meaningful only to the extent that they are routinely invoked to help anchor important conversations and guide difficult choices.

Synagogues will always struggle with choices. Clear statements of their particular mission in the world will not prevent those struggles or inoculate their members against some of the pain of making choices. But if people consistently lean upon those missions and refer to them as guides, the statements will help them immensely, just as the body of Jewish laws anchored the Sanhedrin as they guided the Israelites through a maze of difficult choices. The resulting choices will be based on agreed-upon statements of principles and therefore be easier to make and to accept. Mission statements thus allow synagogues to remain resilient, to move relatively quickly through and recover relatively quickly from potentially disruptive fissures. And the mission statements themselves become stronger and more useful, as they are routinely brought into the open, examined and tested, honed like finely crafted tools used well and often.

The Gift

The president of the board of directors at Congregation Beth El called for a special meeting of the executive committee. He had just met with the eldest son of a lifelong congregation member who had recently passed away. The son, speaking on behalf of his mother and siblings, said that the family wished to create an endowment in memory of the father. The amount of money was significant; the family was wealthy, had given named gifts previously, and felt closely identified with the synagogue. The president was initially thrilled when he received the call from the son. Congregation Beth El, like most synagogues, had a number of wish-list projects and programs; the gift could bring some of them into reality.

During his meeting with the son, the president realized that there might be a problem. The family wanted to fund a "soup kitchen" at the synagogue. The son spoke of how often his father had taken him and his siblings, beginning when they were quite young, into the city and stood with them at the soup kitchens, serving the homeless and indigent. His father felt that volunteering to feed people—to care for them in the most basic of ways—was a sacred and profound duty, and he took great satisfaction in sharing that ethic with his children. What better way, said his son, could their family remember their father's commitment than by building such a program here in the synagogue and providing the children and grandchildren of the congregants with the same experience? The president nodded slowly, rubbing his chin as he listened. He thanked the son, told him he was excited about working with the family on such a meaningful gesture, and said that he would share the news with the rest of the board as soon as possible.

The president told the executive committee of the gift opportunity. The committee members reacted in various ways. Several were immediately enthusiastic. The board treasurer grinned, thinking of the recent decline in membership over the past year and the resulting budget shortfall. He spoke of using some of the money to offset overhead that could be related to the soup kitchen idea. Another member who headed the membership committee spoke of how much visibility and publicity the soup kitchen could attract to the congregation, which might well result in new members. A third member said that the soup kitchen sounded fine—it would fit in with the activities of the *tikkun olam*/social action committee, whose list of projects was not yet filled for the upcoming year.

The rest of the committee was silent. The president turned to one relatively new member and asked her what she thought. She responded that it sounded great in theory—who could be against feeding hungry people?—but that she was thinking about the logistics and wondering how they would be able to pull it off. She made a joke about not wanting to look a gift horse too closely in the mouth, but now that she had, she was troubled. She said that it would be a huge responsibility and time commitment, requiring volunteers seven days a week, dedicated space for the program, and supervising chefs. It made her sad, she said, that she found herself thinking about logistics in the face of a family that wanted to do something so significant, but these were real issues to consider. Another member nodded his agreement. He said that there would also be concerns about the safety of the children in the early childhood center who would be on the premises during the operation of the soup kitchen. There would be a number of outsiders on the premises, he said, which posed a possible danger to the children and, more generally, to the building and grounds as well. He hated to say these things, he said, but it was part of the more general issue of taking on a program that they were not equipped to do.

The president nodded. He told the other members of the committee that he, too, had been worried about whether they would be able to pull it off, given their current resources and the demands on them to staff their current programs, which were more in line with their current mission. They were a suburban congregation, he said. Most of the hunger and homelessness problems came from the downtown area of the city. It was clearly an important issue, he continued, but there were other organizations located in the area and dedicated to the issue that had already focused, with some success, on helping that population.

And there was a larger issue, as well, he noted, that he and the senior rabbi had discussed before this meeting. The congregation had recently reviewed the synagogue's mission statement. Leadership had invited the congregation into that process, held several community meetings to discuss it, amended it slightly, and as part of a Shabbat service, rededicated themselves as a community to that mission. The core of the congregation's mission was, put simply, to provide a dynamic, nurturing, spiritual center for the Jewish community. This mission statement represented a hard-won consensus about the place and meaning of the synagogue in the lives of its members. It was meant to guide lay leaders and clergy in deciding where to invest their energies and direct the resources of the congregation and its members.

The board president sighed and said that while it was certainly possible to argue that developing a soup kitchen at the synagogue would sustain a spiritual center for the Jewish community—as members experienced the blessings of *mitzvot*—it was difficult to argue that it would do so more profoundly than devoting resources to senior congregants whose spouses had died and whose children had moved away or to a sister congregation in Israel whose building had been bombed the previous year. Other members nodded. These were programs they had been working on and were just now struggling to get off the ground. They knew that the soup kitchen program, if they took it on, would overwhelm these and other efforts that were in line with their mission.

The executive committee, after much discussion, agreed to recommend to the board at its next meeting the rejection of the gift. Though the money being offered was significant, they finally agreed that the proposed project would distract the community from its mission.

Congregation Beth El had what is known as a "good problem," but it was a problem nonetheless. Whether or not you agree with their ultimate decision in this matter, we think the way their mission statement guided that decision is clear. Without it, they may have decided to go ahead with this program, soon finding they had little to no communal interest or support for its maintenance. When synagogues do that—go off mission, so to speak—they pay a very heavy price by confusing congregants, turning off donors, and wasting valuable resources in both time and money.

We understand that synagogues must address the reality of organizational survival. They must develop programs that appeal enough to the congregation to sustain them. They have to think about fund-raising, marketing events, and maintaining and living by useful budgets. However, there is a danger in thinking that programs and administration equal purpose. They do not. Instead, synagogues need to learn that programs and administrative support should flow from purpose. Congregation Beth El understood that, and their mission helped to get them to that understanding. The board of directors had some difficult conversations. Its members were split, with some wanting to take the money, which the synagogue could certainly use well, and others wanting to avoid the logistical issues that would likely be quite disruptive. Both sides had good reasons for their conclusions. But it was Beth El's overarching mission to provide a dynamic, nurturing, spiritual center for the Jewish community that ultimately provided the framework by which to make a choice. The decision was grounded in the synagogue's core values and principles.

Healthy synagogues maintain a keen sense of the relative place and meaning of the market-driven ethos. They do not see themselves as organizations that are in the business of creating profits and counting numbers. They do not focus on examining where people are, creating "products" for them to buy, manipulating and sating their ever-changing and often trendy appetites. They are not simply purveyors of programs and services that attract customers/consumers, adding new products and jettisoning others simply to gain market share. Rather, healthy synagogues hold fast to their missions and develop facets—programs, services, projects, schools—that make those missions tangible and viable in the lives of their members and their communities.

When the healthy synagogue experiences the inevitable ebbs and flows—in attendance at services or programs, in class size at Hebrew or day school, in fund-raising efforts—leaders do not, in haste and panic, search for purely market-driven solutions. Instead, they look closely at their mission and look closely at how well the things that they are doing in the synagogue live out those missions. They spend time with congregants, engaging them in this process as well. They do this exploration not as a marketing tool or a come-on, but as a process of real reflection on the mission of the synagogue and the ways in which it is or is not being lived out in what people are actually doing with their lives.

In the end, members and leaders in a healthy synagogue use situations that appear on the surface to be problems or crises as opportunities to reflect on their mission. The healthy synagogue is marked by an ongoing conversation about the tensions that arise between the mission, as it has been stated and traditionally practiced, and the evolving needs and concerns of the congregation. Problems and crises are recognized as signals that such conversation needs to occur. Members and leaders alike address themselves to the mission, as one might hold up a mirror, to reflect on what is seen.

Getting Started

Perhaps you are thinking, "Our synagogue does not even have a mission statement. Is it too late for us?" Or, "We've never had a mission statement, and we have a great synagogue. Why shouldn't we leave well enough alone?" Or, "I think we created one of these when some consultant came to our board retreat, but I haven't seen it since." Here's what we believe: it is never too late for a synagogue to create a mission statement. In fact, doing so could be an excellent way to (re)affirm the principles and beliefs that undergird your synagogue's philosophy of Judaism—just like we do with the Ten Commandments on Shavuot, reenacting the moment when our people first heard them at a mountain called Sinai. Creating a mission statement in an existing congregation offers the chance to build community and clarify shared values in the service of deepening what you are all about. Even synagogues that do have mission statements need to take them out for review and possible update every so often.

Sometimes congregations have an unwritten mission statement built into the very fabric of the organization. Members know it, live it, and can share it with others. But at other times, we think we are all on the same page until we are confronted with a major challenge or a crisis occurs. In these moments, an actual mission statement, a written text, can serve as a focus for the congregation's deliberations and decision making. When a mission statement does not exist, we see powerful members exerting their will on the congregation, while others remain silent, afraid to voice dissent. Other communities take the most expedient route, rushing to decision while ignoring principle, often harming members or staff. Such wounds are costly; they leave institutional scar tissue or wounds that never really heal.

Identifying whether a congregation has a mission statement that matters begins with a simple step: really looking at what people do. When people worship, create programs together, work on committees, create *havurot,* welcome new members, or conduct board meetings, they consciously or unconsciously live out certain underlying principles that have come to be accepted as part of congregational life. These principles may fit, to greater or lesser degrees, a congregation's stated mission. A congregation whose mission statement promotes "a participatory and egalitarian synagogue caring for all its members" may, under close inspection, reveal itself to be precisely that: one whose members treat one another respectfully, care for one another, and make decisions in inclusive fashion. On the other hand, it may reveal itself to operate on the basis of underlying principles that go against the stated mission: lay leaders make decisions behind closed doors, older and younger members have little to do with one another, and the board is composed solely of males.

Regardless of your role—clergy, staff, lay leader, committee member, congregant—you have the ability to watch and listen carefully to what people do when they come together. You can look at the gap, if any, between stated missions and the underlying principles that seem to govern what people actually do—not simply what they say they do—when they come together. You can see whether or not the mission statement truly describes life in your synagogue—how people actually worship, learn, and work together. Mission statements suggest a certain spirit, a certain hope for what a congregation will do and how it would feel to be a member. You can judge for yourself whether that spirit is lived out in daily practice. If it is not, there will be signs. Committees will take forever to get things done. Groups will remain at odds over seemingly inconsequential issues. The synagogue will begin too many projects and complete few of them. People will feel disconnected from one another.

Such a diagnosis offers a platform upon which to build a healthy synagogue. The healthy synagogue grows out of open conversation about its mission and the extent to which that mission is lived out in daily life. You can begin such conversations at any time. You can engage others—in committee meetings, during holidays, after Torah study—in discussion about the synagogue and its culture, its feel, its purpose. With enough conversations, a movement can surface: members, clergy, lay leaders, and staff can engage in meaningful conversations about their community's mission, one that will send them on a journey together toward a destination that they find compelling. If a congregation knows where it is headed, it is far more likely that it will arrive there and that its members and leaders will cherish the journey.

2

BECOMING BUSINESSLIKE
WITHOUT BECOMING A BUSINESS

> These are the records of the Tabernacle, the Tabernacle of the
> Pact, which were drawn up at the bidding of Moses, the work
> of the Levites under the direction of Ithamar, son of Aaron
> the priest.
> (Exodus 38:21ff.)

Once upon a time, and not so very long ago, Jews joined synagogues because they felt it was the right thing to do. Some belonged to two synagogues (although they rarely attended either one of them) because, as they might say, "Jews have to support synagogues." Those days are over. Today people join synagogues to get their diverse needs met—deepening their identities as Jews; exploring or expressing their Judaism in the context of worship and prayer, studying Torah, doing *mitzvot;* finding like-minded others to socialize with, or business contacts, or playmates for their children; fulfilling the commandment to educate their children, especially in celebration of a bar or bat mitzvah; finding spiritual expression for the passages of life. While some of these goals may be accomplished just as well in other settings, it is to the synagogue that people go, consciously or not, to locate and nourish their Jewish hearts, minds, and souls.

This desire of people to have their needs met fundamentally shapes the nature of the synagogue as an organization in a number of important ways. Most obviously, people are there voluntarily. We do not have to be there, in the way that many of us have to be at our jobs in order to earn a living. We do not have to accept the dictates of others, in the way that many of us must pay more or less close attention to those who have authority in our work lives. As adults, we choose to be there. This means that the synagogue itself must operate in ways that make it reasonably easy for us to make the choice, over and over, to be a part of it—to show up, pay annual commitments or dues, become involved. The synagogue needs to function in ways that allow us to continue the journeys that each of us take, in our own fashion, as a member of the Jewish community. Once a synagogue loses that primary task—misplaces it, substitutes another in its place, forgets it—it becomes lost to us, and we to it.

Synagogues must therefore function in ways that honor people's voluntary commitments of time, energy, and money that fit with the values and practices of Judaism and that enable their relationships with one another and with clergy to flourish. When these are compromised in some fashion, members often feel disconnected from their synagogue, from one another, and from their spiritual journeys. The synagogue is a religious institution, or more precisely, a Jewish institution. It needs to operate as such—as a Jewish organization dedicated to deepening the Jewish identities of its members—in order for members to remain connected to those identities.

Yet the synagogue must perform another task as well: it must survive as an organization. It must remain financially solvent. It must attract dues-paying members. It must locate resources and use them wisely. Yes, the synagogue is a nonprofit organization that serves people's spiritual and religious needs. But at the same time, it exists in this world; and as such, it must pay attention to the realities of the marketplace. We often find ourselves reminding synagogue leaders that "nonprofit" is a tax status, not a management style. Those who manage the synagogue—lay leaders, paid staff, clergy—must do so in ways that take into account the financial health of the institution, not simply the spiritual health of its members. Without the former, the latter will be difficult to maintain.

Moses, our first "rabbi" and Jewish leader, understood this well. That is why, at the conclusion of the first successful "building project" in the history of the Jewish people, he demanded, and received, a financial accounting of all the materials used in the construction of the portable worship site known as the *mishkan,* or tabernacle. He understood that in spite of the fact that these donations were voluntary (or perhaps because they were), he needed to demonstrate to the people that their free-will gifts were used wisely and handled appropriately. Thus the Torah portion that ends the book of Exodus, known as *Pekude,* begins with what seems to be an unnecessary and repetitive list of the materials used in the project. In fact, it is a public and open accounting, so that the people will have no suspicions of foul play or misappropriation.

The modern synagogue is no different. Its leaders must care about the internal lives of its members—their religious, spiritual, and moral identities—while meeting the external demands of helping the organization survive. True, these aspects are not necessarily contradictory; however, there is always the possibility of tension between the two. Synagogue leaders must take seriously the notion of financial health and responsible financial stewardship. They must operate the synagogue in a businesslike fashion, the better to manage resources, without becoming a business seeking to create profits and wealth for those whose only concern is the so-called bottom line.

The Mess

Congregation Shir Tikva recently hired Shira Stevens as its new executive director. The outgoing executive director had been at the synagogue for twenty-five years. He had been the first and only executive director and had been universally liked, no small feat in the synagogue community. The lay leaders arranged a large retirement party, which was quite well attended, to honor his work and commitment to the community. Everyone agreed that the new executive director would have to work hard to fill her predecessor's shoes.

After taking a few weeks to settle in and get to know the staff and what they did, Shira arranged to spend some time with the congregation's bookkeeper, Helen Lasky, to go over some of the standard reporting information that she would need on a regular basis. Helen had been at Shir Tikva just over twenty years. She was a congregant as well as an employee and knew a great deal of the history of the place and many of its older members. For the past few years, she had been battling chronic health problems, which had to some degree limited her effectiveness. Shira had had several conversations with Helen, each of which was interrupted for one reason or another—a phone call Helen had to take with a congregant, a doctor's appointment suddenly rescheduled, an approaching storm. The executive director was looking forward to finally conducting a thoughtful appraisal of the synagogue's financial status.

As the meeting began, it was clear that Helen was puzzled by the executive director's request. "What is it you want, exactly?" she asked. Shira told her that for now all she wanted was the basic information, nothing special: monthly income and expenditure statements for the past several quarters, using the typical categories; projections for the remainder of the year based on current budgets; salaries and expenses. Shira expected that Helen would reach into her files and begin to show her the statements. Instead, she was met with a blank stare. "We don't do things that way," she finally said. "After all, we're not a business. We're not here to make money."

Shira was stunned. She assured Helen that she had no intention of seeing whether the synagogue "was turning a profit, like some retail store or manufacturer." She just wanted to know what the finances were, in order to help make some decisions about where the synagogue ought to be investing its resources. Shira smiled and kept calm, but inside she was worried. She did not suspect theft or any particularly immoral behavior, such as embezzlement or sweetheart contracts with vendors. But the fact that she could not easily discover for what and for how much people were billed or where congregants' money went once it got to the synagogue was unnerving to say the least.

After several weeks of pressing for information, Shira finally received some reports from Helen. The records were a mess. They were disorganized to the point that it was not clear which receipts belonged to which month. They were incomplete, and information about members' dues and payments was missing. They used arbitrary and overly general categories to track the money going into and out of the synagogue. There was no way to get a real sense of where and how the money was being spent and how much was budgeted to the various programs and services offered by the synagogue.

Shira knew that this was going to be a problem. The board had recently spearheaded the development of a new vision for the synagogue, which emphasized lifelong learning for congregation members. This meant that the staff would need to create several new programs, such as a Shabbat study group and monthly lecture series, which had been talked about for several years but never developed. The new programs would require funds that would need to be reallocated from the existing budget. Without real data about the current financial status, the developers of the new program—and thus the synagogue itself—would be operating in the dark. Shira needed to do something.

She knew of a new computer software package that might help. She had heard of it from several colleagues at other institutions, none of which were synagogues but, as nonprofit organizations, had similar needs for financial reports. She arranged to have a distributor of the software program come and demonstrate it for her and for the new board president, Stan Levi, whom she had apprised of the situation. The software worked well in the demonstration. It promised to be a tool that could clean up the mess and provide congregants as well as the board with great clarity and openness. Stan agreed and authorized Shira to work with Helen to order the software and get it functioning.

Helen greeted the news of the software with little enthusiasm. She told Shira that she "didn't have the time to fool around with new computer games." Shira suspected that Helen did not feel capable of learning a new system, particularly one so dependent on computer technology and the use of relatively precise categories for financial reporting. She responded calmly, telling Helen that she understood that time would be needed to make the transition, which might be difficult, but that it was very important for the congregation that this information be tracked if the new leaders were to put into place the new lifelong learning programs.

Helen nodded, unconvinced. Shira pressed forward with the conversation, trying to be careful but honest. She told Helen that she understood that her predecessor had not asked for this information but that things needed to be different now: the financial picture was different, the membership was different, the leadership and their agenda was different. "We will all need to work differently, too," she told Helen, "and if that means that we need to give you some support at the beginning, maybe someone to help you track the new categories at first, then we should do that." They agreed on several ways to support Helen as she learned to use the system and to review the process after the first month.

One of the central tensions the synagogue as an organization deals with is how to become businesslike without becoming a business. The executive director at Shir Tikva was struggling with this dilemma. She understood that congregants are, in a sense, customers who are owed a certain level of respectful service, which includes creating and using budgets to responsibly manage the synagogue's resources. It was not that she wanted the synagogue to offer specific services simply in order to make money the way that a for-profit business develops, markets, and sells products. Nor did she want the staff to become so enamored of budgets that they lost sight of the relationships and mission central to the community. She understood that programs must be developed with an eye toward funding and marketing, but also that synagogues must be willing to offer programs that appeal to a few as well as to many congregants. Further, some essential functions, like the religious school, will almost always run at a deficit, yet there are few synagogues without one. These are the spiritual and the temporal tensions that shaped Shira's perspective and, indeed, the nature of the synagogue as an institution. Each part of that nature must be honored in synagogue operations.

How can this occur? How can both the financial health of the institution and the spiritual health of the community be attended to, particularly when there may be inherent tensions between the two? For us, the answer lies in a set of four interrelated principles grounded in Jewish thinking and applied to organizational life. These principles are: stewardship, respectful service, clarity, and responsibility. In this chapter, we show how these principles help guide the operations of the synagogue as a religious institution.

Stewardship/Hanhahlah

The principle of stewardship is that resources must be managed wisely and well. Implicit is the notion that the current generation must invest in their religious communities on behalf of future generations of believers. But stewardship may also be understood more broadly. It is not simply the investment and use of money for the purposes of the financial health of the synagogue; it is also the stewardship of the spiritual health of the community. Consider the following *midrash*:

> A Roman soldier came upon an old man planting a carob tree. "Old man," he challenged, "don't you know that you will be dead long before that tree produces any fruit?"
>
> "Yes, I do," the old man replied, "but just as there were trees for me when I was born into the world, so do I plant for future generations."

As synagogue Jews, we must plant certain kinds of trees: they must be hardy enough to compete for the resources that enable them to survive and lovely enough to gladden us spiritually.

Financial Stewardship/*Hanhahlat mahmone*

Lay leaders and clergy, working together, are the stewards of a synagogue's financial health. Certainly, such health depends on a reasonably steady flow of money into the synagogue. It also requires that more money enters the synagogue than leaves, that is, that synagogues not spend more than they have. Financial health also calls for a financial safety net in place that enables the synagogue to navigate through unexpected expenses. These are all signs of financial health.

Synagogue leaders further act as responsible stewards when they make decisions that show concern for the limits of congregational resources. They live within appropriate constraints. They make difficult choices that move their congregations toward some paths—a particular social action project here, an additional adult learning class there—and away from others. Such choices are, ideally, grounded in their synagogue's stated mission, those agreed-upon and therefore defensible principles and values by which the community makes its intentions known. When a synagogue's mission is clear, as we discussed in chapter 1, distinguishing what the community will pursue from what it will not, leaders have the foundation for managing their resources wisely.

What, in this regard, is wisdom? It involves, certainly, seeking and using resources in ways that allow people to achieve what they set out to achieve. It involves responsibly managing other people's money—money that they have not simply spent, as a purchaser, but have entrusted, as an investor, to the religious community. The executive director at Shir Tikva understood that people invest in a synagogue. They invest not as they do in a company or a mutual fund, buying shares and looking for financial dividends. Their investment is of another sort entirely. They are investing in the synagogue's mission and promise. They are investing in their identities, and those of their children and the Jewish people more generally. They may not be aware of this, of course; indeed, they may believe that they are simply paying dues, in return for which their children receive a Jewish education, a bar or bat mitzvah, and tickets to high holy day services. But wise lay leaders and clergy understand dues paying (we prefer the term "annual commitment") as a gesture of investment in and commitment to the community's stewardship of Judaism and its institutions. And they act accordingly.

They act by paying appropriate salaries to professional staff, clergy, and teachers, determined by an objective analysis of external and internal market comparisons. They act by setting annual commitment schedules according to what is fair for the financial capacities of the members of the community, with sliding scales for different segments of the population and a respectful process that enables members to pay more or less according to their individual circumstances. They act by investigating options before making decisions about how to spend money, whether on books, chairs, computers, grounds maintenance, or any of the other items and services that synagogues need to function. They act by focusing on the value received for the monies spent. And they act by investing money wisely, aware that they need to grow their resources while protecting them for those who are to follow.

These are acts of financial stewardship. They are made mindfully, with leaders aware of both their resources and the mission upon which their congregations have embarked, and with board members aware that they are literally responsible for the finances of a synagogue should it fail. Members sign up to go on the journey and pay for the privilege of doing so. They trust their leaders to make the necessary arrangements, purchase the necessary provisions, and supply and "feed" them on their way.

Spiritual Stewardship/*Hanhahlat ruchahniyote*

Synagogue leaders—and in particular, clergy—are the spiritual stewards of the congregation. As with financial stewardship, this means that they need to make various decisions that are in the best interests of the congregation as it makes its way toward the mission that it set for itself. But the criteria by which clergy make decisions about spiritual or religious matters differ from those used to make financial ones. The litmus test for these decisions is deceptively simple: does the matter under consideration serve the congregation in its collective pursuit of Judaism—its identity, practices, and principles?

Each congregation may answer this question differently. Different movements instruct their synagogues differently, and even within movements, there are compelling differences in how people think about their pursuits of Judaism. Each synagogue must thus determine what the best interests of its members are. Clergy are guided in this work by their own beliefs and training. The synagogue's mission offers guidance. And the lay leaders exert influence as well. Spiritual stewardship emerges at the intersection of these influences. It is practiced in specific, concrete terms as leaders make decisions about where to invest the congregation's resources. A relatively small chapel service is added on Shabbat. A Talmud study class is offered for new members. A *havurah* program is created. A speaker series for interfaith couples occurs. A cantor experiments with musical accompaniment for Shabbat services.

Such moments are created as an attempt to aid our members' pursuit of Judaism. Some programs or events will speak to some members and not to others. Synagogue leaders hope that their attempts to do so will be in the congregation's best interests, generally speaking. They hope as well that these elements of the congregation's life make sense financially, attracting members and resources to pay for them. But they do not create such events simply because they will make money or "break even." They create them because they *ought* to occur, given a synagogue's mission. Indeed, viewed only in financial terms, they might not make sense at all. They might lose money.

The primary example of a "money-losing proposition" in most synagogues is the religious school. Synagogues know and understand that providing for the education of its children is certain to lose money, but because such education is central to the mission, not just of the synagogue per se but to that of the Jewish people, synagogues will fund and operate these schools. By being fiscally responsible in how they create and manage these schools and programs, leaders can take the right steps to make sure that they do not lose too much money. But, to be responsible stewards of the spiritual lives of their members, they must ensure that the programs occur.

Such balancing of financial and spiritual stewardship marks healthy synagogues. One does not exist solely without the other. Synagogue leaders and members do not simply create programs haphazardly and spend money that they do not have and cannot possibly raise. Nor do they focus so intently on financial goals that they are not open to the ways in which they unintentionally impoverish members in their search for compelling spiritual experiences. They find some balance, a point where their obligations to create a Jewishly vibrant synagogue and a financially steady synagogue work together rather than at cross-purposes.

Respectful Service/K'vod HaKahal

In the very first book of the Torah, we learn that the human being was created *b'tzelem Elohim,* in the image of God. This core teaching of Judaism reminds us of the inherent value and dignity of every person. We are, each of us, an entire world, filled with our own experiences, feelings, thoughts, memories, hopes, and dreams. We are unique. No one just like us ever existed before, and no one just like us ever will. Human life is sacred. And treating people with respect is tantamount to honoring the divine image within all human beings, honoring the One who created us all. Thus Rabbi Isaac could say in Talmud Sota 40a, "Let respect for the community always be with you, for you will note that when blessing the worshipers the faces of the *kohanim* were turned toward the people and their backs were toward the Presence of the Holy One."

The principle of respectful service holds that congregants, much like customers, are owed certain levels of responsiveness. In the healthy synagogue, the lay leaders and clergy do not simply dictate what will happen and who will do what, with the congregants blindly following. Congregants are assumed to know something about what they want— what they need to learn, how they might best worship, the types of *tikkun olam* projects that will engage their hearts and spirits. Their input is taken seriously. Their requests for information are attended to. They are given explanations. Their dues statements are timely and simple to understand. They receive annual financial statements. They are brought into conversations and deliberations in appropriate ways.

This is not simply a matter of good politics, although certainly it is influenced by the fact that congregations hire clergy and staff members. It is a matter of principle. People in the process of engaging their identities as Jews through congregational life deserve a certain level of attentiveness, for it is only with the support and respect of their leaders that those identities can be deepened. The synagogue ought not put up barriers to members joining in the life of the institution. Members should encounter minimal bureaucratic hassles, information should be readily accessible, and people's ideas ought to be listened to and responded to. This clears the way for members to bring themselves—to worship, to *mitzvot*, to study, to celebrate—without worrying about things they ought not be worried about. It enables them to feel valued and respected. It affirms them as members of a congregation.

At the same time, the congregant is not a customer in the way that a shopper is, looking to purchase items and make special orders. The synagogue is not a retail store. It does not simply offer items for sale. It is not a fee-for-service operation, with a menu of options and prices: this much for a Shabbat service, that much for an adult learning class. It is not, in the strictest sense, a customer-driven organization, in which the customer is always right. In the synagogue, congregational members *may* be right. What they want—some special Shabbat service, a new social action project, a different educational philosophy or school head—may be precisely what the congregation needs. Then again, it may not. Congregants may be moved by a certain idea or practice that, over time, may turn out to have been a fad, undermining rather than deepening their collective Jewish identities.

The principle of spiritual stewardship holds rabbis and lay leaders to a certain standard and responsibility: they must ensure that congregational practices are in keeping with the values, tenets, and traditions of Judaism as it is lived out within their congregations. The principle of respectful service may seem, on the surface, to raise conflicts. What if a part of the congregation wants something that seems to go against the traditional practices and spirit of the synagogue? What if some members of an Orthodox shul want to contribute synagogue resources to a program for homosexuals? What if some members of a Reform temple want to require *tallit* for Shabbat services? What if some members of a Conservative synagogue press for an educational program for adolescents built around a popular Christian youth abstinence movement? What if a

Reconstructionist group wants to reintroduce the notion of Jewish chosenness in the community's *siddur?* In each case, "customers" may be pressing for a certain program they wish to "purchase." In each case, legitimate arguments, rooted in Jewish values and practices, can be made for or against these programs. How are the principles of stewardship and service reconciled?

The answer, put simply, is communication. The principle of respectful service holds that congregants, as adults capable of helping to determine the direction of their own journeys, need to be engaged in conversation. They are accorded the respect of dialogue. Lay leaders, rabbis, committee leaders, and staff create ways to regularly communicate with congregants about ideas and projects. They engage in what is, ideally, a process of mutual education and influence.

In this process, congregants share with leaders their thinking about the kinds of programs, worship and study practices, and projects that excite them. Leaders—in particular, the clergy—share with congregants the visions of Judaism that underlie the congregation's mission. Each educates the other. What emerges over time and through dialogue, ideally, is a meeting place, some negotiated truth about the synagogue that fits with leaders and congregants alike and satisfies the principles of stewardship and respectful service. (We will address this process more fully in chapter 4 when we discuss the nature of change in the synagogue.)

Clarity/B'hirut

The principle of clarity shapes how synagogues can use resources wisely and helps their leaders move purposefully through their tasks. The principle holds that decisions about resources, programs and projects, worship and study practices, and the like are grounded in understandings of, first, the synagogue's mission, and second, all current and relevant data. Clarity is thus a matter of how well the synagogue's mission is looked to whenever key decisions about strategy and resources are involved. And it is a matter of how well anchored those decisions are in available information about financial resources, demographic trends, past practices, and history of the synagogue.

Let's take these in turn. Synagogues need to make strategic decisions, just as any organization does. They need to figure out how to best serve their mission. Their leaders need to decide how to use synagogue resources to the greatest advantage. They are driven in this regard by their synagogue's mission. If a mission emphasizes education, the synagogue must spend money hiring, training, supporting, and evaluating teachers. If a mission emphasizes the centrality of Shabbat, the synagogue needs to energize staff and lay leaders to develop Shabbat-centered experiences, observances, and programs as well as support them with the appropriate resources. If a mission emphasizes *tikkun olam,* the community must invest time and money in programs that activate the community to advocacy, social action, and education. And what if the community's mission emphasizes all of those and more, like so many congregations do? Then there needs to be oversight on the part of lay leaders and staff to make sure the appropriate balance of time, staff, and resources are maintained.

The clarity here is in terms of what the congregation chooses to invest in. Leaders and members need to hold fast to their mission. They need to envision how to pursue that mission and then seek out or create a vision to make that mission come alive. When they hold clearly to their mission, they can do this. They will help themselves make decisions that adhere to their stated purposes. This is not a simple proposition. Different segments of the synagogue's population will clamor for competing interests, and the overarching mission might well be lost. As Jews, we have some familiarity with this struggle. The children of Israel were redeemed from Egyptian slavery for one purpose and one purpose only—to serve Adonai their God in the land of promise. At several junctures they demurred from this task—when they desired to return to Egypt at the Sea of Reeds, when they built and worshiped a golden calf, and ultimately, when they lacked faith in the mission itself. When we lose our clarity of purpose, we lose our way, often with disastrous results. When we hold fast to our mission, much good can happen.

The other sort of clarity has to do with the financial basis for key decisions. The healthy synagogue respects and recognizes the value of budgets. Budgets create a sense of meaning and order. If followed and updated, they provide valuable, indeed necessary, information about the synagogue and what it values. We could argue that the true mission of any particular synagogue—the mission that people follow, not simply the one that they say they follow—is found in how both money and time are actually spent. If you invested enough time in looking at where the synagogue spends its money and hours—in exactly the same way that you looked at an individual's checkbook and calendar—you would know what they find most important.

Synagogue leaders need to know this. They need to know how the synagogue's money is being spent if they are to know whether its real mission is being served. They are well served by reports that track spending, using appropriate categories, and show sources of income, which should always be well documented. These relatively simple financial reports need to be alive—updated, consulted, lived by. They are not simply reports to be filed with the auditor during tax season or to be ratified by board members once a year. They ought to provide information necessary to elicit what the synagogue is actually doing. They should enable leaders to make responsible decisions. They provide the information leaders need to make choices about what to fund and what not to fund. They impose useful limits. Without them, people are, like the leaders of Shir Tikva prior to the arrival of the new executive director, operating blindly, with unforeseeable consequences.

Ultimately, financial reports and the budgeting process frame conversations for people as they struggle to make choices that enable them to steer successfully by the principles of stewardship (maintaining congregational health and tradition) and respectful service (attending to congregants' needs and wishes). A clear understanding of what a congregation can afford, or ought to afford given its stated mission, animates those conversations. At the same time, of course, leaders must make sure that they are not slavishly following the dictates of a budget. Some choices, as we noted earlier in comments about the education program, may not make sense financially and do not easily fit into the budget but have real implications for the spirit and mission of the synagogue. In such cases, synagogue leaders can, responsibly, choose heart over mind.

Responsibility/Ahcharayut

The principle of responsibility holds that people are answerable or accountable for the actions they take and the decisions they make. Like our heroes from the Torah, when called upon they say, "*Hineini*/Here I am!" A synagogue cannot survive unless people assume responsibility. Clergy are responsible for creating the settings for worship and study, and more generally, for helping congregants to explore their Jewish identities. Lay leaders are responsible for ensuring the synagogue's organizational vitality: attracting members, hiring and firing key staff, managing finances, setting policies, helping to create programs that fit the mission, and the like. Congregants are responsible for joining in the life of the synagogue and filling it with their voices: attending services and programs, making their wishes known, and engaging in the ongoing conversation about Judaism with one another and their leaders. Staff members are responsible for performing the roles for which they were hired. Each of these groups is vital to the life of the synagogue. Each is responsible for its portion.

What does this responsibility look like, in practice? Generally, people are clear about what others have entrusted them to do. They have job descriptions, they set goals, they meet regularly in teams or with their supervisors to maintain focus and commitment. Others may appropriately go to them and not be told to go elsewhere. They have access to information as well as answers to questions that might legitimately be asked of them, or they go find out. There are, of course, different levels of accountability. Staff members and clergy, for example, are held accountable for their work in ways different from the ways lay leaders and committee members are held accountable, given that clergy and staff are paid and synagogue volunteers are not. Staff undergo performance reviews, with implications for salary and contracts. Still, everyone, including volunteers, who agrees to be responsible for getting some piece of the synagogue's business done needs to be held accountable. They need to take ownership, not blame or avoid.

The idea of ownership is central to the principle of responsibility. In the healthy synagogue, people feel that they are, collectively, the institution. There is no separation between those who run the organization, managing day-to-day operations, and those who work for or attend it. Rather, people understand that they each have a stake in what happens, regardless of what roles—member, rabbi, board leader, secretary, teacher—they occupy. They are thus each responsible not simply for what they do but for the synagogue more generally. As a result, the synagogue member interested in starting a new program that might be quite costly takes the time to learn about the synagogue's finances and priorities before deciding whether or how to proceed. The lay leader who runs the committee that would potentially approve that new program takes the time to speak with the member and learn about her interests and the interests of others like her within the synagogue community. These are acts of responsibility. They show people's concern for the whole enterprise, of which they are only a part.

People are often reluctant to assume responsibility and might need time to grow into their roles, just as children need time to develop. Consider the bar and bat mitzvah tradition. The reality is that the age at which children become bar and bat mitzvah is not the age of true adulthood. It never was and never will be. Rather, it is the age of responsibility. Our rabbis understood that by the time a child turned thirteen (twelve and a half for girls), they knew the difference between right and wrong. Though they would not always choose the right thing to do, still they knew the difference. And because they did, they could be held accountable for their actions. Such a moment is considered a *simcha,* cause for celebration. But it took time to get there.

It is equally a cause for celebration when our synagogues are places where leaders and members alike assume responsibility and hold themselves accountable for their portions of the work that maintain the financial and spiritual health of the community and ultimately for the mission. Judaism is very big on accountability. We see it in one of the very first stories in the Torah. After committing the sin of eating from the forbidden tree of knowledge, God asks Adam, "Where are you?" Adam tries to hide and then blames Eve. Eve, in turn, blames the snake. Both are punished. Perhaps if they had taken responsibility, we would still be living in the Garden of Eden.

The Principles as Interrelated

We have spoken of these four principles as separate and distinct, but that was only to better explain how each one works. In truth, the four are interrelated, one affecting the other—like the human being who consists of body, mind, heart, and soul. We may talk about these human energies as separate, but we know that each affects the other in significant ways and that life would be negatively affected, even cease to be, if one of these "parts" malfunctioned or stopped working altogether. Similarly, if we wish, for example, to be good stewards of our synagogues' resources, we need clarity of purpose and roles, to take responsibility for our actions, and to provide appropriately respectful service. Or, if we want to assume responsibility, we must first agree to be stewards of our synagogues who understand the synagogue's mission and purpose. Each principle affects the other. They are not multiple-choice options from which we may choose.

Putting the Principles into Practice

Our work as synagogue leaders and members is to create places for Jews to be Jews: to be as spiritual, religious, prayerful, and searching as they wish to be. At the same time, we are responsible for maintaining the organizations in which those journeys may occur—for finding and using resources wisely, for attracting and retaining talented clergy and staff, for ensuring adequate membership. Finding the right balance in all this requires us to have important, sometimes difficult conversations. It is only through such conversations that we are able to put the principles we have discussed here into useful practice. It also means that as a community we sometimes have to make quite difficult choices.

How do we do that? We first need to raise issues that seem to matter to the long-term health of the synagogue. We can do that no matter what our role. We just need to find the right setting in which to raise them. This can happen when a new person assumes office, as in the case study. This does not mean, necessarily, that everything in the past was wrong; rather, it indicates an opportunity to look at things with new eyes. The Shir Tikva executive director wanted financial reports that are normative in any business. She found ways to include the bookkeeper that were private, giving her the opportunity to learn and grow with her job.

We also need to use the four principles articulated in this chapter as a lens through which to look closely at the different dimensions of the issues. This means that we need to ask a number of simple questions. Are we acting in the best interests of the congregation, in terms of both financial and spiritual sustainability (*stewardship*)? Are we treating congregants respectfully, as adults capable of thoughtful choices based on relevant information, while holding to the spirit of our congregation's mission (*respectful service*)? Are we making choices consistent with the mission and based on good information about financial resources and consequences (*clarity*)? Are we each acting responsibly, holding ourselves and one another accountable (*responsibility*)?

Our answers to these questions ought to clarify the tradeoffs that we inevitably must make in the choices about what we and other stakeholders in the synagogue are doing. There are always tradeoffs. One of the challenges of communal life is to make choices that honor the mission of the whole over and above the needs of any one person without causing undue and unfair harm to particular individuals. This is hard work. It may, at times, require the assistance of a third party, someone not involved or invested in the eventual outcome. With or without outside help, the process of clarifying the choices that we are making, and the consequences of those choices, is a matter of engaging in useful, sometimes difficult conversations with as many people as possible.

We began this chapter by noting that synagogues must honor people's voluntary commitments of time, energy, and money in ways that fit with the values and practices of Judaism, while still creating an institution that survives in the marketplace. Consistently striking such a balance is difficult. It involves finding and losing and finding again solutions to problems that challenge the abilities of leaders and members alike to create a spiritually and financially healthy synagogue. By remaining with those problems and looking beneath them to see what they reveal about choices and consequences, we can stay connected to the mission and purposes of the place we call "my synagogue."

3

IS THIS A PLACE YOU WOULD COME IF YOU DIDN'T ALREADY BELONG HERE?

Bruchim habayim, b'shem Adonai. Berachnuchem mibet Adonai.
We welcome you in the name of God.
May you be blessed in this, God's house.
(Traditional greeting of the bride and groom as they enter the *chuppah*.)

When you drive east on Westchester Avenue, the first sign you see when you approach Temple Beth Am is "Do Not Enter." When we pointed this out to the synagogue's leaders, they at first denied the sign existed. They had become so used to driving past the temple's exit that they no longer even saw the sign. But anyone approaching the synagogue for the first time—a visitor or a potential congregant, someone who was "shul shopping," or even someone who had been a member but never really involved—sure did. And though perhaps they would realize it was just a traffic sign marking the exit, they had to wonder: *Is this synagogue sending a subtle message? Is this an open and inviting place, or are they content to be what they are with who they are? Or as we would phrase it, Is this a community anyone can enter?*

This is just a small sign, so to speak, and we might make nothing of it. But our synagogues send messages, in lots of ways, about how inviting they are. Take, for example, the quote at the start of this chapter. Does a couple really need to hear that they are welcome at their own wedding? Probably not. But we do so to let them know just how we feel. We also remind them that the home they will build together, symbolized by the *chuppah*, is also God's house. We thus connect them and what they are doing on a personal level to the totality of the Jewish people. When someone chooses to join a synagogue, whether an individual or a family, we need both to welcome them and to remind them that we truly value their participation.

Synagogues have cultures. They are marked by habits of thought and action that are often unquestioned by members and leaders alike. These cultures are like underground rivers. Unseen, they contain powerful currents that reveal themselves in habits and customs (*minhagim*), moving people to do things in certain ways that, over time, come to be seen simply as "the way we've always done things around here." Culture is inescapable. Organizations routinely develop cultures as people come together and figure out ways to work and relate with one another to create sustainable routines and systems that allow their organizations to survive and thrive. Synagogues are no different. Over time they develop routines that become embedded in people's minds and are transferred across generations of members and leaders.

The culture of a synagogue reveals itself in various ways. According to Edgar Schein (*Organizational Culture and Leadership*), there are three levels of organizational culture. The first level is that of artifacts, what people actually see as they observe the workings of the synagogue. Synagogues are filled with artifacts. These include the procedures and processes by which members and leaders go about their tasks; the language they speak; the classes, services, and programs that occur; the ways members relate to one another; and anything else that might be observed, ranging from the bulletin boards to the physical layout of the synagogue itself. All of these are clues—artifacts, tangible and real—by which underlying, enduring patterns of belief and action are glimpsed. They are windows into cultures. They give us hints of what lies beneath.

The "Do Not Enter" sign was, on one hand, simply a traffic controller, helping to stop vehicles from dangerously entering the exit. But it may also suggest another, unconscious message: that the synagogue is a closed community, easy to join but difficult to enter. After all, the sign could have simply said, "Exit Only." That it did not might well be meaningful. The only way to know, of course, is to have lived long enough within the synagogue to answer the question, "What does it mean?"

The second level of culture is that of espoused values, that is, its professed strategies, goals, and philosophies. Espoused values swirl around the congregation, shaping the conversations that people have with one another. They serve as touchstones for people: in the midst of potentially difficult conversation and decision making, they offer ways to ground people in a shared framework. Formal statements about what the synagogue stands for and its mission in the community and the world offer a lens into its culture. We can see it on the wall of the main office or in the congregation's bulletin, or hear it in the rabbi's sermon. Once accepted, the values that a congregation and its leaders espouse contain the members, hold them steady and together, even as those people come to contain the values themselves.

The third and deepest level of a synagogue's culture is, at its most basic, a set of underlying assumptions: the unconscious, taken-for-granted beliefs, perceptions, thoughts, and values that motivate people's behavior. It is the synagogue's very own "oral Torah," passed down through generations. Every synagogue has one. Certain choices were made early in the life of each synagogue that, since they led to successful outcomes, set in motion other choices that, since they, too, led to successful outcomes, confirmed the first choices and led inexorably to later ones. Over time, members forget that choices had been made in the first place. They simply come to believe that the way it is, is the way it has always been and the way it ought to be. Over time people find behavior based on any other premise inconceivable. The histories of their institutions unconsciously pull synagogue members toward certain patterns and away from others.

It is not easy to see these basic assumptions directly. Instead, this third level of the synagogue's culture reveals itself through its artifacts and the values the organization espouses. In this chapter, we take seriously the notion that synagogues have cultures that range from openly inviting to relatively closed, with real implications for how vibrant and healthy they are as synagogues. We discuss the various artifacts and espoused values that are worth looking at for what they might, under close inspection, reveal about underlying cultures. We believe that a significant aspect of the healthy synagogue is the spirit of invitation. Members are invited into the life of the synagogue in a myriad of ways. They are welcomed sincerely, never forced. They are brought into the place, made to feel that it is theirs to engage with, to change, to embrace. They are themselves engaged, as though they have much to offer. They are ushered into the middle of the place and its activities, and to the extent that they are comfortable being there, they are welcomed, time and again, to remain there as much as they wish.

The Nature of Invitation

One of the first stories we teach children in religious school is the one in which Abraham and Sarah were kind and hospitable to three strangers. This is clearly a Jewish value known as *hachnasat orchim,* "hospitality." Yet it is often not until we are adults that we realize that Abraham was in the midst of a "visit" with God when he "got up from his place, ran to greet them, brought them water, bathed their feet, and helped prepare a meal for them" (Gen. 18:1ff.). Are people more important than God? Hardly. But when we take care of others' needs, we are celebrating the God image that they are. In serving others, we serve the One. That, too, is a Jewish value. Perhaps that is what Abraham saw when he looked up. Not just three men, but three representatives of the One God who is in every human being. That is our challenge as well. Will our synagogues be places where every person is truly "seen" and honored?

What does this welcome mean, in practice? It looks different for different members, at different times. New members, for example, are quite literally welcomed. Even before they formally join, they are invited into the life of the community. There are open houses, in which the synagogue opens itself up to others in genuine ways. People do not simply put on name tags, introduce themselves, and politely listen to the rabbi and board president talk about the synagogue's goals for the year. Rather, they are asked about what they would like out of the synagogue— their hopes, their fears, their past experiences. These are taken seriously and addressed honestly. Current members spend time with prospective members, talking candidly about their own experiences, their own efforts to create meaningful partnerships with other members, lay leaders, and clergy. It is in the context of such conversations that prospective new members feel taken seriously, rather than simply "sold"; they experience themselves as witnessed and seen.

Once they join, their checks are not simply received and cashed, followed only by a membership brochure and welcoming form letters by the rabbi and board president. They are invited to new member dinners, Shabbat services, and programs to get to know one another as well as the leaders. If they are in the synagogue itself—filling out paperwork, completing intake forms, getting information about Hebrew school or adult education classes—the clergy are alerted by the staff and come out to meet these new members and learn a bit about who they are, what they do, their interests in the synagogue. They are well met. They are then brought into the network of the synagogue community. Introductions are made between new and current members based on like interests, and connections are formed. The clergy, board members, and members of the membership committee help run those networks. They understand that the more embedded the new member is in the networks running throughout the synagogue—the overlapping webs of relationships among members—the more quickly and meaningfully that member will join in the life and activities of the place.

Not only are new members invited and welcomed, but in the healthy synagogue, current members are as well. Members are, for example, routinely invited into programs, even those that they might not, at first glance, think of participating in. Adult education classes, caring committees, *minyans*, innovative services, social action initiatives, softball leagues—all are fair game, all are places where members are welcome to involve and invest themselves. These occur in plain sight, nothing hidden. Lots of information swirls about such programs, with flyers, brochures, phone calls, and the like. Activities are announced in synagogue mailings and on Web sites. People know when and where events are to take place and who to call for information and registration. Fees are minimal, as appropriate, to minimize financial barriers. When possible, scholarships are made available, especially to expensive fund-raising events, such as the annual gala or dinner, to allow for maximum participation. People are invited again and again and are given many chances to say yes.

One of the biggest complaints we hear among synagogue leaders goes something like this: "Everyone around here wants this and wants that, but no one wants to do the work. The same people volunteer for everything!" Yet in those same synagogues, when we ask uninvolved folks why they don't take a more active role, they invariably respond, "No one ever asked me." Or, "When I first joined, literally in the first month, someone—I can't remember who—asked me to be a part of a committee that held no interest for me. So I said something like, 'No this is just not the right time for me.' After that, I was never asked again." For us, this is like the sign saying, "Do Not Enter." Leaders, people in the inner circle of synagogue life, often see their synagogue as easy and open. They forget what it might look or feel like to someone who knows no one and who has not been around forever and ever. While we might believe this is a problem only in large synagogues, surprisingly we find it equally true in smaller synagogues.

Healthy synagogues know their members' talents and interests. A member who owns a plant nursery may very well want to be on the

House Committee for Grounds and Maintenance; after all, it is an area of his or her expertise. On the other hand, he or she might welcome an opportunity to do something non-work-related or follow an area of avocation. We know of one synagogue whose gift shop was run by a dentist whose hobby was sculpture. *Chochkies* and sculpture! The question synagogues need to ask themselves is this: "Are we appreciating and honoring everyone's gifts?" Sadly, in many places we see, leaders do not even know what those gifts might be. On more than one occasion, we have heard of folks joining a synagogue, filling out "time and talent forms" indicating interest in various activities, and never getting called about anything they said they'd be interested in. If congregations aren't going to follow up on those "time and talent" forms, they are better off not asking people to fill them out in the first place.

In healthy synagogues, members are also routinely approached to get involved in creating ideas and programs. They know early on of opportunities to develop activities and initiatives. A few people get together, talk about a program for which they have some energy—a social action project, a holiday program, leadership development for new committee chairs— and quickly spread the word, through word of mouth, Web sites, and flyers, that they are looking for others with energy to be a part of something new. These are invitations for members to give more than just their money. People approach one another, even if they do not know them well, because they have heard of others' particular skills and interests and want to see if they can get them involved.

Though they take time, continual awareness, and much effort, these invitations we just discussed are the easy ones. There are tougher ones, as when members are invited into potentially difficult conversations with one another. Synagogue members and leaders are inevitably confronted by issues that, like lightning rods, attract much heat and energy. The mission of education and how it is practiced; the design and spirit of worship services and synagogue rituals; the respective authority of the rabbi and board; the agendas of the brotherhood or sisterhood in communities with great and diverse needs. Any of these, and other similarly key issues by which a synagogue defines and lives out its mission, have the potential to trigger differences and conflict. The culture of the healthy synagogue welcomes these differences. Leaders invite disparate views. They hold forums or town hall meetings where those views may be publicly aired and discussed rather than locked away in closed committee meetings. They help frame those conversations, identifying issues and alternatives and choices and the questions that need to be resolved. But they open up those conversations to lots of people whose voices and ideas are valued. They put difficult issues and choices before the whole community.

This process is not always easy or placid. Not all of the people with energy around certain issues expend that energy in positive ways. Some congregants or leaders are likely to be negative, only willing or able to push against ideas and opinions they do not like rather than joining with others to develop constructive alternatives. In a healthy culture, these people are still invited into the process. They are listened to respectfully. They are assumed to have some valid information even if it is not presented clearly or is not easily taken in and worked with. Leaders and members look first for what is true in what disagreeing (and disagreeable) others are saying, based on the notion that even if they are misinformed or off-base in what they are saying, the fact that they have certain perceptions or feelings means that they care. In a culture of invitation, people are not simply dismissed or ostracized even if what they say is off point or thoughtless. They are accorded respect.

A final dimension of the inviting synagogue culture is the way members are invited into celebrations. The celebrations of the synagogue— the holiday gatherings of *Simchat Torah, Purim, Sukkot,* and the like; the installation of the new rabbi; the consecration of a new sanctuary; the *brit* and baby namings, *b'nai mitzvah,* and other life-cycle events; each Shabbat—are ideally understood as community gatherings rather than events that honor only some segments of the congregation. These moments are not marked by rigid boundaries between those who are formally or informally invited and those who are discouraged from attending—or, more likely, not truly encouraged to attend. In some cultures, celebrations—no matter whose they are or the reason for joy, music, laughter, and food—are simply excuses for the community to come together. The occasion itself is important, but more important are the hands reaching out toward one another in the midst of celebration. While we understand that practically and economically this can become prohibitive, sponsoring an *oneg* or *kiddush* in honor of a family milestone, having an *aufruf* before a wedding, receiving a blessing for a birthday or anniversary at a Shabbat service, or simply having opportunities to share a family's good news—all can be accomplished easily and inexpensively while being inclusive of the entire community.

Creating the Inviting Culture

How do these inviting synagogues form? There are various ways. In one scenario, people discovered early in the life of a synagogue that truly inviting, welcoming, and embedding members in the institution's activities was a successful strategy. Members joined, paid their dues, brought in other members, made the synagogue an exciting and joyous place to be, created innovative programs, and invested themselves fully into the congregation. Through skill or luck, the first leaders of the synagogue hit upon the practice and spirit of invitation and welcome, of embracing members rather than holding them at some distance, with compelling results. Those successes reinforced the practice of invitation to the point that it rooted deeply, becoming an unquestioned, collectively held underlying assumption. Along with the synagogue's Torah, that assumption was passed down through generations of members, giving both meaning and momentum to ongoing practices.

A second scenario offers a less than smooth portrait of a synagogue's creation of a culture of invitation. In this scenario, differing access to the rabbi evolved as the synagogue grew. The founding members remained at the core, insisting that the rabbi meet their needs for particular types of worship practices, life-cycle moments, and educational programs. Newer members were relatively peripheral. Their needs were met only to the extent that they fit with the prevailing culture. This inequality went on for some time. Only when a large group of members left the congregation to form another were the lay leaders and clergy forced to look carefully at what had happened. The congregation was in crisis; suddenly there were not enough members to keep the synagogue solvent. A new group of leaders emerged to lead the congregation in a process of reflection and change. This not only led to a clarification of the mission statement, but more important, modeled a process by which all the remaining members were brought into the conversation. The distinctions between core and peripheral groups faded away, and over time and with some difficulty, the synagogue developed a culture of invitation and welcome.

The two scenarios show how synagogue cultures work. Cultures, because they tend to be enduring and self-reinforcing, create stability. They help people incorporate familiar habits that they do not have to think much about. They create order, reduce uncertainty, and offer guidelines by which to make decisions and choices. They create familiar landscapes into which people can easily settle: the comfort of worship services that remain unchanging, committee work that is routine and predictable, relationships among members and with clergy and staff that are easy and familiar. When these landscapes are inviting to all members and to all clergy and staff, the culture of the synagogue acts as a current, gently bringing everyone along, connecting the past to the present. This is the first scenario we described above. The synagogue's culture, rooted in the spirit of inviting and embracing all members and what they had to offer, remained that way, to the health and joy of the institution. The culture in the second scenario functioned in the same way as in the first: it created stability, familiar ways of doing things that, although painful or disrespectful, were "comfortable" after a fashion because people knew what to expect. Until the crisis, the culture in the second scenario acted the same way as in the first: the river just keeps on flowing along! In fact, that's what led to the crisis. Rooted in the favoring of some members over others, the synagogue arrived at an imposing waterfall, so to speak, and was forced to change by the threat posed to its survival. It was the crisis, the threat to its very existence, that finally changed the culture.

Repair

A decade or so ago, Temple Emmanuel, a Conservative congregation, had won a host of awards for its social action projects. A dynamic, charismatic lay leader whose passion for community projects had inspired a following among the congregation had revitalized the social action committee. He had taken on much of the work of driving the vision for the committee, although certainly others had assumed responsibility and leadership on particular projects. Many of his friends in the synagogue joined the committee, and together they created programs, several of which gained attention both nationally and in the surrounding community for their innovation and effectiveness. The committee held fast to its guiding vision, which focused largely on the local homeless population and recent Russian immigrants. This vision remained even after the lay leader resigned from the committee for personal health reasons.

In recent years, participation in the social action programs had fallen off. The same people who helped revitalize the committee a decade earlier were still running many of the current projects and programs. They complained that the social action focus of the synagogue had changed, and not for the better. "We used to get hundreds of people to our Mitzvah Day," said one of the committee members. "Now, no one wants to work anymore. And very few show up." They also complained that the new rabbi was only paying lip service to social action, not even attending their committee meetings (which they refused to reschedule, even though they were meeting on the rabbi's regular day off). The committee had begun few new projects; the energy that did exist remained focused on the traditional projects of the community homeless and the Russian immigrants, in spite of several other, and larger, community agencies serving the homeless and a significant decrease in the number of immigrants.

Several of the longer-serving members of the social action committee declined to serve another term. The remaining members elected a new chairperson who, as a relatively new member, was neither personally tied to the founding lay leader nor active in shaping and implementing his guiding vision. She understood from her experiences on the committee over the past few years that the committee had too little passion left for the vision but also had little sense of what the new vision ought to be. She decided to consult with the rabbi of the synagogue. The rabbi had often made clear his interest in the social action component of the synagogue but had done his best to let the congregation and its lay leaders own the social action agenda. He did, however, welcome the opportunity to consult with the new chairperson about how to inject some life into the committee and its work.

After a series of conversations with the new chairperson, the rabbi suggested the creation of a task force to reinvent the committee as the *Tikkun Olam*/Repair of the World Committee. He encouraged the chairperson to hold a series of town meetings for the congregation, at which members could discuss what that committee might do on behalf of the synagogue. And he especially urged the chairperson to reach out to people actively involved in the greater community in civic betterment and advocacy issues but not as active in the synagogue as they might be. He encouraged her as well to continue to involve the remaining social action committee members who were interested in developing a new mission, vision, and strategy.

With some misgivings, the social action committee agreed to support the proposed process. With the rabbi's help, the chairperson designed and ran a series of town hall meetings over the course of several months. The meetings were reasonably well attended. Congregants who had rarely ventured into the synagogue for services or other programs showed up and participated. Some were clearly committed to social action in their personal lives and were intrigued at the possibility of meeting those needs in the context of the synagogue. Several volunteered to join the task force.

After six months, the task force recommended restructuring the way the congregation sees and understands social action. Instead of one committee being responsible for all efforts on behalf of the congregation, the reinvented social action group would work with every arm of the synagogue to adopt or create a project based on an annual synagogue-wide theme. In addition, in their own quarterly newsletter, they would highlight individuals from the synagogue who were involved in good works in the community. They also recommended that the rabbi make a *tikkun olam* project a requirement for every bar and bat mitzah.

The task force's recommendation was enthusiastically received and adopted.

The Center Holds

Too often, synagogues keep new people away while professing openness and a desire for "new blood." It is not that the individuals involved are mean-spirited and cliquish; rather, they find it easier to call on and work with the people they know—the ones who cannot say no to them. Often, we like to work with the people we know have the needed skills, who have proven themselves reliable, who will gladly take on responsibilities, or who do not require much direction. As in the case study, the weight of history presses upon people. The initial leader of the social action committee had a certain vision and certain methods of achieving that vision. He attracted others to the committee who went along willingly with, and even those who were enthusiastic about, his vision. The committee's projects were successful, which helped cement both its vision and methods. Its members reached out to others they knew, with whom they felt comfortable. The committee simply continued along the path it had chosen until it hit a crisis created by its failure to make its culture inviting.

A truly invitational culture creates and propagates relationships within the community that enable *all* members to have access to the various arms and functions as well as functionaries—staff, clergy, lay leaders—of the synagogue. Often, we find that members have the sense that some people are "in"—at the center, the core, around which all revolves—and that others cannot get access, are not really wanted. Further, there is no clarity around how someone might gain access. The system is closed. In our case study, the social action committee walled itself off from the rest of the synagogue community. Its members forgot that they were a representative committee, authorized to do work on behalf of the synagogue as a whole. Over time, it coalesced around its initial leader and then around a core group of his followers. Others were implicitly kept outside. The committee thus lost its original purpose as a representational body and substituted another in its place, propagating the initial leader's vision. In taking that vision so seriously, the committee closed itself off as well from awareness of the demographic trends that were taking place in the community more generally. It lost valuable information and resources, and foundered.

We see such disconnections occurring in several ways in synagogues. They occur in the formal structures that make up synagogues, such as when committees become closed shops and are not meaningfully connected to others in the synagogue. In such cases, congregation members have no obvious access to the congregation's formal systems for making decisions and developing policy. And we see disconnections occurring in informal networks, such as when relationships among members create invisible webs linking some people and not others. This often can be seen in the opportunities that some people have and others don't, such as being invited into a lay leadership development process, or may be manifested as cronyism, with some individuals having more access to resources and information than others.

If either formal or informal groups maintain relatively impermeable boundaries, if they are more closed than open, they tend to become stagnant, like the social action committee in the case. Healthy synagogues are marked by permeable boundaries. Members have access to other groups within the system. The "center" of the synagogue expands to contain and hold all members to the extent that they each wish to become involved. Events and meetings are open and well publicized; people are invited to become a member of the ritual committee that influences clergy; members are invited to join in any wide-ranging discussions about their synagogue and its mission. Committees share information freely and invite board members, representatives of other committees, clergy, relevant staff, and the community more generally into their worlds as appropriate. The committees are not archipelagos—disconnected islands in the sea of the synagogue. Instead, they form a chain of islands connected by bridges of openness, trust, and understanding.

Similarly, the informal networks of relationships that exist below the radar of the synagogue—old friends, study groups, parents of same-grade children, choirs, softball players, ushers—form and bond but are not so closed off that others are pushed away from synagogue life and activities. No cliques are so strong that they act as informal power centers, where relationships determine influence and access. There is no shadow government. Activities at the heart of the synagogue are never "by invitation only." On some level, of course, this openness may go against our natural desires for comfort and familiarity. We tend to gravitate toward the same people and over time, trust them more than we trust those with whom we have no experience. But we need to fight against this tendency and seek out the relatively minor discomfort created when new people and ideas are incorporated in our synagogues.

In synagogue life, there is often yet another twist on the nature of influence. It is widely (and sometimes accurately) assumed that the big givers in synagogues have the most influence and access to clergy. The natural inclination is to accord them outsized influence, to treat them as an inner circle and attend more carefully to their wishes, as well as put their names on plaques and name building wings after them. The danger of doing so is that it excludes others, rendering them less important to the synagogue; it creates a class system, suggesting the possibility that special relationships corrupt a more transparent decision-making process and undermine the reliance on the mission as anchor. Such "big givers" may make it possible for the synagogue to be financially healthy, but if the overall culture is not healthy, this financial well-being will only serve to alienate some members at the expense of catering to others. This pattern creates casualties: people who are kept on the outside become alienated and drop out or distance themselves. This sends a message to the entire community: people need to compete for the center, in which there is often limited room.

It is thus crucial to a healthy culture that the center is expansive and its boundaries are somewhat permeable. What does that mean? That the synagogue is flexible enough to invite and include a variety of people: older members, new singles, young parents, social activists, the keenly observant, intellectuals, and so on. Each group must feel as if they can join activities and decision-making processes that matter to them. In our case study, the rabbi's key intervention was to open up the process. He helped the committee invite all sorts of others into the social action work and in so doing, expanded its viability, vibrancy, and ultimately its influence in and representation of the synagogue's mission more generally.

Are We an Inviting Congregation?

Most synagogue leaders as well as veteran members believe theirs is a warm and welcoming congregation; after all, they were welcomed in, became members, got involved, and have remained loyal. They also know that a synagogue's very survival is dependent on its ability to attract and engage new members. And so, to believe otherwise, to regard their beloved home away from home as anything but warm and welcoming, is to entertain its certain demise. As is true in much of Jewish life, we prefer to examine actions and words rather than feelings to determine what is real and what is not. Judaism is a "show me" religion, relying on deed rather than creed. We describe here some of the ways in which invitations are issued—or not—in synagogue life.

The Intake Form. Most synagogue intake forms ask for names, addresses, and dues level. Some contain a list of committees one might consider joining. However, few synagogues ever really ask about a person's interests, talents, hobbies, and the like. While most list occupations, by and large they do not ascertain what a person actually does at work. We might know someone is an attorney, for example, but not what kind of law he or she practices. Or we might assume that members are part of traditional Jewish families and grew up that way and thus might request everyone's Hebrew names, implicitly excluding intermarried couples. Or it might use the language of "husband" or "wife," implicitly excluding anyone living with a partner. Or it might ask for one's childhood synagogue affiliation, implicitly excluding those who became Jews by choice. Intake forms thus need to be examined for the messages that they send about who is invited in and who is not. Not every synagogue needs to be open to everyone in the extended Jewish community. *Halachic* norms might dictate who can be a member and who cannot in a specific synagogue. This needs to be communicated openly and honestly, and the intake form is a clear place to do so: it lets prospective members know immediately if a synagogue really wants them.

Office of First Impressions. Whatever we call it, that's what it is. So who and what do people see when visiting your synagogue? How are they greeted? Where do they wait to see the rabbi or the principal of the religious school? Even prior to that, what is the first voice they hear when they call the shul? If they hear an automated answering service, as is increasingly the case in many synagogues, is the voice someone from your staff or computer generated? Are the prompts easy to understand and use? Is the information timely and useful? Does it give an accurate impression of the activities and life of the congregation? Does one have to wade through lots of prompts that could be meaningless to the average caller? We call lots of synagogues that have no greeting but force the caller to listen to service times and Hebrew school calendars before allowing us to leave our message. Imagine what that might sound like to an unmarried individual without children wanting some information on an advertised program.

The Entrance. We know that many synagogues are rightfully concerned with security these days. This should not mean, however, that a visitor needs to guess the location of the entrance. We worked with one synagogue that claimed to be in need of new members but required an

adventurous and determined spirit just to find a way to enter the building. And once we found the secret portal, it was anyone's guess where to
go to find a receptionist, the rabbi, or any other human being. Again,
this "secret entrance" may seem like "no big deal" to those who know
their way around, but it may be sending a cultural message about the
nature of invitation that perhaps is not intended. Messages are sent in
other ways as well. Are spaces clearly marked in the synagogue parking
lot? Are there spaces set aside for visitors? Are buildings accessible to
people in wheelchairs, on crutches, the elderly? Are those buildings neat
and clean? Are the grounds well maintained? Are waiting areas comfortable, free of clutter, with interesting things to read? If there is art on the
walls, is it inspiring? Does it create warmth and a sense of home or community? Is the message one of welcome, that people are wanted, invited
in and made comfortable, or is it a perhaps not-so-subtle message of "stay
away" or "members only"?

   The *Shmmes* or Greeter. Growing up, we remember Mr. Feingold,
the ever-present beadle or *shmmes* of the shul who was always at the door
of the sanctuary handing out *siddurim,* showing bare-headed males the
collection of *yarmulkes* or *kippot,* helping someone put on a *tallit.* Having greeters at the entrance of the worship space not only sends a message
of welcome, but it allows newcomers to enter a little less nervously, take
an appropriate seat, and ease into the worship experience itself. This is
often an awkward moment, even for the veteran shulgoer; how much the
more so for a new visitor, a non-Jew, or a recent Jew by choice. A friendly
smile, a Shabbat shalom or *gut Shabbos,* and a hand pointing in the right
direction go a long way in turning this potentially uncomfortable moment into a pleasant one. Just as we would never allow someone to come
into or leave our home without being greeted, so no one should be able
to do so in our communal home, our synagogue.

   Web sites. Web sites offer a relatively easy way to invite others into
the culture and activities of a synagogue. However, if they are difficult to
navigate, that sends its own message. In considering your Web site, ask
the following questions: Does it contain information that is both accurate and timely? Does it allow one to get to know the institution—its
history, its mission, the values and principles that guide its decision making, the main players? Does it have contact information, including the
contact person's name, title, phone number, and e-mail address? Are all

inquiries responded to in a timely fashion? No one who sends an inquiry—to the rabbi, the president, the membership chair, the director of
education—should have to wait more than forty-eight hours for a response. A quick response may well be the single most important factor in
determining if prospective members actually join a specific congregation.

The Worship Service and the *Oneg/Kiddush*. We often hear from
unaffiliated or even marginally affiliated people that they attended a service at such-and-such synagogue and no one came up to them to say
hello, either during the service or even afterward at the *oneg* or *kiddush*.
That should never happen. While each synagogue will have to figure out
the best way to do this in their own congregation, here are the questions
you might want to consider: Are newcomers to a service or program
identified with a "visitor" name tag? Are there regulars whose task it is to
greet people they do not recognize? Or does this just naturally happen? Is
it part of the worship service experience? We heard of one congregation
that taught members to say, "I don't think I know your name; I'm so-
and-so"—a neutral greeting that made room for the possibility that the
person being greeted was already a member! Are visitors offered honors
during the service—to open the ark or have an *aliyah* to the Torah? Are
newcomers invited to peoples' homes for Shabbat? Is there someone who
can respond to their inquiries about the synagogue? Will someone introduce them to the rabbi or cantor? How welcoming a synagogue is does
not depend on its size. We have heard of many large institutions that
have a system for making everyone feel welcome and smaller ones that do
a poor job at this. The inviting synagogue makes everyone feel welcome
and glad they came to shul that day.

Committees. Committees are the lifeblood of the healthy synagogue.
Ideally, no program or no activity should take place without a committee
to support it. The issues here focus on the nature of people's involvements. Is it clear to members how they can become involved? Are all
committees open to anyone who wants to join them, or do they have to
be invited by the committee chair or president? If an invitation is required, how does one get invited? Do committee members have "job
descriptions"? Do they know what is expected of them? Successful experience working on a committee helps turn a member into an engaged
stakeholder, yet we often find that the method for joining a committee is
one of those well-guarded secrets that prevents rather than encourages

participation. Healthy synagogues invite people into meaningful committee opportunities.

Honors and Plaques. Synagogues seem to have a penchant for plaques, walls of honor, trees of life, and so on. Other than *yahrtzeit* boards (which are, in one form or another, a necessity), we need to examine the messages that these plaques convey. The central issue concerns what people in a synagogue community are honored for. Are they honored for monetary gifts? Service to the community? Study of Torah? Where and how are these honors displayed? Do we see the same names again and again? While we say giving time is as important as giving money, the bad joke about the Jewish community is that synagogues are governed by the "Golden Rule"—he who has the gold, rules. Plaques, newsletters, and Web sites might well communicate that rule without intending to do so. We understand the need to honor those whose generosity extends to their temple. When someone is generous, he or she deserves recognition. And being grateful is certainly a Jewish value. The question is, do monetary gifts allow for greater access and privilege? And if they do, what sort of message does that send to the congregation as a whole, as well as to a prospective member? We think it goes something like this: the only people who count around here are those who can afford to write big checks. In healthy congregations, access and privilege need to be equally open to all.

Seeing the Rabbi. We are often surprised by people's assumption that they do not have access to the rabbi in their congregation. They assume that the rabbi is too busy to be bothered, except in time of life-cycle need, *simchas* or sorrows. While not every rabbi can have an "open door" policy, in healthy congregations, rabbis are available and relatively easy to see. How one schedules an appointment to see the rabbi should never be a secret known only by the select few initiated in synagogue mystery. Rather, it should be uncomplicated and well known to every member. The rabbi needs to be the rabbi for everyone. Of course, in larger congregations with more than one rabbi, people may have attachments to different rabbis. However, every member of the congregation should hold the feeling that one can see the senior rabbi when one wants or needs to.

Membership Policies. The gates of different synagogues are not the same width. Every synagogue needs to decide who can and cannot be a member. Criteria must be clear and broadly communicated. These decisions are often determined by *halacha* and how synagogue leaders interpret those laws in the context of the stated mission. A synagogue may be an open and welcoming place, but that invitation may go out to only a limited segment of people. If a gay couple, for example, would not feel comfortable at the synagogue's annual dinner dance, that needs to be carefully and lovingly communicated before they join or before the dance. A synagogue might strike a particular stance about welcoming those not born into Judaism. One of the realities of the twenty-first century in North America is that the Jewish community is increasingly comprised of individuals who were not born Jewish—both those who chose Judaism as an adult, as well as the non-Jewish spouses in interfaith couples. Add to that children who are not being raised Jewish but who have a Jewish parent and/or grandparent, together with those who are discovering "Jewish roots" and are now exploring Jewish life, and the extended families of all these people, and what was once a small fringe is now a significant number of people who are being newly touched by Jewish life today. Whether or not these individuals will have a place in a particular synagogue will depend on members' espoused values (often determined by *halacha*) and underlying assumptions. Synagogues need stated policies about who can actually be a member; who can serve on the board or on a committee; who can go up on the *bimah* or have an *aliyah* to the Torah; and who can attend religious school or day school (e.g. children who are not being raised Jewish or who are being raised in two faiths). Such questions cut to the core of who can be a full-fledged, participating member of a synagogue.

Language. The ways synagogue members and leaders talk send messages about the extent to which they truly invite and welcome others. These messages are encoded in the very language that they use. In some synagogues, for example, words like *goy, shiksa,* and *shaygetz* are used openly. One member might say in passing to another, "Once a *goy,* always a *goy,*" and the remark goes unchecked. Or people disparage others on committees ("The membership committee is a bunch of . . ."), across generations ("The new leaders don't know half as much as we who built this place do"), or in different social groupings ("The Jews from the West Side aren't very sophisticated"). The use of such language—categorizations, stereotypes, projections—builds invisible walls that block people off from one another. It creates barriers where none ought to exist, robbing the synagogue of the energy it requires to be a vibrant institution.

Town Hall Meetings. Synagogues, because they are not-for-profit corporations, are required by law to have an annual meeting of the membership. In some synagogues, these are well-attended, big events. In other synagogues, blink and you miss them. But when difficult decisions need to be made—regarding the purchase of land for synagogue expansion, the creation of a soup kitchen to feed the city's homeless, a major shift in focus in the religious school curriculum—what is the role of the "rank and file" members of the congregation? Has the decision, in fact, already been made and now only need to be "sold" to the members to make it kosher? Or do the leaders, having thoroughly investigated a course of action, really want to hear from members? The healthy congregation invites real input at several stages along the path of congregational decision making. While appropriate authority is taken up by leaders, both professional and lay, the thoughts, insights, values, and feelings of each member of the community are sought and genuinely considered because they are truly valued. A town hall meeting ought not, therefore, be just a show. It needs to be a meeting place for hearts, minds, and spirits to engage in what is important to and cherished by them—their synagogue community.

The Bulletin. Not everyone reads the temple bulletin, but a lot of people really do. Most bulletins are the work of a single individual (paid or volunteer) and contain a message from the rabbi and other senior staff plus the president of the congregation. The rest of the bulletin is usually devoted to announcements of future programs, highlights of past programs, *yahrtzeit* lists, upcoming *b'nai mitzvah*, photos, and donor lists. Very rarely do we see articles or letters by congregants. Almost never do we see anything that remotely resembles controversy. We suspect that this is not a result of everyone always agreeing with everything happening at the synagogue. The bulletin has the potential to be a place for inclusion: a place where congregants offer their feedback on the rabbi's sermons, their assent/dissent with a new program or policy; their own interpretation of the weekly *parasha*. The bulletin can be a community newsletter—*by* the community, not just *for* the community. And this concept can be expanded to the synagogue's Web site as well. Chat rooms, text message postings, *simchas* and sorrows boards all can be used to help develop a spirit of community and invitation, breaking down some of the isolation and alienation that are so much a part of contemporary life.

Inspiring a Healthy Culture

Creating a healthy synagogue culture is difficult but important work. It means paying attention to each of the areas that we just described. Each posts signs of how inviting the synagogue is to the various groups of people who enter it to meet their needs and interests. When such attention is not paid, certain disquieting symptoms and patterns emerge. Groups of members agitate to be heard, resorting to unpleasant methods, such as passing out leaflets or petitions. Some groups become alienated and withdraw from the community. Committees isolate themselves and act independently. A board grows out of touch with the membership. People stop volunteering, to the point that the same few people shoulder all the responsibility and others do very little. These are all signals about the culture of the synagogue, for better or for worse.

Altering a culture takes time. Cultural dimensions are embedded in a synagogue's DNA and get handed down through generations. They change only when people make a concerted effort to do so. People need to begin with espoused values—what they say, the missions they articulate, the visions they say they will pursue, the slogans they coin. And they need to begin with the artifacts—the observable aspects of what they actually do. Over time, they can then work more deeply into an understanding of the underlying, basic assumptions that have driven their thoughts, perceptions, feelings, and behaviors for so long.

Inspiring an inviting, healthy culture depends primarily on people committing themselves to opening up their synagogues to multiple voices. This is not easy. When there are lots of voices, it gets loud. It gets noisy. There is a cacophony, and less often, harmony. People disagree, and struggle, and take a long time to resolve issues and make decisions. Yet this is the mark of a synagogue that is vibrant, alive to various interests and possibilities, inviting to all sorts of people, and welcoming to all the aspects of who they are and wish to be. People are not circumscribed; they do not need to fit into some box that makes them easily understood. When this is done, they may be taken in, but in the process important parts of who they are may be left outside the synagogue's walls. When congregants are truly invited in and welcomed, they are liberated to think, to feel, to pray, to study, to mourn, and to celebrate as fully as they possibly can.

4

WHY CAN'T WE SING THE TRADITIONAL *OSEH SHALOM?*

Customs are more powerful than laws.
(Talmud, Yebamot, 61a)

Synagogues are places where Jews go to pray, learn, and become part of a religious and spiritual community. But they are more than that. They are also places where we go to feel a deep sense of comfort and familiarity. Many of us find great pleasure in singing the prayers and songs as well as humming the melodies with which we grew up. Holiday festivals stir up deep-seated memories of our childhoods. Rituals offer us a sense of connectedness to generations in our pasts, our own and those of the Jewish people. Even the physical surroundings—the light coming through the stained glass, the feel of the seat cushions, the way the ark opens, the smell of old wood—all these sensory experiences create in us a sense of the way a shul should be.

In such ways, the sights and sounds of a synagogue can be emotionally powerful for us, just as the scent of a cigar might evoke thoughts of our grandfathers, the whiff of perfume our grandmothers, or the taste of chicken soup the holiday meals where we were surrounded by our families. When we settle into our seats in the sanctuary or file into the communal *sukkah*, there is always some part of us that longs to hear songs or words that are profoundly familiar. It is that familiarity that keeps us connected to our past, and to the extent that we let it do so, touches us deeply.

This experience of deep familiarity is part of what we often find comforting and meaningful about synagogues. It is what keeps many of us going to synagogues when we have so many other ways to find community. It is also what makes synagogue life so complicated at times. The comfort that we find in tradition is often in tension with our need for change. We wish to be part of Jewish communities that are vibrant, growing, and in step with the world around us. This vibrancy often requires change—in programs, worship practices, educational curricula, and holiday celebrations. Yet such changes may disturb the familiar. They may disrupt the very sense of comfort and familiarity that attracts members to their synagogues.

This tension between the familiar and the new exists in every synagogue. Clergy, lay leaders, staff, and congregants each carry the tension, with some more aware of it than others. Decisions both large and small occur against the backdrop of the trade-offs between what is traditional and familiar—the way that Jews in this or that synagogue have been practicing for years, or Jews more generally for thousands of years—and what seems new and vibrant, given shifting demographics and cultural trends. The central question, in relation to this tension, is how we can honor and build upon the past while embracing innovations that serve the shifting interests of congregants and clergy. As the quote above indicates, changing long-standing patterns of behavior—customs, the way things are done around here—is more difficult than even changing a law.

Between the Past and the Future

Religion itself is caught in the historical tension between its nature as a conserving force and its nature as a force for change. The driving force for change during the civil rights movement in this country came from the pulpits of churches and synagogues, just as it did during abolitionist days. Yet others, citing the Bible's acceptance of slavery, urged a continued subjugation of the races. Today "family values" is a loaded term that means "the traditional family unit" for some, with others pressing for new definitions of family to include gay unions, with or without children, single-parent families, couples who live together and have children, as well as blended families. In these instances, as well as many others, religion is challenged to be a voice for tradition and consistency on the one hand and a voice for societal change on the other.

Certain demographic changes in the American Jewish community over the past century have also placed a fair amount of pressure on synagogues to change. The decline, and in some cities the disappearance, of the Jewish neighborhood has redefined the whole notion of community. With the exception of some orthodox enclaves, most Jews today feel a part of several communities that compete for their time and loyalties.

Early in the twentieth century, the large influx of uneducated Jews from Eastern Europe, accustomed to the authority of the rabbi, helped maintain Jewish norms. Today a highly educated native-born American Jewry, whose participation in synagogue life is totally voluntary—that is, who feel few pressures, either social or economic, to belong to a synagogue—is far less dependent on the authority of the rabbi. It is safe to say that in almost all parts of the Jewish world, a rabbi's power is persuasive at best, and hardly authoritative.

But that is not all. The feminist movement, combined with a quality Jewish education for women, has raised expectations of women's equality and participation in Jewish life. Women rabbis, cantors, educators, and synagogue leaders have become normative almost universally in the Jewish world. These factors, together with women's increased role in the workplace, have created new parenting styles with fathers much more hands-on in the raising of their children. Our fathers did not even know where the diapers were kept in the house. We (Bill and Terry) have changed our fair share and never referred to our alone time with our children as "babysitting." These changes in men's and women's roles mean that synagogues have had to become more family friendly, with equal opportunities for both men and women to participate.

Day school education and Jewish camping have raised expectations for both involvement and participation in synagogue life as well. We have a laity that is better versed in Jewish tradition and more capable in Jewish practices, living a more focused Jewish life at home that desires the synagogue to be a partner with them (not a dictator) in creating a sense of community. The growth and influence of the *havurah* movement in the 1960s and 1970s, as well as the Jewish renewal movement today, demonstrate that contemporary Jews want to take ownership of their Jewish lives and identities. They have become far less dependent on the power and authority of the rabbi and synagogue.

Perhaps one of the more divisive issues to confront the Jewish community in the past few decades has been the question of who is a Jew. The successes in combating discrimination against our people have culminated in a society that is open and desirous of Jewish membership and participation. Whereas once upon a time, universities, exclusive neighborhoods, hospitals, country clubs, and certain industries endeavored to keep Jews out, today they actively recruit us. One result of this open society is intermarriage. While once that meant a Jew was trying to distance himself or herself from the Jewish world, that is no longer the case. Today tens of thousands of children are being raised as Jews by Jewish fathers and non-Jewish mothers. Most of these children think of themselves as Jews or at least as "part-Jewish." What will be their role in the Jewish future? Will they be accepted without the benefit of a formal conversion? Our guess is that their numbers will continue to grow. How will synagogues accommodate them?

These demographic trends have not been simply and wholly embraced or accommodated. Various synagogues and the Jewish movements that inform and shape their practices and beliefs digest them in different ways. Indeed, the differences among the movements themselves can be understood in part according to how they react to pressures to change. We want to be very clear. *All* the denominational movements face this pressure. All note conflicts between the generations. All need to deal with issues surrounding change. And the decisions of one movement do affect the deliberations of the others since, no matter what the stance of the rabbis, laity from various movements do interact with one another.

While we do not want to oversimplify, we do believe the history of these denominational movements helps us see how they have played out their roles as "protectors of the tradition" on the one hand and "innovators with the tradition" on the other. Reform Judaism began in Europe to do just that—"reform" Judaism—by accommodating certain practices that its leaders believed were in keeping with a spirit of modernity and at the same time true to the spirit of their ancestors. With the reform movement coming to North America, the pace of change intensified, so that by the end of the nineteenth century, the Pittsburgh Platform could state:

> We recognize in the Mosaic legislation a system of training the Jewish people for its mission during its national life in Palestine, and today we accept as binding only the moral laws and maintain only such ceremonies as elevate and sanctify our lives, but reject all such as are not adapted to the views and habits of modern civilization.

In one fell swoop, Reform Judaism did away with almost all ritual particularism. Such changes were resisted by more traditional Jews, giving rise to both the conservative movement, which sought to "conserve" the essence of the tradition in a spirit of historic change, and Orthodoxy, which, seeing itself as a bulwark against the shifting sands of modernity, intended to define the "correct doctrine" that was not subject to change. Later in the twentieth century, following the thinking of Rabbi Mordechai Kaplan, the Reconstructionist movement was created to reframe Judaism in an American context, revisioning Judaism as a culture or civilization and the synagogue as a center of community. And now, with the advent and growth of Jewish renewal, as well as new nondenominational seminaries for the training of rabbis, one could argue that each of the denominations has created its own norms, which are now resistant to change.

None of these movements is monolithic; there are often marked differences from synagogue to synagogue or rabbi to rabbi. Further, offshoots within each of these branches define themselves very differently from one another. This is especially true in Orthodoxy. Nevertheless, the movements to which they belong shape how particular synagogues manage the tension between tradition and change, by their importing certain stances and philosophies into their underlying structures and shaping, implicitly or explicitly, their individual missions and strategies. At the larger level, each movement shapes and constrains the abilities of synagogues to entertain the very idea of change. In some movements, shifts in values and practices are readily embraced; in others, they are met with a degree of resistance that matches the degree of pressure for change.

These shifts reveal themselves in a variety of ways, both large and small: the amount of prayer in the vernacular versus prayer in Hebrew during worship services; the use of music and musical instruments, especially on Shabbat and holy days; foods permitted or forbidden on synagogue property; the voice of *halacha* in determining actions taken or not taken by the community; who wears a *tallit* or a *kippa*; the school's curriculum; the social actions on behalf of Jews versus the community as a whole; the role of women in the synagogue; the power of the rabbi versus lay leaders; the relationship of the congregation to Israel—just to name a few. And while most of the twentieth century saw greater universalism (i.e., emphasis on "ethical monotheism" and rationalism) and Americanization within all of the denominations, today we see movement toward greater particularism and recovery of traditions once thought to be abandoned or no longer relevant. However, regardless of which way the proverbial pendulum swings, the challenge of institutional change remains the same.

Across the movements, then, synagogues and their members must come to terms with the twin desires for sameness and change. The issue remains complicated, as individuals long for both a sense of tradition and a sense of relevance in their religious and spiritual lives. Synagogue members look to their institutions for comfort. They want to pray just as they always did and in doing so feel connected to a people and a tradition larger than the sphere of their own life. Synagogue members also look to their institutions as places where they may be able to work out the complications that their thoroughly modern lives pose for them. The healthy synagogue is one in which both parts of this equation—Judaism as an island of stability rooted in tradition and familiarity, Judaism as a source of relevance rooted in a comprehension of modern life—remain operative.

The Experience of Change

Think about the *Oseh Shalom* that is sung at your synagogue. It has a certain tune and melody. It may be sung slowly, as congregants close their eyes and sway, or sung more briskly, in an extended burst of energy, congregants clapping throughout. Imagine that, however it is sung, it has "always" been that way at your synagogue, ever since the first group of young families joined together and beckoned their founding rabbi to join them. Imagine those young families growing, the children turning into parents, the parents turning into grandparents, and throughout that time, the singing of the *Oseh Shalom* remains constant, each generation teaching the next its words and tunes and phrasings. The prayer-song becomes woven into the fabric of the synagogue. We call it the "traditional one" because it is literally part of our tradition.

Now imagine that your synagogue has grown, so a cantor joins the clergy team. She is of a new generation, different from those who came before. She went to Jewish camps and learned to sing traditional songs with new melodies. She has even written some of her own. With the rabbi's permission, the cantor wants to introduce a new melody for *Oseh Shalom*. She has good reasons. It is part of her tradition; it is the melody that has been woven into the fabric of her own Jewish life. The tune is wonderful, she says. It is more vibrant, more moving, and easier to sing along with, which is what the younger families want. Besides, it will help introduce the camp-singing tradition to the congregation, she says, perhaps even inspire the children to go to those camps and deepen their Jewish identities. That is something the rabbi has been pushing for years. The cantor will play guitar, not the organ. Though the *Oseh Shalom* will not sound as it did, it will be beautiful nevertheless.

Against this sort of backdrop we can imagine the experience of change in a synagogue. Significantly changing people's deep experiences—how they worship, learn, engage with one another, encounter rituals, celebrate holidays—will inevitably trigger various emotions. At its core, its heart, change is emotional, particularly when change threatens to disrupt our sense of connectedness to who we are as Jews. The *Oseh Shalom* we sang as children, that our fathers and mothers, and their fathers and mothers, and theirs, too, also sang—that is part of our identity, how we define ourselves in relation to them and the religion they bequeathed to us. To the extent that this is true—that any one prayer, practice, or ritual cuts to the core of our sense of ourselves as Jews—any change in that dimension has the potential to disturb us emotionally.

The disturbance that we often feel is related to a larger issue, of which we are often unaware: the ways the changes at our synagogues are intimately related to the ways of passing generations. When we change our position for saying the *Sh'ma,* how we sing *Oseh Shalom,* or what *siddurim/* prayer books we use, music we play, or countless other aspects of synagogue life, we are implicitly moving further away from the generations that came before. We turn our synagogues into places that may be less and less recognizable to previous generations. This is both a concrete reality and a metaphoric abstraction. Next to us sit people from our parents' or grandparents' generation. More abstractly, we hold within us the sense of our own background, our own pasts. All change is, in some respect, a movement from the past to which we have some attachment, toward some future for which we have only hopes and fears.

The larger lesson here is that change evokes a sense of loss. Adopting new practices means halting old ways. When we are attached to those old ways, we feel a sense of loss as we leave them behind. We may leave them regretfully. We may leave them sadly. We may leave them angrily. We may leave them with relief, determined not to look back. Or we may leave them feeling guilty as though we are betraying our pasts or killing off previous generations. How we react depends a great deal on how we, as individuals, react to loss more generally. We have all these feelings, of course, but for each of us, some feelings are usually more prominent than others.

This makes life complicated for synagogues making changes. As we said, change triggers a host of emotions: sadness, relief, excitement, anger, and guilt. Since it is difficult for any of us to hang on to all of those feelings at the same time, we tend to emphasize and express one and not the others. Some people seem only excited and thrilled at the change. Others seem only angry. Still others seem only sad and despondent. What often happens is that these feelings seem to get distributed across people in a synagogue undergoing some change. The rabbi and cantor intent on changing the *Oseh Shalom* are excited. The past board president is upset. The adult children of the synagogue founders are saddened. The youth choir is thrilled. The director of the youth choir feels guilty. Each of these individuals or groups feels a certain emotion. Together they comprise the spectrum of emotions that are triggered by even the smallest of changes but that feel significant to many.

This distribution of feelings across the synagogue may be inevitable. It is simply too difficult for individuals to hang on to all the emotions triggered by change. The problems appear when people square off against one another. Those who are sad or angry blame those who are excited for the change. Those who are eager to try something new blame those who feel guilty for slowing the process, or those who are angry for resisting it altogether. People get defensive and may react by attacking others. The change gets personalized. Our internal struggles—feeling both glad and sad about a change or both angry and excited—are externalized and play out as struggles between people or groups in the synagogue.

Patience, Patience

Meaningful change requires a fair amount of patience. Time is a key component. People need time to absorb the fact that they need to change. They need time to mourn what they are leaving behind. They need time to find aspects of the change that they can get excited about and own, at least in part. Mostly, though, real change takes time because of how long it takes to change our habits of thought and action. We get used to doing things in certain ways, and the more used to our habits we are, the longer they take to reshape. This is particularly true in synagogues, where our habits may have formed over generations.

The cultures of our synagogues are marked by habits that we often call "*minhag hamakom.*" Synagogue cultures allow for stability and familiarity. Yet the strength of culture is also its weakness. A synagogue's culture renders real change difficult because people must struggle against the weight of history if they are to alter the underlying assumptions that shape what they perceive, think, feel, and do. Assumptions are difficult to change, precisely because they are so deeply rooted in people's unconscious. Unless they are seen and recognized as assumptions—as deeply held beliefs that were once actually a series of choices—they can be neither confronted nor debated. People will follow familiar, predictable routines, even when they lead to unpleasant outcomes. They will change those patterns only when they have to. Faced with some crisis, a threat to their mission or survival, they will, often with much struggle and difficulty, attempt to change what they do. They will make relatively superficial changes (in the artifacts); they will make changes over time in how they talk about what they do (in their espoused values). And with persistence, they will change how they think (in their underlying assumptions). Lasting change thus takes a lot of time, as underlying assumptions are shifted and altered.

The harder truth is that such lasting change cannot occur until the previous generation has stepped aside and made room for the next. This is one of the underlying messages of our Torah. The generation that left Egypt were not sinners, at least no more so than any other group of Israelites before or after. Nevertheless, a generation born into slavery and used to the life of a slave in which everything was provided, proscribed, and determined by others, could ultimately not handle the freedom of the desert and the demands it made on them. Though slavery could not possibly have been a positive or healthy experience, the Israelites continued to romanticize their past, wishing to return to Egypt at every difficulty or temporary impasse. Their desire to go back in time, their fantasy of physical return to Egypt, teaches us that change is difficult, regardless of the circumstances. Sadly, and in spite of God's plan to the contrary, this generation of Jews that Moses helped out of Egypt needed to die in the desert, because they were too hooked into the culture of slavery. We often see that in synagogue life as well—cultures hooked by their past, even to their own detriment.

The Change

For as long as anyone at Congregation Beth El could recall, Kabbalat Shabbat services were at 8:15 on Friday nights, led by one of the rabbis and the cantor, with a formal sermon delivered by the other rabbi. Since Congregation Beth El was part of the Reform movement, the service was the primary vehicle by which congregants worshiped; there was no Shabbat morning service other than bar and bat mitzvah services, which became, for all intents and purposes, invitation-only services.

Over the course of the years, as a new generation of men and women renegotiated their roles at home and in the workplace, parenting styles shifted. Shabbat was no longer viewed as a chance for parents to attend services, uninterrupted by children left home with their babysitters or grandparents, but was valued as an opportunity for families to spend quality time together. Under duress, the founding rabbi had, five years before retiring, reluctantly added a 7:30 "family service" on the first Friday night of the month to replace the later service. The other Friday night services continued to be at 8:15 and were geared toward adults without young children.

The arrival of the new senior rabbi represented a decided shift in the synagogue toward the younger generation's values. The board asked their new rabbi to develop a vision for the congregation. A key component of that vision was to position Shabbat as the center of the community. This vision was shared with the congregation in a series of town meetings and finally approved at the end of the rabbi's first year at the congregation. That approval was muted by the message to the rabbi that it was acceptable to add earlier services but that the traditional 8:15 service must remain as well. The board president was explicit about this. "It's okay to add opportunities," she told the rabbi, "but let's not undermine the Beth El tradition. We've been at this a long time, and it's always worked for a lot of us."

The demographics of Beth El continued to support the new vision, as young families replaced empty nesters in the congregation. The 8:15 p.m. service was simply too late for families with young children, and they could not commit to coming regularly. The rabbi, who himself had young children at home, did not blame them. On the other hand, he knew that there was still a fair amount of grumbling among the older congregants who liked coming to a service undisturbed by young kids. Yet the later services were not attended particularly well. A handful of regulars came, mostly empty nesters. A few people attended on particular weeks to say *kaddish* for a *yahrtzeit*. But the bulk of the attendees were the bar and bat mitzvah families, their friends, and their out-of-town guests. The regular committed core of attendees was small and dwindling.

The rabbi decided, after the first summer, to staff the ritual committee. With his input, the committee decided to add a 6:00 p.m. service on nights when there was also an 8:15 service. The 6:00 service was held in the chapel, a smaller, more intimate space than the formal sanctuary. This service was led by one of the rabbis and did not involve the cantor, who was expected to help lead the later service in the sanctuary. The rabbi who led the earlier service went home after it concluded; the other led the later service. The committee wanted to see what the congregation would support through regular attendance.

The 6:00 service was instantly popular. It became so well attended that by the end of the year, the worshipers could not all fit in the chapel. The bar/bat mitzvah families were starting to ask if they could attend that service as well, rather than the 8:15, for it allowed them to then have a dinner afterward for their relatives and guests. The chapel service lent itself to more informality; people dressed as they wished, with family members meeting one another after work, worshiping, and then going home or out together. Rabbi and congregants sat in a circle together, sang a cappella, and learned through engaging sessions of questions and answers instead of a sermon. The service invariably finished by 7:00 or 7:15, befitting the attention span of the younger children. By the end of that second year, the popularity of the 6:00 service was pressing the physical limits of the chapel. The clergy and the board needed to make a decision.

The clergy proposed a rotating schedule of services. On the first Friday of each month, the family service would be held at 7:30 p.m.; on the last Friday, service would be at 8:15 p.m.; and on the other two or three weeks, depending on the month, services would be held at 6:00 p.m. All services would be in the main sanctuary. The board's concern was that this would disenfranchise the older people because only one service a month would be in "their" style. After much discussion, however, they approved the schedule for a one-year trial. They decided that they would measure the results by attendance.

It became increasingly clear over the course of the year that the 6:00 p.m. service was the most successful. It had the most regular attendance, attracted a core group of young families, and pleased the bar/bat mitzvah families. On weekends when the only service was at 8:15 p.m. and there was no bar/bat mitzvah to celebrate, hardly anyone attended the service. Eventually, on those nights the clergy moved the service to the chapel because of the poor attendance. The attendance data showed that the 6:00 service had the largest average, the 8:15 the smallest. The difference between the two was significant. The families who had attended the 7:30 family service—the original concession to an alternative worship style and time—began shifting their allegiance to the 6:00 service as well.

The attendance data were presented to the board. One of the longest serving board members angrily tossed the spreadsheet on the table. "There are plenty of people who do not always make it to services, but they should have the right to go to them when they can. That's not a matter of numbers. It's a matter of what's right for everyone." A newer member to the board responded. "It seems that people are voting with their feet, and we need to take that seriously." The conversation went back and forth between those who wanted to keep the 8:15 service as the primary service and those who wanted to install the 6:00 worship as the primary service. Finally, the board president proposed a compromise solution, which the board accepted as a reasonable alternative: keep the variety schedule for another year as a continued experiment. The board wanted to be able to say to the older members that there was still a place for them to go if they wanted to celebrate Shabbat in the ways and time to which they were accustomed. The board asked the clergy to do two services in the sanctuary on the 6:00 p.m. days, with the second one occurring at 8:15 p.m. if there was a constituency that would attend. The cantor was required to help lead both services.

The clergy felt disappointed, like it was a step back from the vision. They had already begun to add things after the 6:00 p.m. services—speakers, potluck dinners, Israeli dancing, concerts, and sing-alongs—to extend the sense of family and community that had been building as more and more families attended. Adding the later service disrupted such events. "Look," the rabbi told the board at the first meeting in the fall, "the 8:15 service goes against the vision of building Shabbat community. We all agreed to that vision. That vision was one of the reasons you hired me." Several board members nodded. The rabbi went on. "We've tried to honor the past here. But it really is the past. There's no longer a critical mass. Those who complained don't show up anyway. There isn't the support for the later service, just the memory of it." The board president nodded. "That may be true," he said, "but we have to honor that memory."

The clergy committed to trying the board's recommendation for a year. The bar/bat mitzvah families were given their choice about which service to attend on those evenings when there were both 6:00 and 8:15 Shabbat services. They invariably chose the earlier service. The executive director tracked the number of congregants who attended the services. The numbers for the later service continued to be small. By midyear, the rabbi decided to move the 8:15 service back to the chapel, telling the board that it was embarrassing having only sixteen people in the large sanctuary. He reduced the clergy to one rabbi, feeling it was a great imposition on the cantor to have to lead a second service for so few people. The board members themselves did not show up for the later service even when they had a *yahrtzeit* that week. They received the news of the move to the smaller space with little protest.

By the spring of the rabbi's fourth year in the synagogue, he reported to the board that at the previous 8:15 p.m. Shabbat service only one couple showed. He announced that they were discontinuing the service; henceforth all the Shabbat Friday night services would be at 6:00. Board members nodded. They had little to say in response. They knew that, as a board, they had not supported the later service in word or in deed and that there was no real support for it. That fall, after the High Holy Days, the change was made. It has since remained that way.

Conditions for Change

This case offers a study of clergy trying to implement a vision—of Shabbat services integrated into the lives of families, of parents and children worshiping together on Shabbat—that threatens the traditions and history of a synagogue. Embedded in this case study are a series of lessons about the process by which synagogues make significant change—that is, change that deeply affects their cultures and has the potential to shape many aspects of people's experiences of Jewish life and its meaning in their lives.

Marvin Weisbord, a noted organizational development author, suggests in his book *Productive Workplaces* three conditions that must be met for meaningful change to occur.[1] First, there must be *committed leadership*. Leaders must be willing to take significant risks to make something happen. They must involve themselves as champions of the change, not simply delegate and stay distant so as not to be associated with possible failure. And they must commit resources, both in time and money, to support transformation. Second, there must be some significant *organizational opportunity*. Opportunities may appear as gifts (e.g., a cooperative program with another institution or new funding) or as painful or confusing dilemmas (e.g., dwindling attendance or budget problems). Third, there must be *energized people*. That is, people need to be excited about the process of change for anything significant to occur. This is the trickiest, most important dimension and one that the change agent needs to spend most of the time working to get right.

In our case study, each of these conditions was met to some degree, and together they enabled the change process to occur. There was committed leadership, initially provided by the rabbi who was asked by the board to develop the vision, and later joined, in different ways, by the board president and the chair of the ritual committee. Together they found ways to keep the change process moving. There was also a significant demographic shift that provoked the organizational opportunity for change. The influx of young families looking to make Shabbat a family experience, combined with the shifting trends toward more egalitarian child rearing, exerted pressure on the synagogue to create an accommodating structure for worship. Finally, there were people who had energy for this shift: the families who wished for (and were willing to support with their attendance) this new worship structure, the bar/bat mitzvah families, and the clergy themselves. It was the confluence of these forces that offered both meaning and momentum to sustain the change process over its four years.

The Change Process

Certain steps in a change process make it more likely to ultimately be successful. John Kotter discusses many of these steps in his book *Leading Change.*[2]

Step 1. Establish a Sense of Urgency. Synagogue members and leaders must understand that the change is significant and necessary. This is often a matter of pointing out that cultural, communal, and/or demographic changes require shifts in how synagogues serve their members, which is what the rabbi in our case study did. Members' needs change; demographics change; the society in which we live changes. Thus, synagogues must be responsive to these changes. They must issue invitations to the new, even when they find such newness threatening. Otherwise, synagogues grow stagnant. What was once vibrant fades to dull routine. People go through the motions: they attend services (less frequently), send their children to Hebrew school (less enthusiastically), and take their turns on committees (less productively). The synagogue struggles with inertia. New ideas are stifled by the weight of the past. People who represent new directions and energy are turned off. These are all signs that the potential pool of new members is shifting. Synagogue leaders must become aware of their communities as they really are, not how they once were or how they wish them to be.

Step 2. Form a Powerful Guiding Coalition. No lasting significant organizational change occurs because of one person. Any change agent requires a coalition of others who can offer useful support, resources, advice, and guidance. In our case study, the board was a coalition, as was the ritual committee. Both included people who could offer feedback and guidance, even if it was not necessarily of the type that the rabbi wished to hear. A coalition enables all viewpoints to be represented. This is crucial when developing plans that take into account the various wishes and needs of stakeholders across the synagogue.

Step 3. Create a Vision. Meaningful change is anchored in a vision of the future. There is some cogent articulation of a future that people will prefer to inhabit. When the opportunity arose for a new rabbi to succeed the one who was retiring, the search committee stated that they wanted a rabbi who could be a visionary. As part of his larger vision for the synagogue, the rabbi in the case study developed a plan for Shabbat, disseminated it, and got buy-in, at least in principle, from the congregation early in his tenure. Indeed, he entered that conversation during the hiring period, which makes a good deal of sense, in that it offers a clear and early indicator of the fit between a synagogue and its spiritual leader. His preliminary ideas were compelling because they reflected the deeper needs and wishes of the synagogue's leaders. Later, as the vision was fleshed out, it spoke to others' need to belong to a synagogue where they did not have to choose quite so dramatically between time with young children and time in worship during Shabbat. Such visions have the capacity to inspire.

Step 4. Communicate the Vision. Only when synagogue members share a vision can that vision come to reside meaningfully in the synagogue more generally and become part of a collective desire. Of course, not everyone in the synagogue will buy into any particular vision. But if it is communicated effectively enough, in settings that enable people to digest it, look at it from different angles, and respond to it in ways that allow them to feel heard, it may then become collectively owned. The small town meetings that the rabbi in our case held offered such settings. He put the vision in writing, disseminated it in the synagogue's bulletin as well as sermons, and gained agreement for it from the board and the congregation. Synagogue members spoke to the vision. They questioned it and offered amendments. Ideally, even those who might have disagreed with the vision as first proposed felt heard, felt that their input was valued. When visions are communicated in such ways, they allow people to be brought from different places and perspectives into the change process.

Step 5. Empower Others to Act. If the energy for change remains located within one or several people, even if it is the clergy, or board president, or within a single committee, it is not likely to result in lasting change. Instead, change occurs most effectively when the energy for the change is dispersed throughout the synagogue. When the majority of the spies returned from the land of promise with a negative report, even Moses could not effect the necessary changes. Those who create and communicate a vision also need to work on plans for implementing that vision that emphasize the involvement of as many people in the synagogue as possible. In the case study, the rabbi joined the ritual committee, which expanded the process of involving other people and empowering them to develop ideas for bringing the vision into reality.

Step 6. Plan for and Create Short-Term Wins. Change does not happen all at once. It happens in pieces. The pieces come together over time, building on one another as a result of small successes that blend into larger ones. Synagogue members need to float trial balloons, small experiments that offer opportunities to gather information about what will work and what will not. These are called short-term wins. They build momentum as people get excited about what they are seeing and want to do more. They enable people to collect information about what to continue and what to halt as they continue the change process. In the case study, the ritual committee helped create and implement an earlier service that allowed for informality, teaching, and intimacy appropriate for young families. They built on that energy by offering bar/bat mitzvah families the choice to attend as well and, in so doing, added another constituency that supported the change and its anchoring vision.

Step 7. Consolidate Improvements and Produce Still More Change. A certain momentum gets built when synagogue members begin to see positive results from the first changes they implement. This momentum needs to be sustained and built upon if a synagogue is to make the shift from small changes to a larger, more significant change that would bring a vision into reality. In the case study, the clergy worked with the board to design a final experiment. At the same time, they began to add to the earlier services by arranging speakers, dinners, Israeli dancing, hors d'oeuvres *onegs,* concerts, and sing-alongs to extend the sense of family and community that had been building as more and more families attended. This created greater energy and excitement for the vision of a family-friendly Shabbat and made the change seem inevitable and right.

Step 8. Institutionalize New Approaches. A change needs to outlast the specific individuals involved in enabling it to occur if it is to be of lasting value to the congregation. It must be institutionalized in some fashion, woven into the very fabric of the synagogue in ways that connect it to the ongoing life of the institution. In our case, this was a relatively straightforward process. The new service became, over time, the only Shabbat service. Other events grew up around it—the dances and speakers, the bar/bat mitzvah celebrations—that rooted it even more deeply in place. With enough time, that service may well be all that people remember, as the next generation grows up under its influence.

It is through such steps that significant changes in synagogues occur. The change process is not, of course, as linear and smooth as these steps might suggest. It is filled with twists and turns and steps that feel to some as though they are moving backward, such as when the board in the case study asked for another year with double services. But, over time, with enough energy and momentum spreading throughout the synagogue, change does happen, through processes that can themselves be quite inspiring and meaningful.

Understanding Resistance

Throughout any significant change process in a synagogue, resistance inevitably appears. We need to understand it rather than simply dismiss it or be overwhelmed by it when it occurs. We need first to think about where resistance comes from. Of course, at first it represents people's attachments to their habitual routines. We do not easily give up our familiar, instinctive patterns of thought and action. Resistance is also a matter of people's fear of the unknown. When we do not know what we are getting into and are asked to venture into unfamiliar territory, we may try to do exactly what we are already doing, hoping that the change will fade away or leave us unharmed. And too, people resist because they may fear that a proposed change may cost them too much—in their power base if they benefit from the existing system; in time if the implementation will occur in stages; in recognition and prestige if they are associated with the status quo; or even in money if there are financial implications associated with the change.

How we understand or frame resistance will affect how we respond to it. We might well simply think of those who resist, actively or passively, as obstacles who seek to undermine, diminish, or destroy a change process. When we frame resistance in this way, we believe that those who resist change need to be overcome, worked around, or in other ways marginalized. Alternatively, we might think of resistance as natural self-protection, a normal response of those who have vested themselves in maintaining the current state and are guarding themselves against its loss. Framed in this way, we might be more proactive about reaching out to others, acknowledging their potential losses, and finding ways to help them see the positive dimensions of the changes. Or, in yet another frame, we might think of resistance as a positive step toward change, a first step toward adaptation, since people are engaging rather than disengaging altogether. In that vein, resistance is energy to work with and, moreover, information critical to the change process. The strength of people's resistance often indicates the degree to which we have touched something that is valuable to them. In this case, we need to redirect that energy by getting them involved in making the change process better.

Working with resistance is, of course, easier said than done. And it may not always be successful. Resistance may be built into the culture of the synagogue itself—all change is resisted. Or sometimes people are simply following traditions whose roots they no longer remember but feel strong attachment to nonetheless. We are reminded here of an old joke.

During a service at an old synagogue in Eastern Europe, when the *Shema* was said, half the congregants stood up and half remained sitting. The half that was seated started yelling at those standing to sit down, and the ones standing yelled at the ones sitting to stand up. The rabbi, although learned in the Law and commentaries, didn't know what to do. His congregation suggested that he consult a housebound ninety-eight-year-old man who was one of the original founders of their temple.

The rabbi hoped the elderly man would be able to tell him what the actual temple tradition was, so he went to the nursing home with a representative of each faction of the congregation. The one whose followers stood during *Shema* said to the old man, "Isn't the tradition to stand during this prayer?" The old man answered, "No, that is not the tradition." The one whose followers sat said, "Then the tradition is to sit during *Shema!*" The old man answered, "No, that is not the tradition." Then the rabbi said to the old man, "But the congregants fight all the time, yelling at each other about whether they should sit or stand." The old man interrupted, exclaiming, "*That* is the tradition!"

The joke reminds us quite neatly about the ways the underlying assumptions of a synagogue's culture can seem immovable. People get locked into traditions. That is, in part, the joy of traditions: they are familiar, offering satisfying bridges to previous generations. It is also the trap of traditions: their very familiarity leads people to believe that there are no other ways in which to think and act. They forget that, once upon a time, the practices they follow were simply the result of a series of choices they made. They forget that they, too, can make choices. And they forget that the choices they make have real implications for how inviting, how welcoming, how embracing their synagogue is to all members.

Enabling Change

Synagogue change can begin anywhere. It does not need to begin with a rabbi or board president (although it will need to involve them at some point). It can begin with anyone who senses some opportunity, some gift or dilemma, and is able and willing to take on the role of change agent. In chapter 10 we address the special role of the rabbi in charting a course and leading the synagogue, but in a healthy synagogue anyone can take on a leadership role; that is, see an opportunity and begin to mobilize others to struggle through a change.

Doing so requires particular leadership skills. These include the following dimensions, which we illustrate in terms of the case described earlier in this chapter.

Taking on the Role of Change Agent. We take on the role of change agent when we decide that is what we wish to do and no longer wait for others to step up and lead the effort. In the case study, the rabbi quite deliberately thought of himself as a change agent, someone who could and would find allies who would support the move toward a new vision. He did not simply become frustrated and cynical because others weren't making the vision happen, nor did he simply order people to do things they weren't prepared to do. Brought to the synagogue to develop and implement a vision, he thought of himself as an agent of change and acted accordingly.

Teaching Others about the Larger Forces That Impact Them. We also need to help others see the larger trends that create the need for change. The rabbi helped others understand the changing demographics and the cultural shifts that led to the need for changes in worship practices. He did this respectfully rather than condescendingly. He did this with real concern and passion for the synagogue, its vision, and its future.

Vision Casting or Choosing Specific Programs or Arenas That Would Make the Vision Concrete. A vision remains abstract until it is linked to actual programs and projects that make it real. In the case study, the clergy felt strongly that an earlier service would make the vision come alive for the congregation. They decided to create a service that would show, in practice, what the concept of a family-centered Shabbat actually looked like. Congregants could attend the service and see and feel for themselves what the vision meant.

Identifying and Moving toward Key Stakeholders. It is a fact of congregational life, and organizational life more generally, that key stakeholders must be attended to if any significant change is to occur and last. Key stakeholders are those who care about a situation and, if they wished, could mobilize to affect outcomes. The rabbi and board president in the case understood who the key stakeholders were: the congregants with young children, the empty-nester congregants, the ritual committee, the clergy, and the board. We must move to involve stakeholders and encourage them to share their criticisms and resistance as a necessary part of the change process.

Using Existing Structures. Effective and lasting change in synagogues is made possible by using existing synagogue structures. This ensures that a change is perceived as integrated with, rather than an attack upon, existing structures. It also ensures that the change is in line with other initiatives. In the case, the rabbi used the ritual committee, which was part of the existing structure, to move the project and vision ahead. He involved others in developing solutions; in doing so, he found support in the existing committee, so the new program was not all about him. This makes good sense.

Creating Compelling Cases Based on Information and Data to Justify Actions. It is not enough to assert that a certain change is necessary and will work. We must show it to be so. We must develop test projects that demonstrate to others, supporters and critics alike, that our ideas for change make sense in practice. In the case study, the clergy, ritual committee, and board developed experiments to provide evidence to support their case for the change. They wanted to be able to say that they provided every opportunity for others to prove them wrong. That having been said, we still need to make certain to acknowledge people's feelings, attitudes, and beliefs, which are not necessarily going to be changed just because someone shows up with a lot of facts. Not everyone makes decisions based on logic and facts.

Framing Changes in Terms of Issues, Not People. It is always tempting to think of those who oppose us as the enemy. The changes we seek are quite reasonable, we like to believe, and those who do not support them must be irrational or motivated by bad intentions. We must resist this impulse, for it only makes change more difficult. The rabbi in the case study was careful not to personalize the issues. He did not make it only about the board member who opposed him. The rabbi understood that he was implicitly representing a portion of the congregation. Nor did he blame the older members, inertia on part of the board, or relations between new and old members. He was aware of all of these factors but did not get caught up in them. Instead, he remained calm, rational, and present with others, so the focus remained on the change itself rather than on the distracting and counterproductive interpersonal issues.

Honoring the Past While Driving toward the Future—with Patience. Finally, we must practice a great deal of patience when we take on the role of change agent. When we get caught up in our enthusiasm or struggle for change, we often want to move quickly from the present and into the future we envision. In the case study, the leaders made sure not to disregard the past entirely nor to dishonor the traditions of their synagogue. However, those traditions were not considered inviolate; they were thought to have served their time and place. The leaders thus patiently moved toward creating new traditions that responded to and generated energy in others. This process takes time, often a great deal of time. Honoring our past cannot be rushed.

Moving toward Organic Change

Most synagogues have to confront change at some points in their histories. This means that synagogues must evolve as their membership does. Of course, some shuls will remain stuck and just get by, in spite of their leaders' best intentions otherwise. But it need not be that way. We believe change in a synagogue can evolve as it continuously searches for ways to live out its mission and remain connected to the changing nature of its community and membership.

The synagogue's mission is what grounds this process. Every synagogue will be presented in various ways with numerous opportunities for change. Some will appear as gifts. A donor wants to fund some new program. One congregation wants to merge with another. One synagogue or Jewish Community Center wants to create a community-wide education or social action program. Each of these is an appealing gift that leaders need to examine closely to see if it fits with the broader mission. If it does, the gift is accepted gratefully. If it does not, several possibilities emerge. The gift can be rejected, or it can be amended in one fashion or another. Or the mission itself can be changed to accommodate the gift.

Opportunities may also appear as dilemmas. The budget is woefully inadequate, and difficult decisions must be made. A longtime staff person abruptly quits, citing harassment from several board members. A social action program creates discord within the congregation. The Jewish population is moving away from the city where the synagogue is located to a new suburb. Each of these is a dilemma requiring solutions. All of these, gifts and dilemmas alike, are chances for synagogues to examine their missions, calibrate their relevance in light of important trends or events, and make decisions that honor the past while moving the community into the future.

The healthy synagogue moves toward rather than away from those opportunities. It is led by people who embrace those opportunities for what they might reveal about how well their synagogues are living out their missions. These people help others talk about the cultures they have created. They help put forth the choice to maintain those cultures or to alter them. They lead conversations about their shared history and about how to acknowledge and honor that history without being enslaved by it. They help the synagogue move gently, firmly, and inclusively toward change in ways that patiently build on rather than destroy what has come before.

Notes

1. Marvin Weisbord, *Productive Workplaces* (San Francisco: Jossey-Bass, 1987).
2. John Kotter, *Leading Change* (Boston, MA: Harvard Business School Press, 1996).

5

THE PLACE AND SPACE OF
THE COMMUNAL HOME

Asu li mikdash, v'shanti b'tocham.
Build for Me a sanctuary and I will dwell among you.
(Exodus 25:8)

People often ask, "If God is everywhere, why do we have to have temples?"
Three answers may be given. First, since we ourselves are physical beings,
we require physical structures to live out our relationship with God. We
can call this "embodied spirituality." Judaism teaches that God is without
any physical form and cannot be depicted. We thus create other tangible
places (outside structures) and spaces (inner structures) that enable us to
feel closer to God.

Second, creating and maintaining community is facilitated by establishing regular meeting times in designated spaces. Most synagogues began with groups of people congregating in other peoples' places—homes,
schools, other synagogues, churches. Their development as a congregation is often marked by the important step of creating their own space,
where they have control over when and how their members congregate
for worship, study, and community action.

Third, we build places to contain and mark ourselves as Jews. Consider the Torah text above. We would expect it to say, "Build for Me a sanctuary and I will dwell in it." But it does not say that. Instead, it says, "I will
dwell among you." In this context, the "you" is plural (like "y'all" in the
South or "yous" in New York). Our communal action of creating sanctuaries invites the presence of God to dwell within us. It may seem ironic, but
if we truly want God to be everywhere, in every human being, then we
need to create or designate specific spaces to gather and to worship God.

The House

The home of Congregation Shir Tikva is exactly that, or almost:
an old Colonial house on a tree-lined street marked by rows of

stately Victorian and Colonial homes. Shir Tikva's building fits
its history quite well. The congregation began as an offshoot of a
Hillel. A group of faculty and graduate students formed a cooperative Hebrew school as an adjunct to their college's Hillel. Several years later the school became a separate entity. Its members
met in a building on the college campus. Families without an
affiliation with the college joined and enrolled their children in
the Hebrew school. The cooperative grew to thirty-five families.
It began to add adult education classes and occasional Friday
evening and Saturday morning services in addition to *b'nai
mitzvah* services. A decade after its conception, the congregation
grew to 80 families. It began to support life-cycle events—*brit,*
baby namings, weddings, conversions, funerals—as well as regular High Holiday services and monthly Shabbat services. The
congregation was unaffiliated with any one Jewish movement or
denomination.

As Shir Tikva continued to evolve from its inception as a
school, its leaders engaged the community in a strategic planning process. The community decided to continue to loosen its
connection from its original school-based mission and embrace
the elements of a full-service community. Not all families agreed
with this decision. Some wished to revert to small groups meeting in one another's homes, where they would lead their own
services and read Torah. The community divided, after which
there were 45 families that decided to join together and create a
full-fledged synagogue. An educator who, over time, assumed
rabbinic duties led them. The congregation left the college campus and settled into a local church on an interim basis. A year
later, the community, numbering 50 families, acquired and moved
into its current home. The community began to grow again over
the next decade, its second in one incarnation or another. It currently numbers 85 families.

The synagogue building is a ramshackle affair that could use
a coat of paint. The house itself is large, sprawling over three
stories. Visitors are greeted by an expansive front porch leading
to a front door. That door is not used, however. Visitors must
find the way to the actual entrance, doors located along the sides

of the building. A small lot on one side of the house accommodates several cars, packed like sardines. Most parking is found on the side streets. The other side of the house, where most congregants enter, is reached via a sidewalk that is shared by several other nearby homes. Newcomers often make the mistake of ringing the wrong doorbell; they are greeted with a simple nod and a finger pointing them to the correct entrance. The few signs that direct visitors are not easily visible to those who do not know precisely where to look.

The inside of the building is typical for old, sprawling Colonials. Multiple staircases tucked behind corners wind their way through the three stories. The rooms vary in size. On the first floor is a library, of sorts, with shelves stacked with a great variety of books: Hebrew texts, Torah commentaries, modern novels by Jewish authors, children's books, a few stray magazines. At times, students study and congregate in the library, sharing pizza during study sessions and meetings of one sort or another. Just across the hall is the part-time administrator's office. Papers, spiral binders, coffee cups, and stacks of folders compete for space with the file cabinet, water dispenser, and computer. There are mailboxes for the current part-time rabbi, the full-time educator, and the board president. The kitchen, a well-used space just down the hall, is large and relatively organized: stacks of mugs, silverware, plates; a large refrigerator with notices reminding people to clean up after themselves; several ovens; a generous sink, a dishwasher.

The community meets for services, committee and board meetings, community gatherings, large education classes, speakers, and the like in a large, unremarkable room at one end of the first floor. Long tables are scattered around the edges of the room, with fifty or so folding chairs stacked against the walls. The congregation recently rescued an old ark that another synagogue was discarding; several members rented a truck and picked it up and, with much fanfare, installed it at the front of the large room, where it now contains a Torah donated by another synagogue. This lived-in, familiar, worn room is the center of Shir Tikva. For important community events, members bring large rugs and plants to the room and lay platters of food atop the side tables, creating what seems like a living room large enough for the whole congregational family.

The second and third floors of the building contain a maze of rooms. Converted bedrooms are now used for Hebrew classes. The part-time rabbi and the educator have offices, replete with desks, bookcases, assorted tables and lamps, and drapes donated by various members. It is not easy to find these offices. No signs or posted maps in the building direct visitors to the various offices and people. Visitors need to find their own ways, poking their heads into various rooms and offices until they stumble onto the place or the person they are looking for.

Shir Tikva is a congregation in transition. The community is large enough to occasionally strain the limits of its building but not so large that it has enough money to buy land and build a more functional space for itself. The founding rabbi has left the congregation, and a new part-time rabbi and a full-time educator have been engaged to lead them. A small, committed core group of members is trying to press the congregation to examine and choose from among a number of options: sell the building and look for another space, merge with another small congregation, join one of the movements, develop a strategy for attracting more members, or begin fund-raising.

The community has limited energy to invest in struggling with these decisions, given how many tasks there are to do and how few people are willing to do them. The building itself shows this. In spite of resolutions made, the front entrance remains impassable, jammed with empty bookcases and boxes; paint peels; books spill out over the library tables and are randomly piled in corners; carpets fray; used mugs line desks. The space is familiar, worn, and filled with the random castoffs of people's lives.

The Meanings of Space

Physical spaces communicate. They tell us a great deal about the people who utilize them and dwell in them. They tell us about priorities, what is important and what is not. They offer clues about the cultures people have created. There is a great deal of meaning in the ways spaces are designed, how they are used, and how people live within them. If we look closely enough at the physical nature of synagogues, we can gain a great deal of insight into what they mean to those who congregate and work there.

Our case study offers an example. We were asked to help Shir Tikva with a strategic planning process. The physical space helped us understand much about the underlying nature of the congregation. The setting itself, a house on the block of a residential neighborhood, suggested that they saw themselves as an extended family, connected to and caring for one another. They cared less for the building itself. The peeling paint, the worn carpets, the scattered dishes and mugs, and the piles of books in corners and on floors all suggested a certain lack of care or focus on the space they created together. This attitude can be understood in various ways. Shir Tikva is a small congregation with few resources. Its origin as a school housed in other institutions also led to a certain lack of ownership of and responsibility for the communal spaces in which the congregation might worship, celebrate, study, and meet together.

As our work with Shir Tikva progressed, we discovered that the space held deeper meanings about the identity of the congregation. The congregation was in the midst of growing pains. Members were conflicted about how large they wished the synagogue to grow. Some supported real growth, enough to raise the capital necessary to renovate the building or buy another altogether. Others wished the congregation to remain small to maintain the sense of community and intimacy that marked members' relations with one another. This was the same struggle that had led to the congregation's historical split. Pulled in these different directions, the congregation remained ambivalent. The ambivalence expressed itself in the lack of welcome and direction to visitors and potential members. The small, almost hidden sign at the front of the building; the blocked access to the front door; the badly marked side entrance; and the lack of signage throughout the building were all hallmarks of the wish to keep outsiders at bay. Only if potential members were persistent or knew someone in the congregation who would guide them into and through the building would they find their way inside.

There were other sorts of growing pains as well. The congregation had long grown dependent upon its original leader, who had been the driving force in the congregation and was almost solely responsible for creating social action initiatives, making decisions about worship practices and life-cycle events, and taking care of all administrative functions. When she left, there was a void. The congregation had gotten used to her doing many things for them, in the way that teenagers get used to their mothers picking up after them. Growing up means taking responsibility. The scatterings of books and dishes, the messy desks, the empty pizza boxes stacked atop full garbage cans, the empty bookshelves that blocked doorways—all were signals that the congregation had not yet decided to grow up. They had not outgrown their collective desire to be taken care of, picked up after, nagged. Their wish that their new part-time rabbi would do this for them and her thoughtful refusal to do so were part of their growth struggles. They needed to grow up, to take responsibility for their own growth as Jews and as a congregation. The building and its upkeep was simply a manifestation of that need.

The physical space of a synagogue can thus tell us much about the underlying nature and issues of a congregation. The history of a synagogue, and the culture set in motion by that history, is often on display in ways obvious (plaques, dedications, pictures of founders) and, as in our case study, not so obvious. The issues confronting synagogues as they go about trying to grow or change are on display as well if we know how to look closely enough around us. One of the things we look for is the nature and depth of people's commitments to their synagogues. Fortunately, the signs of commitment are relatively easy to observe. People take good care of what they value. They invest money, time, and energy to make spaces clean, comfortable, and attractive. We knew by the way the Shir Tikva congregation did not take care of the facility that there was ambivalence in the members' commitments to the institution. The place looked like an afterthought. It existed at the periphery of members' lives. And that raised our concern. Synagogues that exist somewhere closer to the center of people's lives appear that way. They are held in people's minds as valuable and meaningful; the spaces they inhabit reflect that sense of importance.

Building It So That They Will Come

How does a congregation create a space that reflects its importance to the community? Synagogues must be *uplifting, practical, accessible,* and *well tended.* To the extent that these dimensions are manifest in a synagogue, they help create places to which members are powerfully drawn.

Uplifting

Rabbi Abraham Joshua Heschel wrote in his book *The Sabbath,* "Judaism is a religion of time, aiming at the sanctification of time. . . . Judaism teaches us to be attached to holiness in time, to be attached to sacred events, to learn how to consecrate sanctuaries that emerge from the magnificent stream of a year. The Sabbaths are our great cathedrals."[1] We agree. Though there are many beautiful synagogues throughout the world, Judaism has not been the religion of cathedrals. We have chosen to celebrate time rather than space. Yet space is still important to us. The original tabernacle in the desert may have been nothing more than a portable tent, but it was a beautiful one, filled with handcrafted ritual items, made with great intricacy of detail and even greater care.

The tabernacle—and many of its successors—sought to stimulate certain emotions within Jews who worshiped there. Part of the experience of being in a synagogue is the opportunity to feel specific emotions that we might not normally experience in the course of our daily lives. We may experience a sense of awe as we worship together and recite the prayers of our ancestors. We may feel close to others as we move together through the cycles of our lives. We may feel inner peace and contentment as we celebrate or pray. We may feel profound grief and sadness, and deep comfort, too, as we recite *kaddish.* We might feel a sense of connection to a community as we study and learn. We might feel a sense of peace as we settle into a deeply familiar rhythm of song and prayer and meditation.

The synagogue is a place—and for some, the only place—where such emotions can be felt. Jews have been drawn to synagogues not simply for what occurs there—worship, study, community gatherings—but for what they feel when they are there. We wish to be uplifted, elevated to spiritual or emotional heights. Judaism offers us the opportunity for precisely this experience—to be lifted up from the ordinary concerns and preoccupations of our daily existence and to consider our lives and our communities from heightened perspectives.

Judaism elevates through its rituals, practices, celebrations, and Torah. The synagogue itself—the buildings, their contents, the use and decoration of space—contributes a great deal as well. We are physical beings with many senses, each of which has the potential to transport us. We can feel close to God gazing upon a sunset, looking down from a mountaintop, seeing a flower inching its way through the ground in spring. We can feel a sense of spirituality, of something powerful moving under the surface of our lives, when we hear a haunting melody, ancient prayers, somber or joyous choruses, or something moving us closer to our relationship with God. We can feel blessed by artistry, in paintings and stained glass, woodwork and sculptures. We are physical beings, and as such, our physical surroundings affect us. Aesthetics are not merely background material; they can lift us up spiritually, liberating us for a moment from the daily lives in which we are grounded.

The synagogue can be a place where this uplifting occurs. Consider the space itself. Sanctuaries may allow space for God to enter. They can be expansive, allowing congregants to open themselves up, to cast their eyes upon different dimensions of the space around them. When we are in cramped spaces, we withdraw; we circle and protect ourselves. We are distracted from the experience of worship and prayer. Sanctuaries can also uplift by offering windows, literally, that enable congregants to look at the natural world. In fact, the Talmud teaches us that it is forbidden to pray in a room that has no windows. The experiences of seeing trees move in the wind, snow falling, leaves turning different colors, and the movement of sun and clouds enable some of us to feel closer to our spiritual selves and to God as we pray and sing and worship together. And, too, sanctuaries can uplift by what they contain. Arks and *bimahs* that draw the eye, that stand out from their surroundings, can usher us toward a sense of grace and beauty. Artwork, woodwork, stained glass, and the like can move us toward a sense that a sanctuary is an extraordinary place, a *makom kadosh,* and we can be extraordinary within it.

Other synagogue spaces can be similarly uplifting. Chapels offer the opportunity for intimacy, for meaningful connections between congregants that enable them to find God in relationship with one another. Social halls, meeting rooms, and other places where communities gather can allow for celebration and joy. Space that allows people to connect with one another—to see and hear one another, to sit and be comfortable with one another, to dance and sing with one another—moves people toward a sense of connection and spirit. Windows, artwork, and architecture in these spaces are the portals through which people's spirits may be moved. Libraries, and the quiet and comfort they afford, are places where people's minds may flourish and insights flower. Libraries, and offices and classrooms more generally, that are comfortable and attractive enable people to work amid a sense of order, calm, and beauty. They lift people up and call them to their most profound work and relations. And clergy studies that allow people to feel a sense of *shalom* in the midst of congregants' stormy lives allow for healing that leads to wholeness and peace.

Practical

Synagogues need not be gaudy or ostentatious to be uplifting. Nor ought they be impractical spaces that are large or stunning but do not serve the real needs of a congregation. The original tabernacle, as beautiful as it was, was at its core a practical space. Everything in it had its purpose; everything was used for the bringing and reception of offerings that allowed the individual to (re)connect with God. Similarly, synagogues need to be well used and used well. They must meet the needs of the community.

Form should follow function. We create programs, attract people to them, and then make certain we have the spaces to accommodate them. A synagogue without a religious school hardly needs many classrooms. An urban congregation may want a large space that opens up into the street to facilitate its soup kitchen. A synagogue in a retirement community requires adult lounge areas for its daily schmooze (lunch and table games hour) as well as adult classrooms for its annual elder hostel. In each of these cases, the physical spaces within the synagogue building need to match the functions for which they are used, not the other way around. Inasmuch as the functions flow from their sense of mission, there ought to be no conflict, no tension between the daily activities and the physical structures built to house them. This is one hallmark of a healthy congregation. When we attempt to build structures and spaces first and then try to create programs to fill them, we often wind up spending time doing lots of things no one really believes in just to "fill the space."

The principle that form ought to follow function applies to congregations of any size. We find that many synagogue buildings are underutilized, standing empty most days for most of the day. Synagogues have to be "big enough." At the same time, we do not build a facility that drains precious resources in both construction and ongoing maintenance costs. That means we do not build facilities *for* the High Holy Days, but we keep those days in mind when we do build. Still, we may decide that for two or three days a year, the congregation will pray in the local civic center or a large hotel's ballroom so that the entire community can pray together in a single service.

Just as we can tell a great deal about a person or a community by looking at their daily calendar and their checkbook, we can also obtain clues by looking at the space they inhabit. Parents who create a home that does not contain a bookshelf can hardly be serious about inculcating a love of reading in their children. In the same fashion, synagogues offer clues about their core values, what they really care about, in the ways they create and use space. Synagogues that care about learning create libraries and classrooms where people want to sit. Synagogues that care about celebration create spaces where people can gather for joyful singing and dancing. Synagogues that care about worship create sanctuaries where people can, without distraction, easily pray and attend to their rabbis, cantors, and one another. And as priorities within a congregation inevitably shift and change over time, so the spaces that house them must be rehabilitated or created anew.

A practical space is thus one that draws people toward rather than away from certain tasks and experiences. The classroom fits precisely the needs of teachers and learners, the sanctuary the needs of clergy and congregants, the offices the needs of staff. In a practical space, one does not have the awkward, uncomfortable sense of meeting or working in a space that was designed for some completely different activity. What we do—praying, planning, celebrating, studying, working—is infinitely enhanced, often in ways too subtle to name but crucial nonetheless, when we are in precisely the right space, exactly where we need to be.

Accessible

Synagogues are accessible to the extent that they present low barriers to entry. People need to find their way to and through synagogues. We mean this literally, of course, as well as figuratively. It should be reasonably easy for visitors to find and follow directions to the building. Those who drive to shul should be able to park their cars. It should be quite clear where the synagogue's entrances are. There should be ramps and designated parking spaces for handicapped and elderly visitors and members. Synagogues that have multistory buildings need convenient elevators as well as staircases. These are basic, albeit essential requirements for enabling people to enter synagogues with a minimum of distraction and aggravation.

Synagogues thus make themselves accessible when they help people find their way to where they need to go. This accessibility is partly a matter of architecture and partly about the use of physical space. Tables and couches in community spaces are placed in ways that allow people to congregate without disrupting the comings and goings of others or the activities of those in adjacent rooms. Corridors are well lit and uncluttered so that congregants and staff can easily move about. Such factors might seem insignificant in relation to other dimensions of synagogues—their cultures and leadership, the vibrancy of their missions, the demographic changes that shape their activities. Yet such small physical realities shape the daily experience of people as they inhabit their synagogues. More profoundly, they shape how people find their ways more or less easily to the intellectual, spiritual, and emotional experiences they seek in worship, study, and collective action.

A final dimension of accessibility is the extent to which people are guided throughout the synagogue. In our case study, people trying to find their way into and around Shir Tikva were constantly lost. People new to the building hunted for offices or classrooms, often wandering and feeling frustrated and, more subtly, not welcomed. Synagogues that do not offer various roadmaps in the form of signs, floor plans, and other postings or friendly faces (staff and congregants) to help people navigate their buildings send similar messages of unwelcome. Once people enter the building, they should be able to see clearly where they need to go, a central office or desk of some kind, to find someone willing to guide them.

Entering a synagogue is difficult enough for many of us. It is in synagogues that we bring our troubling questions—about meaning, God, the nature of our relations with one another. It is in synagogues that we are confronted with rituals, texts, and practices that, while comforting, may also seem alien or impenetrable. And it is in synagogues that we allow ourselves to feel deeply—grief, joy, sadness. None of these is a simple experience. None is easily approached. To the extent that our synagogues are accessible, inviting us in and welcoming us, we move with more purpose and confidence to acceptance and comfort with our Jewish identities and practices.

Well Tended

How we take care of physical space sends a powerful message about the extent to which we care about it and what it means to us. In the ancient and medieval worlds, the grandest building in a community was the house of worship. Today it is most often a financial center. Modern banks, trading firms, and financial service buildings are often stunning in their architecture and appointments. They gleam. They are meant to display wealth and hint at the riches that lie within. We are not suggesting that synagogues need to look like places that store and make money, yet we are convinced that a community that takes pride in its synagogue will take good care of it. And when it does, it will likely also take good care of the people, congregants and staff alike, who call it home.

Several factors are worth pointing out here. A focus on the spiritual qualities of synagogues need not mean that their physical dimensions are neglected, in the way that the ascetics and mystics of earlier times let their bodies waste away in their zeal for connection to God. Synagogues are not-for-profit institutions, but they need not look downtrodden. There is a classic not-for-profit agency look. Piles of papers everywhere, posters in warped frames, books leaning against walls, bookshelves bowed in the middle, walls that need painting, bathrooms a decade or more out of date, fluorescent lights glaring, and a smell in the air that is part musty, part old cigarette. Hidden beneath such appearances is the unspoken notion that donors' monies cannot be spent on looking good. The wish is that people will view those who work in such places as selfless and humble, caring only about the noble work they do and not about their own comfort.

Unfortunately, another, more powerful, message is sent by such an environment: that nothing of great quality could ever come from a place that looks sloppy, unkempt, and uncared for. When we cannot organize our surroundings, keep them orderly and appealing, we often cannot organize ourselves to do good work. When people settle for messiness and disorder in their surroundings, they often do so as well in the quality of their work and relationships. In other words, their standards for the spaces in which they work parallel those for the work itself.

There is a powerful lesson here for synagogues. Synagogues are healthy and vibrant to the extent that congregants, clergy, staff, and lay leaders invest time and effort in who they are and what they do in their synagogues. They take themselves seriously, as though what they do, individually and together, really matters. Such investment is manifested partly by how well their synagogues are tended—maintained, cleaned, tastefully decorated, updated. The basic premise here is that a community that joins together to do the most basic of tasks related to housekeeping and upkeep of the place where members "dwell" together is poised to join together on far more complicated tasks as members accompany one another on their journeys of joy, sadness, celebration, and spiritual growth.

The other dimension worth acknowledging here is our notion of a synagogue as a communal "home." We all grow up with particular understandings of what home is, what it looks like, and what it means to take care of it. What is common, however, is the centrality of home in our lives. We reside there. It helps identify us. We take care of it as an extension of who we are. The same holds true for synagogues. The synagogue is a home in multiple ways: it is the place where Jews return to worship, study, and spend time together; it is the place where they become a social unit; it is a place that offers refuge and a sense of one's origins; it is a place where one's identity, or a piece of it, is formed and maintained. We define home in all these ways. All are found in the synagogue as well. And all are reasons to keep our communal homes clean, orderly, maintained, and, literally and figuratively, well lit, just as the menorahs gave light to the ancient temple in Jerusalem. In fact, after the Macabbees cleared and cleansed the temple, the first thing they sought to do was light the menorah.

In practice, tending the physical dimensions of a synagogue is pretty simple. It means maintaining the grounds. It means painting and fixing inside and outside. It means people picking up messes, regardless of whether it is their job to do so. It means keeping spaces clean. It means maintaining some degree of orderliness, in spite of the many forces of disorder—youth group parties, committee meetings, large worship services, overflowing bulletin boards, and the like—that mark a busy synagogue. It means keeping information up-to-date on Web sites and bulletin boards. It means, above all, a collective mindfulness that the spaces inside and outside the synagogue are holy, *kadosh*. If people are so mindful, they cannot help but tend well to their synagogues, inside and out. And they cannot help but tend to their own Jewish identities, which their synagogues exist to nurture.

The Spaces of Work

Synagogues are places where people are nurtured in faith and formed as communities. They are also places where people work. Staff, clergy, and lay leaders meet to develop strategies and programs, supervise others, solve problems, deal with financial matters, and counsel and teach congregants. Much of the activity we have discussed in this chapter occurs in the public spaces of the synagogue. However, there is, or ought to be, a "backstage" area as well, a private space where people can, undisturbed, do the work that enables the organization to thrive.

These spaces need to be thought about. Offices, conference rooms, and staff lounges need to be comfortable and adequately lit, heated (in winter) and cooled (in summer). They need to be reasonably well appointed, with desks, tables, and chairs that people would not be ashamed to use. Offices need to be clean and organized. And the typical complement of office tools—computers, copiers, and phone systems—need to be reasonably up-to-date and well maintained. These basic requirements are necessary not simply for people to get their work done, but also to adequately provide for staff and clergy. They have demanding jobs and are often expected to care for a variety of congregants' needs, large and small. To the extent that they themselves feel valued, cared for, and invested in, they are more likely to work on behalf of others without resentment. Everyone benefits when staff and clergy can enjoy working in spaces of which they are proud rather than being resigned to working in spaces they feel are demeaning in one fashion or another.

These workspaces need to be separate from the public spaces of the synagogue for at least two reasons. First, it is simply easier for people to get their work done when they are not constantly on display. Clergy and staff members, as in any organization, need time to think, write, meet, and converse without distraction. Second, and more particular to syna-gogue dynamics, clergy and staff need to be able to form connections with one another that enable them to withstand the constant, often contradictory waves of information, requests, and demands that stream in from congregants. They need time to digest and make sense of all that comes at them. They can best do this when there are some boundaries that separate them from the other, more public parts of the synagogue. Appropriately designed space can help with this. Staff lounges, confer-ence rooms, and offices spacious enough for meetings offer useful borders.

At the same time, however, we need to think about the integration of volunteers in the work of the synagogue. Volunteers do much of the work of congregations, yet we are continually surprised by the lack of space dedicated to congregants who do such work. Too few synagogues have volunteer desks with access to a phone or a computer. Even fewer have a volunteer office. Some do not even have a mailbox for the board president. While most congregations have marked parking spots for staff, very few have them for volunteers who are on and off campus frequently during the week. These physical realities send messages. They suggest that congregants must struggle unnecessarily to contribute their time and energies. They suggest that volunteers are not valued enough to have dedicated space. And they suggest a separation rather than integration of paid and volunteer workers. If we want volunteers to take their work at the synagogue seriously, we need to provide serious physical resources for them to get the job done.

Invitational Spaces

In an earlier chapter we wrote that the healthy synagogue is marked by a culture of invitation. People are ushered into experiences that enable them to affirm and deepen their Jewish identities. In this chapter, we suggest (and hopefully make the case) that the actual spaces synagogues create influence the extent to which people feel invited into those experiences. The layout and design of sanctuaries can move us toward the experience of worship, prayer, and insight; social halls can move us toward cele-bration and a sense of community; classrooms can move us toward one another and our teachers in the spirit of inquiry and learning. These spaces can be conducive; that is, they can guide us toward the intellectual, emotional, and spiritual places that we seek in ourselves and our synagogues. And too, the workspaces that support synagogue life can invite people to take up their identities as competent, valued workers who care for others in ways that they themselves feel cared for and invested in.

Surroundings matter. They send powerful, if subtle or unconscious messages, about what is valued and what is not in synagogue life. People respond to those messages. They experience them as expectations and react accordingly. If a library is messy, contains few volumes, and has little space for comfortable reading, the implicit expectation about the extent to which people are expected to care for books and, perhaps more generally, learn from sacred texts, is low. People will live down to that expectation. If a sanctuary is cared for, looks lovely, and offers comfort, the implicit expectation about the extent to which people are expected to engage in meaningful worship is high. People will live up to that expectation. Our physical surroundings issue invitations that call for us to behave in certain ways.

We can all be mindful of what types of experiences the physical spaces of our synagogues move us toward or away from. To the extent possible, we can press for changes in those spaces in how they are filled up and how they are used. Changes need not involve a great financial investment. A synagogue does not have to be wealthy to enable congregants, clergy, staff, and volunteers to get their needs met and do good work. But like our own bodies, which house our souls, synagogues must be cared for and nourished. If we are proud—not vain, but proud—of how our synagogues look, we are far more likely to be proud of what we do within them.

Note

1. A. J. Heschel, *The Sabbath* (New York: Farrar, Strauss, and Giroux, 1951), 8.

Part 2

Healthy Congregants

6

RELATING TO AUTHORITY

Moses received Torah from Sinai and delivered it to Joshua,
and Joshua to the elders, and the elders to the prophets, and
the prophets delivered it to the men of the great synagogue.
(Mishna Pirke Avot 1:1)

Healthy synagogues require healthy congregants. We mean something
quite specific by this: people who approach the synagogue as a place in
which to meet appropriate needs and are willing to assume the role of
congregants in doing so. People of all ages can legitimately approach the
synagogue to deepen, enrich, and cherish their identities as Jews. They
can worship and study. They can learn Torah. They can celebrate. They
can pursue *tikkun olam* in the context of social action projects. They can
engage in the rituals and practices by which they define their Judaism.
They can seek and contribute resources, support, and community for
life-cycle events. They can involve themselves in teaching the next generations of Jews and in building strong programs and institutions to sustain those generations.

These are all quite reasonable needs and ought to lead people toward
synagogue life. Yet people can bring other kinds of motivations to their
synagogues as well that are less appropriate, as we shall see in the next
several chapters. Such motives include, for example, the need to be taken
care of completely and abjectly by others or, conversely, the need to strike
out against or in other ways undermine other people. These motives render congregants less healthy. They get in the way of their becoming present,
willing, and able to participate in shaping and being fully engaged in the
life of those synagogues.

Indeed, such ability and willingness lie at the core of what it means
to be a healthy congregant. The beloved Talmud story of Rabbi Hillel
(Tractate Shabbos 21a) has him responding to a prospective proselyte
who wished to learn the entirety of Jewish law in the time that he would
be able to stand on one foot. Hillel replied, "Do not do to your neighbor

that which you do not wish to be done to you; this is the entire Torah, and all else is the commentary. Now go and learn that." Had Rabbi Hillel been asked what it means to fully be a congregant, he could have instructed, "Participate, fully and lovingly, in the life of your synagogue; all the rest is commentary. Now go and do that." The willingness and the ability to participate—to bring one's competent, joyous, and reflective self into the synagogue, in some fashion or another—lies at the heart of healthy congregants and healthy congregations.

We will examine this idea more carefully throughout part 2 of the book. At its core, participation means creating relationships. Healthy congregants strive to create productive, meaningful relationships with clergy, with one another, with teachers and other staff, and with Judaism itself. This represents a shift across the generations. The quote at the beginning of this chapter contains no reference to the Jewish people, the original congregants. Rather, it speaks to the authoritarian pattern of leadership, with rabbi as keeper of the Torah, which gets passed down from rabbi to rabbi. This pattern dominated the first 18 centuries of Jewish life. Previous generations of rabbis at times actually owned the synagogue building. Rabbis were often unapproachable but highly respected. Vestiges remain. Many *bimahs*, to this day, have the clergy emerging from behind the wall, not walking in the way the congregants have to do. The participation of the congregants was by and large limited to praying, celebrating life-cycle events and holy days, and supporting the rabbi.

New generations of rabbis and congregants, beginning with those raised in the 1960s, wanted a different sort of partnership with one another. They wanted to cocreate the synagogue, with each contributing something unique and important to the partnership. This requires a certain degree of participation on the part of congregants. They are asked not simply for their money, but for their labor, their ideas, their energy, and their voices. They are asked to be meaningful partners. This gets defined differently, in practice, by particular denominational movements and synagogues, but all told there is an expectation that congregants will be participants more than simply audiences.

There are, of course, both healthy and unhealthy ways in which to participate as a congregant, just as there are both healthy and unhealthy ways to create relationships of any kind. In this chapter, we examine one particular dimension that influences the nature and underlying health of congregants' participation—*authority*. People create certain relationships with those who are in authority, which shapes to a large extent what they do and how they feel. In this case, we are focusing on how congregants create certain kinds of relationships with clergy as figures of authority.

We define authority not in terms of hierarchy or power, but rather in terms of the right to do work. Rabbis and cantors are authorized by congregations (or more precisely, by boards of directors, who themselves have been authorized by congregants) to perform certain tasks. They are given the authority to do work, and to make decisions and delegate tasks in the service of that work. In a thoroughly rational world, such authority would be used and responded to in reasonable, appropriate ways. In a thoroughly rational world, clergy and congregants would create reasonable, appropriate relations of authority.

The synagogue, like other complex organizations, is not always marked by thorough rationality. People may respond to one another in ways that, considered rationally, do not seem to make much sense. They may come on too strong to one another. They may avoid useful, if difficult conversations. They may create relationships that do not help real work to get done or important needs to be met. When such occurs a great many factors may be involved. What we have noticed, however, is that more often than not difficult or unproductive relationships in the synagogue— particularly those between congregants and clergy, but with lay leaders and staff as well—can be partly traced to issues involving how authority is understood and worked with. Let's explore those issues in depth.

The Authority That We Imagine

It should be a relatively simple process. Congregants select from among themselves a group to represent their interests. These are boards authorized to make decisions that serve the organizational needs of the synagogue as a whole. In turn, boards select clergy to serve as spiritual leaders. Rabbis and cantors are authorized to make decisions that serve the spiritual needs of the synagogue as a whole. For their part, congregants authorize themselves to participate fully in—and take some responsibility for—the practices of study, worship, social action, celebration, and the building of the synagogue community. This interlocking system of authority provides a reasonably clean set of distinctions about roles and responsibilities. Everyone is responsible for assuming appropriate, reasonable authority according to his or her role in the synagogue.

It does not always work this way, of course. The process of authorizing people in reasonable, appropriate ways is too often distorted. The distortions revolve around how clergy, and rabbis in particular, are perceived by congregants and lay leaders, and indeed, by themselves as well. At play in those perceptions are various assumptions, beliefs, and images of which people are often quite unaware. People look to rabbis (and to a slightly lesser extent, cantors) as saviors, as father and mother figures, as caretakers, or as forbidding figures of authority. Such images powerfully shape what occurs in synagogue life, even as people are not consciously aware of them and are more than likely to deny their existence.

Where do these images come from? We first need to look at what synagogues represent to people. As congregants, we bring to our synagogues not simply the conscious wish for opportunities to study, pray, celebrate life-cycle events, and engage in social action. We bring as well our longings to be cared for—to be healed, taught, comforted, and ministered to. We wish, at some level of awareness, to be protected. We wish to believe in the omnipotence of clergy, as if they are one step closer to God. Holding such wishes and longings, congregants—and this includes lay leaders—regress. We return psychologically to an earlier time in our lives when we were dependent on others whom we perceived as strong and protecting. We often unconsciously model our relations with rabbis in particular on the basis of earlier patterns, when our parents met our needs in certain functional or dysfunctional ways.

This is not a new idea, of course. Freud described the psychological concept of *transference*. People transfer images and patterns of previous relationships onto current ones, mapping the present according to the past. This is a sophisticated way of describing what we often see in synagogue life: rabbis and congregants (including lay leaders) relate to one another in ways that are startlingly reminiscent of parent-child relationships. Congregants who may be extremely capable in their outside lives as doctors, homemakers, attorneys, professors, social workers, or some other role, often wait for the rabbi to take care of things, like program details and managing their own committee's agenda, that they themselves can easily handle. Rather than authorize themselves to think proactively about events they volunteered to handle, they wait for the clergy to take charge and make decisions. They seem to leave their adult, responsible selves outside the door of the synagogue and assume that the clergy will handle things.

There is, of course, an understandable pull for this. People often come to synagogue to be taken care of by the clergy: ushered through life-cycle moments, helped in counseling situations, led in worship, blessed and prayed for, educated. We entrust our children and ourselves to our clergy. For some of us, the synagogue is a somewhat unfamiliar world, about which we know some things but not others—and those others, like the simplest ritual action or Hebrew blessing, may leave us feeling infantilized by the entire synagogue experience.

It is no wonder, then, that we map onto our relations with our clergy an image of them as parents, in one fashion or another, and of ourselves as children. In some ways, this regression is necessary. It allows us to accept guidance, comfort, blessing, and *halachic* decisions. On the other hand, it may also get in the way of creating healthy relationships with our clergy. We may become too passive and empower our clergy at the expense of our own growth and competence. Or we may become angry and frustrated, as children do, and turn away from or act out against our clergy. When we draw on the parent-child pattern, as we inevitably do, we may thus regress in ways that may or may not be useful to what we need from our synagogues and clergy.

Congregants and lay leaders are not alone in creating these sorts of relationships. Rabbis and cantors collude with them as well. They bring their own sets of assumptions, beliefs, and images into the equation, of which they are often quite unaware. They may look at congregants as needy and dependent, as demanding and entitled, as lost and searching, as yearning. These images, too, shape what occurs in synagogue life, in ways of which clergy may not be consciously aware. Such images reflect their own experiences with authority, in the context of their own early family experiences and influences thereafter. They reflect as well the psychological action of countertransference, in which clergy's own wishes and feelings are stirred up by interactions with congregants, and they react in ways that help them manage the resulting impulses. They do so by adopting certain stances and roles relative to congregants.

Thus, some clergy are personally drawn toward taking on a parental role that feels familiar to them. They might say they are simply "doing their jobs" by being very parental in taking care of and seeming to know everything, even as it inhibits congregants and lay leaders from assuming appropriate responsibility. Other clergy are personally drawn toward a more distant, unapproachable role, which also feels familiar to them. Such roles enable clergy members to retreat to types of interactions and relationships that feel psychologically comfortable to them. Clearly, this has certain consequences, healthy and unhealthy, for the relations they create and for the synagogue more generally.

We are suggesting here that there is much, very rarely if ever talked about, that goes on beneath the surface of how congregants and rabbis go about interacting with one another. Underground currents of emotions, fears, hopes, and longings course beneath what we can easily observe about synagogues—their buildings, programs, and services, and what people do together to make them work. Our focus here is on how congregants navigate those currents, through creating certain types of relationships with their clergy. The following case study offers us a way into further examination of such relationships.

The Contract

It was time for contract renewal at Congregation Beth Israel. The rabbi had led the congregation for seven years, and much had been accomplished in that period. Outreach programs to the community, a sharpened educational mission for children and families, and a vibrant social action agenda had been implemented under the rabbi's leadership. He was well regarded by his congregants and had established personal ties to many of those who served in leadership positions or who were otherwise involved in the synagogue community. The few performance reviews that had been undertaken had gone well, and the rabbi had taken the feedback seriously.

It was thus with some surprise that the rabbi received the personnel committee's contract offer. The offer was for a one-year contract renewal with only a cost-of-living increase. Previous contracts had been for two, two, and then three years; each with a significant salary increase as well. There was no mention in the contract of a sabbatical, in spite of the fact that the rabbi and past board president had informally agreed, in negotiating the previous contract, that the next one would include a six-month sabbatical. The rabbi had been expecting something much different than what he received. He was not pleased.

The rabbi spoke with the chair of the personnel committee. He told her that he was unhappy with the contract offer and that it was much less, in terms of both time period and money, than what he had expected. He asked her the reasoning behind the offer. She explained that the offer was not a reflection of his performance, but that the committee was concerned about making a long-term commitment to him, or to any rabbi, given the state of the synagogue's finances. The rabbi knew some of the financial situation, even though he was often kept at arm's length from the synagogue's finances by the board. He knew that membership had been more or less stagnant over the past several years, given the community's demographic decline. And he knew that with the help of several significant donations, the synagogue was just breaking even. This did not strike the rabbi as that different than previous years or, for that matter, than other synagogues that he knew about from his colleagues in the area. He was left dissatisfied with the committee chair's response.

Over the course of the next few weeks, the rabbi gathered more information. He did not have to look far. Several members of the personnel committee each called to tell him that they did not personally support the committee's decision about the contract, in spite of the fact that he had been told by the chair that it had been a unanimous vote by the committee. Several congregants stopped by his office as well, telling him that they were appalled at the committee's actions. A supporter on the board told him that the executive committee was gathering some more financial information that would help them figure out how to handle the discrepancy between what the rabbi was wanting and expecting and what the personnel committee had offered.

The rabbi listened to what people had to say, nodded, and went about his work. Privately, he was upset. He knew that the way in which the personnel committee, and the board more generally, were handling this was poor. The contract offer was insulting. To go from a three-year contract to a one-year contract was, to his mind, a demotion. It suggested that the synagogue was lessening its ties and its commitments to him. This left him feeling badly—it was a rejection that he had not seen coming, nor did it seem warranted, given the positive feedback that he had been given over the years—and in turn it left him less interested in a long-term relationship with the synagogue. He began thinking about leaving; he would rather be in a place that wanted him and what he had to offer.

It was thus again with some surprise that he received the revised contract offer. The terms of this offer were quite different. The contract called for four years, a reasonably significant raise for the first year and thereafter, and a six-month sabbatical in the second year of the term. The rabbi was pleased but stunned. He did not understand why this offer was so different or, for that matter, why it had not been the offer in the first place. Over the course of several days, he thought not about the offer—it was exactly what he wanted and, indeed, more money than he had been expecting—but about the process by which it had come about. That process left him uneasy for reasons he could not fully pinpoint. He finally accepted the offer and, in doing so, requested a meeting with both the committee chair and the board president to examine the process and what it meant for their relationships going forward.

Move Closer! Go Away!

At first glance, this case study is a portrait of a frustrating (and all too familiar) contract negotiation process. It shows a committee that was not particularly thoughtful about the messages that it was sending the rabbi of its congregation about his worth and value. It suggests duplicity on the part of the committee chairperson, or its members, or both. It shows what happens when a committee goes ahead and engages a process without having done its homework, both in terms of the rabbi's expectations and the synagogue's true financial conditions and plans. And it reveals the power that a negotiation process has to disrupt a good working relationship between a rabbi and a congregation. One might look at this case and simply be glad that it worked out, or seemed to, for the rabbi, and ultimately for the synagogue.

There is much moving beneath the surface of this case study, however. If we look closely enough, we can see messages about the authority relations that the congregation is creating with its rabbi. One set of messages, sent via the initial contract, diminishes the rabbi's authority and importance. The contract signals rejection. It signals a lack of appreciation. It signals disrespect. If we interpret these signals through the lens of authority relationships, which are always at play between synagogues and clergy, we can see the synagogue, through its personnel committee, asserting its power over its rabbi. The tables are turned. The rabbi's power—to soothe and comfort, admonish and teach, lead and inspire—is offset by the congregation's power to render him helpless and frustrated. The rabbi becomes dependent for a job and money. The congregants, for the moment, act as if they do not need him.

A second, confusing set of messages is sent when individual members of the committee contact the rabbi, saying they were not a part of the vote. This reminds us of little children telling their mommies and daddies that their big brother "broke the vase" while they were behaving themselves. Or perhaps even worse, that there are "good cops" and "bad cops" on the committee, and the rabbi needs to both know and ally with the good ones who will protect and take care of him.

The third set of messages is sent via the second contract. The congregation, again acting through the personnel committee, reverses itself and reaches out to the rabbi. The new contract is for more money than he was expecting. The revised contract signals desire. It signals shame and guilt. It signals the wish to keep the rabbi, to make amends. We can again interpret this through the lens of the authority relations between congregation and rabbi: the congregation is anxious about not losing their rabbi, on whom they are dependent, and showers him with incentives to remain. They act as if they do, indeed, need him and cannot bear to have him go.

At the end of the case, the rabbi feels uneasy about what has happened. He ought to. He was caught in the undercurrents of his congregation's reactions to the authority of his role and unpleasantly swept this way and that. The congregation gave him a double message: go away, and come here. The congregation sought to reject and then cling to its rabbi. Presumably, this was not an isolated event. It suggests a larger ambivalence—a simultaneous desire to embrace and push away the rabbi—which gets acted out in several other ways as well, such as limiting his access to the finances of the synagogue or the personnel committee offering him an insulting contract while having several committee members act as if they are outraged. The congregation brings him close and keeps him distant simultaneously.

Patterns of Authority

The lens we use to look at this case, which focuses on how people react to authority, is not a simple one. It requires a willingness to believe that people, and the congregations and committees and boards they create, can be motivated to act in ways of which they are not consciously aware. If we believe that is possible, then we can examine some of the underlying patterns of authority on which people may unwittingly depend, and how those patterns create healthy or unhealthy relationships.

Dependence

In this pattern, congregants act as if clergy are the parent in a parent-child relationship and must meet certain needs of congregants. Rabbis and cantors must protect their followers from danger. They must give comfort upon demand. They must provide resources. To maintain this illusion, congregants seek out and strive to follow what their clergy desire from them. They must be followers, in the fashion of children, taking little responsibility for their religious and spiritual journeys. This pattern has a long tradition. After all, the Jewish people are called *b'nai Yisrael*—the *children* of Israel—in the Torah. Wandering in the wilderness, they regress: they complain about the lack of water and food to eat, are frightened, demand to go back to Egypt, and petition Moses and Aaron to save them from their fear and pain. They act like children. God and Moses take care of and provide for their every need and, like parents, take turns getting angry when the children act out or disobey.

The dependence pattern is most visible in synagogue life when members look to their clergy to do for them what they as normally functioning adults ought to do themselves. They behave as if they cannot think and act for themselves. Committee chairs wait for the rabbi to give them guidance about what their committees ought to be working on for the year. Volunteers working on special programs wait for the rabbi to tell them how to organize themselves, what they ought to do to prepare for the program, and the like. Task forces created to lead major events wait for the cantor to provide guidelines for how and when music should be used. The board of directors meets and develops plans but does little else, expecting the clergy and staff to implement them on their own. In each of these arenas, everything the clergy provides—direction, advice, and suggestions—is welcomed and accepted with little comment, challenge, or improvement.

At the heart of this pattern is a certain degree of passivity on the part of congregants. They wait. They take little action on their own. They remain stuck or paralyzed when they try and develop or implement ideas. They expect to be taken care of and their needs fully met by the clergy. For their part, clergy perpetuate the dependence pattern by meeting all of those needs. They fill the void left by lay leaders and congregants. They meet others' expectations to be their caretakers. They act as if congregants or lay leaders have little to offer. They are the saviors, the heroes. This pattern can spread throughout the synagogue, to the point that paid staff members similarly regress and expect the clergy to do their work for them. Or, more generally, congregants may treat their lay leaders in the same fashion, expecting them to do all the work and own all the responsibility for the congregation's efforts. The rabbi is held at the center of the synagogue, and all revolves around him or her.

There are both healthy and unhealthy dimensions to dependence in a synagogue. Regression makes a good deal of sense in some situations. The congregant whose spouse is battling depression has every right to feel afraid and confused and to reveal herself as such to her rabbi. A committee assigned to develop a new prayer book for the congregation is smart to turn to their rabbi and cantor for guidance and support. A new member volunteering to lead a new Shabbat program ought to feel anxious and depend a great deal on those who have more experience. At such moments, leaning on others and waiting for their guidance is exactly right. Similarly, it is reasonable to expect that some congregants will work hard on behalf of the synagogue because they look up to their rabbis and wish to be noticed by them. This too, within limits, is appropriate and healthy.

However, there is an unhealthy dimension of this pattern that makes it difficult for members and leaders alike to evolve, to grow past the limitations they set upon themselves and others. Rabbis and cantors cannot develop congregants' capacities to think and act for themselves. They do their work for them. They hold on to knowledge, information, and visions. They become overinvolved to the extent that they, rather than their congregants and lay leaders, exist at the center of events and situations.

Counterdependence

In this pattern, congregants minimize their dependence on rabbis and cantors, as if they are not truly significant figures in the life of the synagogue. This can happen in several ways. Clergy may be put into very specific, limited roles as spiritual leaders who preside over life-cycle events and lead worship or develop programs. They are kept outside the "business" of the synagogue. Or clergy may occupy significant roles in theory, but in practice their authority and expertise are questioned, resisted, or acted out against, as if what they have to offer is not needed. Beneath the surface, their authority is minimized, undermined, and devalued by congregants and, to the extent that the pattern spreads, by staff as well.

The counterdependence pattern is most visible in synagogue life when congregants turn away from their clergy in one fashion or another. Boards of directors make decisions without so much as consulting or getting input from the rabbi, who clearly has expertise and a unique, important perspective on the spiritual and religious dimensions of the synagogue. Committees create programs without attempting to coordinate their agendas with rabbis and cantors. Or they create programs with clergy input and then ignore the plans completely, doing what they wish. In such ways, congregants and lay leaders deny their needs for assistance or support. They are counterdependent: they turn away from any real dependence on their clergy. We see signs of this in publicity materials such as announcements of synagogue events, brochures, and Web sites that leave out or minimize mention of clergy as well as other staff and their work.

There are traces of aggression in this pattern. It can appear in passive ways. Clergy are invited into the synagogue but held at arm's length. Their legitimate authority—based on their expertise, training, insight, and religious perspectives—is diminished. This may be done gently, even caringly, as congregants believe that they do not wish to burden their clergy. They may wish to protect them, as if rabbis are less than capable of engaging in, say, financial discussions ("Don't worry about that, Rabbi;

we know this is not your field"). Such caring does, however, diminish the rabbi's appropriate role. So, too, do the efforts of congregants to become close friends with clergy. While such friendships often make people feel good, clergy included, and help people to get to know and trust one another, other dynamics lie beneath the surface. The clergy's formal roles may drop away at work and be subsumed by personal relationships. This may not be useful for congregants, who need to depend on rabbis and cantors *as* rabbis and cantors, and is not useful for clergy either, as they seek to lead from their roles.

Congregants may also express aggression directly. They may openly resist the efforts of their clergy. They may distribute leaflets or circulate petitions. They may act out around contracts, as in the case study above. They may seek to drive their clergy away altogether. They may assume roles—as resisters, gossips, rebels, blockers—through which they express resentment toward the clergy and the authority they represent. Such resentment and, indeed, the aggression that fuels the counterdependence pattern, comes from various places. Individual congregants bring their own negative reactions or predispositions to authority into the synagogue. People also have anger about needing others. If dependence is about longing, counterdependence is about frustrated longing. We wish to believe in the hope and illusion of our clergy's omnipotence, but unable to sustain that illusion, we grow frustrated and angry. We turn against those who cannot possibly meet all our expectations and hopes.

For their part, clergy can perpetuate counterdependence in several ways. They can be unapproachable; they can respond badly to requests for emotional support; they can brush people off. Congregants respond by getting angry and keeping their distance. Clergy can also act fragile, as if they cannot handle too much. Congregants protect them by keeping their demands, and their dependence, low. Clergy can also draw too close to members by becoming their friends or becoming intimate with them. Even as congregants grow close in return, they withdraw their needs for clergy to be their rabbis or cantors. There is a seduction here. Clergy can seduce congregants into taking care of them. Or they allow themselves to be seduced by gifts, cash, tickets to sporting events, and the like. This meets certain needs: congregants get to be successful adults relative to their rabbis and cantors, who in turn receive needed income and enticing perks. The danger here is that clergy and congregants step away from how they ought to relate with one another; the latter become benefactors rather than congregants. Taken to an extreme, clergy abandon their roles and their congregants.

Counterdependence, too, has both healthy and unhealthy dimensions in synagogue life. It makes good sense for lay leaders, and congregants more generally, to take some ownership in what they and the synagogue do. Committees ought to pursue appropriate agendas without waiting for rabbis to lead them. Boards of directors need to implement leadership development processes without constantly turning to rabbis for their design. Congregants volunteering to run programs involving music ought to seek out those who have done so successfully in the past, rather than wait for the cantor to manage the process. At some moments, taking responsibility and not depending on clergy is precisely what ought to occur.

The unhealthy dimension of this pattern, of course, is that by pushing them away, congregants might well not have rabbis and cantors to help them when they need or ought to be helped. We need clergy to help us create and live out our Jewish identities. We need rabbis to counsel us, to lead us in prayer, to help us study and learn Torah. We need cantors to help us with our life-cycle moments, to lead our services, to teach our children to chant and sing the Jewish tradition. If we treat them as limited or fragile or needy, we cheat ourselves of their help and take from them the pleasure of doing their work. If we draw them too close in friendship or shower them with gifts (always a tricky and slippery slope to navigate) we alter our relationships and their ability to assume their roles properly as our clergy. If we draw too far away from them, projecting our own fears or resentments upon them, we also diminish their ability to work. When clergy colludes with any of these dynamics, they participate in that diminishment.

A Third Way

Each of these two patterns represents a choice that clergy and members implicitly make about how to negotiate dependency needs. When people choose to act as if clergy are parents and congregants are children, they are negotiating terms of surrender to authority. When they choose to act as if congregants are completely self-reliant and clergy are fragile, untrustworthy, or withholding, they are negotiating terms of escape from authority.

Congregants may follow either of these patterns briefly, during various transitions in their synagogues, or routinely, as their synagogues create certain cultures that persist over time. Some parts of the synagogue might follow one pattern, while other parts follow another. A board of directors, for example, might take on a counterdependent relationship with its rabbi, routinely shutting him out of their decision-making processes, while several committee chairs in the same synagogue strike a more dependent stance, waiting for the rabbi to provide direction and momentum. A congregation might also alternate, as in our case study about contract negotiations, by pushing clergy away and then running to bring them closer, or vice versa.

In each of these scenarios, and others like them, a congregation finds some way to embrace one part of its ambivalence toward authority (in the form of its clergy) and push away the other. They may fall into a pattern of embracing, or rejecting, but not both. Or some part of the congregation—board, committees, youth groups—takes on one pattern and another does the other pattern. Or there is a yo-yo effect, as in the case study, with the congregation expressing one side and then asserting its need for the other side. In each of these cases, it is difficult for congregants to hang on to both needs—to draw close to their clergy, and to remain independent of them—at the same time. So they split the two desires in one fashion or another, expressing one at the expense of the other.

There is another way, however. A pattern of interdependence is marked by a healthy respect for the need to be both connected to and separate from authority. Congregants are able to think and act independent of their clergy. Rabbis and cantors provide useful support in appropriate ways and at appropriate times. Together they create useful partnerships in which, like healthy marriages, they at times operate separately, each attending to particular tasks, and at other times join for support, planning, and action.

So what does interdependence look like in a synagogue? A congregant has an idea for a new program to attract young singles to the synagogue. She brings it to the cantor, who encourages her, connects her to others who have launched programs, and gives her some advice about the political landscape in the synagogue. The volunteer gathers a committee, makes the appropriate links with the standing social committee, and moves ahead, checking in with the cantor as needed for guidance. The program takes off. A board president is having difficultly recruiting new leaders to replace outgoing members. He consults the rabbi, who has some ideas about how to attract the newer generation of members. The board president takes some of the suggestions, changing them to fit his own style and perspective, and asks the rabbi to give a brief *d'var Torah* at the start of one of the events. A rabbi, preparing for her contract renewal process, meets with several members of the personnel committee to discuss the process and create mutual expectations about how it might be conducted in a manner useful for both sides.

Each of these examples is marked by a real partnership between clergy and congregants. No one clings too much to another; no one pushes another away. They each take up a completely appropriate role and do what they ought to do in relation to one another. They assume responsibility, each as they ought, given their roles in the synagogue.

Interdependence is created and maintained in part by congregants' devotion to the purposes of the synagogue as the place for study, prayer, and social gatherings. If congregants focus on those purposes, they have no choice but to take up a certain partnership with their clergy and, for that matter, with the lay leaders who represent them. The terms of the partnership are, or ought to be, clear: congregants offer ideas, invest energies, provide feedback, take and defend reasonable positions, seek out one another and their clergy, and show up and engage in the life of the synagogue; clergy provide direction, spiritual and otherwise, meet their congregants' needs as best they can and within reasonable limits, and do not allow themselves to be pulled away from their given roles and responsibilities.

We are suggesting that when such partnerships do not exist, congregants are not focusing so much on the purposes of the synagogue but on something else altogether. They have become distracted by their reactions to the authority represented in the form of their clergy. Transference, ambivalence, psychological baggage—whatever we wish to call it, there is often underlying "stuff" that gets in our way of creating appropriate, productive partnerships with our clergy, in which each side both depends upon and is independent from the other in healthy ways.

Healthy congregants are defined partly by their ability and willingness to recognize such "stuff" and how to deal with it appropriately.

Moving toward Healthy Ways of Relating to Authority

In chapter 14, we will focus on the clergy's responsibility to lead in appropriate ways. Our concern here is with how congregants can move toward increasingly healthy ways of relating to authority, that is, of creating good working partnerships with their clergy and one another. There are several parts to this process. The first has to do with congregants actually recognizing when those partnerships are flawed and their own part in making them so. This is a diagnostic process that requires congregants to reflect on their own behaviors—individual and collective—and their effects.

There are three types of signs to aid the diagnostic process. First are the repeated patterns in how congregants are treating rabbis and cantors, over time and across situations. A congregation might find that it is losing its third rabbi in six years, each of whom leaves complaining of not being trusted or worked with very well by lay leaders. Another congregation cycles through cantors who leave because they are burned out by a dynamic in which congregants say they want them to do many creative and innovative things but do nothing to support or even show up for these opportunities. Congregants may find themselves complaining over and over that their clergy are never doing enough, are too distant or unapproachable, or do not seem to know enough about what is going on in the synagogue. In any of these scenarios, congregants face a certain choice. They can believe that they just don't have the right rabbi or cantor, and that if only they found the right person, all would be well. Or they can think about why their relations with their clergy seem to follow certain patterns and what those patterns might mean.

Second, congregants may hold on to certain ways of seeing their clergy despite evidence to the contrary. One congregation believes that its rabbi is the central figure around which the synagogue revolves. This image remains even though there is a reasonably strong board of directors, director of education, and cantor, all of whom help create and implement vibrant programs and services. Another congregation believes that its cantor is too detached, not giving enough, even though she works especially hard with bar/bat mitzvah children and the adult choir, and is loved and appreciated by all. Yet another congregation believes that its cantor is fragile, unable to do much, even as he teaches a full schedule of classes and helps lead services. In such cases, congregants wish to believe in certain images of clergy—as figures upon whom they can depend to meet all their needs, as figures who cannot possibly meet any of their needs—in order to maintain certain patterns in the synagogue.

Third, there may be excess emotion. When congregants are stirred up to a response beyond what a situation ought to reasonably evoke, there is often much going on beneath the surface. We are referring to those interactions between congregants and clergy that are filled with emotion that seems out of proportion with actual events. A cantor misses an appointment with a board member, and suddenly the entire board is up in arms, upset with all sorts of things about her performance. A rabbi asks for a sabbatical to be made part of her next contract and is besieged with requests to delay it for several years or indefinitely because the synagogue simply cannot function without her. The clergy experiment with a new musical format for Shabbat services, and the congregation erupts in debate over whether or not they had the right to do so. In such cases, reasonable dialogue is overwhelmed by swells of emotion that seem only partly related to the event at hand. Such emotions exist beneath the surface like underground rivers and are released like geysers by events related to how leadership and authority are viewed and imagined.

These three types of signs can offer congregants, if they so choose, an opportunity to look carefully at the types of partnerships they have created with their rabbis and cantors and other senior staff. They can try to make sense of the patterns they have unwittingly constructed. To do this well requires us as congregants to look at what we have done with curiosity rather than certainty. We typically have favorite ways of explaining events: we chose the wrong rabbi; the cantor doesn't fit our traditions; the gap is too large between this generation of rabbis and the previous generation that we are used to. To interrupt unhealthy patterns in how we work with our clergy, we must hold loosely to our favorite explanations. We must allow ourselves, and others, to explore multiple interpretations for events. In this way, we can try and locate how we as congregants are helping to set up relations with our clergy in which we depend on them too much or too little.

Armed with such awareness, we can do something to interrupt un-healthy patterns. We can speak openly with one another and with our rabbis and cantors about what our partnerships ought to have. We can create a shared model of leadership, describing what it ought to look like given the work that we need to do together to fulfill the mission of the synagogue. We can then make sure that we try and create that model in our interactions.

In this process, we may find that there are some areas in which we need to move toward our clergy, involving them in matters that they ought to be involved in. We may find other areas in which we need to depend less on our clergy; in these areas, congregants need to take more personal authority on the notion that they, too, are partly responsible for the synagogue to which they belong. This is not so different than the relation between God and the Jewish people. We have a partnership with God. We retain responsibility for the lives we live, the communities we create, the good that we do. We depend on God but must depend on ourselves as well. It is in that image that we must try and create our relations with one another in the synagogue as well.

7

BEYOND MEMBERSHIP:
WHAT DOES IT MEAN TO
BELONG TO A COMMUNITY?

Al tifrosh min hatzibur
Do not separate yourself from the community
(Pirke Avot 2:5)

Judaism presumes community. Consider the *minyan*. We cannot begin our prayer service until the requisite number of Jewish people arrive and take their places as worshipers. The traditional quorum necessary to recite certain prayers consists of ten adult Jewish men. While today many denominational movements include women, the essential gesture of ten Jews coming together to create an entity remains the same. Jewish law states clearly that the public aspects of prayer—reading Torah, saying the *Kaddish* aloud, the *Barchu* call to worship—can only occur with a *minyan*. *Minyanim* are the building blocks for the Jewish community. That community is defined not so much by certain places—we can gather in homes, in synagogues, in parks—but by the people themselves. We need just ten Jews, the minimum number of righteous people in Abraham's pleas with God for the lives of the Sodomites (Genesis 18:32), and we begin to form as a people.

Holiness thus involves community. We can be holy through solitary acts as well, of course, but we are strengthened when we pray and practice with others. As *b'nai mitzvah*, we enter into the Jewish covenant in the presence of the community of our people. We are married as Jews in the context of our community. When we are sick or hurt, are dying or grieving, we are held by others; our pain is absorbed and dissipated through communal prayers and rituals that hold us steady. We celebrate the passing of seasons and our days within the extended community of the Jewish people. As Jews, our experiences of God are bound up with our experiences of being with one another in prayer and study and the living out of our faith.

It is intriguing to note that the *minyan* simply requires ten adult Jews, without specifying who those people might be. They could be learned or not; young or old; *Kohen* or Israelite; joyous or grieving. There is anonymity in this. Judaism survives because enough Jews show up at enough communal places for prayer, study, and acts of *g'milut hasadim.* We are sustained as a people not by the particular acts of any one individual but by our collective engagement with traditions and practices that have marked Jews for centuries. All that is required of us as individuals is that we identify ourselves as Jews, for it is within that community that Jews are best able to embrace and develop their identities as Jews.

One implication of this, of course, is that the synagogue must function in ways that honor the community that people create with one another. Jews affirm and deepen their religious and spiritual identities in relationship with one another. Celebrations, services, life-cycle events, holy days—all imply communal acts meant to enable people to feel joined with others, to feel not alone, to feel witnessed and valued. At the core of the synagogue, therefore, is a set of relationships whereby people feel joined, uplifted at times of communal prayer, and challenged to think and question and to give and be ministered to. Synagogues need to operate in ways that enable those relationships to flourish. Their practices need to be evaluated in terms of their implications for the health of people's relationships with one another and with those who lead.

In part 1 of this book, we discussed how synagogues might create communities to engage their members. In this particular chapter, we take a different perspective: how we, as synagogue members, are obligated to take up our memberships in ways that help create the communities that sustain Judaism and the Jewish people.

Partners in Community

Communities are increasingly a matter of will. People choose to belong to communities. They must be proactive about joining them and making them work. We are no longer simply born into a certain time and place with the expectation that we will remain there—in our places within a community that have been reserved for us by our parents and their parents in turn. This is a societal phenomenon. Relative to previous generations, we are more mobile as a society. People change jobs and careers three and four times in their lifetimes. Women have more options than ever before. There is more focus on individual happiness, fulfillment, and success. Urban centers have given way to expanding suburbs. All this and more have led to a gradual erosion of community as our grandparents, even our parents, understood it.

The breakdown of the traditional community and its organizing structures has added to our freedom to make our own decisions about the lives we choose to live. Such freedom has brought advances in human dignity, but at a price. We see it in the high divorce rate, the upheaval in traditional family structure, and the lack of sustained relationships with people and places. As Jews, we can see this most clearly in terms of where we live. Not so very long ago, Jews lived in well-defined communities. There was Delmar Boulevard in St. Louis's University City; Baltimore's Forest Park and later Pikesville with its Park Heights Avenue; Shaker Heights in Cleveland; Denver's West Colfax; the Grand Concourse in Bronx, New York; Skokie in Chicago; and many more.

But community was not just geographical. It was a social mentality. As a Jew, you knew where you belonged. These were your people; their stories were your own. You socialized together, ate in the same restaurants, played in the same parks and on the same streets, went to (and were excluded from) the same clubs, and sent your kids to the same schools. Your community was simply a given, a part of the world into which you were born and whose existence was unquestionably part of the way in which you would live your life.

All that has changed. We no longer have the luxury—and the constraint—of the automatic community. In its place are intentional communities: settings that people seek out in order to meet needs that were once met unthinkingly by the communities into which people were born. For Jews, synagogues are one such community. We join synagogues to be among other Jews, not only for the purposes of Torah, *t'fillah,* and *tikkun olam,* but to capture for ourselves the sense of being among our own people. We seek to regain that which was lost when traditional communities lost their hold and we were dispersed by larger societal forces.

As Jews, we have some deep familiarity with what it means to have to create communities for ourselves. We know what it means for people to leave their homes and make their ways to safer places, across continents and oceans. Throughout the Diaspora and for the last two millennia, our grandparents, our great-grandparents, and those who came before them recreated, to the extent that they could in foreign lands, their *shtetls.* They created synagogues. We, too, must do that, albeit in a different social and historical context. We, too, must join with one another to create the types of synagogues of which we would like to be members.

There are two basic ways to understand what synagogue membership means. For some, membership is the means of access to receiving services. Members join, pay dues, get tickets to High Holy Day services, attend services and programs of interest, and get involved in projects and committees that attract them. Clergy and staff members serve expressed needs by developing and putting forth programs and services. Members hire and pay them, and they deliver. In such synagogues, members show up. They come to receive that which their dues pay for: opportunities to pray and study, sermons, workshops, classes, life-cycle events, and other offerings from the synagogue menu. Implicit in this process is a transaction model, echoing the marketplace. Members are consumers; they purchase services, and if dissatisfied with the quality of those services, feel free to take their business elsewhere. While we recognize the reality of this scenario for many synagogue members today, we see it as unfortunate.

However, membership in a synagogue can also be framed in a different way: as partnership. Members' dues offer them access not so much to services that they purchase, but to the opportunity to create, along with others, a community that will sustain and nourish them. They become part owners of the synagogue. They partner with other members. They allow some members to represent them—the lay leaders—and hire clergy and staff to help them create a functioning, vibrant religious and spiritual place. But they do not simply consume. They partner. They use a different lens to think about their synagogue and their place within it. They understand that they are part of what occurs around them, rather than bystanders; that their experiences as members are influenced not simply by what others do for them, to them, and with them, but by what they themselves do as well; and that while they authorize others to do work, as lay leaders, clergy, or staff, they themselves retain the authority and the obligation to act and speak on behalf of themselves. In this model, membership is active rather than passive.

We believe that this second way of thinking about membership offers a path toward healthy synagogue life. It suggests a way of thinking about what it means to belong to an institution. Belonging means suitability; we belong when we fit in. Yet it also means that we are owned by a place; when we belong to synagogues, they have a rightful claim upon us. They can call upon us; they can ask us to truly join. We use here the deeper meanings of "join": we meet and merge with others just as creeks join rivers; we are connected as points are connected with a straight line; we are brought together to make continuous or to form a unit, as when two boards are joined with nails or joined hands form a circle; and we are engaged with one another, like armies joined on the battlefield or lovers joined in betrothal. These deeper meanings go far beyond simply filling out membership cards and paying dues. They involve partnering with others to create, not just inhabit, our synagogues.

There is precedent here in Judaism. As Jews, we are God's partners. We are taught that God created the world and that we continue to create it as we improve ourselves and those around us. In his book *Being God's Partner*, Rabbi Jeffrey Salkin describes ways in which Judaism requires people to continuously complete God's work. He notes that when Jews circumcise their sons, they are completing the act of creation by bringing the boy into the covenant; that when we recite *kiddush*, we proclaim the creation, and in doing so, make it so; that when we create wine from grapes and bread from wheat, and bless them with *motzi* and *kiddush*, we participate in the process of creation. In such ways, Jews are partners (or, as Salkin puts it, junior partners) with God. It is through our actions, our practices, and our prayers that God's ways are revealed.[1]

This partnership model is the basis for creating synagogue communities, as well. Rabbi Salkin notes that Moses and God together made the tablets of the Law that the Jews ultimately received: Moses carved the tablets, God inspired or wrote the words. Our tablets would not exist without that partnership. That partnership endures. God inspires us; we interpret and live out the words and principles of our religion, completing creation in every ritual and every celebration. In the same fashion, we create the Jewish people, over and again, when we join together—in the deeper meanings of the word—to fashion communities. When our synagogues are vibrant, engaging, and alive communities, we have found ways to join and partner with one another, as well as with God.

Split Decisions

These partnerships are not simple. They demand that we struggle with a particular facet of human nature: our simultaneous impulses to be separate from and connected to others. Psychologists note how people waver between wishing to be closely held within relationships, families, groups, or communities and wishing to be autonomous and self-reliant, independent and on their own. We contain both impulses. At certain points in our lives, we emphasize one and not the other: as infants and young children, we seek to be protected and nurtured, while as adolescents and young adults we seek autonomy. We continue to move back and forth between the two as we age, and in every institution—marriage, work, extended families, religion—we feel the tension between wanting to be autonomous from and wanting to be in close relation to others.

It is no different in our synagogues. Jews struggle with their joint desires to remain both inside and outside synagogues. Our chapter began with an admonishment: *Do not separate yourself from the community.* Our rabbis understood the temptation, the inevitable tugs on us to move away from others, to go our own ways. Men and women alike feel those tugs, particularly in Western culture with our admiration of the rugged individualist. We admire the person who follows his heart, who does not buckle to the power of the majority, who follows her dreams. Personal autonomy—the making of informed religious choices based on individual conscience—became the organizing principle of Reform Judaism, influencing the other streams and most of North American Jewry as well. We honor personal autonomy partly because it speaks directly to our wishes to remain outside the constraints inevitably imposed by our belonging to any group or community.

Yet Judaism survives because enough of us choose to belong. Enough of us pray as our ancestors have prayed, celebrate as they did, struggle with the same texts and moral issues as they did. Enough of us make the trade-off. We join synagogues, which provide a larger context for our lives. In doing so, we lay aside some of our personal autonomy. We go along with the needs or good of our synagogues. We adopt their practices. We send our children to the teachers they select. We worship with clergy they have chosen. We live within the rules, the mission, and the principles of our synagogues. We subordinate ourselves to a larger entity—not just the synagogue, but to the Jewish people. In doing so, in giving up part of ourselves, we find ourselves as well.

Indeed, this is how the Jews first survived as a community. A group of wounded, frightened, imperfect, and confused Israelites huddled at the foot of Mount Sinai as Moses ascended again, after his people had worshiped falsely. Moses climbed toward another covenant. This renewed covenant was, seemingly, on God's terms. God demanded many sacrifices. We must worship only one God. We must do so in particular ways, at particular times. We must redeem our firstborn; we must redeem ourselves, over and again. We must observe legitimate festivals, beginning with the one of unleavened bread. We must not appear before our God empty-handed or empty-hearted. We must tear down altars, pillars, false images of false gods, and so on and so forth; we have 613 ways to serve and connect. In return, we were given God's love and God's law, a land of promise, and a pledge of concern that would last forever.

Such is the covenant. Its terms are clear. There is much that we as Jews must give up. Yet within the constraints lies much possibility. It is only within boundaries that commitment may occur. It is only when our eyes remain fastened upon another that intimacy—a depth of knowledge about both self and other—is possible. The *brit* between God and the Jewish people allows for this depth. It requires discipline, a lifelong practice of rituals and routines and learning. In this respect, the discipline of our covenant is not a punishment visited by God upon the wayward Jews but a set of practices, like water flowing over rock, that smoothes and polishes. We turn away from the golden calves and the shining reflections of ourselves they offer, toward God and one another. This makes *mitzvot* possible. It makes learning possible.

The covenant that Moses struck on our behalf is thus our price of admission to a faith and to a people, and to a relationship with God. When we join synagogues, we rejoin that covenant. When enough of us choose to do so, it is possible to create true community, in which we struggle together with how to live traditions and beliefs. We do not simply accept that which has come before. In subordinating ourselves to a synagogue, we do not act blindly. We create communities, not cults. We bring ourselves emotionally, intellectually, spiritually, and physically into the life of the synagogue, and there we engage, having accepted both that the institution itself is more important than our own particular wishes *and* that we have the right to shape the institution.

Healthy congregants thus allow their synagogues power in and, at times, over their lives, while holding in reserve the ability to act alone on issues of conscience or moral stances. More to the point, healthy congregants remain in conversation with one another, even when they feel most like running away and slamming the door on their involvements. There are times when we disagree with something our rabbis did or said, a decision they made, a certain stance they took. In a healthy synagogue, we open up dialogue with our rabbis and others. We do not simply shrug and walk away, upset or angry. We do not simply give in to cynicism that what we have to say makes no difference. We do not sow dissent, gossip, or vent behind the rabbi's back. We engage. We stay in relation. We reach out in curiosity and desire to understand and make meaning of events to which we react. We remain in conversation with others and, in so doing, create and create again the essence of the synagogue community. We will say more about the nature and language of these conversations in chapter 8.

This is one choice, of course. There are others. Some members join a synagogue for brief periods of time, corresponding to certain events— the bar or bat mitzvah of a child, the year of mourning after a parent's death, a *tikkun olam* program—and then disengage. Other members make certain split decisions within their families. A wife might engage quite a bit in the synagogue, and her husband very little, or vice versa; teenage children might engage in the youth group, while their parents maintain their distance. This pattern occurs in a larger form as well. Synagogue communities are themselves often split into groups of people who inhabit the center and those who inhabit the margins. In each version of this pattern, people emphasize one impulse—moving into, or staying away from, communities—and push away the other. They may even push away from those who seem unlike them as well: those in the center deplore those in the margins, and vice versa. Our internal tensions become external, located in the splits in our families and synagogue communities. These types of choices tend to weaken our ties to the synagogue and to one another.

A Matter of Interpretation

The board president at Young Israel, an Orthodox shul, looked in disbelief at the e-mail that he had just received. It was sent by the executive director at the synagogue, who was inquiring about some of the logistical issues related to the upcoming *Simchat Torah* service and celebration. The e-mail read:

> Hi. I just wanted to touch base about some of the details for *Simchat Torah*. I typically wouldn't bother you with these, but I need your okay to spend some money that I had not originally budgeted. Since we've decided this year to allow girls under the age of twelve to carry a *sefer* Torah on *Simchat Torah*, we'll need to make some extra space for them during the celebration. I'm pretty sure that we'll have to open up the other parts of the sanctuary, which means that we'll have to have some extra maintenance staff involved, which will cost more. I just wanted to give you a heads-up. If there's a problem with that, let me know. Otherwise, I'll just assume it's fine. See you there!

The board president rubbed his head. There must be some mistake. The shul had no policy about allowing pre–bat mitzvah girls to carry a *sefer* Torah. He had been a member of the congregation for over twenty-five years and a member of the board for the last eleven. Never had this been an issue before, and certainly not a policy. He decided that there must have been some mistake and that the executive director had misunderstood someone or something. It was not like him to do that, but then again, it was the only conceivable explanation.

The president called the executive director and left a message that he would like to speak with him as soon as possible. Later that day they finally connected by phone. The president asked where the executive director had gotten the idea that the girls under twelve would be carrying a *sefer* Torah during *Simchat Torah*. The executive director said that he had assumed that the president had already known about the issue, given that he received the weekly reports from the synagogue's chair of the ritual committee. The president said that no, he had not heard of this before, that it came as some surprise, and that it represented quite a significant shift in the synagogue's policy, at least as he understood the accepted beliefs about what rituals the young girls were allowed to publicly join. The executive director suggested that he talk with the ritual committee chair.

The board president did so. He had always held the ritual committee chair in high regard. The chair was a Talmud teacher in the local Jewish community high school, well respected in the community for being thoughtful and articulate as well as quite learned. They met together the day after the president spoke with the executive director. The ritual committee chair explained that several of his students had asked him why pre–bat mitzvah girls did not carry the *sefer* Torah even as their brothers did on *Simchat Torah*. He thought it a good question. After studying the *halacha* on the issue, he decided that, indeed, the girls ought to be able to do so; he found no compelling reason, other than the synagogue's own tradition, that they be prevented from the practice. He told the president that the *Mishna Berura* (the commentary on the *Shulchan Aruch* written by the Chofetz Chaim) writes that even the children (who normally are not called to the Torah until they are thirteen) are all collectively given an *aliyah* in order to educate them in the reading of the Torah. There was no reason to believe that girls were excluded from this practice or from the joy in the beautiful gift of Torah. Smiling, he told the board president that he found it encouraging that the students raised the issue and were able to have an impact on the practices of their shul.

The board president said very little during much of the meeting. He wanted first to understand why the ritual chairperson had made the decision and to get some sense of his thinking. After he heard the explanation, the president asked why he had gone ahead and made the decision without consulting with him, or at least with the rabbi. The ritual chair looked at him for a few moments and then said that he understood the role of his committee in the shul to make exactly those kinds of decisions without burdening others with such issues.

The ritual chair continued, saying that while he understood that the decision went against the tradition of the shul, it fit within the guidelines of *halacha*, and that seemed more important in terms of what they were trying to teach the children and, indeed, the larger community in the shul. The president said that he understood the wish to be responsive to the children, but that it seemed likely that there would be an outcry from a large proportion of the adult members, particularly those from the older generation who founded the shul. He told the chair that the board was meeting the next night and that he would appreciate it if the chair attended the last half hour of the meeting to discuss the matter further.

The board meeting the next night went over its allotted time. They kept the ritual chair waiting in the hall for over an hour before they finally called him in. The president told him that the board had discussed the matter extensively, and while they understood that he was being responsive to the students who had raised the issue, the board found his actions inappropriate. They asked him to tell the students that pre–bat mitzvah girls would not be allowed to carry the *sefer* Torah on *Simchat Torah*. The president would take care of telling the shul's executive director, and there the matter would end.

The ritual chair was quite surprised by this turn of events. He left the meeting not having responded one way or the other to the board because he wanted some time to think about what had transpired. Over the next several days, he thought about the issues and the board's responses. Finally, though he knew himself to be correct on *halachic* grounds, he decided to obey the request. He went to the next religious school session and spoke with the students who had originally sought him out to talk about *Simchat Torah*. He told them of the decision. The leader of the students, a thoughtful girl who happened to be the daughter of one of the board members, asked him why they could not carry the *sefer* Torah, particularly when she had gotten the impression that he thought it would not break *halachic* principles.

The ritual chair knew that, in the context of a prevailing culture that prized autonomy and principled dissent, his answer would sound odd, but he gave it anyway. Sometimes, he told the student, the needs of the community must override the desire of any individual.

The chairperson of the ritual committee faced a certain choice point. He could stand his ground and defend his decision on *halachic* grounds. He was certainly within his rights to do so. He could press forward, rallying the female students and their families, and bring pressure to bear on the board members. This would have created a tremor, of sorts, on the board, that may or may not have built into a quake for the shul more generally. The ritual chair chose not to take this path. He moved away from controversy and let the tremor subside. He acceded to the board's request. In doing so, he put the needs of the community ahead of his own wishes and beliefs.

One might debate whether the choice was correct or not. We could argue that the ritual chair made the wrong decision. Perhaps by pressing the issue, he would have helped the shul look more closely at itself and at what it means to be orthodox in the modern world in ways that it might not have done so previously. Some members of the shul may have been ready, indeed eager, to be pushed in just such a way. The students may have needed him to offer a model of what it means to use *halacha* to make a principled argument and stand by it. Yet we could also argue that the ritual chair made the right decision. He may have sensed that the shul may not have been able to withstand the impact of the forces unleashed by such discussions. The shul may have been at a particular point in its history—healing from the loss of a group of members who split off to form their own synagogue, for example, or just finishing a yearlong process of writing bylaws—that left it unable to take on another challenge. The ritual chair may have been sensitive to this and acted accordingly.

Yet this debate is, in a profound way, beside the point. The point is not whether the ritual chair's decision was correct but whether it was his place to make such a decision at all. The board made a decision. They were authorized by the shul to do so. For the ritual chair to have pressed ahead, mobilized the community, and gone against the board would have been to place himself, rather than the community, at the center of the shul. The board must be at the center, as the group authorized to facilitate discussion, convene people, and involve them in examining problems and developing solutions. The board in our case study may not have performed particularly well along these dimensions. Nevertheless, if the ritual chair wished to pursue the issue, he needed to do so in extended, persuasive, even contentious dialogue with board members. Such a process would put the needs of the community first and foremost, even as it protected it from unsettling quakes.

The Nature of Our Engagements

We engage in our communities in two ways. The clearest, most observable way is to engage in community practices. Synagogue members attend services. They take classes. They observe rituals. Such engagements maintain the community. The second type of engagement deepens a community, making it vibrant and alive, if at times chaotic. Such engagement occurs when we bring ourselves—our emotions, beliefs, perspectives, intellects, curiosities, and quests—fully into our communities. We express those parts of ourselves as members and hope that others will as well, the better to struggle and learn and grow together. Both types of engagement define healthy congregations: people show up and engage in synagogue practices, and they bring themselves fully into the role of members when doing so.

This is a complicated process, and we need to break it down into its various components. The first component is relatively simple, and we have discussed it throughout the chapter: members show up and engage in synagogue programs and practices to the extent that they are willing and able to do so. The synagogue is alive, bustling with activities and energy.

The second component is simple for some, more difficult for others: members say what they are thinking and feeling and engage in dialogue with others. This sort of engagement is very Jewish and always has been. Our Torah is filled with stories of Jews arguing with great passion and great intellect over matters great and small, until they consulted rabbis who then argued points of law with one another, with much gesturing and posturing, until they consulted the great rabbinic court, the Sanhedrin, which engendered yet another series of passionate debates, until some decision was made and recorded and then, of course, questioned and debated through time immemorial. This is our legacy. Judaism has room for many voices, many passions, and many disagreements. Our religion seems chaotic and often is because of how much permission it gives for people to think and act for themselves.

Yet, while the boundaries around our religion are elastic and allow us to strain against and question its rituals and beliefs, the boundaries hold. We remain Jews even as we question Judaism. We remain members of the community even as we press against it. The Torah teaches us that great and terrible arguments among Jews, over points of law and how we treat one another, do not end with people resigning their memberships in the religion. They ultimately accept the rulings, knowing they are made on behalf of the Jewish people. This is the third component of our process: in healthy congregations, people remain members. As members they speak their minds. As members they show their passions. As members they argue, persuade, even annoy. And as members they accept the legitimacy of the structures that, like pillars, hold up their community: the board, the committees and task forces, and the roles and responsibilities of the clergy and other staff. The ritual chair in our case accepted that legitimacy, after having tried, with intellect and passion, to make his case. He placed the needs of the community, and its legitimate structures, at the center.

This is not often an easy idea to accept. Some of us believe that it is our right, even our duty, to reject a representative body such as a synagogue board when we believe that it is incompetent, corrupted by cronyism, or out of touch. When we believe this to be so, we have several choices. We can assume that we have no chance of changing the situation—persuading people or getting different people to represent us. We can withdraw and not engage much with the synagogue. We can find like-minded others and form a splinter group, even going so far as to form our own synagogue community. Or we can engage ourselves even more deeply in the synagogue and try to make changes, using our passion and ideas and intellect.

We believe, of course, that the last option—using our voices to try and influence our communities—is often the most productive path to pursue. But we are not blind to the limits of this strategy. There are times when we must withdraw, when we give up too much of ourselves to belong, when there is not enough room in the community for who we really are and what we really believe, in spite of our efforts to push the boundaries of that community so it offers us a place to be in it. Then it makes sense to leave. That is how some new synagogues have been born from others. A culture forms, with a set of practices and beliefs, and leaves little room for those who do not fit in. When enough members feel like outsiders, they leave—sometimes amicably, other times explosively—and create a community where they can feel they are inside. Sometimes this is exactly what needs to occur, as some members outgrow a community that cannot change or a community outgrows members who do not wish to change.

People may also disengage from their synagogues, through passive withdrawals or active leavings, not because of legitimate differences, but because they cannot or will not simply stay the course. We speak here of commitment. Healthy relationships occur only after people commit to remaining within them. They assume that there will be ups and downs, periods when they feel wonderful and those when they feel frustrated and upset. They assume that in a long-term relationship, there will be deficiencies on both sides, and that with enough work, honest communication, and respect, they can often be overcome. We suggest here that this is true for our relationships with our synagogues, as well as for our personal relationships.

What does this mean, in practice? Mostly, that we accept our synagogues for what they are and for what they are not, and commit to making them places where we wish to be. To do this we must let go of the wish for perfection, for Eden, saving it as one vision of *yemot haMashiach*, the messianic age. In the creation myth, which begins the Torah, God evaluates each day's creation with the single word "good." With the sixth day, God adds the adjective "very," but nowhere does the text say "perfect." As miraculous as creation is, neither it nor anything in it, including us human beings, is perfect. Indeed, as imperfect human beings, we have less-than-perfect lives, form less-than-perfect relationships, and create imperfect institutions. The synagogue is one of them. If people expect perfection from their synagogues, they will inevitably be disappointed. That is not a pass for synagogues to stop trying to be the best they can be; rather, it is recognition that mistakes, missed opportunities, hurt feelings, disappointments, and unmet needs are to be expected. Moreover the needs of individuals will conflict with those of the community. While synagogues cannot afford to trample on individuals and their particular needs, they must always weigh them against the needs of the total community. The whole will—and ought to—win out over the parts.

We remember in a particular school there was a problem with bullying in the fourth grade. One of the parents accused, "This should not happen here. After all, this is a Jewish day school." We responded that children inevitably display childlike behaviors wherever they go. Bullying is part of the normal development of preadolescent behavior. What ought to mark a Jewish day school is not the prevention of such expected behavior, but the way it responds to the bullying. Jewish institutions are subject to all the same human foibles and imperfections that we find in society in general. God did not choose the Jewish people because we were "mightier or better" than the other peoples of the earth. If people expect synagogues to always be "better," they are bound to be very disappointed, hopping from one synagogue affiliation to another until they finally alter their expectations and make real commitments to join and work with imperfections, or they drop out altogether.

Just as there are no perfect synagogues, there is no such thing as a perfect fit between an individual or a family and a synagogue. In one synagogue you might love the rabbi's sermons but not the religious school. One might have an outstanding youth program, but the *davenning* is lackluster. The physical space in a particular synagogue reminds you of the one in which you grew up, instantly giving you warm feelings of belonging, but the people are rather standoffish and cold. When deciding on a synagogue—shul shopping—one ought to create a hierarchy of needs. What is most important, what's next, what's least? To the extent that some needs may be met by other synagogues or institutions (e.g., taking adult education classes at the JCC or another synagogue), one ought to take advantage of that. But we need to be careful. While learning with several rabbis from across denominational streams can represent a true growth process, a desire to expand one's understanding of Jewish possibility, more often it represents a kind of "spiritual adultery," an inability to commit to a real relationship with a synagogue or its spiritual leader. Besides adding confusion, what most often happens in these all-too-common situations these days is that the individuals hear what they want, not necessarily what they need.

Saying "I Do"

Our point here is rather straightforward: it is through commitment that relationships work. We mean this literally. Commitment means that people in relationships have decided to *work,* to make their relationships strong enough to enable each person to grow and change and still remain with the other. This is like marriage. We look for someone that feels right, to whom we are attracted enough to make a commitment to being with him or her. We say, "I do." And then we do; we try to make the marriage work. We search for ways to change ourselves, to be better partners. We look for ways to help others change and grow. We create healthy marriages marked by commitment and the ongoing willingness to keep at it. The same is true for healthy congregations. Synagogues thrive when people truly commit to being members. They thrive when members want their relationship to the synagogue to survive and are willing to work at it.

The search for perfection is a defense against such commitment. It allows people an easy excuse to disengage. They can simply blame others—the board, the rabbi, the teacher, or the congregation—for the synagogue's inevitable imperfections. When we expect others to meet our needs perfectly, we set them up for failure. Indeed, we subconsciously wish for that failure: it lets us move away from being in some relationship about which we are ambivalent. We get out of such relationships while holding ourselves blameless for their failure. This characterizes a fair number of Jews, who are ambivalent about what it means to be members of a synagogue. For any number of reasons—frustrating or boring experiences with synagogues when they were younger, difficulties engaging issues of faith and God, lack of models in their lives, unresolved anger at authority figures, or the like—some Jews are deeply ambivalent about synagogue membership. They manage that ambivalence by seeming to approach synagogues but then remaining outside them because of their wish for perfect synagogue experiences.

Healthy congregations are filled with ambivalent Jews, of course. The difference is that these are Jews who have decided to commit to the institution, make good faith efforts (indeed, to make efforts to find good faith), and see what they can contribute and gain from the relationship. They commit not to perfection, but to their synagogues and the people who inhabit them. When we truly join our synagogues, when we take up our memberships with purpose and intent, we cut our synagogue communities slack. A synagogue is not a fraternity or a sorority, nor a country club or co-op apartment building. No one gets blackballed or refused admission. It has an open door, open to anyone who wishes to join. We accept people as they are, not as we wish them to be. This is both the beauty and sometimes the bane of synagogue existence. Every synagogue represents a cross-section of the Jewish community. And in spite of all the dedication and devotion, there are plenty of behaviors about which to get upset. Beyond the ability to get our needs met, being part of a community may push us to the limits of our acceptance, where we get to explore just how generous our spirits are when we are not getting what we want. Such moments also lend us the opportunity to look inside to determine what it is we are doing that gets in our own way.

What we would like to suggest is that when we experience flaws in the fabric of synagogue life, we view them as opportunities to make a difference. Synagogues are one of the last bastions of true democracy; everyone has a voice and a vote. We have seen it time and again. One person is often the difference between something coming to fruition or it remaining one of those "good ideas" that never see the light of day. If each of us engages in the conversation, we can make that difference. We can push for evolution. We can support the growth and change of our synagogues even as we support the structures that keep them stable. We can engage in the tradition of Jews: to learn and honor our faith and the houses in which we practice it, even as we push against it and make its connections more powerful in our lives.

Note

1. Jeffrey Salkin, *Being God's Partner: How to Find the Hidden Link between Spirituality and Your Work* (Woodstock, VT: Jewish Lights Publishing, 1994).

8

FINDING AND USING YOUR
VOICE, APPROPRIATELY

Moses sent for Dathan and Abiram, but they said, "We will
not come." Moses was much aggrieved. Then Korach gathered the whole community against Moses and Aaron at the
Tent of Meeting.
(Numbers 16:12ff.)

In the previous chapter, we suggested that commitment to a synagogue
means joining others as partners who create, with energy and purpose,
the community they wish to have. We concluded that chapter by noting
that it is only when we engage our voices—make ourselves heard, clarify
our experiences and wishes, and have meaningful dialogue with others—
that we create real partnerships. In this chapter, we explore what it really
means to use one's voice as a member of a synagogue. We believe this is
crucial for a healthy congregation. Increasingly, synagogue members are
asked not for "dues" but for "annual commitments." This is more than
an alteration of language; it denotes that belonging to a congregation is
an act of commitment. Committing to a community requires a commitment to speak and to act, to engage in the life of the community, moving
its mission forward while satisfying one's personal needs and goals.

Engaging one's voice is, of course, a choice. It is not a choice that
everyone makes. Some people choose *exit*. They decide that the synagogue is not the place for them for any number of reasons: their original
needs (like a child becoming bar/bat mitzvah) have been met, and no
other needs have emerged to hold them to the synagogue; they feel like
they do not fit with the mission or culture of the synagogue in some
important way; their energies are taken up by other events in their lives;
they are hurt or angry about some slight they feel; or they feel that synagogue programs or services do not serve them particularly well. They
leave. Some people choose *loyalty*. They remain at the synagogue out of
loyalty to its tradition, its clergy, their friends, or their memories. They
are good citizens, attending events and giving their opinions when asked.

They do not engage deeply, as partners, but remain steadfast and loyal. Others choose *neglect*. They remain synagogue members but barely. They attend only infrequently. They are largely indifferent and pay little or no attention to the state of the community. They drift in and out.

People who choose to use their voices may do so in different ways. They may communicate clearly and directly, or not. They may provide useful feedback in ways that are constructive and sensitive, or not. They may raise issues at the right time with the right people, or not. They may have insights that they try to share with others, or not. These choices determine whether congregations are marked by healthy dialogue or fragmented by gossip, complaint, and blame. Voices are instruments. Each congregation is powerfully shaped by how those instruments are used, and for what purposes.

The text at the beginning of the chapter helps us understand that the question of how one's voice is used is not a new problem for Jews. In the time of the Torah, a man named Korach challenged Moses's and Aaron's leadership, claiming that the priesthood belonged to the people of Israel and that no one family of Levites ought monopolize it. "Too much is yours," Korach accused Moses. Korach himself was a Levite and, moreover, the first cousin of Moses and Aaron. Left out of the long-term right of succession, he mounted a rebellion, drawing support from others from different tribes who wished for other reasons to create a civil uprising against Moses. Korach sowed seeds of discontent among the people, and rather than speaking directly with Moses, sought a public showdown, a win or lose situation. The results were disastrous, as the earth swallowed up Korach, his supporters, and his entire family.

The story is instructive. Viewed one way, it is a simple story of an individual's Machiavellian grab for power. This is a story that Shakespeare has written several times over: a cousin schemes to dispose of the king, in one fashion or another, and take his place on the throne, gathering others to his cause by pretending that their agendas are his. It is also a story of two brothers surviving a political fight by purging those who wished to destroy them and take power for themselves. These stories are old. They have been restaged over and again, in various guises, and can be glimpsed in struggles for power throughout our world today.

Viewed another way, however, this is a story of how communities struggle with difficult issues. Korach raised important issues that the Jewish people needed to figure out. How should power be transferred across generations? What is the authority of the Levites, relative to one another and the children of Israel more generally? What are the roles and responsibilities of the various tribes of Israel, relative to one another? These questions were crucial for the new regime, as its leaders and members sought to understand the new world into which God delivered them. They engaged those questions in an all-too-familiar way, by splitting off into warring factions, until God intervened, choosing Moses and Aaron and striking down the rebels. Wisely, God then clarified the Levites' duties and the regulations concerning them, and their relations with the priests.

We can thus understand Korach as having served a useful purpose, in spite of his self-serving intentions otherwise. He brought into sharp relief the Israelites' need for clarity and order in relation to how they would be led and how the various tribes would relate to one another. Every community and every organization needs clear understandings of the rules by which it will be led and by which leadership will be maintained across generations. Korach exploited people's anxiety about not having that clarity and order; in doing so, ironically, he ultimately led to the community's creation. He did this by removing himself from the community, literally pitching his tent outside the Israelite camp, as a way to demonstrate to others that there was an alternative to the existing leadership structure. He distanced himself from the community. From that place, he attracted others to his cause and led them to their peril.

In this chapter, we consider questions related to members using their voices to strengthen their synagogues. We have a clear perspective of what this means: speaking directly, clearly, and respectfully to others the truth of one's experiences, beliefs, and ideas in the service of creating synagogue communities that meet the collective needs of their members. Korach did not do this. Indeed, as Everett Fox notes in his commentary *The Five Books of Moses*, Korach himself is never portrayed in the text as saying a single word on his own.[1] He works behind the scenes, talking against Moses and Aaron but never to them. What led to his unwillingness or inability to do so? What leads to similar behavior today? How do we, as congregants, find our voices and use them appropriately?

How Synagogues Evolve

Judaism has a three-thousand-year history of evolution. Our religion is steeped in tradition: we are constantly referring to the Torah as an ancient source of stories, wisdom, and teachings. Yet our religion evolves as well. Our rabbis strive to apply the laws of Judaism to contemporary situations, and those laws have proven over and over again their relevance to modern Jewish life. We reinterpret the Torah, again and again, enabling it to evolve and maintain relevance in our lives. We reimagine our religion—its rituals, its principles, its meaning—and in doing so continue to breathe life into it and let it breathe life into us. We reinvigorate our religious community when we challenge it to remain relevant and meaningful to our lives.

Consider the story of Zelophehad (Numbers 27:1-7), who died in the wilderness and left five daughters, who subsequently claimed the inheritance of their father. The tradition up to that point was that when a man died, all property was to be inherited by his sons, which kept all tribal lands within the tribe. Knowing that those who took part in the revolt of Korach were exceedingly objectionable to Moses, Zelophehad's daughters argued that their father was not of Korach's assembly. Moses consulted God about the matter and was ordered to satisfy the daughters' demand. This established a legal precedent in Judaism, namely, that when a man dies without any sons, his daughters will inherit his land holdings. The daughters pushed for that change. They brought their issue to the community and, in so doing, challenged it to evolve based on circumstances not envisioned in the original precepts. They did so as members in good standing, which enabled them to speak directly with Moses in a way that Korach could or would not. They acted as part of, rather than separate from, their religious community, posing questions that pushed that community to reconsider its practices.

This story offers a useful framework for understanding how synagogues evolve. The evolution depends first and foremost on community members believing that the religion belongs to them. It is theirs to internalize, to make work for them. This is not a simple matter. We often see members very hesitant around the Torah scroll. They feel uncertain and uncomfortable; they do not want to make a mistake and look foolish or irreverent in front of others. It is then that we remind them that it is, literally, their Torah. It belongs to them, as members of that congregation. It is theirs to uphold, defend, learn from, feel unfamiliar with, and make mistakes around. It belongs to them.

We can extrapolate from individuals to the synagogue as a whole. Synagogues belong to the congregants. Yet somehow we have professionalized these institutions such that we think they belong to the rabbi or the board. But both rabbi and lay leaders are there to serve the needs of the Jewish people and, more specifically, the needs of their congregants. They are there as servants of God. Zelophehad's daughters understood this. They came to Moses knowing that they had the legitimate right to ask their question, to voice their needs and concerns.

Such is the ideal for our synagogues. People raise concerns and issues. They take it upon themselves to challenge or question congregational leaders. They do so not by withdrawing from or marshalling forces against the leaders, as Korach did, or just giving up and assuming that they had no way to influence others. They find the courage to raise their issues. They understand that they have that right, as members of the synagogue that belongs to them. At the same time, they understand the limits of this: that the synagogue belongs to others as well, to the congregation as a whole, which authorizes people to assume roles of leadership and responsibility. This is the ongoing way synagogues evolve. People raise issues, speaking of their experiences and needs, while respecting the needs of the congregation more generally. This requires trust and faith that the congregation, acting through its leaders, will digest those issues and experiences and, over time, find the wisdom to do the right thing.

None of this occurs if individual members do not speak directly, openly, and respectfully to leaders and other members of their congregations. The voice, however, is a complicated instrument. Rabbi Gamliel once asked a disciple to go to the market and buy the best kind of food. The disciple brought home a tongue. The next day, Gamliel asked him to buy the worst kind of food. The disciple again brought back a tongue. When asked for an explanation, the disciple replied: "There is nothing better than a good tongue and nothing worse than an evil tongue." In our synagogues, the voice is an instrument that can clarify, yet it can also create much noise. It can inspire, yet it can also inflame. It can join in evolution, yet it can also incite revolution. How we as congregants use our tongues—and our intentions in doing so, of which we may be only partly aware—matters a great deal to the health of our synagogues.

On Guard

Several months after the September 11, 2001, terrorist attacks, members of Beth Tikvah raised the issue of security for the synagogue. Several members came to the board president with reports of various synagogues that had suffered some disturbance—a fire that had broken out, a cemetery that had been vandalized—and wanted to know if Beth Tikvah had a plan to prevent such incidents. The board president realized that, with High Holy Days and the beginning of religious school fast approaching, it made sense to look into the matter sooner rather than later. He consulted with the board, and together they decided to create a task force that would look into developing a security plan for the synagogue and make a recommendation to the executive committee.

The chair of the task force, a former captain in the army of the former Soviet Union, believed that many congregants did not attend synagogue services and events because they felt that the synagogue was an easy target for terrorists and anti-Semitic groups. He told the other task force members that their task was to help create a sense of security that would allow people to feel safe enough to come to the synagogue whenever they wished. The other task force members agreed with this. Several suggested that they needed to explore the different ways that "security" could be defined and work from there to decide how best to enable people to feel secure. The chair nodded, but by the end of the first meeting, the agenda had shifted: it was agreed that he would investigate several local security companies and see what they could offer.

A month later the task force reconvened. The chair had spoken with several security companies. He described the various services that the security companies offered—guards on the premises, sophisticated alarms, video surveillance, technologically advanced entry badges, and the like—and how the companies compared in terms of reputation and price. He then recommended a security company that would put an armed guard on the synagogue's premises for a reasonable price. Several members said that they did not feel comfortable going down that route so soon, since they had not spent much time exploring other ways of thinking about security and what it might mean in the context of the synagogue. The chair brushed this off with a joke about how Americans, unlike Israelis and Russians, thought security was stock that one owned in a company. The meeting adjourned soon thereafter, with the chair thanking the other members but making no plans for a future meeting.

The chair presented the recommendation to the board president and the executive committee several weeks later. The executive committee engaged in a lively discussion, spurred on by the very real concerns of several of its members that having an armed guard would be, in the words of one, "overkill," and likely to make congregants more rather than less anxious about security. They asked the task force chair to reconvene the committee and offer other, less extreme measures for them to consider. The chair was upset with the request. He told the executive committee that people would only feel safe when they saw an armed guard as a visible sign of strength. The chair said that he would reconvene the committee but that he could not, in good conscience, continue to lead it since he saw any further work that it did as a waste of time.

Two weeks after that conversation, the board president received an e-mail from a congregant with whom he was friendly, who was forwarding an e-mail that he had received from the task force chair. The subject line of the e-mail read, "Have you seen this???" The message contained the following:

> I am bringing to your attention an important matter that is of particular concern to you, as a parent of young child attending Beth Tikvah religious school. I recently served as the chair of the Synagogue Security Task Force. Our committee was created in order to investigate various ways in which to alleviate the concerns that congregation members have raised since the 9/11 attacks about security at the synagogue. After some deliberation the task force recommended that we hire a local, reputable security company to provide an armed guard, implement essential security precautions, and install basic security devices. We felt that these steps were essential to create a secure environment. We brought this to the executive committee, whose members seemed more concerned with financial costs than the safety of our children. I am writing to you because I believe that you should have this information.

Together, we can force the executive committee to rethink its priorities and do the right thing. Our children deserve that.

The board president was furious. The task force chair had misrepresented the executive committee in the pursuit of his own agenda. Over the course of the next few days, the board president received countless e-mails and phone calls from congregants, wanting to know why the board had made such a decision, and from board members themselves, furious about what was being said about them. The board president finally had to call a public meeting to discuss the issues of security with the congregation as a whole. Speeches, angry diatribes, and very little problem solving marked that meeting and the several that followed. Finally, months later, Beth Tikvah created a new task force, which the original chair refused to attend, calling it an "illegitimate meeting," and slowly moved toward a security program that focused on the community policing itself, with the aid of technology, training, and good relations with the local police department.

Our case study illustrates how an individual—the chair of the task force—made a decision to push his own agenda and inflamed the congregation. The chair was a modern Korach: metaphorically pitching his tent outside the community, he presented himself, through his e-mail, as an alternative to the synagogue's given leadership structure. He sought a rebellion, hoping that the community would rise up and overturn the executive committee. What occurred instead was the releasing of a great deal of free-floating anxiety into the community. The earth did not open up and swallow the chair and his supporters. The consequences were messier than that. The community was bogged down in blame and accusation, and only after some time were members able to understand that their problem was not one another but the issue of how to enable a sense of security in ways that honored rather than diminished congregants. The task force chair used his voice to frighten people about an issue rather than help clarify it. He lost one task—that of helping the congregation identify and choose among various alternatives—and substituted his own ego and agenda in its place. It is a story as old as Korach.

Missed Signals

We often hear synagogue leaders and members complain, "We just don't communicate enough." This is a standard, if generic complaint. We have a more precise way to define communication: *the process of clarifying the signals that people are sending to and receiving from one another, such that what is said is exactly what is meant and is exactly what is heard.* This is simple in definition and inordinately complicated in execution. We discuss three dimensions of how signals get missed (and what makes communication so complicated) in synagogue life: excessive noise, the silencing of others, and the silencing of ourselves.

Noise

Synagogues can be very noisy places. Congregants can make sounds that are loud, unpleasant, unexpected, or undesired. They can cause commotions that distract rather than clarify. They can create disturbances that obscure or reduce the clarity of a signal, or offer irrelevant and sometimes meaningless data. They can lodge complaints or protests, spread rumors, talk to hear themselves talk. It takes a fair amount of work to hear and to transmit clear signals when such noise is relatively high. Sometimes it is only those who speak the loudest and are the most insistent that get heard, to the detriment of the synagogue community more generally. Much gets lost amid the noise.

Noise is the antithesis of direct and clear communication. In synagogues, noise often appears as gossip. Gossip occurs when we say something about another person when he or she is not present. If it is true, it is gossip. If it is false, it is slander. Gossip, whether true or false, may seem innocuous but often has unintended consequences. Person X says to Person Y, "I had a great time with our friend Z last night. Beautiful dinner she prepared." Y responds, "That's interesting. When I called her earlier in the day to get together, she said she wasn't feeling that well." X's words were true, but spoken without Z present, without Z's permission, they constitute gossip. This goes beyond defining gossip *(lashon hara)* as saying only negative things about another person or spreading information we are not absolutely certain is true. We offer a different sort of rule: do not talk about another person unless that person is present or has given permission. A caveat here may be the ability to speak openly about others to one's therapist, which occurs both in the service of one's own growth and healing and in the context of clear boundaries.

This is, admittedly, extreme but worth considering for what it suggests about how we use speech. It means that we limit our conversations, at least those involving others, to ourselves—our experiences, thoughts, perspectives, and reflections. This may expand what we talk about and force us to go more deeply into our experiences and beliefs. It cuts down on the noise gossip creates in a synagogue.

Relationships get triangulated as people speak about one another to third parties rather than directly with one another. Such triangles are inherently unhealthy. The one who gossips may need to say what is on his mind, but the recipient almost never needs to hear it. The one who gossips may feel unburdened by what he has said, but in reality he has simply handed the burden to someone else. Usually, this leads to more "sharing," which vastly multiplies the original damages.

This reminds us of the Hasidic story of a person who went to a rabbi and confessed, "I have been guilty of gossiping against my friend for months, and now I wish to undo the wrong I have done. Please tell me what to do." The rabbi told him to bring a feather pillow and said, "Go outside, rip the pillow open and shake out the feathers." The man did this and asked the rabbi, "Now what should I do?" The rabbi told him "Go outside and gather all the feathers, and then return them to me." The man looked startled and asked, "But how can I gather all the feathers now that they are scattered to the four winds?" The rabbi answered: "Now that you have spoken gossip, how can you recall it, since the rumors you started have now been spread by others to every corner of the community?"

Some synagogues are filled with many feathers. We know of a rabbi who signed a discretionary fund check for deposit and was accused of "pocketing the money." A congregant, in appreciation for something the rabbi had done, had sent him a donation for his discretionary fund. The rabbi, having changed banks and having not yet received the official stamp, decided to deposit the check anyway. When the congregant got the canceled check back, he saw the rabbi's signature and assumed the rabbi took the money, which would have been a violation of the synagogue's policy and the congregant's intent. He told several of his friends, who then directed him to a board member, who then told the president, who then confronted the rabbi with a photocopy of the back of the canceled check. The rabbi calmly produced his new discretionary fund account number, which matched the number on the canceled check. The president apologized but felt he was just "doing his job." The rabbi replied, "Just ask our congregant to tell all the people he told that he was mistaken and ask each of them to tell all the people they told." Rumors of the rabbi's indiscretion persisted for more than two years after this so-called "incident." A simple act of direct communication—the congregant picking up the telephone and asking the rabbi for a logical explanation, suggesting that perhaps there was a mistaken assumption that the check was a gift and not a donation—would have prevented a great deal of damage.

Such incidents can harm not only the subject but also those who gossip, by inflating their egos to outsized proportions through the assumption of being "right" or "in the know." Gossip can prevent others from willingly sharing about themselves and can rend the fabric of relationships. The victim often isn't aware of the damage until it is too late for repair. Gossip can harm, in the end, the synagogue community itself, whose members must struggle to hear important signals about how the synagogue is serving congregants' needs amid the noise of rumors, gossip, and innuendo.

Noise, finally, can also occur in the form of useless complaints. Congregants complain about the shul, the rabbi, the cantor's voice, the religious school curriculum, the high cost of belonging, too much Hebrew in the service, too little Hebrew in the service, *ad infinitum* (and *ad nauseam*). Complaining may be a Jewish pastime, but it is rarely productive and almost always eats away at the fabric of good that synagogues often provide. Complaining helps identify problems, certainly, but it also leaves them to others who may not have the time, energy, knowledge, or skill to solve them. When we complain, we are showing that we care at least enough to be disappointed or frustrated. But when we leave it at this, the hit-and-run interaction, we use complaint as a way to avoid constructive engagement. This might make us feel good about ourselves—we were smart and caring enough to notice something and complain about it—but it leaves the issue for someone else to handle. When we raise issues in a constructive manner with those who are in positions to make or influence appropriate changes, and take some responsibility for situations and their resolutions, we can make real contributions. When these conditions are not met, we are simply contributing to the noise.

Silencing Others

We also miss signals in synagogue life when we silence those who, if listened to closely enough, could offer valuable opinions and insights. We silence others by turning away from them. We tell ourselves stories that allow us to dismiss what they have to say. We keep them outside of the places where decisions really get made. We label them in ways that leave their input devalued. We think of them as having minority opinions that ought to be considered but not really incorporated. We use silencing techniques in different ways, some more subtle than others, and move on with our projects, unaware of what we lose in doing so. For example:

- A member of the finance committee suggests that the traditional annual fund-raising event is of limited value, raises less money each year, has little appeal to the newer members, and needs to be examined in terms of the overall strategy for attracting new members. The chair and other committee members nod in agreement but, over the course of the next few meetings, continue to plan for the traditional event. The member slowly disengages from the process to the point that he misses several meetings.
- The synagogue is struggling with how to attract new members. Several long-term members who were involved in the founding of the synagogue want to join the membership committee to offer guidance based on their own experiences of attracting members several decades earlier. The chair of the membership committee resists their involvement, citing the fact that the committee is already full and its agenda is already jammed with the planning of several events. Privately she tells several other members, "These guys don't have a clue as to what it's like now to try and get new members. We can't waste time hearing old war stories."
- The parent of a religious school student tells the education director that she is concerned that her child's teacher is losing some of his faculties. The teacher is beloved in the school, having helped found it several decades earlier and having taught generations of

its students. The parent says that the teacher is repeating lessons, assigning homework that is far too simple or far too complicated, and has forgotten class several times. The education director dismisses the parent's concerns. She tells her assistant that this parent, who has occasionally helped out in religious school classrooms, wanted to be a teacher herself and is probably just envious of the older teacher's reputation in the synagogue.

- A senior rabbi gives his administrative staff few directives and fails to build a shared sense of vision with them, then becomes angry when they do not produce the results he is expecting. Several staff members leave their jobs over the course of a year. Each time, the rabbi tells the remaining staff that he is glad the others have left, since they simply "weren't able to do their jobs properly." The executive director and board president each attempt to help the rabbi see the effects of his leadership style. The rabbi gets defensive, blaming those who have left. The executive director and board president each stop giving the rabbi feedback. The rabbi's contract is not renewed.

- The leadership development committee, whose mission involves identifying and training potential lay leaders for the synagogue, takes its clues from the existing board members. The committee chair asks each board member to provide several names of synagogue members whom they know well and who might be interested in serving in a leadership capacity. The committee uses this list as its only mechanism for contacting and selecting potential synagogue leaders.

- At a board meeting, a longtime member objects to a proposed policy change. As soon as she does so, some members begin to roll their eyes, others start passing notes, and one rather loud whisperer says to another, "There she goes again. No matter what it is, she's going to be obnoxious and object!" Hurt, the longtime member resigns that night from the board.

Much moves beneath the surface of these examples. The finance committee avoids what could potentially become a very constructive conversation and does so in a rather passive-aggressive fashion by ignoring the member who raised the issue. The chair of the membership committee turns away from some long-term members, dismissing their contributions by stereotyping them as out of touch. The education director similarly dismisses a concerned parent's report by invalidating her as a legitimate source of information. The senior rabbi silences others who might otherwise offer useful feedback, becoming defensive and unapproachable in ways that undermine his rabbinate. The leadership development committee creates homogeneity by seeking out only members who are likely to resemble, in belief and perspective, those already on the committee. The board members stereotype a longtime member, locking her into a particular role that prevents them from listening to her ideas and finally silences her altogether.

In each case, a synagogue loses legitimate dissent. This can be quite common. We often try to simplify our worlds, thus reducing information or ambiguity that might otherwise overwhelm us. We do so by inadvertently pushing away perspectives, beliefs, or information that might force us to examine the choices that we have made or the paths that we are pursuing. In synagogues, this often means that we push away others. We tell certain stories that help us keep others and the dissent that they represent away: someone has an ax to grind, is out of touch, obnoxious, egotistical, incompetent, misguided, or just plain wrong. These stories protect us from having to consider the validity of what others have to say. This is costly. We lose others' valuable information, insights, and energy. Our decision making is less robust and thoughtful. We risk alienating others, causing them to withdraw, or we scapegoat them outright, branding them as troublemakers and driving them away in order, seemingly, to protect the community from their views. In such ways, we silence others; we, they, and the synagogues we create together are the worse for it.

Silencing Ourselves

Our synagogues also miss signals when we silence ourselves. This might be as simple as deciding not to say anything. We see a Hebrew school teacher berating a student and say nothing. We attend an annual board meeting and feel that nothing meaningful is discussed there and vow never again to attend one. We read the temple bulletin, think that it is just one advertisement after another, and decide not to waste any more time in the future reading them. We attend a fund-raising event, feel out of place because it is geared only toward a certain generation, and stop giving to the synagogue. Our child is bored with Hebrew school, and we tell her that she just has to go and suffer like we did when we were her age. In each case, we remain silent. We move away from the synagogue itself.

Whenever we silence ourselves, we wind up telling ourselves something that makes us feel okay about not engaging with the synagogue. We tell ourselves that saying something will do no good, that we cannot really change anything, that the people in power are concerned only with themselves, or that the situation is hopeless. These are "cover stories." They provide cover for our unwillingness to move toward our synagogues in constructive ways that would inevitably require more involvement and commitment than when we turn away. To respond constructively to situations in the synagogue we have to involve ourselves: speak to the teacher and her supervisor, learn about the nature of board meetings, write an article for the bulletin, join a fund-raising committee, speak to the rabbi, volunteer to help in our child's classroom. Each of these involvements requires us to move away from our cynicism, our hopelessness, or our ambivalence. Each requires us to stop telling ourselves cover stories that are fundamentally dishonest, rooted in what we wish to believe rather than in some demonstrated reality. Their primary purpose is to let us off the hook.

We may also silence ourselves not simply because we wish to limit our involvements but because we do not feel comfortable engaging in dissent. We may dislike conflict. We may dislike ambiguity, which often shows up when different but reasonable perspectives collide. We may wish to keep our views of situations and people simple and uncomplicated. We may not wish to engage with others and learn that we are wrong or that we have to rethink deeply held beliefs. We may not believe that it is appropriate for us to disagree openly with others, particularly those in leadership positions. (We have often heard of congregations in which someone or some group of individuals is upset with their rabbi but are unwilling to speak directly with him or her.) We may feel that if we speak up, we will be labeled as a "troublemaker" and not get the attention we deserve when we really need it. Any of these reasons may feel valid to us, based on our personalities and experiences. To set any of them aside and move ahead often takes some faith—that it will be all right, things will work out, people will survive just fine—and some courage. It also requires a clear awareness that if we are not part of the solution we are part of the problem. When we silence ourselves, we have decided to agree with that which is occurring within our synagogues.

Encouraging Voice in Our Synagogues

The use of our voices—to say what we think and feel, to contribute our ideas and perspectives—is not simply a matter of our courage, faith, or egotism. It is also a matter of how much room there is for our voices. Others may silence us. Leaders may not pause, inquire, or listen. There may be no ongoing structures that enable us to speak in ways that will matter. Viewed this way, the lack of direct and clear communication lies not only with those who do not speak but also with the synagogue more generally. Perhaps the story of Korach is not simply that of a man grasping for power. It could also be the story of congregational leaders making little room for a transparent discussion of how leadership is conferred, the different roles and responsibilities of the tribes of the congregation, and the differential power of the priests. Viewed through this lens, Korach's actions may be understood as an attempt to address important issues in the only way that he felt was available to him. Rebellion becomes an option—for some, the only option—in the absence of opportunity for more direct means of communication.

Every synagogue has certain patterns of communication. Most patterns inevitably represent certain ways of encouraging some voices in the congregation and not others. To encourage all voices, we must look carefully at the patterns in our synagogues and try to understand which voices they encourage and which voices they do not. This may require us to tell ourselves and others more complete stories about what occurs in our synagogues. When we see communication patterns that strike us as odd, irrational, or ineffective, such as petitions, gossip, inappropriate e-mail, or clandestine meetings, we tend to tell certain stories that allot blame to certain individuals or groups. When we analyze those patterns for what they can tell us about how certain voices get encouraged or discouraged, our stories become more complete. We can think about why people may feel as if they cannot communicate more directly to others. Korach may have longed for power, yes, but he may also have had no other way to raise important issues to the community and its leaders. To develop this more complete story, we must allow ourselves to be *curious,* rather than simply certain, about why certain events happen or patterns are repeated.

If we do allow ourselves to discover how our synagogues encourage some voices and not others, we can develop thoughtful solutions for encouraging congregants to use their voices. We can create different structures or processes—different meeting formats and times, neighborhood visits with the rabbi, more reliance or less reliance on e-mail, and many other possibilities—that enable other types of communication to occur and a multitude of voices to be heard. We can make sure that there are ongoing opportunities for constructive dissent.

Doing these things reduces the likelihood of creating more Korachs in our congregations; by involving dissenters in the conversation, we reduce their needs to employ hit-and-runs, amass power behind closed doors, or engage in destructive political processes. Constructive dissent requires direct communication. It is a democratic, transparent, and thereby slow process. But if members really want to resolve conflicts, move the agenda of the congregation forward, and involve the community in new ways of realizing its mission, they need to work with those who can be change agents—the elected board volunteers and professionals in leadership roles. They need to engage rather than disengage.

Often enough, solutions involve the use of committees. We are fond of saying that nothing important happens in a synagogue without a committee to do the work. Healthy congregations provide access through committees for people to meet their personal needs. If a committee does not yet exist, and the unmet need does not contradict the mission of the synagogue, there should be a process for creating a new committee. One congregation's mission, for example, speaks of lifelong learning as a value consistent with the highest ideals of Judaism. When a group of empty nesters approached the rabbi to create a monthly study group for them and others, he and the synagogue president helped them create a subcommittee of adult education, which began to offer a monthly get-together with others in that demographic grouping. The only condition the congregation placed was that, at least for the initial year, all programs had to be self-sustaining. The group is now in its third year and has a small budget from the congregation itself.

Committees and their "cousins," task forces and planning groups, enable people to join together and develop a collective voice. Individual voices, joined with others, become modulated and form a chorus. Committees allow for this. They protect the community more generally from an unruly cacophony of individuals shouting; when we speak only for ourselves, too many voices get lost amid the din, and too many of us feel unheard. When we join together on some piece of work undertaken on behalf of the congregation and make sure to include as many voices as we can to represent the different parts of that congregation, we can create a chorus that speaks to all of us and lets all of us speak to the congregation. Voices play off one another, singing with and against, but always in the context of the same piece of music. Our committees are not so different. They gather information, run experiments, and build support, all with transparency and working within the system that, with dissent, grows stronger. Properly conducted, they are filled with agreement and disagreement, passion and hope, and they are always pointed toward the same goal.

We also understand the limits of any structure or process to fully contain all community members. Sometimes, in spite of the fact that all avenues for appropriate and direct communication have been taken, a congregant may find that the synagogue is unable or unwilling to seriously engage them or their idea. If this is a temporary condition, the congregant may choose to wait. A board member may raise an issue, for example, and fail to persuade the others of its importance. Ideally, the board member will feel fairly dealt with and fairly listened to and heard. And, ideally, the member will support the board's decision as if it were his own. Over time, the board member will, hopefully, continue to join with others in the context of a shared mission that they all find meaningful.

If, on the other hand, there is a recognition that what the congregant desires is incompatible with the mission of the synagogue—as when a member wants an alternative *mechitza minyan* in a shul committed to egalitarian worship, or another wants only one day a week of religious school while the congregation is committed to a three-day-a-week program—there may be a need for that individual to find another community. Healthy congregations are able to part gracefully with those who need to belong elsewhere, blessing them on their way, without the need to call upon God to open the earth beneath their feet. This need to leave is, we hope, a last option, one explored only after congregations and their leaders have examined how they encourage and discourage the voices of their various members.

Note

1. Everett Fox, *The Five Books of Moses* (New York: Schocken Books, 1983).

9

SUPPORTING INSTITUTIONS
THAT SUPPORT US:
PAYING YOUR REAL DUES

> When you take a census of the Israelite people each shall pay
> God a ransom for their enrollment. . . . This is what every-
> one shall pay—a half shekel by the sanctuary weight. Every-
> one who is entered in the records, from twenty years of age
> and up, shall give this offering. The rich shall not pay more
> and the poor shall not pay less.
> (Exodus 30:12ff.)

The tabernacle was the original sanctuary of the Israelites, a tent into which the community could gather to bring their offerings for sins, for well-being, and for gratitude to God. It was merely a tent, of course, of animal skins, goat hair, and rope, supported by acacia wood poles. Yet it was also the enduring symbol of the Israelites' relationship with God and of their increasingly moral relationships with one another. The tabernacle offered a focal point for the community; it was the place at which people gathered, learning to fashion a shared understanding of what it meant to be chosen by God. And the tabernacle was the place where the Israelites, as a people and a community, came into existence.

It is equally true that the community was the place where the tabernacle came into existence. The construction of even so simple a dwelling required the collective efforts of the Israelites. More accurately, God demanded that the Israelites each contribute in some fashion to the creation of the tabernacle. He understood that if the tabernacle, and Judaism itself, were to belong to the Israelite people, then each Jew would need to contribute in some way to its construction. Once they invested in the creation of the religion, they would wish to follow that investment with energy and commitment; thus, the half shekel, a ransom tax that God insisted upon as payment for the lives of those who had been saved and delivered unto Mount Sinai. In a sense, God had the Israelites "pay" for

157

the privilege of joining the covenant, for the opportunity to live as Jews in the world that the Holy One would help them create.

According to the rabbis, the half-shekel tax was used to create the bases of the stands into which the poles of the tent of the tabernacle were inserted. The tabernacle itself was created from the free-will offerings of some of the Israelites. The bases on which it stood represented the whole of the Israelite people, those who gave their half shekels willingly, as well as others who may have done so grudgingly. The symbolism here is clear. The entire community was involved in creating the bases upon which the tabernacle and the tablets of the pact it contained, the religion it sustained, were raised and supported. The tax was at once practical—it shared the burden and forestalled resentments among the Israelites—and deeply symbolic of everyone supporting the construction of an institution that would support the entire community. It was also prescient. God understood that the covenant would demand much from the Jewish people in the way of sacrifice and discipline and that they would need to stay the course amid much difficulty. Their half-shekel investments might well help them do so.

The story of the tabernacle continues to resonate for the Jewish people. The modern synagogue is the tent, the shelter within which Jews congregate to worship, study, pray, and reconstitute their community and their religion. People still make their own choices about whether and how much of their time, money, and abilities to invest in Jewish institutions. Some Jews remain unaffiliated with any particular Jewish institution, preferring to invest in other dimensions of their lives. Those who choose to join synagogues pay the modern equivalent of their half shekels to ensure that the bases upon which their institutions rest are strong. Some go further, offering gifts that build capacity, beautify, and strengthen the place and meaning of their synagogues in the world. The Jewish people have thus far been fortunate to have enough individuals willing to invest in synagogues as the places where the tabernacle and the covenant that it represents live on.

It is the sum of these individual choices that determines the fate of the Jewish people. God's requirement that every Jew contributes a half shekel simplified the process by which the tabernacle was constructed and supported. Absent that, we are left with many individuals rather than one community. There are those who join synagogues. There are those who do not. There are those who join and invest a great deal, putting the synagogue at the center of their identity in the world. Individuals make choices that fit with who they are, with their personal histories, with their beliefs and values. At the same time, there is the larger community, the tent under which all Jews are gathered by dint of their birth. This is the tent of the Jewish people, expansive enough to contain any and all, regardless of where (or indeed, whether) they wish to reside within it. This tent is a complicated structure relative to the first tabernacle. Its space has more divisions. Its walls are flimsier, less able to hold fast in the face of assimilation, intermarriage, and disbelief. Its bases are less well supported by the entire community.

We believe that the modern synagogue together with the home is the place where Jews are created, nurtured, and sustained. By supporting synagogues, Jews are trying to retain the place and meaning of the tabernacle in their lives and in those of generations to follow. They are trying to maintain the bases of a tent that has grown complicated, unwieldy, and increasingly crowded out by other, stronger, secular institutions. In this chapter, we focus on the role that the synagogue plays in maintaining the tabernacle of the Jewish people and on the struggles that congregations have with the various aspects of that role. These struggles are important; they exist, they are real, and they reveal much about the functioning of synagogues. The more that we understand these struggles, the more able we are to engage them in healthy ways.

Open Door

The new treasurer of Congregation Beth Shmuel looked at the spreadsheet on his computer screen. It showed the financial information from last year's gala, the synagogue's annual fund-raising event. He was reviewing the numbers in preparation for his meeting with the chair of the fund-raising committee, who was now starting to plan this year's event. The numbers were not great. There had been plenty of members at the event, they had sold all the tickets they had, and the function room they used had been bursting. The band was great, people were dancing, and by all reports it was a great event. It just hadn't made as much money as they had anticipated.

When the treasurer looked more closely at the numbers, he understood what the problem had been. The planning committee had done a reasonably good job of keeping expenses down. They had solicited multiple bids for the catering and the band and received the usual range of items for the silent auction. With costs for events going up as they inevitably do, and the number of staff expanding, the problem was one that had been lurking in the corners, embedded in one of the traditions of Beth Shmuel: the "open-door policy." Ever since anyone could remember, Congregation Beth Shmuel had a policy of letting staff members (many of whom were congregation members as well) and their families attend Shabbat dinners, Purim carnivals, second night seders, and other synagogue events free of charge. The staff often attended these events, sometimes in the role of staff liaison, sometimes simply as members of the community. Staff considered the policy as one of the perks of a job that they occasionally found quite demanding.

There were clearly financial repercussions of this practice, however, which the new treasurer was beginning to understand pretty clearly. When he met with the chair of the fund-raising committee the day after reviewing the data from the previous year's gala, he had some startling news to share. "We have some choices," he told the chair. "We can do what we did last year and raise less money than we planned for in the budget process. We can raise the average ticket price pretty significantly. Or we cannot have staff attend the fund-raiser for free."

The committee chair looked surprised. "I thought we were right in line with our projections from last year."

The treasurer nodded. "We are. And last year we didn't do that well, at least in terms of what the budget had called for. We had to go to several donors for help at the end of the fiscal year. I don't want to have to do that again."

The fund-raising committee chair had been on the board in various capacities for over fifteen years, and he knew how much the staff liked being able to attend events for free. The practice had been in place for so long that the staff now considered it their right. He told the treasurer that he thought they should just raise the ticket prices a bit. "A bit?" responded the treasurer with a smile, shaking his head. "It will be significantly more than a bit. The average ticket price right now will be about one hundred dollars, with some people choosing to pay more and others a bit less. If staff are allowed to attend this fund-raiser for free, the average ticket price would have to be raised some forty dollars each. That's a lot more than a bit!"

The fund-raising committee chair inwardly groaned. He knew there was going to be no easy way to solve this dilemma. He did not want to put all this time into planning a fund-raiser that wasn't going to raise much money. Nor did he want to raise the ticket prices so high that it would scare off or upset the members of the congregation. That left the staff members and the open-door policy. He was not looking forward to taking that on but knew that it was the most viable alternative on a list of unattractive options. He also knew that he did not want to do this on his own. He first met with his committee. One member suggested not inviting the staff, but others recognized that several of them had been asked to "help out" with the event and were looking forward to being there. After much discussion, the committee suggested that those staff who were helping with any event could attend that event for free, but their families and other staff members who were not required to be there needed to pay for their attendance.

The chair knew that he would need some support for this new policy, both formally, in terms of how policies needed to be changed, and informally, in terms of getting some help in dealing with the staff and their disappointment. He called the president of the shul, and with support from the treasurer, convinced her to bring the committee's suggestion to the board for a policy revision. The board approved the revision. Over the course of the next few weeks, the policy was explained to and discussed with staff members, some of whom were upset while others were understanding of the financial implications of the old policy. Over time, the new policy was more or less accepted, and the gala and other synagogue events contributed more to the financial stability of the synagogue.

At first glance this is the story of a congregation figuring out how to create a fund-raising event that would actually raise money. The treasurer, appropriately, looked closely at the numbers from the previous year and identified a significant area of concern: the synagogue's open-door policy, created as a way to invite staff members into the life of the congregation, had the unintended consequence of creating a financial burden for the congregation. From this insight came necessary changes in the policy itself and, presumably, in the process of developing and analyzing budgets for future events.

Yet beneath this story lies another one whose theme involves the process by which a synagogue is supported. The treasurer, in pointing to the costs of the synagogue's open-door policy, was inadvertently raising the question of what it means for a community to support itself. The question he raised pointed to the issue of fairness within a community. Who ought to bear the burden of ensuring that a synagogue survives as an institution? Should everyone contribute equally or ought some bear the burden on behalf of others? Are there different "classes" in a synagogue community, with some people able and willing to give more than others? Can a community honor its diversity, with some people contributing in some ways (e.g., with money) and other people contributing in other ways (e.g., as staff members or volunteers)? These questions are not new to us. They hark back to the tabernacle, to the half shekel that each Israelite was required to pay, and to the gifts that some chose to give and others to withhold.

These questions remain difficult. Synagogue leaders and members struggle with how to create communities that honor differences in people's abilities and willingness to support their synagogues while also creating cultures of fairness and equity. The tension at the heart of this struggle is that between inclusiveness and exclusiveness. The synagogue strives to include all members, inviting them to join in activities, programs, and other dimensions of synagogue life. Cost structures are often flexible, sensitive to people's financial circumstances. Clergy and lay leaders work hard to create inviting communities for those wishing to join in shared practices, beliefs, and values. At the same time, congregants make choices about how much to become involved and how much to give of their time and money that inevitably lead to some members being more fully "inside" the institution than others. Congregations often end up appearing as concentric circles of exclusivity, with some members more closely tied to the synagogue sitting closer to the core of its leadership and others ringed outside according to their levels of involvement.

We offer this as descriptive rather than prescriptive. It simply reflects the choices that individuals make and the results of those choices on the dynamics of an institution. Behind these individual choices is a larger issue that we wish to highlight. Put simply, it is the fact that synagogues cost quite a bit to maintain in the world, and the dues that individuals and their families contribute can seem quite high. Why is that so?

The Dues We Pay

Answering the question of why we pay high dues is both simple and complicated. The simple answer is that it costs money to operate synagogues, as it does any complex organization. There are buildings to maintain, staff to hire, programs to develop and implement, and schools to run. For most synagogues, 80 percent or more of their budget is salaries and benefits. Synagogues are employers. They employ rabbis and cantors, educators and administrators, secretaries and custodians. While these staff members are certainly attracted to their jobs because of the place and meaning of synagogues in the world, they expect and deserve to be fairly treated and adequately compensated. Rabbis do not take vows of poverty. Synagogue professionals require the same considerations (health insurance, benefits, pension, and the like) that any of us seek from our employment. Indeed, much of Jewish law deals with how to appropriately take care of one's employees—"Thou shall not withhold a workman's wages over night" (Deuteronomy 24:15). Jewish law deems taking advantage of a worker an abuse. Synagogues need to role model this behavior by the way they take care of their employees.

Congregants pay as well to maintain aspects of the synagogue that are not, in the language of the business world, "profit centers"; that is, they cannot cover their costs with the money they attract. A synagogue educational program is the clearest example of this. When it comes to education, whether Harvard University or our local synagogues, we can never charge enough tuition to cover the real costs. Every educational program is subsidized by someone or some fund. In synagogues, the members who are relatively uninvolved but still paying dues are helping to subsidize the cost of every child's education. Similarly, the congregation as a whole subsidizes the synagogue's efforts at *tikkun olam* in the form of various social action or community projects that bring much meaning and satisfaction but no money into the synagogue. In both instances, whole congregations are investing in bringing into the world two dimensions—study and acts of kindness—that define Judaism and its people. Indeed, we recently read a synagogue's "dues reminder" letter that made this explicit. The letter read, in part, "Our temple activities of worship, study, social action and community gatherings have been wonderfully successful this year. Dues and fee payments by our members fund these important programs which are central to our Jewish life together."

Our congregations invest in Judaism in other ways as well. We support rabbis, not simply to work in our congregations, but to exist in the larger community as well. Rabbis have a presence in the community, performing rabbinic roles apart from their work with congregants. They may officiate at life-cycle events for nonmembers. While some synagogues have policies against doing so, living with it is quite another matter. What does a rabbi say to a previous member when he calls after his mother has just died? What about that couple, new to town, looking for a rabbi to marry them? How about someone in the hospital who needs a blessing? How can rabbis possibly say no? Our rabbis struggle with these questions but do so without having to think about financial implications. Embedded here is an old model, in which the *shtetl* community took care of the rabbi's material needs, freeing him to study, pray, and wrestle with complicated questions on behalf of the community. The congregation is the new *shtetl,* supporting the rabbi to work on behalf of the larger community.

In some ways, our congregations are carrying an unfair burden. Congregants are investing a disproportionate amount of the resources—money, time, and energy—to maintain the people and practices of Judaism. They are paying their half shekels; others are not. How can we understand this? One way, of course, is to divide the world of the Jews into those who care ("the practicing Jews") and those who do not ("the nonpracticing Jews"), and act as if they are two separate groups whose members have or ought to have little to do with one another. This may, however, be a false dichotomy. Modern Jews across the movements routinely struggle with the place and meaning of Judaism in their lives; some struggle in the context of the synagogue, and others do not. A second way, then, is to believe that the differences between the groups are slight and that Jews who are unaffiliated, used to be affiliated, thinking about becoming affiliated, or would like to but cannot afford to be affiliated ought to be reached out to and brought closer *(keruv)* through and into the synagogue.

What we choose to believe matters a great deal in terms of what we do in our synagogues: what proportion of synagogue offerings are for the community at large, how much we support not only our own synagogue but synagogue life in general, and what role the individual synagogue plays in maintaining a vibrant Jewish presence in a world of assimilation.

The *midrash* told earlier of the old man in ancient Israel who was discovered by a Roman soldier planting a carob tree on a hillside applies here as well. "Old man," says the soldier, "don't you realize that you will be long dead before that tree can bear fruit?" "Yes, of course I do," responds the old man. "Then why are you wasting your precious little time left on earth planting trees?" accuses the soldier. The old man replies, "Just as there were trees that I did not plant when I was born, so I plant for the next generation that will come after me."

The truth is that we are all inheritors. Very few of us created the synagogues in which we study, celebrate, and congregate, or the institutions that support the Jewish community, such as the Jewish community center, the cemetery, and the federations. Yet they nourish us because someone had the foresight and the generosity to create them. We need to see ourselves in the same way. Our synagogues cannot simply be places in which we get our needs met. Rather, they need to be seen as parts of a forest whose trees we need to grow and protect so that they will be there to provide the natural resources for the next generation who will enhance them with their love and commitment. While we harvest fruit for our families and ourselves, we need to be planting trees for those who will come after us. This is more than just a metaphor. There was a time not so long ago when supporting the relatively new State of Israel meant sending money for the planting of trees on its land. Many of us gave knowing that we were helping to sustain generations of the Jewish people and that we ourselves might never see the trees that we had helped to plant.

When we maintain our synagogues with our dues, our time and commitment, and our expertise, we are planting trees. We are creating the bases for the tabernacle, inside which the ark resides. We are investing not simply in buildings, but in the synagogue as an idea; we are ensuring that the synagogue and all that it represents outlives us. There has been too much history—the Exodus, the Diaspora, the rebirth of the State of Israel, the Holocaust—to do otherwise. We are stewards, holding fast to that which we were given at Mount Sinai. Our synagogues are the places in which our inheritance and our tradition reside, and we who have chosen to congregate together gather to keep it safe and holy. We do this because we feel we should. We believe that it is our obligation, and for some, our joy, to invest in and maintain Judaism and its institutions. We do this for ourselves, yes, and for our children and grandchildren, but also on behalf of the Jewish people, even those who do not care so much. In many ways, joining a synagogue and paying dues is an act of faith, a step taken in the belief that it will make a difference not simply to oneself but to the Jewish people more generally.

The Price of Admission

The notion of "dues" is itself quite interesting. We understand dues as a charge or fee for membership in an organization. Synagogue dues are, in effect, the price of admission: they enable people to become congregants, subject to the same opportunities, rights, responsibilities, and obligations as other members. When we pay dues, we are granted access—to opportunities for prayer and study, for learning, to relationships with clergy and other congregants. Our dues represent the beginning, not the end, of our support of the synagogue.

Though many in the modern world would like to see them as such, synagogues are not and have never been "fee for service" institutions. They are membership communities, supported by annual commitments made by their members. Partially, this is a matter of practicality: it would be difficult, if not impossible, to charge enough for the services that the synagogue provides and still make the synagogue open to anyone who wished to join. On another level, though, "paying as you go" would detract, if not outright negate, the nature of the synagogue as a community. Communities are where one lives, where one belongs, *not* where one shops. Further, "buying" synagogue services, such as a bar mitzvah or a worship service, would cheapen these moments, turning them into commercial transactions.

While the demarcation between a fee-for-service and a membership organization seems clear enough in theory, for some members of the synagogue the line can seem blurry. In many synagogues, members are offered events and programs for which they are asked to pay fees in addition to their membership dues and religious school tuitions. The list can be quite long: congregational dinners before special Shabbat events, adult education classes and seminars, guest speakers and concerts, retreats, school events, Purim carnivals, and so on. These fees are neither unreasonable nor unexpected. Most of these events require extra funding in that they do not fit neatly into synagogue budgets. Some of the events may be fund-raisers. The fees also enable synagogues to apportion costs according to who benefits from attending certain events, rather than to the membership community more generally, which already absorbs many other significant costs.

Yet while the pay-as-you-go system makes sense, it also leaves some synagogue members feeling uneasy and others feeling exploited. Why, they ask, must they pay so much more, after having already paid what may be a great deal of money as annual dues? What does their paid membership provide for them? We have already suggested an answer to these questions: dues are a commitment to both a particular synagogue and to the existence of synagogues (and thus the Jewish people) in the world. But we suspect that this answer will remain unsatisfying to a certain percentage of congregants who are either unfamiliar with or uncommitted to the idea of being asked to make such commitments, to plant trees from which they themselves will not benefit. We suspect as well that the ongoing sense of exploitation is familiar to some members and shapes their membership experiences, much as it did for some of the first Israelites who questioned what exactly they received in return for their half shekels. Indeed, the answer then was the same as the answer now: as synagogue Jews we pay for the privilege of creating the bases into which the poles that hoist the tabernacle are placed. We pay to create a space for the Jewish people.

Then, of course, congregations need to figure out how to pay for what occurs within the space they have created. As with the original tabernacle, there are opportunities for congregants to give as much as they wish, according to their abilities and desires. Our synagogues offer many opportunities to give money. There are discretionary funds, memorial funds, funds that honor individuals and causes, scholarship funds that offset tuitions, fund-raising events, and capital campaigns. Congregants also often write checks to the synagogue after a *simcha,* such as a wedding, bar or bat mitzvah, or naming of a child. When they do so, they are keeping faith with the notion of a *zevach sh'lamim*—a free-will offering or gift through which people express gratitude to the Holy One for the great joy that came into their lives. Such offerings, like prayers, enable congregants to remain connected to God and to one another through the vehicle of the synagogue. These offerings help maintain and sustain the shul and those who work on its behalf.

Our Fair Share

Creating and maintaining the tabernacles in our lives—our synagogues— is not solely about money, of course. It is about all members of a synagogue community finding ways to support that community, according to their gifts, resources, and desires. Members will choose to contribute in certain ways. Some will pay their dues—their half shekels—and leave it at that, participating in some events and not others without investing more of themselves in their synagogues. Others will volunteer their energies, serving on committees, working with areas of the synagogue that appeal to them, and throwing themselves into particular efforts and programs. Others will become lay leaders, trying to guide their synagogues in certain directions. Still others will involve themselves in capital campaigns, endowment planning, or expansion efforts, each of which represents an investment in the stability of the synagogue and its ability to remain central to the future generations of congregants. As long as there is a community to support and be a part of, there will be members who take different paths in doing so.

We hasten to point out that the different contributions that congregants make to their synagogues are just that—different—rather than unequal. There are many ways for congregants to contribute their fair shares. It is often tempting for congregants to measure the contributions that they and others make in financial terms; indeed, it is easy enough in some synagogues to keep track of financial contributions through the monthly bulletins that list what members gave to what funds, campaigns, or events. It is more difficult but no less important, however, to track other kinds of contributions—volunteer work, program planning, being part of the weekly *minyan* or Torah study group, and showing up and lending a hand to events—that are vital in the life of the institution. People may be recognized for such contributions, but often not as prominently as those who give money (and perhaps little else). There is, or ought to be, room enough in congregations for all kinds of people who offer all kinds of gifts; for the tent of the tabernacle is truly wide and deep enough to contain us all.

We end this chapter by underscoring an important point that has been implicit throughout: the dues that we pay, in their various forms, are crucial not simply to support synagogue communities, but to securely bind individuals *as* community members. When individuals contribute to a community, they invest in it; and in so doing, they invest part of themselves in it. They then see themselves in that community and are bound to it, as they are bound to their identities in the world. The synagogue becomes an extension of themselves. They feel *a part of* rather than *apart from* the synagogue. They would as soon see their synagogues fail as they would themselves.

As we pointed out at the beginning of this chapter, God understood this. The Holy One understood that the half shekel meant something, financially, in its purchase of the bases for the tabernacle but that it meant much, much more in its purchase of the Israelites' loyalty. Our synagogues need to hold fast to this knowledge. We need to remember that every congregant needs to feel as if he or she is contributing, not simply "paying their dues," to the synagogue community in ways that matter, that dignify them and their synagogues. When we find ways to ensure that this occurs, we bring people into the tabernacle; indeed, we bring the tabernacle into them, such that they feel part of what it means to be taken into Judaism, its practices and its people and its relation to God. We maintain the holy tabernacle, in our synagogues, and in whatever forms it will continue to appear for generations to come.

Part 3

———————————————————

Healthy Clergy

10

CHARTING THE COURSE AND LEADING US THERE

As Pharaoh drew near, the children of Israel caught sight of
Egypt advancing upon them. Greatly frightened, the Israelites cried out to Adonai. And they said to Moses, "Was it for
lack of graves in Egypt that you brought us out here to die in
this wilderness? What have you done to us taking us out of
Egypt? Is this not the very thing we told you when we were
still in Egypt that it would be better for us to serve the Egyptians than to die here, like this?" And Moses replied, "Have
no fear! Stand back and witness the deliverance Adonai will
work for you today!"
(Exodus 14:10-13)

How many times have you heard someone say, "I belong to Rabbi ———'s
shul"? While there is no congregation in America that we know of that is
named after its current rabbi, still many Jews identify their synagogue
with their rabbi. Perhaps it should not be that way; after all, even in the
best-case scenarios of long-lasting relationships, rabbis do come and go
and the synagogues they served continue to serve the community. But it
points to an unconscious reality. As rabbis link their lives and their work
to a particular synagogue, those synagogues link themselves to their rabbis. Therefore, in writing a book about healthy synagogues, we recognize
that a key ingredient to that health, perhaps *the* key ingredient, is a healthy
rabbi. What do we mean by "healthy"?

In this section of the book, we offer various answers to this question.
In short, healthy rabbis are thoughtful and reflective, balanced in reason
and emotion, available to others in both personal and spiritual ways, and
respectful and giving within appropriate boundaries. They create healthy
relationships with others—congregants, lay leaders, other clergy, and
staff—and thus model ways of being and working with people that others can intuitively follow in their own lives. They recharge themselves

rather than allow themselves to become burned out; they remain alive in their work and in their personal lives. Like Moses in the above quote, healthy rabbis remain clear-headed in the face of doubts and challenges that will inevitably come their way. They have a sense of gravitas without losing their sense of humor. While they listen to and take seriously what others say about them—the good, the bad, and the ugly—they stay grounded in their own honest and reflective sense of themselves. And finally, healthy rabbis seek enough support from others to take on the demanding role of visionary leader.

The Rabbi as Visionary

In this chapter, we focus in particular on the rabbi as a visionary, some-one able to create a compelling preferred picture of the future of the synagogue to which congregants are and will be attracted. While honor-ing the past, visionaries create images of what people and communities can become, images powerful enough to engage and energize. They link their vision to the ongoing narrative of the congregation it will serve, providing continuity even while there is change. Visionaries do not sim-ply offer a sense that what has come before is wrong; rather, they offer a sense that what will occur in the future is, inevitably, exactly right.

While rabbis do not create visions by themselves (we explore this more fully in the following section) they are, by necessity, the focal point. However, while this is necessarily so, rabbis must remember that the vi-sion can never be about them. Their personal passions must be contained within the vision, but the vision itself must be about the future of the community—the specific one located in the congregation, and the larger one of which each synagogue is a part.

As visionaries, rabbis ought not to harangue their congregations about all that they are not. Rabbis do not simply point out the weaknesses of congregations, leaving members feeling ashamed and guilty. Rather, ef-fective rabbis articulate visions of what we can be and continually point to that vision when people fail, falter, and doubt. That is exactly what Moses did in the story quoted above and what he will continue to do in the journey ahead. He will point, again and again, to the future, to the land of promise, helping and encouraging the people to strive to make real and concrete their yearnings as a people, assuring them of God's continual love and concern. Similarly, in their visions for their communities, rabbis must offer a sense of what extraordinary places their synagogues can be, enabling us to thrive as congregations and as a Jewish people.

A Vision Sampler

The mission of Temple Beth Am is "to maintain a Reform religious institution that will meet the spiritual, educational, social, and cultural needs of its members and to be a positive contributor to the community in which its members live." We offer here a piece of the overall vision created toward the conclusion of the rabbi's first year at the synagogue.

> In the last few decades, we have turned Judaism into pediatric pabulum, which we feed our children because "they have to know who they are." Then, when they are "done" (bar/bat mitzvah or confirmation), we drop out of the synagogue because "we no longer need it." This mind-set demonstrates a complete failure to understand the meaning and purpose of Judaism and in the end will also wind up failing the very population it purports to serve, our children. You see, Judaism, like any great religious system, was designed to give meaning and purpose to life. It was meant as a guide for adults, who would teach it to their children through example and experience. Our children would learn the messages of their faith by participating with their parents in life-cycle events, Shabbat, and holy day celebrations. Their life decisions would be influenced and informed by Jewish values that had been part of their deliberations and discussions with their parents and teachers.
>
> How far we have come! Today a largely Jewishly illiterate adult population sends their children to synagogue schools and day schools to be filled up with Jewish knowledge. The schools do their best, and the kids perform well with minimal complaining. And then the dissonance between what they have been taught at synagogue and the lives they are living begins to be the substance of irritation and mild rebellion. "Do as we say and not as we do" has never worked. Our children see through that and reject it. And I, for one, do not blame them. Unless and until we adults commit ourselves to learning and living a

life of Judaism, we are wasting our resources and our children's time. We have to get serious about our own Jewish lives.

Synagogues have to become places for adults of all ages and children—in that order. Day schools must expand their mission to include the parents through family education and expectation. Gone are the days when we could afford to educate our children alone. Synagogues must become "shuls with schools" and not the other way around. The tail has wagged the dog for far too long.

At Beth Am, we have already made some strides in this direction. But we have a long way to go. I propose the creation of a lifelong learning center with its own full-time educator. Such a center would provide opportunities for adults and families to learn both together and separately. Every adult in our congregation (regardless of age) would be considered a student, participating at his or her own pace in the *mitzvah* of *talmud* Torah/the study of our sacred sources and becoming literate in Hebrew. We could create an entire curriculum of basic courses and electives available both at Beth Am and throughout the community. Let us use the technology available to us to have lectures at home, on video and cassette recordings. Adults would have a counselor (rabbis, cantor, educators, etc.) to guide them in their interests and needs. Milestones would be recognized and certificates awarded. Those who study to enrich their lives should be our heroes and our role models. Their example needs to be emulated and expanded.

This, we believe, demonstrates a vision, grounded in Jewish values (the study of Torah and lifelong learning) and a particular relationship with God; connected to various trends in the larger community (dropping out of temple life after bar/bat mitzvah, combined with an aging population of adults with more discretionary time); and flowing from and moving the congregation toward the synagogue's historic mission as a community of learners of all ages. The vision is abstract enough to relate to the synagogue's mission and concrete enough to guide the expansion of specific programs.

What Do We Mean When We Say "Vision"?

Visions are powerful because they provide meaning and direction to people. They help them make sense of their lives, as individuals and as part of communities. The rabbi is crucial here. Living at the intersection of Torah and the world of the everyday and ordinary, the rabbi has a particular perspective that others do not. Occupying that place, the space between what a congregation could be if its members were truly living a God-centered existence, striving toward holiness in each of their daily moments and interactions, and what it is, the rabbi invites others to visit that intersection and reside there, even temporarily. It is because such gaps exist, and always will in an unredeemed, imperfect world, that we need rabbis among us. For it is they who willingly step into those places, much like Nachshon ben Aminadab stepped into the Sea of Reeds, and in partnership with God lead us to a vision of who we, in our higher moments, wish to be.

The narrative of the Jewish people is the context, the sweeping backdrop of our lives as Jews, and rabbis need to use this narrative as the foundation for their visions of what congregations can be. This narrative we call "Torah." It is read to us and by us each week throughout the year and, once ended, begins again. This narrative both orients and holds us steady through the cycles of planting, growth, and harvest, of gain and loss, of exile, hope, and redemption. Rabbis help us make sense of this narrative and find our places within it; they help us see the links between the lives and words and stories of our ancestors and ourselves. The narrative of the Torah—of how we Jews were found and lost and then found again (and lost and found again and again) entering into a covenant with God, striving to make real its terms in our lives—is a narrative that provides meaning. It is a way to make sense of how we, as Jews, now continue to struggle to live in covenantal relationship with God and by extension with one another. This larger narrative helps us understand why we choose, as faithful Jews, to build and worship in our modern tabernacles called synagogues.

The smaller, more specific narratives that rabbis offer are those that enable us as congregants to make sense of who we are as congregations, finding our places in the larger story. These narratives are shaped by the particular denominational movements in which rabbis have been trained and by the affiliations, missions, and histories of their synagogues. They are grounded as well in the traditional functions of synagogues as Houses of Study, Prayer, and Gathering. They are, finally, shaped by individual rabbis' own senses of what is most important to them and to the Jewish people they will serve—the possibilities for Jewish life and renewal, and the meaning of their own personal rabbinate. Rabbis bring these "visions," often inchoate and unarticulated, into their work. Their work and their roles as leaders demand that they find voices to express those visions.

In framing visions, rabbis must remember that the purpose of the synagogue is to do holy work, create holy space, and foster holy partnerships between people and between ourselves and God. Yet visions can never be "cookie cutter" in nature. What may work at one point in time in one synagogue may be impossible, even counterproductive in another. Visions need to be big, but not so much so as to be unrealizable. If a vision is well beyond the capacities of the people, it will serve to frustrate them into giving up even before they begin. Visions must challenge and inspire, making the synagogue and its members reach. But if it requires too much of a reach, the congregation is likely to fall. Getting back up can be a difficult, even debilitating task.

The Visionary

For Rabbi Simcha Katz it was music to his ears. After five years in the rabbinate, working first as an assistant then associate, he was finally going to be in a synagogue that wanted him to be a real rabbi. They said it in their listing for the position, and then he heard it again and again in the interview process—Beth Tikvah wanted a visionary, someone to lead them into the twenty-first century! It had been five years since the congregation had a real leader. After their founding rabbi (now emeritus) had retired, his successor turned out not to be much of a mensch, and his successor just did not have the "right stuff." Beth Tikvah needed a take-control type of guy. Simcha knew he was ready for this.

Though they were not very well attended with so many people out of town, the summer coffees went very well. The people were friendly and very receptive of him and his family. While some members expressed their hopes for the synagogue, most of his conversations were social, introducing himself and his family, recounting aspects of his growing up, sharing why he became a rabbi—the usual kinds of things rabbis talk about at these events.

Since there was not much to do over the summer, Simcha spent much of his time drafting his vision for the congregation, which he planned to reveal at the High Holy Days. He divided his sermons into three parts—self for Rosh Hashanah, synagogue community for Kol Nidre, and community at large for Yom Kippur day. His sermon on self would focus on adult and family learning, in which he would announce his plans for changing religious school into the *Bet Sefer Mishpacha*, a school that would require parents to learn along with their children. His sermon on the synagogue community would feature his plans for Shabbat. Rabbi Katz loved Shabbat and was convinced that this was the only way to build a real community, something Congregation Tikvah sorely lacked and needed. And finally, on Yom Kippur day, he would talk about revitalizing the synagogue's historic role as a leader in social action, only he would call it *tikkun olam*, in line with what a lot of other synagogues were doing these days. He was really excited.

But his excitement was matched only by his sense of deflation when soon after the holidays the president asked to see him with two or three "important congregational leaders" whom he had never met to speak to him about "those sermons."

"Rabbi, please don't get us wrong. Your sermons were very interesting, but they are not who we are. This is not a congregation of Torah scholars; Friday night is not a time we come to shul; and while we are involved in our community, we believe in helping Jews first, not *goyim*. I don't know where you got those ideas."

"But in all the interviews you said you wanted a rabbi to vision the twenty-first century. This is what is happening in the Jewish world today. I merely put together—"

Rabbi Katz was interrupted by one of the gentlemen who accompanied the president to this "meeting." "I don't know about any interviews, but I do know this congregation. You are way out on a limb, young man, and if you do not want to go crashing to the earth without a net, you are going to need to modify those sermons of yours."

The Visioning Process

Articulating visions is holy work. It requires rabbis to take up their personal authority in the role of spiritual leader to point their congregants toward a better, more fulfilling way of life together. This is not to say that rabbis, and only rabbis, are allowed or are able to articulate visions for the Jewish future. Others—clergy, laypeople, communal leaders—may do so as well. Jacob had a dream, a vision if you will, and it inspired him and quite likely others as well. So too, congregants can be moved in certain ways, inspired to develop visions that speak to them, offering ways to live increasingly Jewish lives. Yet it is the rabbi who has the moral authority to craft visions on behalf of a congregation. It is the rabbi who most often maps the intersection between the demands of Torah and the pulls of the outside world and popular culture. And it is the rabbi who must be enlisted, in some fashion or another, for a vision to be woven into narratives that define the Jewish fabric of our people and our communities, our synagogues.

Ideally, then, the visioning process begins with the rabbi and gradually expands to include others. Creating the vision has three initial steps.

Respect and Know the Past. While sharing one's personal vision for the Jewish people must be part of any interview process, to determine if there is a proper fit between rabbi and congregation, the actual visioning process should not take place until the rabbi spends a good deal of time getting to know the synagogue, its mission, and its story. This, along with building relationships with staff and congregational leaders—official and unofficial—is the primary task of the rabbi's first year. Knowing the past, and knowing how this community has dealt with change, is necessary, for the vision must be part of the congregation's ongoing narrative. And demonstrating respect for the past is an indication of the rabbi's wisdom and *menschlichkeit,* or common sense. We have seen too many great visions fail because they failed to take past history into account, seeing it as an impediment or an irrelevancy. Just as with individuals, the past of a synagogue tells us much about its collective identity, a very powerful force. Also as with individuals, synagogue history is very difficult and sometimes impossible to overcome.

Understand and Assess the Present. Assessment requires a great deal of data collection on the part of the rabbi. Who are the leaders, both professional and lay, already working in the congregation? What are their strengths and their learning curves? How well do they deal with change? What are the demographic trends? Who is moving into and out of the community? What are some of the larger communal concerns? Unless one knows one's people and the communal realities in which they sit, and places the vision squarely within their reach, it will be doomed to fail before it ever gets off the ground.

Imagine and Dream the Future. The vision itself involves setting a course that the rabbi believes in and that can be realistically achieved in the future. Before it becomes final, the rabbi will have to share and "vet" the vision with key leaders and decision makers, seeking their input and commentary. We discuss this in detail in Part 4. Once again, the vision, in order to garner passion and energy, must require the congregation to reach. But unless it is graspable, very few will even attempt it. Even so, sometimes there is failure. The promised land may have been only an eight-day journey. The Torah may have been located in the people's hearts and minds, not over the sea or up in the heavens, but that slave people could not overcome their history to realize the vision both God and Moses had set before them.

In our case study, Rabbi Katz failed not because of his ideas. Rabbis rarely do fail for that reason. His concepts for the synagogue were excellent, inspiring, and truly visionary. He failed because he did not understand the process by which visions come to take hold. He thought that since the synagogue's search committee called upon him to be a visionary, he had a mandate from the congregation to go forth and lead. Search committees often represent the vanguard of a synagogue; they are not always truly representational. And even when they are, rabbis have a lot of work to do before even one word of a vision plan is uttered. Rabbi Katz ran before he walked through the steps. No wonder he fell so hard.

Articulating the Vision

The visioning process begins but does not end with the rabbi's initial creation of the vision. Visions need to move from narrative and imagery to greater specificity and meaning for particular congregations. They must become widely accepted, having enough support to be made real. They must be reinforced through words, symbols, and actions. Key figures in the congregation and sometimes even the greater community must be identified with them. How this process happens usually occurs in one of three ways or forms that vary in terms of the nature of the collaboration between rabbis and other key players in the synagogue's hierarchy.

Rabbi-centric. In this first form the rabbi drives the process and is largely left alone to refine and implement a vision. Others may provide some input, but the vision is accurately perceived as "the rabbi's vision," which others may subscribe to but do not immediately see as their "own." The rabbi leads the process of both creating and articulating the vision into an easily understood philosophy, suggesting concrete ways of implementing that philosophy into programs and projects, motivating others to embrace them. All the while the rabbi, like our Rabbi Katz, remains clearly at the center of the process. Depending on the extent to which these visions become accepted and ingrained into the lives and practices of the congregants and are espoused by lay leaders and staff, they are more or less likely to fade as the rabbis who developed them leave their congregations. What begins with the rabbi and stays with the rabbi usually leaves with the rabbi as well.

Partnership. In a second form, the rabbi articulates an initial vision and is then joined in a meaningful collaboration by lay leaders, staff, other clergy, and sometimes other interested or invested congregants in finding ways to make the vision come alive in concrete, specific ways. People invest time and energy in making the vision right and meaningful. They engage in important, sometimes difficult conversations, challenging and joining with one another to make the vision fit their collective sense of what the congregation is and what it ought to be. The rabbi is a significant force but not the only significant force in this process. The result is a vision that not only reflects the congregation more generally, but a cadre of people who have a sense of ownership over that vision as well. It is not only the rabbi who stands above and apart, seeing what others can only glimpse. Others now stand alongside looking to the imagined future together.

Lay Leader-centric. In the third form, the rabbi is more marginalized. The lay leaders keep the rabbi at some remove, taking a vision that either already belongs to them or one they have collectively created, according to how it fits with their perceptions of what their congregation is or ought to be. The lay leaders may request that the rabbi and other staff leaders lead services and/or run programs, but the lay leaders remain at the center as the visionaries and the decision makers. Oftentimes these visions are not tightly connected to the narratives of the Jewish people and their covenantal relationship with God and one another, or of that particular synagogue as an embodiment of the tabernacle, that are integral to a compelling, lasting vision. And, in as much as lay leadership turns over frequently in most synagogues, this form runs the risk of having no lasting passion and energy behind it.

These patterns are related, of course, to the nature of the collaboration more generally between rabbis and lay leaders in particular synagogues. In some congregations, collaboration between clergy and lay leaders comes relatively easily; in others, it is more difficult and may not occur much at all. Since most congregations begin with a group of lay leaders whose initial vision is what creates the energy to form the synagogue in the first place, the way they "hand off" visioning power to the rabbi (or fail to do so) will determine what form a congregation takes. We believe that when congregations are able to create a useful collaboration among rabbis, lay leaders, and staff—similar to the second form we just described—the resulting visions are deepened, more widely accepted and owned, more representative of congregational needs and capacities, and long lasting.

In our case study, Rabbi Katz acted as if he had a mandate to create the vision all by himself. We cannot know, of course, whether the congregation colluded with that, seducing him in the interview process to come and be "their visionary and savior." While Rabbi Katz's vision was grounded in the narrative of the Jewish people and was in line with contemporary needs of the Jewish community in general, he rushed the process. He did not get the kind of buy-in necessary for the vision to go forward. And he misunderstood that there were other significant and powerful leaders, elders of the congregation, with whom he never spoke, perhaps never even met. Had he spent the requisite amount of time building relationships and getting to know the synagogue and its players, he may have been able to present the same vision at his second High Holy Day services with great acceptance and appreciation. Did Beth Tikvah really want a visionary to lead them forward? Or was this a congregation that really operated as a lay-led system and did not wish to admit it?

That, too, we cannot know, for Rabbi Katz became the third failed succession, wondering what went wrong.

The Nitty-Gritty of the Visioning Process

A number of technical aspects of the visioning process remain the same regardless of who is in the driver's seat. While they are relatively straightforward, there are no shortcuts. Congregations put in peril the overall vision if they think they can fast-track any of these steps.

Get People Together in Lots of Different Forums. When Rabbi Katz came to Beth Tikvah, he was introduced to the community in several coffees that took place in congregants' homes. This is necessary but nowhere near sufficient. These coffee forums tend to be social in nature, often giving the rabbi an opportunity to introduce himself or herself and do most of the talking. There also need to be forums, like town hall meetings, in which the rabbi is able to ask congregants what they think, listening to their concerns and needs. Congregants need to feel that the leadership is interested in their input. If not, individuals will either seek the rabbi's ear in private or go underground. The former leaves the rabbi with data that he or she may not be able to process; the latter leaves the rabbi uninformed, walking over potential land mines. Both are dangerous.

Support Experimentation. In any change process, it is essential that new programs, formats, or ideas are presented as "experiments," not "the new way we are going to do things around here from now on." Experiments say, "Let's try it"; "the new way" tells people, "You are either with me or against me." By creating experiments, the congregation understands that the visionary is not a know-it-all and that nothing will be forced down their throats. Experiments invite feedback as data is collected. This gives everyone an opportunity to feel that their input will be considered as the congregation moves toward the new vision. Rabbi Katz's High Holy Day sermons made it seem that he had decided the direction for the congregation. Even if they liked his ideas, many people may have felt, "How dare he come to our community and tell us what to do!"

Encourage Others to Get Involved. We like task forces and think tanks. They allow people to get involved in their congregation without having to be on the board of directors. Boards can have only a limited number of people. Committees are great when people are ready to make a commitment to work. But task forces and think tanks allow anyone who is interested an opportunity for involvement. Of course, these cannot be pseudo-teams. Their work must be carefully considered and implemented whenever possible. On the other hand, participants need to understand that the board must approve their input and that such approval is not automatic. The greater clarity and transparency used in this process, the more likely real involvement will occur.

Delegate Tasks. Rabbi Katz's vision was well constructed and quite comprehensive, yet he seemed to hold the vision, and its implementation, to himself. He needed to create a structure of delegation. For example, he and the president may have empowered separate groups to consider specific aspects of the vision and its implementation. This would have given Rabbi Katz an opportunity to teach others about the realities of the Jewish world as he saw it and to enlist their help in getting there. Their excitement and investment in the process is a necessary component in the ultimate acceptance and success of the vision. One group could have been working on the family curriculum, together with the educator and the school board, a second with the social action committee to come up with new projects, and a third with the adult education group to create a menu of learning opportunities for congregants. This delegation of tasks is both healthy for the rabbi and essential for congregational buy-in.

Bring People Together to Celebrate. Each completed task needs to be recognized and celebrated. So, for example, if Beth Tikvah had decided to experiment with a family education track in its religious school (as opposed to changing the curriculum altogether), the first program or semester could have concluded with a little *sium* (conclusion) publicized in the congregational newsletter. These celebrations are congratulatory to the participants, encouraging them to continue and send a message to the community as a whole, keeping the vision alive in everyone's minds.

Keep the Vision in Front of the People as Much as Possible. We are not recommending that the leaders beat people over the head by repeating the vision ad nauseam; however, a big mistake that synagogue leaders often make is that everyone becomes aware of the vision because the rabbi spoke it so eloquently at the High Holy Days, but it then seems to disappear. Visions need repeating. And various programs need to be attached back to the vision when appropriate. So when Congregation Tikvah announces their Habitat for Humanity Day, someone needs to remind the congregation, "This day is part of our overall vision for *tikkun olam.*"

Make the Vision Part of the Congregation Itself Rather Than Located with Certain Individuals or Groups. It can be the rabbi's vision. In fact, we suggest it ought to begin there. But it has to be the rabbi's vision for the congregation as a whole. By Rabbi Katz failing to include more people in the visioning process and rushing to get it in front of the congregation, he made it look like the vision was all about himself, perhaps representing the views of the search committee, but not more than that. Such visions are likely to fail regardless of their merit. And when they fail, as happened with Rabbi Katz, they often take the rabbi down with them.

When we present this vision process, we are often asked, "Whatever happened to 'real' rabbis who are out in front come what may? This sounds more like a politician than a rabbi!" Synagogues are organizations, and complex ones at that. Organizations have political processes. Rabbis need to learn them and deal well with them, for as we said earlier, politics is the art of getting things done. If rabbis want their visions to be realized, they need to master the politics as well. Perhaps Moses did not have to, since he literally had God on his side; however, we must also remember that Moses did not make it to the promised land.

Be that as it may, we do believe that the rabbi quite deliberately needs to take the role of visionary and change agent. As we noted in chapter 4, changes always should be anchored in a vision, with a real sense of where we are going. The rabbi is perfectly situated to offer that vision. There is the formal authority and influential power vested in the office of the rabbi. There is expertise through training and a finely tuned sense of "torah" in all its manifestations. There is information and relationships, given that the rabbi exists at the center of the network of staff, clergy, lay leaders, and congregants. These are all sources of influence and leverage by which rabbis can move ahead with their visions for the Jewish people in general and their congregations more specifically. To paraphrase Pirke Avot/The Wisdom of the Fathers, "If not them, then who?"

Yet there is messiness in the visioning process as well. The messiness relates, again, to the nature of the relationship between rabbis and congregations. While rabbis may have a great deal of spiritual authority and may have a great deal of organizational authority as well, the fact remains that they serve at the discretion of the congregation and, more specifically, the board of directors as its elected representatives. They are, at once, rabbis to and subordinates of lay leaders. This can be tricky and often is. Rabbis, as we discuss in other chapters, are thus in the potentially awkward position of needing to push people who have significant control over their futures and are paying their salaries to make changes or confront issues that they would rather not face.

This potential messiness makes it crucial that rabbis find ways to collaborate with others as much as possible and as early as possible, such that their visions are widely adopted. Opportunities abound at many junctures for this to happen, from the initial coffees to discussions with board leaders to task forces and think tanks and town hall meetings. This provides useful cover for rabbis and moves the visioning process into the space where it belongs—the congregation itself. It also helps rabbis avoid what we call the "visionary trap."

The Visionary Trap

In describing rabbis as visionaries, we risk placing them in a dangerous position, atop a pedestal. The world is not often kind to those in this precarious place; they see what most of us cannot, or will not, and can therefore be a threat to how we wish to see the world and ourselves. At the same time, people long for visionary leaders. They wish for others to take them to a land of promise and are often willing to follow blindly. In so doing they cast their leader into the role of savior, rescuer, omnipotent healer, "rebbe."

People thus have complicated relationships with visionaries, wanting at the same time to follow them and resist them.

The *visionary trap* occurs when rabbis offer visions and are either cast in the role of omnipotent leader and savior or resisted so powerfully that they withdraw from their visions and the Jewish principles and values that lay beneath them. Of course, much of this is unconscious in the synagogues we have seen and almost never discussed. Instead, it gets played out in a variety of unhealthy ways in which names and reputations are too often damaged or destroyed.

Rabbis can avoid this trap by holding *firmly* to the need for visions that they appropriately set forth while holding *loosely* to the need to be at the center of those visions. The first enables them to stand fast in the face of resistance to their doing what rabbis need to do, which is to insist that Jewish principles and values—the Torah—remain at the heart of what congregations and congregants ought to do. The second enables them to avoid being cast as the savior, which will lead to a crushing dependency on them that can only undermine, finally, the long-term vibrancy of the vision itself.

It was the rabbis of old who dubbed Moses "*rabbenu*/our rabbi" inasmuch as that title did not exist in his time. They saw themselves in Moses's struggle to lead the people from Egypt to a life of holiness in covenant with God. It was as if Moses was for them the ideal (but flawed) mirror for rabbinic leadership. While we can understand and even excuse the people's often immature dependency on Moses—after all, they had been slaves all their lives—nevertheless, from their first complaint about the lack of water to their last, a savior mentality existed in their minds, and we wonder if Moses himself unconsciously fed it. We recall that it was Jethro who had to teach Moses about delegating tasks to competent others. Each time the people complained, it was Moses who "fed them." No wonder when he was away from them on the mountain of Sinai they rebelled. Aaron, instead of holding fast to his brother's vision of one God, gave the people what they wanted, an idol of gold, and thus brought destruction to the community. In the end, Moses was punished for saying to the people, "Listen you rebels, shall *we* get water for you from this rock?" (Numbers 20:10). If Aaron failed by withdrawing from the vision in the face of the people's resistance, Moses failed by allowing himself to be cast in the role of omnipotent savior. It was exactly that for which God called him to task—"You failed to sanctify Me before the people"—punishing Moses by not allowing him to set foot in the promised land.

Congregants may set the visionary trap, but rabbis spring it. Rabbis can be more or less willing participants in creating cultures of dependency in which they, like Moses, exist at the center of their followers' lives. Rabbis can allow themselves to be seduced into the role of lords of their congregations; through flattery, through others acting as if they know nothing while the rabbi knows everything, and through congregants manufacturing crises that seemingly only the rabbi can solve. To the extent that rabbis believe that it is their role to be the primary visionary and to help determine the course of the life of the congregation, they are likely to accept, and indeed invite, other's projections. They will collude with the belief in their own visionary powers.

But it does not have to be this way. Rabbis can stay out of the visionary trap by holding firm to the notion that real change requires followers who become convinced that they also need to engage the change process and not just blindly follow their rabbi. Rabbis need to understand that if congregants have a real sense of ownership, they will improvise new ways to work together on behalf of a shared vision. The rabbi's role is thus to hold firmly to that clear vision on behalf of others. When rabbis do this, and not too much more, congregants can authorize themselves to make the articulated visions their own and together figure out how to make them real.

Effective and healthy rabbis thus hold lightly to their formal authority. They understand that this authority is only on loan and may be withdrawn by followers who experience betrayal, abandonment, or the abuse of power. They also understand that congregants will look to them, at times longingly and at other times angrily, during discomforting transitions. They understand that some congregants and other staff or clergy will pull them toward the status quo to halt the rabbi's quest for the fulfillment of the vision. And they understand that others will question the vision, even challenge their competence or loyalty, stage insurrections, and broker treaties, all in the hopes of forcing rabbis to back away or be distracted from change efforts. Healthy rabbis are aware of such responses. They are not surprised by them, nor do they take them personally, understanding them as people's natural reactions to the threat and anxiety of moving from certain if flawed presents to uncertain futures. They understand this is part of being what Rabbi Jack Bloom calls "a symbolic exemplar." Even with such awareness, however, rabbis, if they are to be leaders, need the courage to continue to challenge others.

The Wide-Angle Lens

Rabbis are, often enough, at their congregants' sides accompanying them on their journeys through life, much as Moses walked with the Israelites for forty years in the wilderness. And yet there are passages, moments in the life of a congregation, when rabbis must separate themselves—the better to receive the visions they can share with others just as Moses did when he went up the mountain called Sinai or spoke with God in the Tent of Meeting. Our modern rabbis, who are asked to be part of the community, who are lauded for being approachable, must also at times separate themselves. They must put themselves in places where they are best able to hear what God has to say to them, to receive or discover the visions that will guide them and the lives of their congregations. In practice, this means that rabbis continue to explore the intersection of Torah and the surrounding societies in which we all live, the world of the holy and the world of the mundane, every day. Our rabbis are our wide-angle lenses; with enough patience and fortitude, they capture for us exactly what we need, the images of who we can be and the tabernacles our synagogues can yet become.

Effective rabbis not only offer portraits of who people can be, they also give people the sense that they have always been on the journey to get there. They offer narratives that help congregants make sense of who they are and what they have done thus far. By doing so, they provide a sense of meaning to where we are and who we are yet to be.

11

STAYING ALIVE

> The role of the man of faith, whose religious experience is
> fraught with inner conflicts and incongruities, who oscillates
> between ecstasy in God's companionship and despair when
> he feels abandoned by God, and who is torn asunder by the
> heightened contrast between self-appreciation and abnegation,
> has been a difficult one since the times of Abraham and Moses.
> (Rabbi Joseph Soloveitchik, *The Lonely Man of Faith*)

The work of the rabbi, and for that matter, the cantor, requires a fair amount of effort, emotional as well as physical and intellectual. Synagogues are, at their core, caregiving institutions that enable congregants to live well through the events of their lives. Our clergy are at the epicenter of that process. They are caregivers, in addition to being teachers, worship leaders, guides, and role models. Congregants, for their part, are also care-seekers; they approach their synagogues, often with great need, difficult questions, uncertainty and confusion, longing, and ambivalence. They are not there simply to buy products, like at retail stores, or be serviced, like at hotels, or be entertained, like at theaters. They are there because they need to join themselves to a tradition that they hope, in ways of which they may or may not be aware, will hold them fast as they go about the cycles of their lives. This very fact, that people bring their very human needs into the synagogue, fundamentally shapes what occurs in their relations with clergy. Our clergy are routinely confronted with the full ranges of emotions that often accompany people's difficult, joyous, enraging, powerful journeys toward growth, healing, and learning.

As caregivers, our clergy, when they are at their best, respond to congregants in certain ways. They make themselves accessible, actively inquiring about and attending to congregants, and receive their experiences with compassion and acceptance. They take in and absorb those experiences, the better to understand their needs and how to meet them, and in doing so, begin to contain parts of their experiences. They empathically acknowledge congregants by identifying with and validating them as they go about their attempts to grow, learn, or heal. This enables congregants to feel known, understood, and valued—cared for rather than simply tended to as part of one's duties. Congregants feel witnessed, in the deeper meaning of the word, and experience themselves as joined, as seen and felt, as known, and as not alone, the core experiences of feeling cared for. And clergy help people make sense of their experiences. They help congregants gain perspectives, through teaching, study, and prayer. They bring congregants closer to Torah and in doing so enable them to develop a deeper sense of that which occupies them, as one climber helps another gain purchase on a difficult mountain slope by steadying him and focusing him on the task at hand.

This requires quite a bit from clergy. They often require relatively high levels of physical, emotional, or mental stamina. That is stressful in its own right, particularly in situations where clergy must perform with little respite, changing *kippot,* if you will, almost by the hour, moving from joyous to sad, from teacher to pastor to community leader or organizer. There is little space for recovering one's balance or for reflection before moving from one situation to another. The pace or the pressure of what needs to be done becomes a source of stress, separate from that associated with how one actually does the work. Another source of stress is the knowledge of the costs of situations that are not handled well. Clergy cannot only inspire congregants but, through their lack of leadership or misconduct of their personal lives, turn congregants away from creating a rich religious life. Our clergy know this; it is a constant, always just behind their consciousness. It is part of their world, like the air they breathe, and it exerts its strain.

Clergy are also subject to the stress of absorbing their congregants. People's needs, experiences, and emotions must be taken in and understood if they are to be cared for, served, taught, helped, and ministered to in effective, lasting ways. This taking in of others—of fully grasping what they know and how they know it, what they fear and are excited about, what their needs and wishes really are—occurs through the creation of relationships. Those relationships are often a source of stress. Congregants bring to their interactions with clergy a host of responses to their own spiritual and religious searches. They bring anxiety about the larger issues related to existential meaning, the conduct of moral lives, and the place, meaning, and outcome of death in one's life. They bring certain emotions related to the rituals and life-stage events (e.g., births, bar and bat mitzvahs, funerals) that mark major transitions. They bring uncertainty and confusion about the definition of a good life, one that balances the pursuit of earthly matters with conduct that is moral and principled. They bring emotions related to the apprehension and experiences of God in their lives: longing, confusion, frustration, awe, and disbelief.

Congregants also bring into their interactions with their rabbis ambivalence about organized religion. They may act out against clergy. They may regress. They may be passive-aggressive. Clergy must simultaneously protect themselves from being harmed by such acts while creating the relationships in which others can effectively heal, learn, grow, and change. They must absorb assaults. Even when congregants are relatively unconflicted about Judaism and synagogues, the seemingly inevitable action of transference attends their relationships with clergy. Transference is an intrapsychic process that becomes an interpersonal one: the congregant acts toward the rabbi as if that rabbi was the individual's father, mother, or other major figure in his or her internal life. This occurs quite frequently in the synagogue. It is quite common for people to have transferential reactions to clergy. When we enter the rabbi's study, we are predisposed to map onto that place the internal terrain we know so intimately: our parent-child relationships. We look to our rabbis as we once used to look toward our parents. It is our instinct.

Together, these sources of strain—the sheer pace and pressure and constancy of the job and its resulting fatigue, the absorption of others' distress, the ambivalence and transference projected onto clergy—place a fair amount of pressure on our clergy. So, too, does the overarching context of the clergy's work: the drive to maintain the Jewish people, which gets more pressing in the face of ongoing assimilation. In the context of such pressure, effective rabbis learn, often after much practice, to develop filters. They learn to establish necessary relationships with distressed others without being flooded by, and taking personally, others' experiences and emotions. They learn what is called in some caring professions *detached concern,* or what the Buddhists call "loving detachment." This enables them to bring others in emotionally but limit the depths of that entry such that they remain their own, separate people, filled with the purposes of their roles rather than with the experiences of those they need to serve.

Yet even with the skill of detached concern, working with distressed people is stressful. Our clergy often cannot help but absorb some of our sadness, fear, anger, and anxiety as they go about helping us with our journeys and life-cycle events. Some remain filled in such ways, particularly those who have not yet learned to limit the depth of their relations with congregants; they learn, slowly, to extricate themselves from others emotionally. If they do not, they develop what is known as *compassion fatigue,* becoming so filled with others' emotions that they cannot absorb any more. Just as containers become worn with repeated use, caring clergy tire of the process of connecting to and then moving away from care-seekers. Just as containers build up residue of what they have contained many times over, our clergy contain within them a lasting memory and experience of others' distress. The proximity to pain and distress takes its toll. Clergy may become burned out temporarily, and if left unchecked, permanently.

We think of burnout in reasonably simple terms. Burnout occurs when the light in us that led us to do the work that we do gradually dims and for some, goes out. When clergy are emotionally drained, giving of themselves until they have nothing more to give, they burn out, becoming physically or emotionally exhausted, negative about themselves and their jobs, and increasingly less concerned about congregants. They withdraw from others. They become cynical or bitter. They become short-tempered, sarcastic, or emotionally labile. They become absent emotionally, and increasingly, physically as well. They disengage. They are deadened to others and to their own emotions and experiences. They are in various phases of shutting down and off. Our clergy may continue working even as they are fading. They may be adequate but uninspiring. They may implode, often with boundary violations, to stimulate the light in inappropriate ways. Or they may leave the work altogether.

It does not have to be this way. Burnout is reversible. It is preventable. The light within us can be protected; it can be rekindled. Clergy need not become so emotionally depleted by their work that they are deadened. There are ways for them to remain emotionally and spiritually alive in their work. In this chapter, we discuss such ways. We do not simply assume that we need to make clergy hardier, more competent, so strong and impenetrable that they cannot possible burn out. Nor do we assume that we need only to give clergy breaks and sabbaticals, as important and necessary as these are for personal and professional revitalizations. These are relatively simple explanations and lead to relatively simple interventions focused either on building clergy members' skills at managing themselves in their roles or giving them more time off. While we believe that these sorts of interventions are useful, they are not enough. In this chapter, we develop more nuanced explanations that allow for other, potentially more effective interventions that enable our clergy to stay as *alive* as possible in their work.

Support

The classic way of thinking about helping people avoid or offset burnout involves support. The quote at the beginning of the chapter by Rabbi Soloveitchik points to how our rabbis are isolated in their spiritual quest; their role of moral outsider and what Rabbi Jack Bloom refers to as "symbolic exemplar" leaves them isolated from the very people they seek to lead. Isolation, left uninterrupted, is suffocating. It is the relationships that we have in our lives that enable us to breathe deeply, to take in ourselves and our worlds more fully, and to make us expansive rather than closed off. This is no less true of our clergy. They, too, need ongoing, meaningful relationships in their lives. Meaningful personal relationships are, like vitamins and exercise, preventative. They build up stores of caring within us. They enable resilience—the capacity to bend without breaking, to give without being drained, to remain alive in the face of sometimes deadening work. And meaningful relationships are restorative as well. They are interventions during difficult moments in the lives of clergy, offering support and replenishment.

Joshua ben Perachyah famously said of rabbis, "Make sure you have a teacher and find a friend" (Pirke Avot 1:6). This is simple, profound advice. He understood that no one could do the work of rabbi alone. Teachers enable clergy to continue to grow and learn, to shape and refine who they are and are becoming. The purpose of having a teacher—Joshua ben Perachyah actually used the Hebrew word *rav*, signifying "master"—is to be able to rely on someone who has traveled down the same path. If we are to grow and learn, we must have someone who can serve as a guide or an authority to tell us when we are heading into a dead end, to warn us of danger, to encourage us when all seems lost or empty. Other clergy, former teachers, even spiritually sensitive therapists can serve in this capacity.

Friends, too, offer clergy the opportunity to feel personally cared for. They enable clergy to be replenished. The psychologist Willard Gaylin wrote, in his book *Caring*, "To be cared for is essential for the capacity to be caring."[1] Friendship and other forms of support enable clergy to replenish their personal stores of caring that they provide to others as a matter of course. Unlike our teachers, they are more like fellow travelers. They can hold our hands in support and empathy, and we can do the same for them. As we will discuss in the next chapter, friendship between clergy and congregants is a complicated affair, requiring the explicit managing of boundaries between who clergy are as people and who they are in their roles. These complications make it difficult for clergy to gain support as individuals, rather than as rabbis or cantors per se. Friendships that are rooted elsewhere—from childhood and school, sports and hobbies, travel and vacations—are usually less complicated and offer relatively clean sources of support. And rabbis and cantors in other congregations, *chevruta* partners from seminary, even ministers or priests of other religions can be a clergy member's friends.

For some clergy, finding support from colleagues or in their community is easier said than done. There are three sources of difficulty that we highlight here: a sense of competition among clergy, the lack of privacy, and the difficulty of allowing oneself to be cared for. We examine each of these briefly.

It Shouldn't Be That Way

One of the ugly secrets in synagogue life, the one that clergy generally do not want to admit or talk about, is the competition for members and for the various honors—like being the one who gets to lead the *motzi* at the federation dinner, or who gets to sing *Hatikvah* at the JCC Israel Independence Day community celebration—that exist in the community. The Jewish people like to think of themselves as a united community and in many respects we are, especially in crisis. But this feeling of competition leaves the professional Jewish community without the natural support that ought to exist. It leaves clergy without a natural source of useful caring and support rooted in a relatively deep sense of understanding and empathy. This is particularly poignant in the case of Jewish communities containing synagogues that form from other synagogues because of demographics, loyalty to rabbis who leave, or differing values and tastes. The antipathy between synagogues and their clergy often lasts long after the original event. When this occurs, clergy lose a natural source of comradeship.

We wish to note that the competition that can exist among clergy occurs within a larger context, in which some institutions assume that they are competing with others for the loyalties of Jews. Healthy synagogues, however, seek to work with other institutions within the community for the greater good. Community high schools, joint trips to Israel, combined adult education programs and learning opportunities are examples of communities working together. Healthy communities welcome choices, realizing that no one institution should need to meet all their members' needs. Choices help individuals clarify what it is they want from their synagogue. Like the man stranded on the dessert island who built two synagogues—the one he liked to *daven* in, and the one in which he would not be caught dead—we like to have choices. With diminishing resources and a shrinking Jewish population in North America, the need to cooperate and share resources is imperative. A thriving Jewish community is one in which all the Jewish institutions are also thriving. We need to switch the paradigm to understand that the vibrancy of the Jewish people requires interdependence rather than competition.

The truth is that people who join usually join more than one institution. Most members of the JCC in every Jewish community are also members of synagogues. Those who give to the federation almost always give to their synagogues. Leadership and volunteer time are often interchangeable. When the organized Jewish community gets along, it is more attractive to those unaffiliated who are watching from the sideline. The opposite is also true. When Jews fight with one another, it is often a turnoff to those same people, even to their own members.

Life in the Fishbowl

Rabbis, and to some extent, other clergy and Jewish professionals, live in a fishbowl. Their every move, and often those of their families, is under constant scrutiny. Part of it is the higher standard to which religious leaders are held. After all, if they preach it, ought they not live up to it? Some of it has to do with projections. Clergy are often parental authority figures in the subconscious minds of their congregants. And some of it is prurient interest. Unfortunately, gossip, *lashon hara,* seems to be a favorite pastime in many communities, and rabbis are favorite targets.

"The Fishbowl"

The fishbowl is not an easy place in which to live. A rabbi and his family are shopping for a Christmas dinner for a needy family in their community. It is a *mitzvah* they do every year, but this is the first time the children are old enough to actually participate. The list of foods is provided by the Coalition for the Homeless: yams, bread for stuffing, cranberries, and on and on. The children enthusiastically pull the items from the shelves and place them in the food basket next to the baby who is in her car seat. The next item is a ham. "Where do we get a ham, *abba?*" one of the children asks.

"They sell them in the supermarket."

"They have meat here?" Keeping kosher, the children think meat comes only from the butcher shop.

"Yes, there is a meat section," their *ima* says. "Let's go there next."

The children decide to take a ham in a can rather than a plastic bag because it does not look as what the eldest child describes as "gross." Then as they are wheeling the cart through the store, the five-year-old asks, "*Abba,* what if one of our congregants sees us and looks in the basket. They might think we eat ham!"

At that point, they decide to hide the ham with one of their coats.

This story is sweet, in many ways, but also quite serious. It suggests the extent to which even the children of our clergy are always aware of the glare of a very public life. Rabbis often benefit from this public life as they are granted access and favors not afforded to "regular citizens," such as free tickets to events, free medical care, and not having to "wait in line" for services. But there is a price to be paid: the loss of privacy. To protect themselves, some clergy withdraw from others, which only leads to further isolation and greater loneliness. The self-protection is understandable, if lamentable. A clergy member's movements and those of his or her family are often the topic of community conversation. Can a rabbi be seen in a psychotherapist's waiting room awaiting counsel? Or go to an AA meeting to deal with his or her addiction? Is a rabbi given permission to be vulnerable at all? We know of several instances in which rabbis "went public" with a problem they were having and soon found themselves embroiled in controversy or looking for a new job. Our experience teaches us that there are very few areas in which the exposure of what might be perceived as a weakness, or indeed, of the personal and vulnerable self of a clergy member is acceptable to most congregants.

The Caregiver's Trap

The third source of difficulty is located within clergy members themselves. Like other caregivers—physicians, therapists, nurses, teachers, and the like—rabbis often find it difficult to ask for help. This difficulty emanates from what we call the "caregiver's trap": some caregivers are fixed so firmly in the role of giver that they have great difficulty imagining themselves as receivers. Since they cannot imagine themselves being dependent on others, which they would experience as a reversal of roles, they do not put themselves in the position where that might occur. They remain at some remove. They do not ask for help. When people try and inquire about them, they tighten their armor and, with greater or less degrees of smoothness or awkwardness, parry and deflect the inquiries. They remain apart. They are trapped inside the loneliness of their own roles, like actors who cannot escape the plays in which they have been cast.

This trap is not simply the making of our clergy, of course. As we discuss further below, the intensity of the clergy's role (and its accompanying burnout) is shaped by the collective, unarticulated wish within congregations that their clergy be a step closer to God—the better for congregants themselves to be brought closer to God's protection and light. This wish, like a crowd surging forward, presses clergy (particularly rabbis) to step away and up; the surge ushers them onto a pedestal. There they remain, taking up an important role symbolically on behalf of the congregation. Our clergy symbolize hope, the promise of meaning, God. They step onto the *bimah*, raised in ways that symbolically conjure Mount Sinai, Jacob's ladder, and other moments in Jewish biblical history that suggest Jews and God striving to connect across the gap between heaven and earth. Our clergy are thrust into that gap. It is not an easy place in which to dwell.

While the caregiver's trap is thus partly rooted in the collusion of congregants and clergy, rabbis may do much to maintain it. By not seeking out or being receptive to care, they collude with congregants to keep themselves up high. They forget that while Moses had to go up the mountain to receive the Torah, real life was lived in the valley below. Unable to allow themselves to ask for and receive care, our rabbis remain on the mountain. In doing so, they unconsciously act as if they are apart, above, and all-powerful and their followers are less competent and able. This split is rooted in the healthy/unhealthy, helper/helpless, powerful/powerless archetypes that lie beneath the helping professions. In hospitals, for example, there is great press upon staff members to be healthy and powerful, leaving the patients to be ill, obedient, and grateful. Interactions are between the helpful and the helpless. The pull then is for caregivers and care-seekers to collude in acting as if the former are all-knowing and the latter helpless, as if such a formula will guarantee the required healing, growing, learning, and ministering. A version of this formula occurs in some synagogues. The formula leaves our clergy cast firmly in the role of helper and thus less able and willing to allow themselves to be ministered to, appropriately dependent, and supported.

Getting Support

If burnout is a lack of support and clergy have difficulty asking for and receiving support, interventions are needed. Some rabbis initiate these interventions on their own. Healthy clergy have healthy personal relationships. They seek out teachers. They have their own rabbis. They continue to learn and grow. They allow themselves to take up roles in which they follow others rather than lead them. They remain alive to the possibility that they will learn that which they do not know.

Healthy clergy also seek out friends. They cultivate friendships outside the synagogue with people who are neither staff members nor congregants. This is not to say that they will not be friendly with staff members and congregants or that they will not form friendships with some of them. They will, as a matter of course, but they must also have significant friendships with others, in ways that enable them to be open and vulnerable. Each of us needs settings in which we can be whomever or whatever we are or need to be, without the worry of how we are seen. Friendship, ideally, offers such safety; it offers unconditional acceptance. Our friendships with our own rabbis are always conditional, even as we are not aware of the conditions that we impose upon them and that they impose upon themselves: that they must be and act in ways that accord with what we expect of clergy members. Those conditions are not the conditions under which we can be most supportive to our clergy, as people. They need other places to go for such support.

When clergy have difficulty finding those other places, they need to look carefully at the sources of that difficulty. It may be, as we have suggested above, that they are unable to form healthy relationships with their own peers—other clergy in other synagogues in their communities—because of a sense of competition. Rabbis and cantors need to step through that sense, as one would step through a mist, and see that it does not have to be so. They need to act as if such competition does not exist, even when they sense it might. This will create a self-fulfilling prophecy; if clergy believe that they can find and offer support responsibly to their colleagues, and act in such ways, it will be so. Similarly, if their difficulty is located in the caregiver's trap, if they are caught within a perception that they must remain firmly in the role of giver, they must act as if that need not be so. They must step down from the place to which they have been elevated and become dependent on others in appropriate ways. This, too, is a self-fulfilling prophecy, which rabbis must, if need be, jumpstart with their own behaviors. If they believe and act as if they are allowed to receive as well as give in their lives, it will be so.

Never Enough

Rabbi Steve Kantor sits at his desk, trying to find the energy to read through his teaching notes for the class he needs to teach later this evening. He lifts his cup of coffee and then wearily sets it down, discovering it has grown cold and bitter.

Earlier that day, Susie Weinstein dropped by while he was trying to multitask—eating his lunch while going over calendar changes with his assistant, Cyndi Goodstreet.

"Do you have a minute, Rabbi?"

Steve did not really have a minute just then. Besides, he had been around long enough to know there is no such thing as a one-minute conversation. But Susie was a young woman who had grown up in the congregation. Her parents were very active, and now she was following in their footsteps by becoming involved in the synagogue's early childhood center where both her children attended preschool. Steve had officiated at her wedding and blessed each of her sons at their *brit*.

"Sure Susie, for you I always have a minute," he said against his better judgment.

As soon as he had closed the door to his study, she began, "Maybe this is none of my business, but you really blew it with my friend Beth Ungar. She told me no one from the clergy reached out to her, and she's really hurting!"

"But Susie, I did call her. In fact, on the day I got the message she had the surgery, the cantor spoke to her—it was her hospital visit day—and I did as well. I had left a message with her nurse, and she called me back. I told her how concerned I was and offered to be there for her. I also told her that the cantor was available; these are not always the kinds of things women feel comfortable sharing with men. She thanked me for my concern, told me about her brother-in-law who is also a rabbi and always took care of family issues. I replied that in case she wanted two rabbis, I would be there for her. I don't know what more I could have done."

"Well, she told me she got no support from her own temple and now wants to leave the synagogue. We can't afford to have young families leaving!" Susie was angry.

"Susie, I reached out to her. You've known me for a long time. Do you really think I ignored your friend? I don't know what more I could have done."

"Why didn't you call her back to see how she was recovering?"

"I thought I was respecting her privacy and her family situation."

"Well, you blew it!" She stormed out of his study.

The Good-Enough Rabbi

Our case study seems simple enough. A rabbi disappoints a congregant. He does what he thinks is right, reaching out to a congregant struggling with a difficult circumstance. He moves toward her, making himself available, at the same time wishing not to intrude upon her. Still, in her view (or that of her friend) he does not do enough; he falls short of what she seemed to wish for. That she did not actually express her needs to him is, it seems, beside the point. The notion is that he ought to have understood exactly what support she needed and provided her with that support.

This story is quite familiar to our clergy. All too often they are presented with examples of their own failures to do enough for congregants. They did not call often enough. They did not stay long enough. They did not teach well enough. They did not preach insightfully enough. They did not sing beautifully enough. They did not react quickly enough. They were simply not enough, in spite of their efforts to perform their roles to the best of their abilities, to do all that they could reasonably, humanly do.

Flooded with stories of their own inadequacies, rabbis move toward burnout. Even as their congregants appreciate them for what they do, clergy are reminded of the myriad ways in which they do not measure up to people's expectations. The sense of inadequacy accumulates, and that sense is draining. Over time our clergy run deficits, giving out more appreciation than they receive. This is the burnout formula: expending more than one receives. The interventions are reasonably simple. Clergy must expend less or take in more, or both. Expending less is a matter of husbanding one's resources so as not to deplete one's stores of energy and emotion. It means giving less, or less fully, as a marathon runner might do, understanding that the race is long and energy must be meted out rather carefully. Taking in more is a matter of getting more support, which we described in the preceding section. Support replenishes that which is drained in the process of giving to others and helps protect against the running of deficits. If our Rabbi Kantor had enough teachers, friends, and colleagues who cared about him, they would at least help offset some of the lack of appreciation he experiences.

This way of framing our case study seems straightforward enough. But there is more beneath the surface of this story. The conversation between Rabbi Kantor and the congregant was driven, we believe, not simply by the particular circumstances of a disappointed friend but by the expectations of congregants more generally about the omnipotence of clergy and, in particular, of rabbis. Our disappointments in rabbis for all that they do not do for us are often rooted in the set of unreasonable and, indeed, irrational expectations that we have of them: that they will be all-knowing, all-providing, all-encompassing, able to hold us and keep us safe and whole. We expect, or more accurately, we wish them to be infallible. We do not hold these expectations consciously; in fact, if asked, we would deny having them. But the depth of the disappointment that we may feel when our rabbi does not call us or leave us alone at just the right time, say just the right thing, or give just the right sermon is a sign that we carry with us a set of expectations and hopes that are rooted more in our longings than in our rational understandings of what another human being can reasonably do or be for us.

It is not too difficult to figure out what these longings are about. We identified some of the key factors in chapter 6 when discussing the nature of authority in synagogue life. We noted that in synagogues, as in other caregiving institutions, there is regression. Care-seekers long to be taken care of. They wish to be held tightly, as parents hold their infants and young children, and made safe and secure. Students want teachers to make their struggles to learn disappear. Patients want nurses, physicians, and therapists to cure them and make their pain go away. And congregants want their clergy to enfold them into a spiritual cloak that will shield them from the pain of loss, uncertainty, and death. They may thus project all sorts of things onto their rabbis, and, if somewhat less, their cantors as well. They (wish to) see their clergy as powerful, gifted, healing, and infallible, in the ways that children (wish to) see their parents. We are called the children of Israel; our rabbis ascend mountains, bringing us closer to God and God closer to us.

These longings and projections are a key ingredient in the recipe for burnout. When we expect so much of our clergy, they cannot help but be met by a sense of disappointment when they prove to be human and fallible. And when they collude with our projections—when they come to believe that they *ought* to be infallible and all-providing—the burnout is hastened. What do we mean by collude? Clergy fall in with the expectations of others and come to believe that they are more responsible, more indispensable, and even more powerful than they actually are. They fall in with the unconscious pulls on them to be sorcerers and magicians, grand healers in the tradition of the medicine man. This is a difficult role to play. In this regard, our clergy, wishing to please and used to helping others, strive mightily to take up the role and complete impossible tasks. They inevitably fail and feel their own inadequacies. Rabbi Kantor did.

There is a way out of this dynamic. Our clergy can hold on to a sense of themselves as "good enough." The notion of good enough is rooted in developmental psychology; it refers to a way of parenting that requires the parent to be present and appropriately caring without needing to be all-encompassing and impossibly perfect. Our clergy, too, ought to be good enough. They ought to do what they can to be present for congregants and to teach, counsel, pray with, and lead them to the best of their abilities without the expectation that they can or ought to do anything beyond what is humanly reasonable. Our clergy are like congregants: imperfect, striving to do the best they can, human, fallible, with resources that are limited rather than limitless. That said, they can be good enough in their work, which is quite good indeed.

The good enough idea leads pretty directly to three types of interventions. First, rabbis and clergy need to hold reasonable expectations of what they can and cannot do. They need to allow themselves to be imperfect. They need to overcome any embarrassment they might have about not always being able to do all things, know all things, and be all things. They need to allow themselves to need help as they go about their work. They need, in essence, to internalize what it means to be good enough.

In order to do these things, rabbis must, at times, interrupt the stories that they tell to and about themselves that lead them to collude with the wish that they be all-providing. We all tell ourselves stories to help us make sense of what we do. When clergy members collude with congregants' wishes, they do so by telling themselves certain stories: that they cannot help but care about others, that no one else can provide what they can provide, that they are selfless, that they have no choice but to give and give, and so on.

Unless such stories are interrupted and understood for what they are—rationalizations that allow rabbis to be willingly seduced onto pedestals constructed by the irrational wishes of others—some clergy will run too fast and too furiously and burn away. If they are able to interrupt such stories and replace them with new ones about what it means to be good enough, rather than impossibly perfect, rabbis can begin to educate their congregants as well. They can push back on others' unreasonable projections. They can help their congregants understand that if they want their clergy to be *menschen,* they must allow them to be the imperfect human beings we all are.

Second, our clergy can develop practices and disciplines that allow them temporary respite. Replenishment occurs not only in the context of our relationships with others but also in the context of various disciplines or practices in which we engage ourselves. Yoga and meditation, exercise and sports, social activities and art—each offers a way for people to be filled with a sense of aliveness that they can carry into other parts of their lives. So it is with our clergy. When they engage in such practices (and take some time off to do so) they help themselves feel alive: creative, engaged, and attuned to themselves and the world in ways that do not require them to minister to others. They have places and spaces to breathe and to be. This, too, offers a foundation for maintaining the good-enough clergy member. When clergy, like any of us, engage in some practice or hobby or sport, they move away from the role of expert. They take on the role of practitioner or learner or dabbler. In those roles they experience what any of us experience: the evolution of learning how to do something, complete with its failures and successes and an ongoing sense of awareness of our gifts and limitations. In short, they get to be human, which is a nice antidote to the sense that others, and they themselves, might otherwise have.

Third, clergy can replenish themselves as they go about their work, to the extent that they are able to reenvision that work. Instead of seeing (and feeling) the myriad of tasks only as outputs of energy and caring, they can see them as inputs as well. What does this mean? Rabbis and cantors can actually *daven* as they lead *davenning.* They can have moments—the chanting of the *Amidah,* "silent" meditation, facing the ark—when they take in rather than only provide for others the experience of worship. Rabbis can learn while they teach, to the extent that they create new materials and discover new resources that will help them go along on a process of discovery with their students. They can gain insight into their own behavior while counseling, to the extent that they are open to seeing similarities with others while guarding against countertransference. To the extent they can be emotionally present without making the event about themselves, they can reexperience or anticipate each life cycle as they lead others through it. They can limit Shabbat and holy day "work" activities to celebration, study, and prayer.

This, too, is a foundation for the good-enough clergy. When rabbis and cantors truly join their congregations in moments of worship, of teaching, of song, of personal connection in counseling and life-cycle events, they live in the valley with their congregants rather than on the slope of the mountains above. They exist with rather than apart. This is important. It makes it more difficult for clergy and congregant alike to hang on to the illusion that the former is so vastly different from the latter. It makes it more difficult to sustain projections that clergy members are somehow more than human or closer to God in some measurable fashion. When clergy are fully present, they, too, are learning and reflecting and wondering and feeling, just as their congregants are. They have or ought to have permission, from themselves and from others, to do just that as they go about leading their congregations as best they can.

We need to complicate this slightly, however. There are moments in our lives when we wish to believe—indeed, need to believe—that our rabbis *are* closer to God, help us come closer to God, and bring God closer to us. Consider this analogy: when we undergo surgery, we do not wish to think of our surgeon as "good enough." Nor do we need to believe that he or she is infallible. We just need to have faith in his or her abilities to help cure us. Similarly, there are times when we need the rabbi's blessing. At those moments, feeling that our rabbis are closer to God is helpful, comforting. We need to be able to hang on to those notions even as we understand that our rabbis do not need to be more than human.

Cultures of Collaboration

Ultimately, clergy protect themselves from burnout by having lots of people join them on the journey of practicing Judaism. We believe that when clergy encourage others to collaborate on their own Jewish practices of worship, of Torah study, of social action, and of life events, the clergy members themselves are released from the pressing force of needing to be much more than good enough. Cultures of collaboration are marked by small rather than large distinctions between those who give and those who receive. Rabbis and cantors do not step away from their expertise or from their rightful use of authority. They do, however, make room for congregants to be, and to become, competent in their own practices. They step away from the mystique that others attach to their roles; in so doing, they step away from colluding with a culture of dependency that might well spring up in some congregations.

We described in chapter 6 the various ways in which congregational life exerts pulls upon clergy and congregants alike to create overly dependent relations. In that chapter we described how that dynamic undermined the healthiness of the congregation itself. Here we wish to emphasize the ill effects of that dynamic for the health and energy of the clergy members themselves. To remain on a pedestal is draining. It requires an impossibly high state of vigilance. It involves a potentially crushing sense of responsibility. It is exhausting. Even with its rewards, overly dependent relations trap clergy just as much as they trap congregants; they remain locked together in an embrace of the helper and the helpless. This is a disservice to both: clergy lose a vital sense of their own humanity, and congregants lose an empowering sense of their own competence as practicing Jews.

A collaborative synagogue culture frees clergy and congregants to both be human and competent, and to journey together. Rabbis work alongside congregants, providing resources and support, guiding and teaching and taking up appropriate authority while guiding others toward their own familiarity and comfort with Judaism, and enabling them to find their own ways in their life-cycle events. For their part, congregants must actively practice rather than expect clergy to practice for them. They must seek, question, and involve themselves in conversation and ritual until they have reached some insight and meaning that offer them satisfaction. The role of the clergy is to be for their congregants a secure base: a place to which to return when they need help and guidance as they go about their journeys. This is more rewarding for congregants. And it is a meaningful role for the clergy. They remain at a safe distance, from which they safely guide others while enabling the others to rely on and develop themselves. They are present and safely distant simultaneously.

Toward Resilience

Staying alive in the draining role of rabbi or clergy means developing resilience. Our clergy need not be invulnerable or impervious to adversity. This is not possible. We do believe that it is possible for them to be able to ride out the inevitable points of stress that threaten to destabilize them and their work. Resilient clergy members are able to return to a steady state of balanced relationship—that stance of simultaneous openness to and detachment from those they seek to help—after being temporarily laid low by stress, the difficulty of their workload, their own emotional reactions, a sense of hopelessness, or some other disturbance. They are flattened, momentarily out of commission, and then they regain their shape and return to their work and relationships.

Resilience derives from a number of sources. Some people are almost instinctively resilient. Through some combination of genetics and family background, personality and character, they move through life with the capacity to weather the storms of their lives reasonably well. They draw upon seemingly unlimited stores of security and optimism that leave them relatively unscathed even as they feel the normal feelings of loss, sadness, hurt, and anger. Other people have more limited emotional reserves. They need more overt replenishment of the sorts described in this chapter: relationships that allow for an influx of care and love with teachers and mentors, friends and family; and disciplines and practices that keep oneself strong. Such relationships and practices replenish clergy, offering an inoculation of sorts from the stress of their work and roles. It is that replenishment that fuels resilience.

Resilience is also a matter of insight and understanding. The synagogue has an emotional life of its own, filled as it is with congregants bearing loneliness, confusion, loss and sadness, hopefulness and longing, anger and frustration. These emotions are brought to clergy as they go about their teaching, worship, and cycles of life. The more that clergy understand how those emotions suffuse their interactions with congregants, the more clearly they are able to see and respond to them without taking them personally, internalizing them, or bearing them on behalf of others. Such insight enables clergy to understand some of the underlying dynamics that, if undetected and responded to inappropriately, can trap them in ever more stressful situations.

We end this chapter by noting the complexity of clergy burnout. Both the causes of and the solutions to burnout are multifaceted. They are located partly in individual clergy members themselves, in how they experience and react to events, create replenishing relationships, and take care of themselves. The causes and solutions are located as well in the expectations of clergy and congregants, in how rational or irrational they are and the extent to which they allow clergy to be good enough rather than impossibly perfect. They are located, finally, in the nature of the relationships between clergy and congregation—the extent to which each is allowed to be both competent and human as they go about their shared journey of congregational Judaism. To the extent that all of us, clergy and congregant alike, can remain mindful of each of these dynamics, we are more likely to tell complex, nuanced stories about burnout and create thoughtful interventions that enable our clergy to stay fully alive in their work.

Note

1. Willard Gaylin, *Caring* (New York: Knopf, 1976).

12

MANAGING HEALTHY BOUNDARIES

Moses said to Aaron, "What did this people do to you that you have brought such a great sin upon them?" Aaron replied, "Let not my lord be angry. You know the people, that they are bent on evil. They said to me, 'Make us a god to lead us; for this man Moses, who brought us up from the land of Egypt, we do not know what has happened to him.' So I said to them, 'Whoever has gold take it off.' They gave it to me, I hurled it into the fire, and out came this calf!" Moses saw that the people were out of control, for Aaron had let them get out of control, so that they were a menace to any who would oppose them. Then Moses stood at the entrance of the camp and said, "Whoever is for Adonai, come here!"
(Exodus 32:21-26)

Practicing Jews choose the various paths of congregational life. They have decided that, to degrees large or small, the synagogue is part of what defines who they are in the world. The clergy's role is to help congregants along their paths, to provide for them ways to engage Torah, to practice *tikkun olam,* to worship, and to experience the events of their lives as Jews do and have done. Rabbis and cantors have various ways to provide such help. They have the technical knowledge and skills to help us study and pray, learn Hebrew, sing, and chant. Their work with congregants is not, however, simply a matter of technique. It is, above all, a matter of the relationships that they create with congregants, relationships that enable us to feel cared for, inspired, taught, valued, empathized with, seen and heard for who we are and strive to be in the midst of our cycles of life. The clergy's ability to create such relationships is intimately tied to the ways in which practicing Jews remain on and experience the paths along which they journey in their congregations.

The fact that the relationships between clergy and their congregants are so central to what occurs in the synagogue means that the *person* of

211

the clergy member—whom he or she *is,* with all that that entails—is put into play in a significant way. Congregants attach to their rabbis and cantors, often enough, as a way of attaching to the synagogue itself; if asked about how we feel about our synagogues, we often answer in terms of how we feel about our clergy and, secondarily, how we feel about other congregants, worship services, religious school, various programs, and the like. Even when asked what shul they belong to, many Jews respond with the name of the rabbi, not the synagogue itself. How we feel about rabbis and cantors is shaped by how they, as people, assume the various roles that they play in our lives as pastors, teachers, counselors, leaders, facilitators of life-cycle events, preachers. Each of these roles allows for certain connections with congregants; each allows us to feel more or less close to our clergy as they help us live out our Judaism.

Clergy members put themselves in play in different ways. They have various ways of constructing and using relationships with congregants. In the Exodus quote above, we see how Moses and Aaron took on quite different roles, as the leaders—the clergy, if you will—of the Israelites. Moses stayed firmly in the role of the religious leader; he held fast to the task of bringing the Israelites into relation with God, to forge them into the Chosen. Aaron assumed a different role, one defined by a desire to soothe the Israelites' fear and anxiety by providing them with a familiar, if false, idol. Moses and Aaron constructed quite different relationships with the people, the former remaining more distant (on the mountain), the other remaining closer (in the valley). In so doing, they made certain choices about their purpose and mission, their relationships, and the trade-offs between the two, with certain consequences for the Israelites and their work.

In this chapter, we focus on such choices and consequences, for not much has changed since the time of Moses and Aaron. How can rabbis and cantors manage the relationships between the various roles they play? How can they bring themselves into personal contact with congregants? These questions have much the same answer: boundaries. For make no mistake about it, boundaries—and the clergy's ability to maintain them in healthy and appropriate ways—will ultimately define one's rabbinate or cantorate. Let us consider how clergy members manage boundaries and the implications for when they do so well or poorly.

Walking the Line

Rabbi Michael Nathanson was looking forward to the next meeting of the day. He had always enjoyed his interactions with Alice Miller, a relatively new congregant who had been a participant in several of his Torah classes over the last few years. Michael found Alice to be thoughtful and articulate and often quite insightful in helping others make interesting connections between the Torah and events in their current lives. He did not know much about her outside of the classes. Her husband, David, was for several years the chair of the finance committee, and now served as a board member. Michael was not particularly fond of David—he found him abrasive, a board member who seemed to cause more problems than he solved. That was neither here nor there; he was here to meet with Alice. Michael did not quite know the purpose of the meeting and found himself curious as to what Alice wished to talk with him about.

Alice sat down in Michael's office and asked if he minded closing the door. Michael did so, took the chair directly opposite her, and asked her what was on her mind. Alice smiled nervously, shifted in her seat, and spent a few moments looking around at the bookshelves and down at her feet before answering. "I'm not sure where to begin," she started, not looking at him. "I'm not even sure what it is that I want from you. I just needed to talk to someone, and I didn't know where else to go."

Alice looked so sad that Michael found himself reaching for her hand but stopped himself from doing so. Instead, he smiled at her gently. "I'm happy to talk with you," he told her. "How can I help?"

Over the course of the next hour, Alice told him quite a bit, the words at times halting and at other times spilling over themselves in their haste to emerge. The story was painful for Michael to hear. He felt deeply for her. Alice told him that over the course of the last year she had been struggling with periods of depression that had, at first, been brief but were now lasting slightly longer each time. There was no family history to speak of, she

said, and she had the sense that it was rooted more in the circumstances in her life at the moment rather than in her chemical
makeup. The circumstances were quite real. Her mother was
dying, Alice said, from a slow-moving but incurable cancer that
was taking her mother away bit by bit, month by month, and
was now approaching the point at which her mother was talking
about taking her own life. Alice was distraught about losing her
mother and just as distraught about her mother being in physical
and emotional pain as she neared the end of her life. Alice wanted
some help from Michael in terms of the Jewish perspective on
end-of-life choices.

There was another issue as well, said Alice. Her husband was
having an affair. She had known for the last four months. The
woman was an unmarried junior partner at the firm at which he
was a senior partner. Alice had discovered the affair quite acci-
dentally. Mixed-up dinner plans, a strange phone call, and a lu-
dicrous story told by her husband led her to ask him, somewhat
in jest, if he was having an affair. She knew instantly that he was
lying when he assured her that he was not. Furious, she had
hired a private investigator, and several weeks later had proof,
with which she had not yet confronted her husband. Alice wanted
help from Michael in thinking about what she ought to do next.

Michael listened, not quite sure what issue he should tackle
first. He did not know if Alice was more deeply upset by her
mother's condition or her husband's infidelity. He sensed that
her depression was at least partly a matter of grief; she was grieving the imminent loss of both her mother and her marriage. He
said as much to her. She nodded, her eyes tearing. Michael reached
over and handed her some tissue. He said that he would be happy
to give her some texts to look at which would help them talk
further about the Jewish response to death and dying. He told
Alice that studying together about those issues might bring some
insight and comfort—for her as well as, he hoped, for her mother.
Michael went to a bookshelf and found the text that he had in
mind and handed it to Alice. He kept his hand on the book and
looked closely at her. He smiled gently and told her that the
book would not, of course, help her in terms of the pain that she

was going through in regard to her husband and marriage. After several moments, he let the book go and sat down. Michael reached for his phone and told the clergy secretary to cancel his next meeting and hold his calls; then he turned to Alice and invited her to tell him more about what she was feeling.

They spoke for another hour. Alice opened up to him in ways that he would not have expected. She told him about her marital difficulties, about how this was not the first time her husband had cheated on her, and how she had previously accepted it because she thought that she might be able to change him. Alice told Michael that she was starting to think differently. During her Torah classes with him, she said, she had slowly come to several realizations, including the fact that there were men—she did not specify who, exactly, she was referring to—who seemed to be strongly anchored in a set of moral tenets that her husband lacked. Michael briefly wondered who she might be talking about—there were several men in the Torah class—but then began asking Alice some questions about her history with men before she had married. As he suspected, she had a history of being with men who treated her badly and of staying with those men well past the point of self-respect. Michael had some training in counseling when he was in rabbinic school, and he understood the insidious effects of low self-esteem, how it led people to choose and remain in relationships in which they were treated poorly, like an afterthought, and how that felt achingly familiar to them, enough so that they were unwilling to end those relationships even when they knew they ought to do so. Michael thought that Alice suffered similarly, and he felt for her.

Alice looked at her watch and realized with a start that she needed to leave to pick up her children. She asked Michael if she could see him again.

He nodded, gesturing to the book in her hand, and told her that she should feel free to make an appointment after she read the text and wanted to talk with him about what she had found.

She smiled, telling him that it wouldn't take her long and that she would schedule a meeting for next week on her way out. She started out the door, stopped, turned, and gave him a quick hug. Michael hugged her in return, briefly, and told her that he would be thinking of her.

Over the course of the next few months, Michael and Alice met every week or two. Their conversations ranged widely. They spoke about Jewish perspectives on death and dying, on suicide, on depression. They spoke of Alice's experiences growing up with an overprotective mother and distant father. They spoke of her marriage and its discontents. Michael found himself looking forward to their meetings. He hoped that he was being helpful. He tried hard not to show Alice that he felt she ought to leave her husband who was clearly not worth her suffering. These conversations were sometimes difficult, but he felt that if anyone could save her, in the midst of her sadness and grief, he could, given how open she was with him.

Michael did find it awkward at times to see Alice and her family at synagogue services and holiday gatherings. He tried to be as friendly as he was with any other family in the congregation, but he could not help but find himself looking on with a sense of protectiveness toward Alice and animosity toward David. He hoped that this did not show. Alice assured him that David did not suspect that she was confiding in Michael. This relieved Michael, but still it was difficult whenever he saw them together; he could not help but imagine them together in their home afterward, which angered him more than he would have predicted. He wondered if this was a sign that he had overstepped some line and drawn too close to Alice. He was happily married, and although he found Alice attractive and enjoyed her confiding in him, he had no intentions of becoming involved with her. Still, he thought, perhaps he already was, in a matter of speaking.

Changing Kippot

Our case study is, on one level, a portrait of a clergy member managing shifts between various roles. Michael is a rabbi. As a rabbi, he moves in and out of various roles. He is a spiritual guide, helping a congregant sift through Jewish perspectives on troubling end-of-life issues. He is counselor, offering solace and support as the congregant struggles with grief, rage, and depression. He is religious leader, directing worship services that the congregant and her family attend. He is teacher, sharing his knowledge of the values and traditions of Judaism with children, teens, and adults. The rabbi shifts through these roles and others as a matter of course. Indeed, clergy move in and out of various roles constantly. In a typical day, many rabbis will function in several different modalities, from teacher to counselor to community organizer to fund-raiser to staff supervisor, just as cantors move between being educators, musicians, counselors, choir directors, and leaders of life-cycle events.

The constant movement between roles cannot help but blur the boundaries between those roles in the minds of congregants and staff as well as in those of clergy members themselves. A rabbi's shifts between counselor, religious leader, and organizational leader in the course of a single conversation with a lay leader, for example, can leave each confused as to which *kippa* the rabbi is wearing at any moment in time. This can lead to what we might call "spillover," in which conversations that occurred in the context of one type of relationship, such as counseling, might leak out and spill over into another type of relationship, such as board colleagues. Such spillover, or the fear that it might occur, can leave congregants feeling unsure about their clergy member's abilities to keep separate the various types of relationships they have together. This can easily translate into awkward, unsettling encounters. Or it can lead to inappropriate influence, such as when congregants listen more to their rabbi than his experience warrants, or conversely, seek to constrict the rabbi's power because they fear such influence. These are issues related to spillover, or its potential, between clergy roles.

We also wish to note that staff members assume various, sometimes conflicting roles as well. Congregants often work for synagogues. They, too, have multiple roles. At times, for example, they seek out the rabbi as their rabbi, and at other times as their supervisor. Synagogues collude with this by wanting or expecting certain staff positions to be held by Jews; lay leaders may feel betrayed or suspicious if staff members affiliate with other synagogues. Jewish staff members may resist that pressure and affiliate at other synagogues to separate their prayer and religious lives from their work. This keeps the boundaries tight around their religious lives, as they have rabbis who are only that for them and a spiritual community whose members do not seek them out to ask work-related questions. Staff members who are also congregants need to find other ways to create and maintain such separations.

Staff and clergy alike are thus in the difficult position of needing to quite explicitly manage the boundaries between the various roles that they assume in relation to others. Boundaries provide containment: what occurs between people when they are in one sort of relationship with one another is contained and bounded rather than opened for inspection elsewhere. This means, for example, that rabbis do not counsel individual members during Torah study classes, fund-raise while officiating at life-cycle events, or assume the supervisory role with a staff member seeking spiritual guidance. These are each, in its own way, a violation of what we would all recognize as appropriate boundaries. The roles themselves—counseling, teaching, fund-raising, supervising—are each important, as long as they occur in their appropriate context.

Placing and keeping roles and relationships in their appropriate contexts may at times require clergy to send signals in order to clear any confusion. This might mean being quite explicit about the various *kippot* that they are wearing. A cantor could make explicit her shift from role of teacher—"Now we're finished studying this section"—to that of choirmaster—"and we're going to move into the sanctuary and meet up with the others to practice for our concert." Or, to take a trickier example, a rabbi could make explicit his shift from pastoral counselor to organizational leader with a lay leader, saying, "We need to move into a brief conversation about our upcoming committee meeting, since that was what we planned to do, but I want to make sure that we finish this other conversation later. Let's figure out a time to do that." This is what we mean by managing boundaries: navigating the transitions among roles, such that people are having the right types of conversations at the appropriate times.

It is not always possible, of course, to manage boundaries as explicitly as one might like or, indeed, to create boundaries that are as tightly contained as they might need to be. What may pass for healthy boundaries in some professions—like therapists, for example—would be considered a failure in the rabbinate. In our case study, Michael, the rabbi, is privy to a great deal of intimate information about the marriage of the congregant Alice and David, her husband, who happens to be a board member. Michael then sees the couple at services and holiday gatherings. A therapist would walk in the other direction. The rabbi has to greet the congregant and wish them a "Shabbat Shalom," pretending he never spoke to the wife. This is boundary management of a different sort. It precludes external negotiations or making the switches between *kippot* transparent. It requires clergy members to outwardly pretend while internally managing boundaries.

Staying in Role

A different sort of issue emerges when clergy members find it difficult to hang on to their roles in certain situations. In the epigraph that opens this chapter, Aaron drops his role as spiritual leader almost completely. He melts away from the Israelites' fear, anxiety, and rage, and invites them to cast their gold into an idol, a false god, the golden calf. It is left to Moses to hold firmly to the rabbinic role. He calls to them quite clearly, "Whoever is for Adonai, come here!" In so doing, Moses stays within role and remains anchored to the appropriate task, which involves fastening God to the Israelites and the Israelites to God. In subtler but equally powerful ways, the rabbi in our case study seems at times to drop the rabbinic role and move into the role of therapist, as Alice invites him increasingly deeper into psychological and emotional realms. Michael seems to cross a boundary between what ought and ought not to consistently occur in a relationship between rabbi and congregant.

When clergy members step away from given roles, they slide into what we might call covert or shadow roles, such as therapist, savior, healer, lover. These roles remain largely unacknowledged. The shifts away from overt to covert roles may be subtle or obvious and profound. Either way, they invariably involve clergy members letting go, in ways fleeting or ongoing, of their ostensible tasks in relation to congregants and crossing boundaries between what is appropriate and inappropriate in the relationship. Aaron let go of the task of ministering to the Israelites and holding them fast to their relationship with the God that delivered them from Egypt. Michael let go of the task of helping Alice examine the various ways in which her grief could be understood and expressed in the context of Jewish principles and practices. Both Aaron and Michael crossed boundaries, with real implications for those they served.

In this regard, we have a great deal of empathy for clergy members. It is no small feat for them to remain firmly in their given roles when they face significant pressures to slide away from those roles. Congregants approach clergy members, particularly rabbis, with a great deal of unspoken, mostly unconscious wishes and expectations—that the rabbis will save or heal them in some fashion, take away their pain, and give them answers for questions for which there may be no earthly answers. Congregants may wish for a rabbi to become the all-knowing leader, guiding all aspects of the synagogue itself, as if he or she were Moses, responsible for every dimension of the people's flight toward their personal "promised land." Or congregants may project a great deal of anger and resentment at their rabbis for not doing what they could not possibly do as a spiritual or organizational savior. In each case, clergy members cannot help but be tempted to turn away from their roles, let drop their tasks, and cross boundaries that if tightly held to are likely to bring struggle and difficulty in their relations with congregants.

These struggles are most closely seen in issues involving counseling. Many rabbis get advanced training in counseling, especially in premarital and marital counseling. Is getting a couple ready for marriage a rabbinic role or a therapist's role? What happens when some of the premarital material borders on counseling? It is very seductive for the rabbi to keep going with the couple, especially when they say, "We already trust you. We are comfortable talking to you. We don't want to start all over with a stranger." An effective rabbi needs to be a good pastoral counselor. They are often warned not to try to be a therapist, however. But how is therapy defined? Is it merely the length of time one spends with a person? Or is it the nature of the material one brings to the interaction? Clearly, rabbis ought to talk to congregants who have lost loved ones. What happens when that same congregant begins to speak about the abuse she encountered as a child? What happens when the abusing parent was active in the synagogue and now the adult child is ambivalent in his or her relationship with religion? How does one separate "spiritual" issues from psychotherapeutic ones?

These are legitimate questions and legitimate struggles. Rabbis develop certain personal relationships with congregants in the context of their pastoral work. They also need to construct boundaries that enable them to maintain appropriate distance; such boundaries protect both the clergy member (from intruding upon others) and congregant (from being intruded upon). Clergy members can construct these boundaries by holding tightly to the tasks that fit with given roles. A series of interrelated questions can anchor this process. These questions include the following: How can the rabbi best offer religious and spiritual guidance to others who are going through emotionally charged experiences? How can the rabbi stay within boundaries of training and expertise? How can the rabbi best retain legitimacy as a clergy member? How can the rabbi best serve the congregant, and the congregation as a whole?

Answering such questions offers a path through potentially thorny relationships. When clergy members take seriously these questions, in self-reflection and conversation with trusted others, the appropriate stances usually reveal themselves. Rabbis in particular will have a clearer sense of the boundaries between what they ought and ought not do in relation with others. They will be able to best serve others, ministering to them when they should and referring them elsewhere when it is best to do so. Indeed, rabbis need strong referral lists; such lists are the lifelines to which rabbis can cling when they feel pulled out of their rabbinic roles.

The Person and the Role

Clergy members need to manage another sort of boundary—between who they are as people and who they are as professionals. This is a crucial boundary. Clergy members will experience moments when they feel tempted to burst from their roles and be "themselves" with others. We see this in our case study. The rabbi, Michael, feels for the congregant, Alice. He is drawn to her. He forces himself not to reach for her hand; he cancels other scheduled meetings to remain with her; he willingly lets himself be hugged by her; he thinks of her often. While none of these are horrible violations, cumulatively they are suggestive of a personal involvement—what we might consider an overinvolvement—between a rabbi and congregant. They are signals that something else might move beneath the surface of a rabbi-congregant relationship, something related to Michael as a person and not simply as a rabbi.

We are not suggesting that our clergy be automatons, people who more or less mechanically go through the motions of teaching, preaching, counseling, life-cycle events, or worship. Nor are we suggesting that rabbis never cry at a funeral, never hug or kiss a congregant, never laugh at others' jokes. That would make for dull and lifeless rabbis and cantors. Congregants would grow frustrated or bored with their clergy. They would sense that there was not much life, passion, or engagement in their rabbis or cantors; they would either resent or come to expect a certain level of clergy disengagement. Clergy members need to be fully alive and present: they need to feel with and for others, engage with others as humans capable of empathy and connection, and truly care for their congregants.

At the same time, our clergy need to connect personally within boundaries. They need to have limits on how much of their personal selves enter into their interactions with congregants. They need to practice what the Buddhists call "loving detachment"—demonstrate real love without making it about them or their own lives. Otherwise, their own needs, wishes, longings, and desires might become so prominent that the appropriate needs of congregants are eclipsed. Congregants may then feel intruded upon, or more disturbingly, feel violated in some fashion (we discuss this in more depth later). The key issue here is balance. How do clergy, and in particular rabbis, manage their intimacy and closeness with congregants? How do they establish and maintain a certain professional distance from others that enables them to do their jobs in a way that is safe for everyone involved, while at the same time enabling enough of their personal selves to emerge so that they can connect as people to those with whom they need to empathize? How do they remain professional even as they themselves have needs and desires?

Such questions need to be consistently explored by rabbis and cantors. Indeed, starting with their seminary and cantoral training, clergy members need to begin to understand the difference between the role of rabbi or cantor as an authority figure versus the rabbi or cantor as an individual, a person, an imperfect human being like all the rest of us. Unfortunately, our clergy members receive little or no training around this definitional issue. They do not learn when it is okay or not okay just to be themselves and, more generally, about the processes by which those boundaries are managed. Ideally, and minimally, they would learn the following lessons in the service of answering for themselves the questions we just posed.

Boundaries Maintain Useful Separations. Without boundaries there can be no relationship: knowing that we can keep ourselves separate from others allows us to move toward them in useful ways, since we know that we can remove ourselves from them as well. This is a matter of safety for all involved: when we know that we can keep others out, we are more likely to let them in. This goes for clergy and congregants alike. When rabbis and cantors know that they will be able to manage the depths of their involvements with others—that their interactions will remain bounded and limited—they are more likely to allow themselves to personally engage with others. Similarly, when congregants sense that clergy members will remain within appropriate boundaries, such as maintaining confidentiality or keeping their own reactions in check, they are more likely to seek help. Boundaries are necessary for clergy to do their work.

There Are Various Ways to Create and Maintain Boundaries. Clergy members help create boundaries in various ways. There are simple structures that help. Meetings start and end on time; agendas are followed; days off are adhered to; doors are closed when others might overhear but remain open otherwise; calendars are used; personal cell phone numbers remain private. Such structures limit the potential overinvolvements of clergy members, creating useful boundaries that hold them and congregants in check during their interactions with one another. During those interactions, there are nonverbal and verbal behaviors that help maintain boundaries as well: seating arrangements that allow for appropriate distance and closeness simultaneously; eye contact and gestures, such as the touching of an arm, that are respectful yet show connection and empathy; and words and tones that show respect for the limits on what ought to be said and not said. Rabbis and cantors may also need, at times, to quite clearly set boundaries, making distinctions about what they feel they can and cannot discuss in particular situations. On a more mundane level, clergy also have to set boundaries, rather politely, in those all-too-frequent situations when a congregant comes up to say hello at the grocery store, a concert, or a restaurant and starts sharing temple or personal "business."

It's Not Personal. Congregants open their lives to clergy members, particularly to rabbis. Rabbinic access to people's lives is a privilege and a sacred trust. Rabbis are allowed into the most intimate moments in the life of an individual and a family. This intimacy is not personal: it is not because of *who* the rabbi is but *what* he or she represents. Congregants need to see the rabbi as a rabbi, not just as a person. This allows them to provide access to the intimate, even unattractive parts of their lives, without feeling embarrassed or intruded upon. Rabbis are more likely to construct and maintain effective personal/professional boundaries when they keep this in mind. If they take the intimacy personally and come to believe that the intensity of other people's reactions to them—positive or negative—is only about who they are as people, they are more likely to press closer to others and overstep the boundaries of their roles.

Get a Personal Life. When clergy members get their personal needs for intimacy, connection, love, contact, and emotional support met outside the synagogue, it makes it easier for them to remain within appropriate, reasonable boundaries. They do not care so much about their own needs for centrality and love getting met in their relations with congregants and staff because those needs are being met elsewhere. Clergy members can thus let the congregation and its members remain at the center of their relationship; the task, not the rabbi or cantor, becomes the focus. The larger truth here is that boundaries are easier to manage when people are not looking to meet needs that ought to be met elsewhere. Such boundaries put limits on unwelcome emotional involvement.

The struggle involved in maintaining personal and professional boundaries is stark when viewed in the special context of friendship. "You are my rabbi and my friend—that's what I love about you." Rabbis hear this all the time. Unlike rabbis of a previous generation who were "respected, feared, and held in awe," the modern rabbi is supposed to be accessible and friendly, a "real person." Even in ancient times, rabbis were supposed to be "householders" so that they could relate to the realities of their congregants. But is it possible to be both a rabbi and a friend? True friendship requires some sense of equality, the possibility of mutuality and reciprocity. Being a rabbi, however, requires inequality; like Moses, rabbis must remain somewhere on the mountain. (This is less true for cantors, whose roles involve less distance from congregants.). While it is possible for someone to be friends with their rabbi, it usually means they have lost their rabbi.

What do we mean by this? Imagine what happens when a congregant, with whom the rabbi has socialized, comes to the rabbi for a pastoral counseling issue. Or the very active congregant with whom the rabbi is working on several synagogue-related projects wants to go out for a drink and get to know the rabbi better as a person. Or the couple with whom the rabbi and his wife have become best friends begins to have marital difficulties, triggered by the husband's gnawing sense of emptiness and isolation. In such cases, the fact that congregants have grown personally close to their rabbis removes a useful, protective, and quite necessary layer between rabbi and congregant. It makes it difficult to see the rabbi as a rabbi, precisely when the congregant needs a rabbi and not simply a good friend. It makes it difficult for the rabbi as well to see the congregant as a congregant who needs a rabbi, with all that that entails.

This is a big problem since congregational rabbis spend most of their lives in the synagogue, and since most people make friends in the workplace. Where else do they find friends? The problem exists for their families as well. Can a rabbi's partner create friendships with congregants? What happens when they talk about their sex lives? Or want to complain about their spouse? In such instances, the rabbi's partner is not just talking about his or her spouse but about the other person's rabbi! And even if they seek friends outside their synagogues, there are generally very few places rabbis can go in a community without being identified as "rabbi." This may very well add to the loneliness and isolation rabbis feel. Such feelings are often the root cause of boundary violations. If rabbis cannot get their needs for companionship met openly like other people do, they will too often get those needs met inappropriately or surreptitiously.

Boundary Violations

Clergy members may cross the boundaries between appropriate and inappropriate behavior. Much has been known to happen in congregations: affairs between clergy and congregants, counseling sessions that become too personally intrusive, embezzlement, careless drinking among clergy and congregants, harassment. These are violations that destroy useful layers of distance between clergy members and congregants. Often they violate the safety and welfare of congregants, leaving them exposed and vulnerable. Violations are serious business. They have the potential to destroy lives and careers, and to rend the fabric of trust throughout a congregation.

Boundary violations may be understood as expressions of a clergy member's own longings and needs that may not be getting met elsewhere. Under certain conditions—when there is no one to go to for help, for intimacy and connection, or when there is crushing loneliness, isolation, and a sense of not being heard, seen, or cared for—rabbis can erupt, seeking to break free. They shatter the fishbowls in which they reside; they slide away from the role of giver and into something else altogether. Violations can also be clergy members' attempts to break free of roles they find limited and constraining. Rabbis in particular get locked in roles, forced into narrow straits of who they ought to be and what they ought to do, as ultimate caregivers and moral standard bearers. Such projections can feel like straitjackets keeping them tightly constrained. Boundary violations are their misguided movements to break free of the arid confines of the rabbinic role. Indeed, the intensity of a rabbi's sense of being confined is often matched by the intensity of his or her boundary violation; the tighter the straitjacket, the greater the force needed to break free of its shackles.

It is too simple a matter, however, to suggest that boundary violations only arise because of the clergy member's own longings, predilections, desires, and frustrations. These are crucial, of course: they make a clergy member more or less available, psychologically and emotionally, for the possibility of violations. Yet there are moments when others are involved as well. Congregants can pull for clergy to move closer to them. As in our case study, they can press for intimacy, inviting clergy deeper and deeper into their personal lives, bringing them into their marriages, their personal histories, their longings. They can seduce clergy members, if not physically, then emotionally, beckoning their rabbis closer and closer. Congregants can engage in such seductions knowingly, or not. They can also do so with ambivalence, wanting to get closer and more personal with clergy members yet to keep them distant enough to ensure that there is no danger of intrusion.

Boundary violations must thus be understood in the context of relationships rather than simply being pinned on the clergy member alone. Rabbis and cantors do, of course, have to assume real responsibility whenever they cross boundaries. But congregants and staff members, and sometimes congregations more generally, must look closely at their own participation or collusion as well. Consider, for example, how there are often various signals or signs that are present before boundary violations. We can recognize those signals. The rabbi begins to cancel meetings, not show up for regular committee meetings, talk a lot about personal financial problems, spend a great deal of time with certain congregants and cut himself or herself off from others. The cantor gets overly involved with a congregant's family during bar or bat mitzvah preparations, drinks a great deal at some synagogue functions, spends a great deal of time behind closed doors with a staff member.

Such patterns of behavior may be meaningless. Or they might suggest a movement of some sort toward the violation of a boundary. Staff, lay leaders, clergy, and congregants routinely make choices about how to interpret those signs and how to act or not act. Often they do nothing, dismissing the importance of what they observe or not wishing to intrude. This might be exactly the right thing to do. It may also be exactly the wrong thing if we believe that clergy members might well be sending signals of distress in ways of which they are not aware. Unfortunately, such signals are not often received or, worse, are ignored. If we hold rabbis to higher standards of conduct, for example, we are less likely to interpret troubling behaviors as signals for help. Rabbis who edge toward inappropriate boundaries and cross them often are scorned rather than helped; people talk *about* them rather than *with* them when inappropriate behavior is observed. Indeed, rabbis may become objects of fury, as if they have betrayed a whole community, whereas if they were ill or suffered a calamity, congregants would reach out to help.

We cannot emphasize enough that when rabbis or cantors violate some boundary between what is appropriate and inappropriate for their roles, we must try to explain those acts both in terms of the clergy members themselves and in terms of how the congregation, including members, leaders, and staff, might have unwittingly aided and abetted such violation. We do so with our silence. We do so by withholding useful feedback. We do so by trying to establish inappropriately close relationships with our clergy and not watching our own boundaries. We do so, finally, by thinking of our clergy as somehow beyond human, without our same need for connection and support.

Holding Fast

While we do believe that all of us are responsible for ensuring that rabbis and cantors hold fast to appropriate boundaries, the burden is often on the clergy member to make sure that he or she is doing so. Others are not often as clear about the issues involved in the shifts between the roles that rabbis play. Nor are others privy to the internal struggles that clergy members wage to bring their personal selves into their professional roles in appropriate ways. There are power differences that make it easier for clergy members, if they are so inclined, to address boundary issues; the power that rabbis have, in particular, through expertise and authority can silence congregants. We conclude this chapter by offering ideas about how clergy members might deal effectively with the burden of managing boundaries.

Let the Task Be an Anchor. When rabbis and cantors hold tightly to their tasks, they are less likely to violate boundaries. Certain tasks require certain types of relationships. Preparing a student for a bat mitzvah, comforting a grieving widow, celebrating a *simcha,* counseling a couple having marriage difficulties, teaching a Torah class—each of these requires a certain level of personal engagement and a certain professional distance on the part of the clergy member. When the rabbi or cantor remains mindful of the task and of the nature of the relationship that can best and more respectfully complete that task, the boundary ought to remain clear.

Seek Clarity and Transparency. Clergy members help clarify boundaries when they name the roles that they occupy at any particular time; this both announces the role to congregants and contextualizes it for themselves. For example, the rabbi could say to a congregant, "In order to answer that question, I need to take off my teacher *kippa* and put on my senior rabbi one." This indicates to the congregant that the rabbi is stepping from one role to another so as not to confuse the congregant with the response, while allowing the rabbi to speak with a sense of clarity about his or her role. Clergy members also need to be able to clarify when they cannot assume a particular role, such as therapist, by saying something like, "I cannot go there with you, because that would undermine my ability to be your rabbi."

Consider Perceptions. We offer here a rule of thumb for clergy members. If your interaction with a congregant was reported in the news the next day, how would it affect your job? If the answer is a negative one, a rabbi or cantor ought to back away from engaging in that sort of interaction. What feels "innocent" may not look that way to someone else. Rabbis, because they are religious leaders, need to err on the side of caution. How they are perceived goes a long way toward maintaining their ongoing abilities to remain trusted, and thus effective, in their roles.

Stay Human. Rabbis in particular are in danger of violating boundaries when they feel as if those boundaries do not apply to them. When rabbis have a sense of themselves as godlike or extraordinary, they leave themselves open to being seduced or to abusing their power. Rabbis often feel they have the weight of "saving the Jewish people from dying out" on their own shoulders. They can thus be seduced by congregants' claims of "You saved my life, Rabbi." Rabbis cannot believe their own press, either good or bad. They need to remain grounded in a normal life—to take out the garbage, play tennis, cook, fold the laundry, and other small acts of normalcy. Such acts allow for humility, a sense of limits on what a person can and cannot do.

Know Thyself. Clergy members can do much to remain within appropriate boundaries by knowing a great deal about themselves: the situations that tempt them, the support they need to withstand temptation, the triggers that lead them to the edge of boundaries, and those that enable them to back away from those edges. This self-knowledge takes a fair amount of self-reflection; it requires a willingness and ability to learn about oneself from one's own personal experiences. To the extent that clergy members are able to develop that self-knowledge, they can prevent potentially complicated situations from developing.

Find Others to Help. Self-knowledge does not often occur in a vacuum. We need others to help us reflect on and learn from our experiences. And we need the support of others in learning to deal effectively with current situations. Yet many clergy members do not have such support. Many have never been in therapy or coaching themselves. Unlike therapists, when they hear congregants' stories, they have no group in which to process what they are hearing. Since most rabbi conversations are privileged information, rabbis cannot easily locate groups in which to discuss their transference or countertransference issues and dilemmas. To the extent that they can find settings—peers, therapy, other clergy in the community—in which to struggle with those issues and dilemmas, they are more likely to remain within rather than trespass boundaries.

None of these strategies is simple. But the difficulty of each is more than matched by the pain, the casualty rate, and the shattered trust that accompanies significant boundary violations in the synagogue. Moses understood this. He understood that, as difficult as it was for him and for the Israelites to have him maintain boundaries between himself and them—and, presumably, between what he ached to do as a person and what he needed to do as a spiritual leader—his task, as set forth by God, required those boundaries. Aaron either did not understand this or was unable to withstand the press of maintaining the appropriate boundaries. Moses asked of Aaron, "What did this people do to you, that you have brought such a great sin upon them?" The sin of the Israelites was simply that of being anxious and frightened; the sin of Aaron was to give way to that, to step aside as they cast their gold and, by extension, their lives into the flames. It is only by holding fast to their roles, their tasks, and their boundaries that rabbis and cantors can help their congregants sustain their spiritual and religious journeys.

13

"Go in Strength": The Meanings of Clergy Transitions

> Then Joshua knelt and Moses placed his hands upon his head
> and called out: "The spirit which God put into me, I put into
> thee. Go in strength and let thy might increase." And Moses
> knelt by the side of Joshua and lifted his hands to heaven and
> prayed aloud: "I thank Thee, O God, the God of our ances-
> tors, that Thou hast granted it to me to see the leader of Israel
> before Thou didst close mine eyes. And I implore Thee, God
> of our fathers and our mothers, to strengthen his hands and
> to be with him as Thou hast been with me until this very
> day." Then he rose from his knees and called out to the people:
> "See your leader, Joshua. Him shall ye obey!" But among the
> people there was a heavyhearted silence. No tumult was raised,
> and no voice was heard save that of Joshua, which lamented:
>
> "My lord, my teacher, my father!"
>
> (Sholem Asch)

The story of Moses's transition of power from himself to Joshua is contained in the latter chapters of the book of Deuteronomy (31, 32, and
34). After Moses accepted the fact that he would not lead the Israelites
into the land of promise, the process was quite smooth and the people
seemingly accepting. In the above commentary, however, Sholem Asch
projects ambivalence on the part of the people: sadness about the loss of
Moses existed alongside appreciation for the wisdom and strength of
Joshua. Joshua himself understood the magnitude of the moment and
prayed for help with what he understood would be a difficult transition.
Even when leaders do the right thing in readying themselves, the community, and their successor, as Moses did, transitions are not easy, un-
leashing as they do complicated mixtures of emotions in leaders and
followers alike.

Judaism understands the complexity of transitions. Every Shabbat we must transition from spiritual rest and renewal to the hectic pace and demands of the ordinary week. Our life-cycle moments—the baby welcomed into the covenant, the young man or woman accepting the responsibilities of adult Jewish life, the partners joining their lives together in marriage or choosing to end a marriage, the seeker choosing Judaism as his or her spiritual path, the bereaved saying good-bye to a loved one who has died—are marked by rituals and words that help us deal with the variety of emotions we inevitably feel. Judaism, in its ritual and its language, creates the bridges that people must cross as they move from one place in their lives to another. Our clergy understand this. They help congregants navigate across their bridges with appropriate ceremony, gravity, and celebration. They help people acknowledge that which they are leaving and move gracefully toward that which they are entering. They help people understand the meanings of their transitions, which enables them to approach those transitions more surely and engage them more thoughtfully.

In this chapter, we focus on how clergy themselves can approach and engage their own transitions into and out of pulpits more surely and thoughtfully through a greater understanding of the various dimensions of those transitions. We believe that clergy transitions, and in particular, rabbinic transitions, may be understood in various ways, all of which have meaning for how those transitions are conducted and experienced. Such transitions are *natural* and inevitable, as both rabbis and congregations move through various stages of growth and change. They are *corrective,* as rabbis and congregations discover who they are and who they are not in relation to one another. They are *emotional,* as rabbis and congregations that have formed attachments of one sort or another struggle to disentangle themselves. They are *historical,* as rabbis and congregations each mark the various periods of their respective lives in terms of their relationships with one another.

Rabbinic transitions are each of these and more. The rabbi makes a personal calculus, in which all sorts of variables—career, family, work environment, finances, geography—get factored into the decision about leaving, staying, going, and entering. The rabbi attempts to sort these variables in ways that help make sense of the particular journey that he or she takes as a rabbi and as a person. These journeys do not occur in isolation, of course, but set in motion a number of other transitions. The rabbi's transition shapes (and is shaped by) the transitions of his or her family as well. The transition impacts clergy and staff at both the synagogues that are left and those that are joined. At a larger level, rabbinic transitions influence the lay leadership of a synagogue, which must find ways to detach from and attach to different rabbis. And, of course, there is the congregation. Rabbinic transitions are interventions in the life of a congregation, in ways large and small, the effects of which are both immediate and potentially quite long lasting.

Rabbinic transitions thus occur at multiple levels simultaneously. Each level may be affected differently, and more or less deeply, according to the particular nature of the rabbinic relationship. The rabbinic transition offers each entity—the rabbi, his or her family, clergy groups, lay leaders, and congregations—the opportunity to learn, grow, and change. The extent to which this actually occurs depends on two factors: first, people's capacities to live with rather than be swept away by the various emotions triggered by rabbinic transitions (i.e., anger, resentment, shame, guilt, sadness, loss, anxiety, and the like); and second, people's capacities to reflect on, and thus make meaning of and learn about, their transitions (i.e., what led up to them, what they signify about the rabbi-congregation fit and relationship, how they were handled, and their place within individual and collective development). Our capacities to reflect are shaped, of course, by how we handle our emotional experiences; the reverse is true as well.

We write this chapter to help both rabbis and others—family members, other clergy and staff, lay leaders, and congregants more generally—approach rabbinic transitions better equipped to learn and grow from the experience. To do so, we examine both the emotional and practical aspects of those transitions. Our experience at Eitzah teaches us that these transitions are often handled poorly, creating "casualties" among rabbis and the synagogues they serve. We begin with a brief case study of a rabbinic transition.

The Release

Rabbi Saul Rosenthal was mildly annoyed. He had left three messages for the board president that had not been returned.

The issue itself was not a big deal, just some scheduling matters, but he was getting a bit tired of feeling as though he and the other clergy were such a low priority with the lay leadership. This lack of responsiveness had been going on for some time, across the tenures of various board presidents, to the point that Saul felt that it had somehow filtered into the culture of the synagogue itself. He finished leaving a fourth message, hung up, and thought about the situation.

It was Saul's sixth year in the synagogue. His tenure there had been smooth enough. He had helped the congregation do some healing after the previous rabbi left amid a conflict with the lay leadership, taking a position at a nearby synagogue, along with a large number of families who had followed him. Membership had slowly risen, from 540 families when he began to the current total of 760 families. Saul had also introduced a number of new programs, helped the congregation identify a vision related to family-centered worship and *tikkun olam,* and supported the development of an award-winning Hebrew school. He felt good about the work that he had done and thought that others did as well. Recently, however, he had noticed a certain boredom and restlessness in himself. He did not look forward to the work as much as he had, nor was he as hopeful about changing the congregation as he once had been. He felt worn by all of the pushing and prodding that he had to do whenever he wanted lay leaders to get more involved and take some real responsibility for making programs and initiatives more engaging and successful. He knew that it would probably get worse before it got better; the incoming board president was someone with whom he had a few run-ins in the past, and he knew that there was quite a gap in what they each wished the synagogue to be.

Without even knowing quite how he had gotten to this point, Saul hung up the phone and began taking seriously the idea of seeking another pulpit. He was in the last year of his current contract. He had assumed that he would be here for a while, but perhaps the time had come. He knew that rabbis left their pulpits for lots of reasons—sharp disagreements with lay leaders and the directions in which congregations were headed, financial problems in congregations, contracts not being renewed, ambition for bigger and better opportunities elsewhere—but none of those were really motivating him. It just seemed time. Saul spoke with Esther, his wife, and over the course of several weeks, they decided that if they were to move, it was better to do so now rather than later, after their daughter had already started at the local high school. Esther was supportive. She knew that Saul was less excited and hopeful about his work.

Saul called the placement office and submitted his name for the upcoming year. He knew that it was a relatively good year to be on the market; for some reason, there were a fair number of jobs open at the senior level in various parts of the country that seemed appealing. He was not thrilled at the idea of the transition itself—of the various reactions that he was likely to get when he told people that he would be leaving—but he knew that it was all part of the business of being a rabbi. Telling his daughter would be difficult as well. She had some good friends, liked the place where they lived, and was likely to have a strong reaction. He would be sure to get Esther's help with her.

Saul began with the current board president. He said that he would not be asking for another contract. The president seemed stunned. Saul explained that he simply felt that it was time to move on to new challenges; the congregation was in a good place, he told the president, growing and successful, and a new rabbi could take it to the next place in its journey. The president said that he was disappointed and urged Saul to reconsider. He promised Saul that he would help make whatever changes seemed necessary to help persuade him to remain. Saul smiled, told him that would not be necessary and that he had already made up his mind. The president asked Saul to attend the board meeting the following week and speak to the board members directly. Saul agreed.

Over the course of the next week, prior to the board meeting, a number of lay leaders called Saul or stopped into his office to speak with him. Many wanted to see if they could talk him out of his decision. Saul listened politely, answered their questions, and assured his visitors that it was the right decision for him, his family, and, he believed, the congregation itself. At the board meeting, Saul reiterated that he thought it was the right time for him to leave, given what he and the lay leaders had been able to accomplish together. Several members said that they thought that he was leaving too soon, in that the congregation had not yet become joined around the mission of *tikkun olam*. Saul told them that might well be true but that he felt that he had taken the congregation as far as he could. Saul felt reasonably good about the meeting in spite of the fact that several board members avoided him completely before, during, and after the meeting. He was not sure what that meant but figured that they would talk to him if and when they chose.

Meeting with the cantor and the synagogue staff was more complicated. They were more clearly sad and upset about his leaving, to a depth that he would not have predicted. The clergy's secretary was upset; the synagogue was her first job, and Saul her first supervisor, and she had come to depend on him a great deal as a mentor. The cantor, too, was plainly sad. She told him that it would not be the same working with another rabbi and that she, too, might consider leaving. Saul told her that she ought to wait and make sure and do what was best for her. The executive director showed little emotion when Saul told him and immediately focused on the practical aspects that would accompany the transition.

Saul began to speak of his decision to others in the congregation as well, beginning with the chairs and members of the committees on which he sat. Many expressed their regret about his leaving. Some were clearly angry. The social action committee chair accused him of leaving something before it was finished. He told Saul that a number of people had joined the social action committee out of personal loyalty to Saul, who had been increasingly vocal about its importance in the life of a congregation that took *tikkun olam* seriously. The chair told Saul that these people would feel betrayed and that it was on Saul's conscience. Before Saul could respond, saying that congregants ought to do social action because it was the right thing to do, the chair turned his back and walked away.

There were other incidents. A congregant accused Saul of betraying her son after Saul had begun helping the boy, who had learning disabilities, prepare for a bar mitzvah that Saul would now not be officiating. A congregant cried in Saul's office, telling him that she would not be able to accept another rabbi as her rabbi and that she needed Saul to remain in that role for her. A congregant told Saul that he agreed that it was time for a new rabbi, given what he perceived as Saul's "lackluster" sermons over the last year or so. Saul attempted to respond to each incident as calmly as he could, even while feeling the guilt, anger, sadness, and frustration it evoked.

Saul also heard of the various stories that were making their way through the congregation about his leaving. One story held that Saul was leaving because the board would not meet his exorbitant demands for more money and a lifetime contract. Another story was that Saul was forced out because he refused to raise funds for a new capital campaign. Still another was that he could not work with the current lay leaders and that they had refused to extend another contract. Another story held that Saul had been offered a much larger salary by a competing synagogue in the area and that he was planning to appeal to members of his current congregation to join him. Saul heard these stories and more. Some he found humorous, others angered him, and still others were insulting and infuriating. He tried his best to put them out of his mind.

The transition proceeded. Saul had several visits with different congregations and was offered a position at two of them. He and Esther finally chose a congregation in a neighboring state. It was at an exciting point in its history. The lay leadership very much wanted to partner with a rabbi with a vision. Saul felt good about his experiences during his visits there and looked forward to the challenges that lay ahead. He spent the last few months at his current synagogue trying his best to support his staff and the lay leaders. They, too, were going through a search process for his successor. He stayed away from that process, although several times he responded to requests from the interviewing committee for information about his role and job

description. Saul offered to speak to any candidates, an offer
that was accepted by several of them, including the one who was
finally chosen. A month before Saul left, the congregation honored him with a dinner. He thanked the congregation for the
opportunity to walk alongside its members during his years with
them and said his good-byes.

The Emotional Life of Transitions

On the surface, our case study is a relatively simple story of a rabbinic
transition. A rabbi decides, for various reasons, that it is time to seek
another pulpit. He informs others. He searches for and accepts another
job. He does his work as best he can. He leaves. Much, however, moves
beneath the surface. Emotions are triggered and released throughout the
congregation. The board president and some of the board members are
shocked, then disappointed. Other board members and some of the committee chairs are angry, feeling betrayed. The cantor and clergy staff
are upset and saddened. Congregants, too, run the gamut of emotions,
ranging from acceptance and understanding to anger and betrayal. Lay
leaders and congregants alike, like the rabbi, do the best they can given
the difficulty of the situation.

Rabbinic transitions often trigger such emotional reactions for a
number of reasons. Transitions are changes; they are terminations, of
sorts, that require people to let go of that which they have held—habits
of thought or action, attachments to others, relationships. People react
emotionally to change and termination. They grow sad in the face of
loss. They are filled with regret or guilt for what has not been done or
said. They are angry or bitter in the face of what they may experience as
rejection or betrayal. They are anxious and confused about the uncertain
future or bitter about what will remain an unresolved past. Some, of
course, are also relieved and glad, excited about what lies before them.
Such are the emotions that significant transitions trigger, both in those
who leave and those who are left.

Rabbinic transitions are particularly emotional, layered as they are
with various transferential reactions by congregants, lay leaders, and staff.
When rabbis are (and they often are) the objects of others' projections—
about parental authority, God, Judaism—their leaving is experienced with

heightened emotion. For some people, a retiring rabbi will be the only rabbi they have ever known—the one who welcomed them into Judaism, stood under the chuppah with them, held them at graveside when they buried a loved one. These congregants, with a deep connection to their rabbi, will feel more bereft, as if their protector has left them to an uncertain fate. They are more deeply wounded. The power of their emotions points to the extent that they experienced their rabbi as closer to God and a figure of authority, in counterpoint to what they feel is their own distance from God and lack of personal authority as practicing Jews. When such projections are in play, people feel abandoned by their rabbi. They are less able to understand how a rabbi may want to make a "career move," need a new challenge, be required by a spouse's job to move to a new city, or simply want to retire. But such transitions are necessary or inevitable, products of the need for rabbis and congregations to continue to grow apart from one another.

The emotional life of rabbinic transitions plays itself out in ways that are often psychologically complex. The complexity derives from the difficulty that people often have in holding on to and expressing different emotions simultaneously. As we noted earlier, transitions tend to trigger certain emotions: sadness, anger, guilt, betrayal, resentment, and relief. We often feel these things at the same time, as befitting the multidimensional relationships that we have with others who leave us. It is difficult, however, to have different, opposing feelings at the same instant. It is hard to feel sad and angry at the same time, or relieved and betrayed. It is difficult to know what to do when we feel both of those things.

To resolve that internal tension, we often split our feelings, holding on to one and pushing away the others. We feel mostly sad or mostly angry. Yet the pushed-away emotions never really get lost. Congregations have a way of making sure that all of the triggered emotions are expressed somewhere. Different people carry various sides of the split emotions. In our case study, some people were disappointed and upset with Rabbi Rosenthal; others were sad; still others were angry and betrayed; and, presumably, some were relieved and hopeful as well. This dynamic simplifies people's internal worlds. They hang on to particular emotions and organize their understandings of the rabbinic transitions around those emotions. This dynamic also makes it difficult for congregations to learn from those transitions.

Wounds and Opportunities

Transitions are at once wounds—gashes in the congregational body—and opportunities for growth—moments in congregational histories that offer choice about what the congregation can and will be. Each of these is a part of the rabbinic transition. What *happens* with the wounds and the opportunities greatly depends on the ways in which people turn toward or away from one another during transitions and their aftermaths. When people remain apart and locked into certain emotions (they are only angry, only sad, or only hopeful) the congregation is likely to remain split as well. Congregants, lay leaders, staff members, and even the rabbis themselves will be unable to support one another and develop a shared, nuanced understanding of the transition and its implications for the past, present, and future of the congregation. Some part of the congregation will remain wounded. When that occurs, the congregation as whole suffers.

Rabbis often leave in the natural course of their career development, moving on to a different position according to the stages of their careers. The choice to leave in such situations is understandable, following as it does a relatively clear path. The wounds in such cases are relatively clean, without ragged edges; blame does not need to be a large part of the leaving process. So, too, are rabbinic decisions based primarily on two-career situations, retirement, or other family-related reasons. Still, there is a wound.

If, however, a rabbi leaves for reasons that are not so obviously acceptable, the wounds are more difficult. Like our Rabbi Rosenthal, rabbis might simply become wearied by their work with particular congregations or, more explosively, have raging conflicts that lead them to resign. Rabbis might not have their contracts renewed, or worse, be fired. These types of leavings trigger more emotion; they leave congregations in difficult places, marked by blame, recrimination, guilt, sadness, hurt, anger, and the like. They create deeper, more complex wounds.

We believe that congregations, like individuals, may choose to or choose not to heal wounds. The choice, and indeed, the nature of wounds and the difficulty in their healing, depends partly on why rabbis leave. Certainly, it is more complicated to repair relationships among congregants or lay leaders when they are blaming one another for causing their rabbi to leave. Gaining a sense of closure is more difficult when there are multiple stories swirling around the congregation that "explain" why a rabbi left or did not have a contract renewed. When rabbis leave under clouds of suspicion or uncertainty, the emotional fallout can be large and unwieldy for congregations. How people deal with that fallout determines the extent to which they wish to heal.

Healing

When congregations choose not to heal, people relate to one another and to their rabbi in ways that leave them unable to *learn* from events and experiences. Transitions are significant opportunities for real learning about a congregation and its values, culture, purpose and community. People may only realize those opportunities when they look closely at rabbinic transitions and with real curiosity try and figure out what they mean for and about the congregation itself. Too often, this does not happen. People act out rather than reflect. Their emotions hijack them, dictating their responses and leaving them unable to work through what happened and what it means for the congregation as an evolving entity. Rather than look at events with curiosity, they look at them with pathological certainty—a type of certainty that cannot be touched by facts—that always prevents learning.

This happened a lot in our case study. Congregants accused Rabbi Rosenthal of betrayal. They sought to make him feel guilty. They turned their backs on him. They attacked him. Such responses enabled people to avoid stopping to think about why the rabbi was leaving and what it might have to do with the nature and evolution of the congregation. They were also, unwittingly, attempting to make the rabbi feel what they felt (anger, sadness, betrayal, guilt) in response to his leaving, such that he would feel those things and they might not have to. Such acting out inevitably maintains rather than heals wounds.

Congregational wounds heal only when people come together to talk through events and experiences and try to make some shared sense of what has occurred. A rabbi leaves. The circumstances are unclear. As in our case study, different people have different reactions. Some are upset, others less so. Various stories begin to emerge. The rabbi was greedy, lazy, or contentious. He received a better offer elsewhere. The lay leaders mishandled the contract negotiations. These are relatively simple stories. They have good guys and bad guys. It is when people come together and begin to make sense of what occurred that the stories become more faithful to the complexity of reality, in which multiple factors and parties always play a part. Rabbi Rosenthal was at a certain point in his career. The lay leadership had, over the years, created a certain culture that the rabbi ultimately found tiring. The congregation was about to undergo a significant capital campaign, which demanded a certain clergy-lay partnership that was not currently in place. All of these factors and more played a role in Rabbi Rosenthal's decision to leave.

This is a more complex story. It is in the process of people coming together to create these more complicated narratives that learning occurs. People can come to understand together the ways in which everyone is implicated in the rabbinic transition and bears some responsibility —the rabbi and his or her family, the staff, the lay leaders, the congregants themselves. They can understand as well how the transition might fit into certain historical patterns in the congregation—the uneasy sense of familiarity that this has happened before—which offers the possibility that such patterns might, with enough scrutiny and understanding, be finally interrupted. In doing this work together and developing a more complicated, nuanced understanding of events and experiences, people can also broaden their own emotional responses. They can claim for themselves the full range of emotions—sadness, anger, relief, guilt, excitement— that would otherwise remain located in bits and pieces in different individuals and groups in the congregation.

These are the hallmarks of congregational healing. People come together to try to make sense of what happened and why they feel as they do. Rabbis can help in this process if they choose. We refer here to both the rabbis who leave and those who join. Each is in the position of helping a congregation and its members come to terms with transitions and what they trigger. Rabbis are best able to do this when they are able to make the emotional life of transitions explicit for others. This means helping people understand that their reactions to various situations that occur during transitions are, often enough, about the transition itself rather than the specifics of the situations. Rabbis can also convene people, such as their staff, and encourage lay leaders to convene congregants, to let them talk about the transition. Doing so provides opportunities for people to express their feelings, hear of others' experiences, and, hopefully, develop well-rounded understandings of transitions and the lessons that they can offer.

The Practical Side of Transitions

Rabbinic transitions are filled with practical matters as well. We describe a few of the practicalities from the rabbi's point of view. In particular, we focus on why and how rabbis leave their pulpits and ways in which they can enter new ones.

Looking to the Next Place

Rabbis make decisions to leave their current pulpits in different ways. For some, it is simply a matter of external factors that exert their own press to leave. A spouse or partner needs to move. An interesting position appears in a desirable location. A larger congregation offers more money and prestige. A congregation does not renew a contract. For other rabbis, it is a more internal process. They want more responsibility or the chance to set a congregation's direction and tone. They sense the limits in the current situation or, indeed, feel hopeless about the possibility of change. They are frustrated with seemingly intractable conflict. Or like Rabbi Rosenthal, they are bored and find themselves going through the motions. These feelings of restlessness, hopelessness, frustration, and boredom are signals, sent by rabbis from within themselves, that it might well be time to leave their current situations. Sometimes these signals can serve as a stimulus to work on and improve or fix a problem within the synagogue setting. Instead of leaving, then, the rabbi decides to stay and together work on the relationship, assuming a different stance toward organizational leadership and change and trusting that the signals will lessen rather then strengthen in intensity.

If the rabbi decides to leave, he or she follows a reasonably predictable path. For most rabbis, this means entering the placement process: calling the placement director, letting at least one board member of the current synagogue know current intentions, networking, and generally starting to look into various options. (Most movements have particular guidelines and rules for this process, which should be adhered to strictly.)

Ideally, the placement process yields several possibilities, and like our Rabbi Rosenthal, rabbis will have the ability to choose among different congregations or other positions. The process then becomes one of determining the best fit between who a rabbi is and what a congregation wishes to be. The interview process offers a way to assess the fit or lack thereof.

Interviews are a kind of courtship. They hold the potential for seductions: for rabbis and lay leaders both to try and entice the other, to win the other over by strategically manipulating the impressions that one gives off. This is dangerous. Rabbis can end up in the wrong place, led to believe that which was not true. So, too, can congregations wind up with the wrong rabbi. The question is always that of fit; and, as in a courtship, the more that the partners learn of one another as they are, rather than who they wish they were, the more likely they will make the correct decision about whether to pursue a future together. This learning process needs to go both ways. Rabbis ought to share their visions of Jewish life, their passions, what they have learned through previous experiences, their strengths and the areas in which they need to learn and grow. Rabbis ought to ask about congregational mission statements, organizational charts, financial records, and sample bulletins.

Edwin Friedman, in his classic book *Generation to Generation,*[1] suggests that during the courtship period, clergy members ought to look carefully for answers to questions about the nature of the partnership between clergy and lay leadership. Such questions include: To what extent are the founding members still in power or in the congregation at all? How many different spiritual leaders has the congregation had, and what were their tenures? What has been the nature of the congregation's previous separations (transitions), and with what fallout? How do members of the congregation talk about their previous spiritual leaders? Friedman suggests that such questions are guidelines for what to ask at various meetings and what to listen for. The resulting information is likely to be invaluable as a source of clues about the relationship a new rabbi is likely to be able to form with a new synagogue.

Ways of Leaving

Leaving a congregation, like leaving any significant relationship, stirs up emotions not simply for those who are left but for those who leave as well.

Rabbis can feel sad, guilty, relieved, excited, angry, or any combination thereof, depending on the circumstances of their leaving. How they manage those emotions, and the loss that inevitably attends transition, shapes the ways in which they leave. Some rabbis act as if the transition is not occurring or downplay its significance; they deny the importance of the change or pretend that they are not really leaving. Other rabbis leave before they have actually left. They disengage, going through the motions of their work and avoiding others who might press them to be emotionally present. Some throw themselves into their new jobs before they have left their current ones. Still other rabbis *create* conflict as a way to manage their own emotional responses to leaving. They pick fights, as it were, with lay leaders or staff or congregants; this, too, allows them to disengage and makes the leaving psychologically easier. They do not have to feel sad as long as they can get themselves to feel angry.

The cleanest way for rabbis to leave, of course, is to choose none of these options but instead to create ways to say good-bye to those they have served. Saying good-bye offers people the opportunity to share what they have meant to one another in ways that may be simple but may also be complicated and nuanced. As we noted earlier, the Jewish tradition is filled with rituals that enable Jews to mark all sorts of transitions—of the calendar, of life cycles, of relationships—and that it might well make sense for rabbis and congregations to use rituals to mark the transition of their own relationship. Such rituals—closure exercises with lay leaders or staff, for example, or last sermons to the congregation—enable rabbis and others to remind one another of what they have meant to one another. We believe that this ought to happen early rather than late, to give people a chance to absorb, digest, and respond to the rabbi's leaving. Presumably, this also gives the rabbi a chance to take in the various meanings of his or her departure well before the event.

Saying good-bye in such ways is not simple emotionally. It allows people to feel what they feel, in all its complexity, and ideally, express those feelings in appropriate ways to one another. The rabbi's role here is significant. People will look to the rabbi to "perform" transition rituals just as they do in the context of other Jewish rituals. This puts rabbis in the difficult position of needing to care for others at the same time they need their own care. They, too, will be reacting to their own leaving, even as they need to permit the reactivity of those they are leaving. In his book, Friedman writes that if clergy do not manage their own emotional reactions well while allowing others their reactivity—that is, they avoid or deny events, experiences, and emotions—they increase the likelihood that both partners will carry emotional baggage into their next relationships. Rabbis can best walk this emotional tightrope during their leaving by getting some personal support from trusted friends, family, coaches, therapists, and the like with whom they can fully share their own experiences. Rabbis need to care for themselves and for their families as they make their transitions out of and away from the synagogue.

Leaving is also a matter of letting go. Rabbis need to give others permission to move ahead and, indeed, to give themselves the same permission as well. This means that rabbis remain gently clear with their congregants that, yes, they are leaving, and, yes, a new rabbi will soon serve the congregation. Rabbis need not turn away from their congregants; they will need to listen to them and absorb their sense of loss but not get so caught up that they are unable to say good-bye in healthy ways that leave both them and others grateful for what they had and clear that the separation is real. Rabbis thus need to resist making promises that they cannot keep. There will, often enough, be commitments that are already on the calendar for after rabbis have left that they will feel pulled to honor. Rabbis need to do the difficult work of extricating themselves from most of these; the rest ought to be cleared with the successor as a way of honoring the successor as the new primary spiritual figure.

Leaving is also an opportunity to set up the next rabbi for success in his or her partnership with the congregation. Practically, this means that the outgoing rabbi works with the lay leaders to ensure smooth transition of ongoing projects and to make room for the next rabbi to have input on key matters related to the future. It also means becoming involved in the creation of the selection process itself, not for the purposes of actually helping to choose the next rabbi, but for helping lay leaders understand the requirements dictated for the rabbinic role as it has come to be defined in their specific congregation. Writing an actual job description, for example, rather than an ideal one, might be quite useful for a congregation as it seeks to learn about the type of rabbi who would succeed. This offers yet another opportunity for congregations and rabbis to learn who they were in relation to one another, even as they go about the process of separation. This helps minimize what Friedman refers to as the "emotional residue" left by separations marked by undiscussed, and thus unresolved, issues.

Finally, rabbis can leave in ways that enable their successors to actually succeed. They can leave referral lists and lists of handy telephone numbers. They can personally introduce their colleagues to others in the community. They can answer questions honestly while being careful not to prejudice their successors against those people they found to be "difficult." They can make themselves available when their successors need them in the future. They can celebrate, from a distance, the changes that their successors make as they go about creating their own relationships with their new congregations. They can resist being triangulated, as former leaders or members attempt to enlist them in some campaign against their successor. They can, in short, do their best to support the new relationship, knowing that it will be different—not better, not worse—and that it deserves respect. This is especially important when the outgoing rabbi remains in the community as the emeritus of the congregation. After all, a person is only called a "successor" if he or she actually succeeds.

Ways of Entering

The first moments, and months, of a new rabbinate are crucial for the tones that are set and the impressions that are formed. It is a chance to build on the good feelings from the interview process—the courtship, as it were—and move into a "honeymoon" period in which the partners in a newly formed relationship begin to learn about, adjust to, and live together as a "couple." The marriage itself will be hard work, as all are, and begins in earnest after the first year; but if, in that first year, rabbis prepare well, they increase the chances of a healthy relationship with their new congregations. The primary task for that first year, as in any marriage, is for the partners to learn to *be* together.

In actually entering a new congregation, a rabbi has a significant window of opportunity for learning about the community and enabling the community to learn about itself. Beginning with the interview process itself, entry allows rabbis to develop a diagnosis of the congregation: how it functions, where it seems healthy or unhealthy, and where it needs to be strengthened. The primary tool by which rabbis develop diagnoses is the posing of questions. Rabbis need to ask a lot of questions, not simply in the interviewing process, but in the first months of their tenures. It is by asking questions in various forums, such as individual conversations, staff meetings, board and committee meetings, and social events, that rabbis can learn that which they need to know: Where are the splits in the congregation and what are they about? How do members think about the lay/professional partnership? What does change mean to the congregation based on how they have dealt with it in the past, and whose buy-in is crucial for change to succeed? What are members' hopes around what the new rabbi will and will not change? Where does there seem to be emotional residue left over from the previous rabbi-lay relationship?

When rabbis put themselves in the position of posing such questions and reflecting on what they hear, they are able to resist pressures, internal and external, to rush into fixing what might not be broken. They take their time. They help staff members identify the areas where they have worked well together and collaborated effectively, and where they have not. They do the same with board members, committees, and the steady volunteers. Rabbis can thus help others reflect and learn by looking anew at areas and perhaps seeing new possibilities in how they function together and what may have been getting in the way before. During this process, rabbis need to begin to develop their own support systems, to help them make sense of and interpret what they are hearing. This might well occur in the context of an independent transition management team that provides rabbis with the necessary support to look carefully at all areas of synagogue functioning. Such a team can be headed by a past president who has some authority and carries a great deal of prestige, one who is committed to the future of the synagogue, not just its past. An outside consultant can also serve in this role.

The entry period is also a time for rabbis to send clear signals about their own rabbinates. We mean this, in particular, on two dimensions. One dimension is the rabbi's vision of the congregation and of the Jewish people. The rabbi has the opportunity to signal what he or she will be as a *spiritual leader* of the congregation. The second dimension is how the rabbi plans to work with lay leaders and staff. A number of moments will present themselves as opportunities for the rabbi to signal what he or she will be like as an *organizational leader*. These are what we call leadership moments: events such as staff conflicts that offer clear choice points, requiring resolutions of one sort or another that show quite clearly how leaders think of themselves in relation to their followers. Rabbis are likely to face those moments early and will be watched keenly by others for how they handle them.

The entry period is, finally, an opportunity for rabbis to create foundations for healthy, effective working relationships in the synagogue. Rabbis need to clarify the roles, tasks, and boundaries of the rabbi(s), cantor, rabbi emeritus, board members, committees, and other staff. They need to create relationships with as many members as possible, particularly those in influence. They need to resist triangulation—by not entering into splits among staff or congregants, dividing their loyalties, or taking sides—that undermines their abilities to function as rabbi for the whole system. They need to keep from being seduced by flattery or guile into taking sides against previous rabbis. If new rabbis are able to move toward clarity and transparency and away from co-optation and intrigue as they go about constituting their new relationships, they lay strong foundations on which their rabbinates may be constructed.

Graceful Transitions

Graceful transitions enable rabbis and synagogues to join and to separate in ways that strengthen their capacities to be in relationship with one another or with other partners. We have suggested that there are both practical and emotional aspects to such transitions. The practical aspects focus on managing the specific tasks related to entering and leaving, and are relatively straightforward. The emotional aspects focus on enabling people to move away from blame or recrimination and toward reparation and understanding. These aspects are more difficult and, when mishandled, contribute to much of the failure of rabbinical transitions. Indeed, there is a great deal of failure. Congregations are often not able to move on and let go of past relationships and unconsciously sabotage successors. Rabbis get hurt, often leaving the rabbinate altogether. Leaders are blamed, often dropping out from positions of responsibility in the synagogue. Members are turned off, sometimes starting breakaway congregations and sometimes dropping out of synagogue life altogether. Rabbis are left sitting with leftover emotions from previous experiences.

Rabbis and congregational leaders both have responsibility to ensure that rabbinic transitions do not fail. We have suggested in this chapter that rabbis can help manage anxiety, their own and others, during and after transitions. They can do their best to be as transparent as possible about the transition process. They can do their best not to leave "messes" behind that might trap their successors. Mostly, they can do their best to hold on to the complicated experiences of transition—sadness and joy, relief and guilt, acceptance and frustration—and not simplify situations and people in ways that do them disservice. This enables others to hang on to complex understandings of transitions and move from blame toward acceptance.

Lay leaders, too, have certain responsibilities in ensuring the success of rabbinic transitions. They must get themselves to a place where they truly partner with rabbis. This process begins with figuring out what they need from a rabbi. Lay leaders ought to involve congregants in a process of clarifying the type of rabbi that best fits with the synagogue's traditions, values, and strategic needs. Leaders then manage the rabbinic search and selection process, making sure to include representatives from the different parts of the congregation, involving as many people as practical in the interview process. At the same time, lay leaders are managing the exit process of the current rabbi in ways, we hope, that allow for closure and gratitude and that honor the various emotions triggered by the transition process. Ideally, lay leaders develop and help others develop nuanced rather than simple understandings of why and how certain rabbinic transitions occur rather than, say, simply demonizing the previous rabbi or hailing as *mashiach* the incoming one.

Managing both the entry and exit processes simultaneously is a lot of work and often pulls people in different directions. People in the synagogue—staff, clergy, leaders, and congregants more generally—are likely to be made anxious by one or another part of transition processes. Anxiety often leads to conflict, as people look to blame others for making them have feelings they would rather not have. This is natural and should be expected. Lay leaders can help normalize this process, spreading the message that anxiety and conflict do not signify that mistakes were made but that congregations are going through significant transitions. Like rabbis, they can also use the entry process of a new rabbi to lay foundations for effective working relationships. And they can work closely with new rabbis to clarify effective lines of authority, decision making, and communication between lay leaders, clergy, and staff. The ability to keep these lines clear, to agree on where they begin and where they end, will be a major piece of the new rabbi's success or failure.

Graceful transitions, finally, depend on the willingness and capacity of both rabbis and lay leaders to try and learn about what makes for a healthy partnership, even as they separate from one another and move on to their next relationships. In this way, they can be very much like a Jewish document of divorce known as a *get,* blessing what was while allowing the future to unfold. Healthy transitions promote insight. They occur through people expressing honest emotions in ways that promote understanding and reparation. They flourish when people stay with, rather than rush through, transition events and experiences, trying to learn as much as they can about themselves and congregational life.

Note

1. Edwin Friedman, *Generation to Generation* (New York: The Guilford Press, 1985).

Part 4

Healthy Relationships

14

LEADERSHIP AND FOLLOWERSHIP IN THE SYNAGOGUE: THE LAY-PROFESSIONAL PARTNERSHIP

> Two men named Eldad and Medad remained in the camp,
> yet the spirit rested upon them and they started speaking words
> of prophecy. A young lad ran to tell Moses what was happen-
> ing, and Joshua spoke up and said, "My lord Moses, restrain
> them." But Moses responded, "Are you upset on my account?
> I wish that all God's people were prophets and that the Lord
> would put the spirit upon them!"
> (Numbers 11:26-30)

The Israelites became the Jewish people through their *brit* (covenant) with God. Our covenant is a binding agreement; it binds us to God and to the principles, practices, and constraints that the Holy One established as the foundation for the people of Israel. Indeed, our relationship with God is held fast by several covenants, each marked by a particular symbol. God's covenant with Noah is symbolized by a rainbow (Genesis 9:13); the covenant with Abraham is symbolized by circumcision (Genesis 17:10); and the covenant with the children of Israel is symbolized by our Sabbath (Exodus 31:13). The covenant is an agreement of mutuality, in which there is both give and get, privilege and blessing, obligation and responsibility. The covenant, as both idea and practice, has given and continues to give shape and meaning to the relationship between Jews and their God.

The covenant offers a model as well for the synagogue. The synagogue, as we have described earlier, is the modern version of the original tabernacle, the tent in which the Israelites gathered to create their relationship with God. The synagogue is the place in which our covenant with God is lived out, over and again; it is the place where we all gather, the men and women and children of Israel, those who have come before and those who will follow. It is the place where we congregate to interpret

God's laws and apply them to our modern daily existence. When we do so within the context of a covenant among ourselves, our struggles to live together as Jews are helped considerably. God created the covenant with the Israelites not simply as a means by which to keep them by His side, but also as a model for how they can be with one another.

In this chapter, we look closely at how the model of the covenant might be followed in our synagogues. Healthy synagogues are characterized by healthy relationships between and among congregants, lay leaders, clergy, and professional staff. We offer a blueprint for healthy partnerships between lay leaders and professional clergy and staff. Such partnerships hold great potential for the leading of synagogues.

The Minyan

Mordechai Starr is the rabbi of Beth Kehilah (House of the Community), a demographically declining and aging congregation but one that is still vibrant and quite active. Rabbi Starr has been there for five years. He is well liked and feels well taken care of by the membership in the shul. Though there are not many younger families like his own, his children are able to attend a local *yeshiva* where his wife teaches. Rabbi Starr loves his "little shul" and the people who are attached to it, but he is concerned. "These *minyanim* are killing me—no pun intended," he intoned recently to a colleague. "I get back from the funeral, which can be half a day, and I have fourteen calls and e-mails to return and a class to prepare for, and then I have to run out and do the *shivah* on top of that. And sometimes they are not even in the neighborhood. I miss dinner. Ruthie, who has been teaching all day, has to pick up all three kids, feed 'em, bathe 'em, and help 'em with their homework."

His friend suggested that the congregants help out.

"They know how to *daven*," said Rabbi Star, "but everybody really wants the rabbi to come to their house, no matter what they say. If I don't show, they are very disappointed."

His friend told him that the congregants would be more disappointed if their rabbi left them from exhaustion. Rabbi Starr knew his friend was right. But how should he approach his leaders? That was the question.

Several days later, the ritual committee meeting was proceeding without much fanfare. A report on *kashruth* was followed by an update on the proposed new *eruv* (the string or wire that creates the legal fiction of a wall) in the community. While not much progress had been made, negotiations were going quite well. Sam Jaffee asked if there was any new business, at which point, Avi Wise, a new member of the committee, said, "I had heard that there was a group of people who volunteer to lead *minyanim* at *shivah* houses. How does that work? Whenever I have paid a *shivah* call, it seems Rabbi Starr is always the *shaliach tzibur* (prayer leader)."

Sam responded that it was up to the rabbi.

Avi said that may be the problem. "This is a community *mitzvah*," he said, "and we all need to feel and take responsibility for this. If Rabbi Starr, who does a great job, is the one who has to decide, then he will always feel that he has to be the one to lead. It should be out of his hands so no one feels insulted if he can't make it."

Another member agreed, pointing out that they do call themselves "Beth Kehilah."

Lots of heads nodded in agreement. And eyes turned to Sam. He told them that he would call Irv Kerschen, the board president. He was concerned about how to approach Rabbi Starr without threatening him or making him feel unappreciated. He and Irv decided to meet with Rabbi Starr. The meeting took place the following week in the Rabbi's study. After assuring him of their respect and admiration for what he was doing for the congregation, Sam related to him the feeling that the ritual committee felt somewhat disenfranchised from the *shivah minyanim*. They felt a partnership had been created but was not being actualized.

Rabbi Starr thanked them for their concern, expressing his feeling that, though it was becoming a great burden on him, congregants wanted him and him alone to lead these *minyanim*.

They decided to put together a small task force to deal with this problem, which would report to the board in three months' time. The task force included some members of the ritual committee and the board, as well as some members at large. After meeting bimonthly for three months, the task force came up with a recommendation for which they would seek board approval. They proposed to create a new group called the "minyanaires" who would be responsible for all *minyanim* after the first day of *shivah*. Rabbi Starr would always endeavor to lead the first *minyan* unless he was out of town. The rabbi would train the minyanaires, enabling them to be well versed in the synagogue's *minhagim* (customs) and *nusach* (melodies). Anyone who was familiar with the *davenning* and had a "pleasant voice" could apply to be a *minyanaire.* All scheduling of the *minyanim* would be handled by the rabbi's secretary.

The proposal was presented to the board for its approval. Some members worried that congregants would miss not having the rabbi there. Others were concerned that the rabbi would lead the *minyanim* at the "important people's homes," but they were assured that the recommendation would be followed without exception. Ida Simkovic, a veteran member of the board, voiced her concerns, saying, "No one in the congregation knows about this. I think they need time to digest such a big change, not just have an announcement that this is the new way *minyanim* are being run." Sam Jaffee agreed. It was decided to hold two town hall meetings, one during the day and one at night, to enable the task force to share its proposal with everyone in the congregation. The board decided to hold off the vote until after the town hall meetings.

While similar concerns were heard at the town hall meetings, there were no serious objections to the proposal as long as the policy was the same for everyone. Congregants seemed to understand that their rabbi was working as hard as he could, and with no *chazan,* they could not expect him to be everywhere all the time. The task force brought these results back to the board, and the proposal was approved without dissent.

Our case illustrates a respectful working relationship between clergy and lay leaders, built on a foundation of mutual interest. Each person has valid concerns; each worries a bit about how others will react to what could potentially be difficult conversations. Rabbi Starr struggles with the personal costs of the demands that he experiences from his congregants and those he places on himself. The ritual committee struggles with the extent to which congregants ought to be empowered to minister to one another. The committee authorizes its leader to engage the issue with the rabbi, in concert with the synagogue president. They and the rabbi agree that there ought to be a way to satisfy everyone's interests. They create a group whose members agree on the need to balance competing demands, and then create a thoughtful proposal that requires a partnership between the rabbi and congregants. The lay leaders and the congregation accept the proposal after assurances that the new *minyan* process will adhere to principles of fairness and equity.

Implicit in this story is the assumption that lay leaders and clergy need one another. Neither the rabbi nor the lay leaders act as if their needs outweigh those of the other. Each side understands that unless all parties are satisfied, the synagogue as a whole will suffer. This understanding is crucial to a healthy partnership between lay leaders and professional staff. It guarantees that as they solve problems, they will keep foremost in mind what they share, rather than the places where they differ. It guarantees that they will not create casualties as they go about their leadership tasks. And it guarantees that they will continue to create covenants that serve, ultimately, to bind them together as surely as their covenant with God binds them to Judaism.

In the following sections of this chapter, we examine particular dimensions of the covenant that, ideally, lay leaders and professional staff live out in their relations with one another. These dimensions include clarity of tasks, roles, and boundaries; effective working relationships between rabbis and board presidents; board development processes; and the processes by which healthy partnerships occur. Each of these dimensions is crucial to how leadership ought to occur in the context of synagogues.

Tasks, Roles and Boundaries

Productive relationships in any organization are created through clarity about people's tasks (what pieces of work they are supposed to do), roles (formal expectations of what they and others do in relation with one another), and boundaries (demarcations between people's areas of work and responsibility). In synagogues, such clarity is necessary to enable lay leaders and professional staff to collaborate on behalf of shared missions; both lay leaders and staff need to know how they are both differentiated (what they each do apart from the other) and integrated (the places where they collaborate). They must understand who is responsible for what, who consults with one another about what, and how they are connected in terms of hierarchy and supervision. Absent such shared understandings, people collide with one another, are confused about who is supposed to do what, intrude upon one another's areas of responsibility and authority, and find themselves caught in various conflicts. In this section, we describe the tasks, roles, and boundaries relevant to synagogue leadership.

Lay Leadership

Lay leadership most directly occurs in the form of boards of directors, representative groups that act on behalf of congregations and in turn authorize various committees to do a variety of tasks. Board members are most often chairs of synagogue committees, though a synagogue could have any number of committee chairs that do not sit on the board. The primary role of the board is to make policy and provide financial stewardship for the synagogue. The board of directors sanctions the governance of the synagogue. Tasks often include legal oversight, hiring and firing of key staff, selection and election of leadership, policy formation, resource development, creation and oversight of an annual budget, evaluation procedures, board recruitment, human resource development, planning, and program development. The particular board structure varies according to the size of the board. Larger boards typically authorize executive boards, consisting of synagogue officers, to develop proposals for consideration by the larger board.

Lay leaders thus govern. Governing is different than managing; in the context of the synagogue, the former requires a democratic process, while the latter requires a process of executive decision making. The lay leadership operates within a context of democracy whereby individuals are elected to represent the congregation more generally, and if they cannot do so effectively, may lose the right to do so. Boards thus authorize individuals—the board president, executive director, and rabbi—to make management-related decisions on their behalf while retaining oversight capability. This is the ideal. There are, of course, synagogue board members who are involved in the management of the shul. This may occur as lay leaders work so closely with program staff on a committee that they edge into management, are drawn to "do something" rather than just make policy, have to pitch in because the synagogue is too small to hire professionals, or simply feel more entitled because they do so much—pray, celebrate, study—at their synagogues and have a sense of ownership over how they function. Such dynamics need to be carefully monitored and controlled lest the lay volunteers wind up managing the synagogue.

An effective board structure is one in which synagogue officers are seen as the "staff" of the president. The board president, acting in concert with the rabbi, sets the overall direction for the synagogue in terms of what programs and projects will best serve the mission of the institution. Synagogue officers, such as vice presidents, treasurers, recording and corresponding secretaries, and the like, work with committee chairs to ensure that their work supports rather than conflicts with the overall direction. Committees are a key component of the board structure. Each committee oversees a certain dimension of the synagogue; each year the committee sets goals in the context of dialogue among the committee chair, the vice president assigned to that committee, and the staff person whose job falls under the committee's purview. "Staffing" these committees with volunteers is a major part of the board's function. Vice presidents provide support and oversight for the committee chairs and report to the president in relation to the progress of the committees and leadership of committee chairs. In smaller synagogues, in which there are no officers, committee chairs report directly to the president.

The board president is responsible for the healthy functioning of the committees, making certain the financial resources are available to carry out the work of the synagogue and creating effective relationships with clergy. Board presidents are most effective when they meet regularly with rabbis to review the progress of committees and staff in light of overall goals they set together for the synagogue each year. When there is an executive director, he or she may also meet with the rabbi and president. The board president also asks each chair to evaluate committee members to help provide the basis for future service on the board. Board presidents also run board meetings (and may be assisted by a parliamentarian or the synagogue's counsel, using Robert's Rules of Order to govern discussions and disagreements). The purposes of board meetings are to review the financial status of the synagogue; discuss, make, or amend policy decisions/bylaws; and hear reports and updates of various committees. Most boards include some learning of Jewish values, discussion of communal issues, and a personal sharing of synagogue and/or life experiences such as *simchas* and family milestones. Board meetings are attended by all board members, officers, past presidents, the rabbi, the executive director, and staff members who may be making a presentation and are open to any member of the synagogue in good standing.

Rabbinic Leadership

The primary role of the rabbi, and the clergy more generally, is to set and carry out religious policies and procedures. This is a significant role, of course; the synagogue exists as a religious institution, and many of the decisions that typically shape organizational life must, in the context of the synagogue, include a religious component. The rabbi is thus involved in many aspects of the synagogue and quite reasonably may be consulted on any number of issues that emerge from the board and its various committees. More generally, the rabbi is, or ought to be, a significant force in developing and articulating the overarching vision for the synagogue, as we described more fully in chapter 10. It is the vision that sustains synagogue leaders as they go about the sometimes difficult work of maintaining a vibrant religious institution in a secular world.

The daily work of the rabbi is as the chief spiritual officer of the synagogue. In practice, this means providing counseling, teaching, leadership of worship services, and officiating at life-cycle events. Rabbis have led in such ways for two thousand years. Their leadership is derived from their abilities to help congregants, singly or in groups, learn to apply the teachings of the Torah to their lives. The authority of the rabbi thus derives from his or her teachings of the Jewish tradition and faith. Rabbis are trained to use such authority through their seminary, yeshiva, or rabbinic school studies. They use that authority not simply with congregants, but also in the context of providing Jewish and *halachic* (accepted legal rulings) guidance to staff and lay leaders. Such authority extends elsewhere as well. The rabbi represents the congregation to the community in the context of community events, local and national programs and projects, and as a spokesperson on behalf of Jewish institutions.

The rabbi is also usually the senior leader/manager of staff members who work at the synagogue. Staff members—educators, administrators, and the like—carry out the mission and policies of the board in the context of daily operations. Staff members are typically assigned to committees to do work on behalf of those committees and serve as liaisons with the rabbi and other clergy. Within the staff, each person will have his or her job description and is supervised and evaluated by the rabbi and/or the executive director. The rabbi is, more often than not, relatively untrained in the ways of organizational management and leadership. He or she thus develops, over time and with a great deal of trial and error, ways of supervising, coaching, directing, and supporting individuals and staff groups that may be more or less effective in different contexts. Ideally, of course, the rabbi becomes a student, in one fashion or another, of leadership, through training programs, appropriate lay leaders who offer guidance and models, or a self-directed program of study and reflection.

Boundaries between Professional Staff and Lay Leaders

The lay leaders (who set policy and provide financial stewardship) and the professional staff (who manage daily operations) form separate systems, each with its own tasks to perform and issues that arise in the context of those tasks. The separation is, in some ways, observable: the professional staff works at the synagogue and maintains relatively stable work hours, while the lay leaders are at the synagogue here and there for meetings, often at night and on Sundays. The separation is useful. It enables each part of the larger system to do its own work. It differentiates the groups, enabling them to create their own identity with which their members connect. The professional staff works on their own areas of responsibility, coordinating with one another in the process of implementing programs and services. The lay leaders meet, in committees or as boards, to review policies, procedures, and the progress of synagogue activities. Hopefully, there is enough separation between the two to enable each to work with its own challenges without being caught up in the challenges of the other.

Boundaries not only maintain separation, they enable certain connections. Effective relationships between lay leaders and professional staff are marked by boundaries that are permeable enough to allow for sharing information and ideas. For this to work well, there needs to be a fair amount of contact between the two groups such that each knows what the other is doing and can find ways to be useful to rather than redundant or contradictory with one another. Integration is key to the healthy workings of synagogue leadership. When lay leaders and professional staff are stepping into one another's areas of work or influence, working at cross-purposes, or simply out of touch with what the other is doing, the synagogue can quite easily come into disarray. Projects do not get done when they fall through the cracks or when people become paralyzed by not knowing who is doing what and who is in charge of any particular aspect. The boundaries between the lay leadership and the professional staff must constantly be patrolled, not simply to keep people out of areas not their own, but to make sure that there is a constant exchange of information.

Ideally, then, boundaries are strong enough to enable people to identify with their particular areas and flexible enough to enable people to connect with one another and identify with the synagogue as a whole. This sounds difficult, and it is. We have seen a fair number of synagogues in which this difficult balance was not maintained, with uniformly poor results for all involved. In some synagogues the separation is too pronounced. The lay leaders work with policies and missions that have little to do with what the professional staff is actually doing, or the professional staff is working on programs and services that seem disconnected from the interests of the congregation as represented by the board. In other synagogues, the two groups are so tightly interconnected that neither is able to separate from and work independent of the other. The lay leaders hover over the professional staff, micromanaging them rather than letting them do their work; or the professional staff micromanage the lay leaders, pressing them toward some directions and away from others in ways that inappropriately influence synagogue missions. When these boundaries are too tight or too loose, the synagogue has a diminished capacity for leadership.

Boundaries are also most useful when, like roles and tasks, they are clarified and widely understood. A reasonable path toward such clarity is the organizational chart that seeks to clarify rather than mystify. Organizational charts offer efficient ways to track the relations between roles.

They identify the authority relationships by which the synagogue operates and allow people to have shared understanding of the locus of decision making and supervision. Useful charts make transparent potentially difficult questions of who has authority over whom, where the decision-making power lies, and who is supervising whom. An organizational chart should be relatively simple, with single lines of authority connecting people to one another. When people report to multiple supervisors, they have the experience of fragmentation, which is offset only to the extent that those different supervisors communicate often and well. While there is often a great deal of flexibility in synagogues, in contrast to a corporate setting, the clarity that comes from simple organizational charts is often quite welcome to staff and lay leaders alike.

The Rabbi–Board President Relationship

The relationship between the rabbi and the board president greatly determines the nature of the relationship between the two groups—professional staff and lay leaders—that they represent, respectively, in the synagogue. When their relationship is strong, the staff–lay leader relationship generally is strong. They provide an effective bridge between the two groups, enabling communication that is reasonably clear and forthright. This does not mean they always have to agree; as committed Jews, they may differ from time to time. It is essential, however, that such differences are carried out privately, with respect for one another and without personal recrimination. Unless they have agreed to represent opposing views, the board president publicly supports the rabbi's vision for the synagogue as a Jewish institution, and the rabbi shares the president's vision of governance. They each interpret the other to his or her constituency and explain to members of their own groups the perspective of the other leader. Under such conditions, it is far more likely that the professional staff and lay leaders will remain focused on what it is they are doing together rather than on the various differences and splits between them.

The effectiveness and health of the relationship between rabbi and board president is closely related to the extent to which their particular roles, responsibilities, and authority are clear and transparent. To avoid confusion, redundancy, and ambiguity, the authority of the rabbi in relation to the staff, to policy decisions, and to program decisions needs to be clear. This means, for example, clarifying the conditions under which the rabbi decides or consults or collaborates on decisions, or the extent to which the rabbi has the power to hire, fire, and supervise staff. Various synagogues will answer these questions in different ways; and indeed, different board presidents may have different understandings of these issues even within the same synagogue. What is important is that the answers are clear and that the rabbi and board president both know what they are.

The partnership between the board president and rabbi is made more complicated by the inevitable fact that there is a power imbalance between the two. The rabbi is an employee of the synagogue, serving at the discretion of the board of directors, as the authorized representatives of the congregation. Absent a lifetime contract, the rabbi remains relatively vulnerable in terms of job security, which serves as the backdrop against which relationships with lay leaders and board presidents are created. The board president is key to managing tensions in the employee-employer relationship with rabbis that often occur when rabbis are dealing with issues involving contracts, evaluations, compensation, and workload. While the rabbi as employee should mostly be in the background—with the roles of spiritual leader, teacher, pastor, and preacher in the foreground—this often shifts during contract time. Hopefully, the board president helps ease this process and enables the synagogue and the rabbi to move through these periods as quickly and smoothly as possible.

The board president can also play a significant role in the rabbi's evaluative process by framing it as an opportunity for mutual reflection on their relationship and on the synagogue more generally. This allows for learning, not just evaluation. It also minimizes the power imbalance; rather than simply treating the rabbi as an employee that needs to be evaluated, the board focuses on the rabbi as a partner who helps lead the congregation toward its stated mission and goals. The president largely sets the tone for this type of process, and ensures that it is not tied to contract renewals. This is not a simple matter. Boards and their presidents are often pulled, by themselves and by dissatisfied congregants, to blame their rabbis for much that is seemingly wrong in the synagogue. Framing the rabbi's evaluation as a reflection on the synagogue leadership more generally is, in many synagogues, an act of courage and fortitude. This is particularly the case when rabbis have received projections of godlike authority from the congregation, lay leaders, and the board president. This makes the contracting and evaluative process more difficult psychologically and may lead to acting out by all parties.

We also wish to point out that the relationship between the rabbi and the board president both shapes and is shaped by the relation between the synagogue groups that they represent. The rabbi-president relationship exists at the core of the relationship between the staff and lay leaders. As such, that relationship may be influenced by what occurs between those two groups more generally. Consider, for example, a synagogue in which the education director, a professional staff member, and the chair of the education committee, a lay leader, are at odds with one another. Each disagrees with the other's philosophy of religious education to the point of personal animosity. Each complains constantly of the other; the director complains to the rabbi, the committee chair to the board president. The relationship between the rabbi and the president is now contaminated, if you will, by that between their constituents. It may work in the opposite direction as well. What happens in the rabbi-president relationship may reverberate through the rest of the synagogue. Consider, for example, a synagogue in which the rabbi and president are at odds with one another, the result of a miscommunication that damaged their personal relationship. Their subsequent inability to speak clearly and directly with one another gets picked up and mirrored by the staff and lay leaders whose relationships become similarly disturbed.

Great potential lies within the rabbi-president relationship. There is the potential to connect a synagogue's mission with the vision of how to make it come true in the world. There is the potential to bridge the interests of the professional staff and the lay leaders. There is the potential to model a certain partnership that may be emulated in other parts of the synagogue, on committees, task forces, and programming groups. Tapping this potential is a matter of hard work—the kind that builds relationships. Rabbis and board presidents need to invest time and effort in clarifying their relationship and examining how they are working together. They develop trust in one another, make transparent the implicit rules by which their relationship functions, and make conscious choices about those rules. This process is complicated, of course, by the fact that new presidents cycle into their leadership roles; with each transition the rabbi must develop a new partnership. It is crucial that they do so. The relationship between the rabbi and president is like the pebble dropped into a still pond, sending out ripples upon ripples in ways that cannot be fully predicted but have a great deal of impact—seen and unseen.

Board Development

The partnership between lay leaders and professional staff is forged, in part, through a board development process that prepares board members to assume their roles. Board development is not simply a process of "leadership development," although it is often framed that way. We take a more encompassing view. Board development involves creating effective structures and processes, as well as expanding members' capacities for leadership. This process entails the following six steps.

1. **Identifying potential board members.** Board membership regularly changes, as lay leaders cycle on and off committees and the board more generally. Potential new members need to be identified; this process often begins when people join the synagogue and some type of intake is provided to ascertain their interests, abilities, skills, talents, and past leadership experiences. Current board members and professional staff may also be good sources for new leaders, based on their programming experiences in the synagogue.

2. **Entry and exit processes.** The entry process for new board members must include an introduction to the purposes of the board, its mission, its ways of operating, and its current agenda. New members usually participate on committees in order to get involved in particular areas of the synagogue; this offers one type of training ground for future leadership. Board members who are successful also need to be cultivated as potential officers. The exit process ought to include acknowledgment of service and appropriate blessing for members who have served in various board capacities.

3. **Role clarifications.** Board development includes a sustained focus on the exact nature of what the role of the board is, generally, as well as on the roles of president, vice presidents, particular committees, and their chairs. The clarification process—of who does what, with what decision-making authority, and in consultation or collaboration with whom among both lay and profes-

sional leaders—is a crucial part of developing an effective board. Too often we see boards flounder because it is not quite clear who is responsible for what. Indeed, it is not simply new members who need an orientation that includes a description of the proper and healthy function of volunteer boards.

4. **Committee development.** Board development cannot be separated from the development of committees as effective, functioning groups. This involves identifying the specific tasks of each committee and how its goals and objectives fit with and serve the mission and vision of the board as a whole. Committees must be both differentiated, that is, focused on specific tasks that differ from those of other committees, and integrated, that is, explicitly connected with the work of the other committees and the board more generally. The board president, working with committee chairs and other synagogue officers, is responsible for the committee development process. This includes giving each committee a "charge" based on the synagogue's vision and accepted budget, and ensuring that each committee creates a plan of action for the upcoming year with specific, measurable, and stated objectives.

5. **Skills development.** Board members develop their leadership skills in the context of getting support from others as they go about working on their assignments. Synagogues should provide mentors for new board members, as well as orientation, training, support, and evaluation. This is not, of course, a simple process, in that volunteers may not appreciate being provided with feedback. Again, it is the board president who needs to set the tone for and model the process by which board members give and receive feedback and support within the context of continuous learning.

6. **Reflective capabilities.** Committees and boards best develop as effective units when they are able to reflect on their work, in terms of both outcomes ("How well are we doing, relative to our goals?") and processes ("How effectively are we working together?"). Reflection enables people to examine the choices they have made about how to work together and provides the opportunity to make different choices.

This board development process requires real leadership on the part of the board president and other synagogue officers. We mean by this some very specific behaviors, for leading in the context of a volunteer organization like a synagogue board can be a tricky business. The leader needs to be very clear about the synagogue mission—what the synagogue stands for—and how that mission translates into its vision of certain programs, services, projects, and initiatives. The leader needs to ensure that the work of other board members, and in particular the committee chairs, are aligned with that mission and with one another. The leader must work hard to clarify roles, tasks, and boundaries among and between different officers and committee chairs, and to ensure that there are mechanisms by which board members are communicating with one another and with relevant staff members. The leader needs as well to ensure that board and committee members are receiving the feedback necessary to reinforce desired behaviors and correct those that are less desirable.

The tricky part is that the board president must do all of this in the context of working with peers—other members of the synagogue who have agreed to volunteer their time and energies—over which he or she has limited authority. In theory, when people sign up to participate on the board, they are accepting the authority of the board president to direct their efforts. In practice, however, synagogue leaders must use a fair amount of persuasion to get others to work effectively within the board context. With little recourse to the sanctions that are more typical of organizational life—financial incentives, job changes, and the like—board presidents and other leaders must build relationships by appealing to others' interests and incorporating their ideas, all the while steering them toward the stated goals. They must also strive to create cultures of openness and transparency, which allow people to communicate directly and to learn from one another on behalf of their collective efforts. This, too, may be tricky, as leaders strive to engage in potentially difficult conversations with peers. We find that when board leaders care deeply about the synagogue mission and are clear about how that mission is to be played out, they allow themselves to assume their roles in ways that honor both the mission and its realization.

Key Dimensions of Healthy Partnerships

At the core of healthy partnerships between lay leaders, clergy, and staff is a set of processes that characterize their attitudes and behaviors in relation with one another. These processes show up in daily interactions—in how people treat and work with one another, how they approach one another, how they react to one another. With enough repetition, these processes become ingrained, to the point that people become accustomed to working with one another in useful, healthy ways; indeed, with enough repetition, synagogues form cultures that sanction such processes as normal, as expected, as simply the way things ought to be done. We briefly describe six interrelated types of healthy processes here.

Transparency. In keeping with our focus on transparency and clarity throughout this and other chapters, we believe that the foundation of a healthy partnership is a clearly shared understanding of how the partnership itself operates. Lay leaders and professional staff each need to understand where authority for particular decisions is located and, as noted earlier, the nature of their own and others' tasks and roles and how they relate to their shared mission. Such transparency in turn enables people to be consistent and reliable with one another.

Openness. People being open to one another is a mark of healthy partnerships. Openness, in this context, means people considering others as potential helpmates, as potential partners, rather than as people who are unable to contribute or to partner. Lay leaders and professional staff work with one another far more effectively when they have mutual respect and believe that the other can make real contributions. Certain conditions make those contributions likely: a sense of humility (others may know things that we do not), benefit of the doubt (others have good intentions), trust (others have our interests at heart), and appropriate boundaries (others maintain confidences and communicate directly and honestly).

Support. Supportive relationships involve a mixture of different elements. People are, first and foremost, available to and for one another: they make time to talk, they listen well, they remain with rather than avoid or rush one another, they challenge one another respectfully, and they can show one another warmth. They also come to an understanding and appreciation of one another; staff members appreciate the time and energy put in by lay leaders who in turn appreciate the dedication of the professional staff. Support also comes in the form of offering salient information, feedback, insights, and interpretations that enable others to reflect on and make sense of situations that they find confusing or troubling. Lay leaders and professional staff can help one another a great deal simply by sitting with and trying to help one another understand situations and potential courses of action. They can also help protect each other as the various politics of the synagogue swirl around them and threaten to destabilize their work and their relationships.

Managing Differences. Healthy partnerships are marked by differences—in perspectives, agendas, ideas, beliefs, and experiences. Ideally, those differences are worked with rather than suppressed or denied. Managing differences well means engaging them directly. Lay leaders and professional staff identify the places where they agree and those where they disagree, and then explore the issues in light of their shared interests and goals. Resolving differences is foremost a matter of getting agreement on the primary objective of any particular program or project, the criteria by which progress on that objective will be determined, and then, finally, the ways in which that objective will be pursued. This last issue is most often the sticking point: *How will we go about getting this thing done?* People who navigate those places well focus on as much objective data as they can in resolving their differences. They do so without creating casualties.

Productivity. Healthy relationships are productive: people get things done in partnership with one another. Lay leaders and professional staff create effective relationships when they focus on the tasks before them. They divide the labor, based on a shared understanding of what they need to do and how they need to work, together and separately. They collaborate effectively, sharing information and attacking problems early and often. They create achievable objectives that are neither so difficult that they are unattainable nor so simple that they pose little challenge or satisfaction. They go after and celebrate their successes. And they enjoy the process of working with one another. Productive partnerships occur in the context of a culture of ongoing regard, in which each individual is celebrated as *b'tzelem Elohim* (an image of God) doing God's work in this world.

Capacity for Learning. Partnerships remain strong and healthy when those involved within them keep learning. In this regard, we mean various kinds of learning. People need to learn the various things that enable them to make real contributions. Lay leaders must keep learning about the synagogue, its members, and one another to continue to run effective committees and create thoughtful board policies. Professional staff must keep learning about their areas of expertise, about the interests of the congregants, and about the effectiveness of their work to keep improving upon their programs. People also need to learn about their partnerships, and discover (and discover again) what is working well and not so well and how their work with others might be improved upon. Last, but certainly not least, all of us need to learn *torah lishmah* (study for its own sake, without hope for reward) to deepen our sense of who we are as Jews and about the tradition that sustains us on our individual journeys. It is this capacity for learning—for reflection, dialogue, and absorption of lessons—that enables partnerships to be resilient, that is, to change and growth in the face of the inevitable peaks and valleys of their evolution.

And God Be with You

> And Moses's father-in-law said to him, "It is not good this thing you are doing; you will surely wear yourself out and these people as well. Now listen to me. I will give you counsel and God be with you! You represent the people before God. You bring the disputes before the Lord, and enjoin upon them the laws and the teachings, making known to them the way they are to go and the practices they are to follow. You shall then seek out from among all the people capable, God-fearing men who are trustworthy, spurning ill-gotten gains. Set these over them as chiefs of thousands, hundreds, fifties, and let them judge the people at all times. . . . And Moses heeded his father-in-law and did just as he said. (Exodus 18:17-24)

Jethro, Moses's father-in-law, had several concerns. He feared that his son-in-law would take on too much work for any one person. He was also concerned that the people would not get their needs met, at least not in a timely fashion, if everything had to go through this one man. Further, he understood that there needed to be a division of labor so that the totality of the needs of the people could be met. We, too, are concerned with these issues. And other than the way in which the lay leaders came to power—Moses appointed them—we see in this Torah text a precursor for our own synagogues.

Rabbis need lay leaders, just as the congregation and its leaders need rabbis. The rabbis bring the laws and teachings of God into the synagogue; the lay leaders act as chiefs, directing energies and resources and making judgments that are in the service of the congregation. It is only through that partnership that the synagogue can remain strong and vibrant. We have offered here various components of a model for what that partnership might look like. We understand that this model is difficult to follow. It requires a great deal of patience, as professional staff and lay leaders struggle to work with one another in situations that may be difficult and trying. It requires a great deal of learning and growth, as people strive to take appropriate responsibility, maturing into their roles. And it requires us to understand that God is with us as we go about creating modern tabernacles that celebrate our religion and protect it as a way of life.

15

THE DISTURBANCES OF
LAY-PROFESSIONAL PARTNERSHIPS

Jerusalem was destroyed because the people despised their rabbis.
(Talmud, Shabbat, 119b)

The rabbis offer a number of reasons to explain the destruction of Jerusalem in their Talmudic commentary on the Sabbath. Jerusalem was destroyed, they wrote, "because the Jews violated Shabbat, neglected to say the *Sh'ma* morning and evening, did not send their children to *cheder* (school), had no shame, did not rebuke each other when rebuke was called for, and ridiculed their scholars and rabbis." The list suggests a community in disrepair, so much that God allowed its centerpiece—Jerusalem, the Temple itself—to be destroyed. The community existed in name only, its children in the streets, its people shameless, turning away from one another, from their rabbis, from Judaism. The destruction of the temple was simply the physical manifestation of a disturbance that had—like a subterranean shifting of the geophysical plates that join the earth—already occurred in the community.

The destruction of Jerusalem was cataclysmic, of course, on the order of the plagues in Egypt, the flood in Noah's time, or Sodom and Gomorrah. Our Torah is replete with moments when God destroys those who turn away and protects those who hold fast to the covenant. The God who demands loyalty and brings judgment does so when a community is so deeply disturbed that it cannot right itself. Destruction of such biblical proportions is, presumably, ancient history. Yet our modern synagogues can still get disturbed in ways that are far-reaching and matter a great deal to congregational life.

In this chapter, we focus on the primary way in which such disturbances are manifested: the relationship between clergy (and other professional staff) and lay leaders. While this relationship rarely, we hope, devolves into one side despising the other, it all too often goes awry in some fashion that undermines people and their attempts to work together. With the best of intentions, people struggle on behalf of ideas and principles that they believe are right. Those struggles may be waged well, or not. When they are not, people turn away from one another in significant ways; it is this turning away that leads to disturbed systems. The disturbances present themselves in various ways, according to particular synagogues and their cultures, leaders, and histories. Inevitably, they make it more difficult for synagogue leaders, clergy, staff, and congregants to struggle well together in creating and inhabiting their synagogues. In this chapter, we examine particular forms of disturbances that are readily familiar.

Outrageous, Part 1

Rabbi Susan Klein sighed. It was going to be another long day. It was still early in the morning, and already her e-mail inbox was full. She had gotten used to this. She was entering her fifth year as the senior rabbi of Temple Ohev Shalom, a 900-plus member Reform synagogue, and she had deliberately set out from the beginning to make herself accessible to congregants. She received an endless number of e-mails per day and tried her best to answer them when she was not caught up in some crisis or the usual allotment of meetings. That was fine. She let out a sigh as she scrolled down the list of incoming messages and noticed that several were flagged "Urgent" from Debbie Scott, vice president of youth at the temple. This was not a new experience. Debbie often thought that much of what she needed to communicate was urgent. This was one of the complaints of the previous assistant rabbi; she felt that she was being micromanaged by Debbie. The previous board president had spoken to Debbie about that, and she had backed off, to the point that she had not even met the new advisor, which Susan found a bit odd.

Susan opened the messages from Debbie. The first one was from 8:00 the night before. The subject line was "Outrageous." The e-mail read:

> Hi Rabbi. I wanted to let you know something that I found
> very disturbing. I was driving carpool this afternoon, taking

my teenage daughter and some of her friends home, when I overheard them talking about Sam Tarloff, the new youth group advisor. It seems that he left the youth group alone last night for forty-five minutes. That is outrageous and completely unacceptable. As you can imagine, I was mortified when I heard this. He may be endangering our kids. Call me.

Susan rubbed her forehead. She saw another message down the list from Debbie and knew that this was going to get worse. She thought about going to get some coffee in order to delay the inevitable but decided instead to just get it over with. The subject line of Debbie's second e-mail—this one from late last night—was "Tarloff."

I did some checking since my last e-mail to you, calling some of the parents of the youth group. It seems that this is not the first time Tarloff has slipped up. I heard a few stories about kids showing up to events and him not being prepared, in terms of what they were going to do or even having food for them for events that were supposed to include dinner. He is also chronically late to the meetings. I know that Rabbi Stone, as the assistant rabbi, is supposed to be supervising the youth group advisor. Is he doing that? Let's try and find out what's going on here. Let's talk soon.

Susan went to speak with the assistant rabbi, Eric Stone. He was on the phone in his office but motioned her in while he finished up the call. Susan then brought him up to speed, summarizing Debbie's e-mails. Eric was surprised that Sam Tarloff was the issue. Throughout the year, he had been meeting pretty regularly with Sam, helping him plan events and learn more about the advising role. He found Sam to be young but thoughtful and clearly committed to helping the temple youth stay engaged with the congregation after their *b'nai mitzvah*. Sam had a lot of energy for the kids and was particularly invested in getting them involved in social action activities around the community. He knew that Sam was not getting much support from the rest of the staff, who were busy with their own programs. He promised Susan that he would call Sam and find out what happened the other night and get back to her as soon as he could.

Several hours later, Eric came to her office and told her that he had had a long conversation with Sam. It turned out that Sam had indeed left the youth group for a half hour or so during the program a few nights earlier. It seems that the youth committee had forgotten to supply dinner for the program and that Sam had taken it upon himself to go out and, with his own money, quickly buy dinner for the group. He had given the group a fun project to do—they created a game of Hanukkah Jeopardy for the younger Hebrew school students—and left a responsible high school senior in charge. He told Eric that there was no one else in the building to help out and that he wanted the kids to have food as they had been promised. He had not liked doing it but didn't think he had any choice because he couldn't think of anyone on the youth committee to call.

Eric said that Sam also told him that sometimes he felt as if he were doing this whole thing by himself. He really liked the temple youth and had lots of plans for new activities for the group, particularly in community social action, but did not feel much support from the congregation. The youth committee was largely absent, the education director and many of the teachers did not respond to his attempts to integrate the youth group with what they were doing, and the kids did not see the rabbis and cantor as much as they hoped to. Sam wondered if he was doing something wrong.

As Susan listened to Eric, she wondered where, exactly, the youth committee was in all of this and why she did not know about the problem sooner. The board had created the youth committee seven years earlier, just prior to Rabbi Klein's tenure, in response to a request from several congregants whose teenagers were involved in the youth group. When it was formed, the youth committee was charged with the responsibility of creating mechanisms that would help keep the congregants' children engaged with the temple after they became bar/bat mitzvah. Initially, the committee did not have to do much since the assistant rabbi at the time was very involved with the youth group and created a devoted following of high school students. She left and was replaced by Rabbi Stone, whose interests were elsewhere. The clergy proposed to the board that they create the role of youth group advisor, into which Sam Tarloff was then hired. It was not clear what the relationship between Sam and the youth committee was at this point. From what Rabbi Stone said, it seemed as though there wasn't much of any relationship at all. Nor was there any integration of the youth program agenda with that of the education department, which had recently developed its own mission statement.

Susan went back to her office to work on a sermon. A few minutes later Debbie Scott walked unannounced into the office. Susan looked up in mild annoyance but welcomed Debbie and invited her to have a seat. Susan was not looking forward to this meeting, but she figured it was better to get it over with.

Debbie started right in. "Have you talked to the Tarloff boy yet?"

"No," Susan replied. "I wanted to gather more information first. But Rabbi Stone has spoken with him about what happened the other night and let me know what he found out."

Debbie smiled slightly. "Great. So what help do you need from me in getting rid of him? I'd be happy to write a letter of some sort to put in his file to make this go more smoothly."

"From what I can tell," Susan said slowly, "there is no need to fire Sam. From all reports, he's doing a good job with the youth group. The kids like him, and they're getting involved in some interesting projects. Rabbi Stone tells me that Sam left the group alone for a half hour or so because the dinner that the youth committee had organized never showed up—it turns out that no one had made arrangements for it—and that Sam went out and got the dinner. He even paid for it himself. The group did a project during that time, and an older girl watched out for everyone."

Debbie grimaced. "I figured Rabbi Stone would cover for him. It's not entirely clear to me that he has been giving Tarloff much supervision. I brought up an issue with him in the fall, and he didn't seem to do anything about it. What's going on here? Who's supervising him? What are you doing about it, Rabbi?"

More calmly than she felt, Susan responded. "I don't believe that the issue here is Rabbi Stone's supervision, or for that matter, Sam's leaving the youth group for a few minutes, as regrettable as that is. Perhaps we need to look at the extent to which the youth committee, and the board more generally, is supporting the youth group. The committee dropped the ball with the dinner arrangements, which left Sam out on a limb. I worry that is a pattern, in terms of the committee's support. What can we do about that?"

Disturbance #1: One Hand Clapping

Embedded within this case is a familiar issue in synagogue life: the lack of shared ownership of a program, project, or mission. In the case study, one group—the staff, particularly the youth advisor—is pursuing a particular agenda, which is to engage the congregation's youth in social action activities within the community. The other group—the lay leaders, particularly the youth committee—is notably absent as a partner in pursuing that agenda. The youth advisor is left to run the program by himself, with little support from a committee that was developed, in fact, to provide support in the form of guidance, resources, and yes, pizza. The symbol is telling: the youth were left without an adult (when the advisor went out for the food) in just the way that the youth program was left by a youth committee that seemed to exist in name only.

Synagogue life is filled with instances of programs, projects, or initiatives that are primarily or solely worked on only by staff or by lay leaders rather than in the form of some partnership. In some cases, this may be appropriate. A cantor does not need to involve lay leaders in selecting or arranging musical offerings, just as the education director need not invite the leaders' input in designing a teacher orientation program. Similarly, when there is no executive director, the chair of the development committee does not need to involve staff in developing a fund-raising strategy, just as the finance committee need not invite staff to submit ideas about how to maintain accounting records or negotiate with banks for the best interest rates. Of course, even in such instances when it is relatively clear that the expertise belongs on one side or the other, it may often be helpful to seek resources and information from others.

In other instances, of course, it is not only helpful to do so but dysfunctional not to do so. There are many areas in which the lay leaders and the professional staff must work together—share information and solve problems collaboratively, develop strategy together, work on programs jointly in ways that we outline in the previous chapter. When this does not occur, the system becomes disturbed in fundamental ways. There is a lack of buy-in from one or the other group to a path that needs to be followed by everyone. The lay leaders or professional staff pursue separate agendas, or act as if they do. One group of people ends up with sole possession of a program, which may lead to resentment both from them (for being abandoned by others) and toward them (from others who feel, rightly or wrongly, left out). Their work becomes less well informed, their ideas become more insular, and the resentment inevitably spills over into the program or project itself. There is simply not enough connection between lay leaders and the professional staff in the support of a shared agenda. One hand clapping may pose a very interesting Zen koan, but it makes for very little applause.

Disturbance #2: Leader, Manage Thyself

Our case study suggests a second type of disturbance: a leader who micromanages members of a group over whom he or she does not have authority. The vice president of youth in the case is a serial micromanager; she drove off the previous assistant rabbi and threatens to do the same to both the new assistant rabbi and the youth group advisor. There are several dimensions to this problem. First, of course, is the issue of micromanagement itself. Micromanagers do not simply look over but perch atop the shoulders of others, dispensing advice, criticism, direction, and argument. They hold on tightly to authority even as they believe they are delegating. They reach in to take care of items themselves that others can and should be working on. They seek control and take it whenever they can. They intrude.

The second dimension in our case is that the micromanager has no direct authority over those she seeks to control. Professional staff members, like the youth group advisor, most often report to one of the rabbis in a synagogue, who in turn is accountable to the board and its elected officers (in our case, Sam reported to Eric, the assistant rabbi). As described in the previous chapter, lay leaders and professional staff function as parallel systems, each supervised by their own members, with the exception of the relationship between the senior rabbi and the board president, who form a bridge at the top of the synagogue between the two groups. The vice president of youth did not have the authority to directly manage clergy or staff and ought not to have been confronting or hectoring them. The boundaries between the two groups were breached and created a significant disturbance in the synagogue, to the point that the youth group advisor and the new assistant rabbi were in some danger of being rendered ineffective or worse by a rogue lay leader. Fortunately, the rabbi in the case stepped in to protect her staff; it is not always so in synagogue life.

At the core of micromanagement is a lack of trust. When we trust that others will perform as they ought, we move away, secure in the belief that events will work out in a reasonable fashion. When we do not believe that others can perform without our direction, we remain close, and, indeed, often too close, to the point that others sense our lack of trust and withdraw. Unwittingly, we create self-fulfilling prophecies. We believe that others cannot act effectively without us; we move in too close and take over, leading them to back away, which ultimately leads them to act less effectively. We are thus confirmed in our initial belief that they cannot act effectively without us. Like an unsteady driver, we drive away, oblivious of the accidents that we caused and left in our wake. Synagogue life may be filled with such accidents, as lay leaders and professional staff alike hold certain beliefs about one another—as incompetent, untrustworthy, naïve—and then move in too close, overstepping boundaries and managing others to the point that they throw up their hands in disbelief and despair. They cannot say what they wish most to say: "Manage thyself, leader, manage thyself."

Disturbance #3: The Unexamined Board

The various dramas staged between synagogue lay leaders and professional staff members often overshadow a more persistent and hidden storyline: the dysfunction of boards themselves. In our case, the dysfunction of the board is obscured somewhat by the noise about the youth group advisor and his actions. But the dysfunction is plain to see if we look even a little closely. The lay leadership is disconnected almost completely from the youth program, which ought to operate in the context of a partnership between staff and lay leaders. The youth group advisor does not know anyone on the youth committee or even the vice president of youth. The youth committee is nonfunctioning. There is no integration of the youth committee with the education committee or the synagogue's education program. These lapses are due as much to the board and its lack of oversight of its committees and officers as they are to the individuals involved. The board is responsible for the relative lack of support that the synagogue shows for its youth program. We also need to look at the leadership, or lack thereof, of the senior rabbi in bringing the professional staff together to work as a team. Clearly, that is not happening in our case study.

Often enough, a board's dysfunctions recede into the background of the struggles of a staff to hold together a program. In our case, there is an interesting sleight of hand, as the vice president for youth castigates the failures of the youth group advisor (and of the new assistant rabbi) rather than taking responsibility for her own failures and those of the youth committee she supervises. It is not clear, of course, whether she does this consciously or unconsciously, but the result is the same: a set of projections about the staff that holds them accountable for failures while leaving the board and its representatives blameless.

We understand this all-too-familiar process in several ways. Boards may have certain dysfunctions that render them less effective than they might otherwise be. They may suffer a lack of real leadership. They may be overly political. There may be infighting between polarized subgroups. They may have too much or too little dissent. They may be unable to make decisions. Effective boards recognize, take ownership for, and develop ways to solve such problems. Ineffective boards deny, avoid, and in other ways leave these problems unexamined, which guarantees that the problems will remain, even as they assume different forms over time. We find that the simplest defense that ineffective boards use against examining and changing their own practices is that of projection: they blame the staff, rabbis, or congregation itself for their own failure or ineffectiveness.

They are rarely called to account for this process, simply because of the power imbalance in synagogues: boards ultimately have the power to hire and fire staff, including clergy. It is no simple matter for staff to confront a board with its own dysfunction, even as staff members are themselves undermined in their work.

The lack of self-examination on a board is understandable, if regrettable. Self-examination requires a certain willingness to look at how one's own decisions, actions, tendencies, and ideas might lead to undesirable or ineffective outcomes, and to take corrective action. On boards, it requires as well a willingness to confront one's peers and hold them accountable for what they do and do not do. Congregants who are elected to serve on the board must thus decide to raise difficult issues with one another, issues that might well test if not outright threaten ongoing friendships. Many board members decide not to do so, preferring to deny that anything is amiss or looking elsewhere to place blame in order not to threaten their relationships with other community members. Such decisions create boards that are incapable of examining and learning from their own processes, to the detriment of synagogues and their missions. In such instances we find that the unexamined board often does as much damage as it does good.

Outrageous, Part 2

Rabbi Susan Klein placed a call to Mel Sobel, the board president. She filled Mel in on what had happened and told him that she was concerned that Debbie was going to try to convince the youth committee to get the board to fire Sam. Mel laughed and told Susan that it was not very likely that the youth committee would do much of anything. Its members rarely attended meetings, and its chair was so ineffective that the education committee refused to have anything to do with the youth committee, charging that its members had no idea what they were doing. Mel said that Debbie was an important person to listen to—her ideas were often valuable, and she had really helped him out on a matter the year before. He thought of her as a future board president. He told Susan that he was busy traveling in the next few weeks and hoped that she could take care of this without involving him.

Susan offered a mild protest to Mel about having to work with Debbie without the support of other board members. Mel became upset, telling Susan that it was her job to get along with the lay leaders. He told her he had heard from a number of board members over the last few months that Susan was protecting her staff so much that it was becoming difficult to work with her. She was just too defensive, he went on, and needed to step back a little and let the lay leaders do their jobs. Susan was surprised, and then angry, to hear this. She tried to calm herself before replying, but there was still an edge in her voice as she told Mel that she found that there were some members on the board who did not and could not do their jobs, no matter what she did or did not do, and that she needed to step in and take care of their work. Mel interrupted angrily, asking whom she was talking about. Susan mentioned the names of Debbie and several others who were supposed to be involved in the synagogue's youth program but who rarely contributed anything useful or did what they said that they would do. Mel said that perhaps those board members did not feel welcome by Susan and the others working on those programs. Their conversation went on in this vein for several more minutes before Mel said that he needed to get to another appointment and ended the call.

Susan was furious after the call. She had long known that she and Mel did not see eye-to-eye on a number of matters, and she was looking forward to the end of his tenure as board president, but he had never attacked her like this before. She was not sure how she could continue to work with him in a productive fashion. She canceled some appointments and went home early, eager to get away from the synagogue and spend time with her family for the afternoon.

At the other end of the building, Eric Stone, the assistant rabbi of Temple Ohev Shalom, stood up from his desk after a long period of returning calls and e-mails. He felt like taking a walk around the synagogue to stretch his legs. In the hallway he ran into Richard Fogel, the director of education at the temple. They talked about the approaching end of the religious school year. Eric asked how the year had been and what changes Richard might be thinking of for the following year. Richard told him that it had been a good year and that the teachers they had brought in last year were working out nicely. He said that his only disappointment was the performance of some of the teaching assistants. The *madrichim,* drawn from the youth group, seemed unsure of what they were supposed to be doing, in spite of some of the direction that they had been given by the teachers they were helping. He thought that the youth group and its advisor, Sam Tarloff, might have something to do with the poor performance. Perhaps Sam wasn't taking the teaching assistant role that seriously and was passing that message on to the *madrichim* as well. He had heard from Debbie, the board's vice president of youth, that Tarloff did not have the proper focus for the job and was more concerned with social action activities than with the educational dimensions of the synagogue. Debbie had also suggested that Sam might not be getting the right supervision. Richard said that he wasn't sure what the solution was but that there was definitely a problem that needed to be fixed.

Eric found himself getting upset. He told Richard that he was Sam's supervisor but that they spent their time together talking about how to make the youth group strong, not how to create better *madrichim* for the religious school. He told Richard that he resented the implication that he was not doing a good job of supervision and that perhaps it was the teachers who were not doing an adequate job of communicating their expectations to the *madrichim* or giving them the proper amount of support and feedback in the classroom. Both Eric and Richard grew increasingly defensive, and the conversation halted abruptly when Richard excused himself to make a phone call.

The next morning Charlene Garfield, the executive director of the temple, called Eric and asked if she could drop by his office. Charlene said that Richard had sought her out the afternoon before and told her about the argument between Eric and himself. Charlene thought that it might be useful for Eric and Richard to get together and talk about their differences in the hopes of avoiding future confrontations. She would help mediate that conversation. Eric said that he would be happy to speak with Richard—he, too, felt uncomfortable about their conversation—but that he did not believe that the focus ought to be simply about their relationship. The executive director who had a previous background in conflict management and mediation disagreed and said that there clearly was a lot of emotion triggered between Richard and Eric and it was best to get that out on the table sooner rather than later. To not do so, she suggested, was probably resistance. Eric shrugged his shoulders and told Charlene that he would give it a try. They set a date for later that week for Richard and Eric to work out their differences.

Eric had lunch that day with Susan and told her what had happened. Susan was quiet for some time after Eric finished his story. After lunch she sought out Charlene and told her that she did not think that a meeting between Richard and Eric was the right intervention. Charlene disagreed, telling Susan how upset Richard had been after his hallway conversation with Eric. Susan nodded, saying she understood that people were getting upset, but that she thought there were larger issues that were making them upset and that she wanted a chance to work on them first. Charlene said that as the executive director, it was her job to make sure that the professional staff was working together effectively and that she needed to follow her instincts on this. Susan disagreed, saying that the professional staff reported to her and that she would handle the matter. Charlene shook her head and said that unless she heard otherwise from Mel Sobel, the board president, she would go ahead and meet with Eric and Richard to get this issue behind them.

Disturbance #4: Faulty Bridges

The key relationship between the lay leaders and the professional staff is that between the board president and the rabbi, as we described in the previous chapter. They serve as the bridge, across which information and ideas flow and upon which problems are identified and solutions are developed and implemented. When that bridge is in disrepair, the relations between lay leaders and staff become fundamentally disturbed. In the second part of our case, that disturbance is patently obvious. The rabbi and the board president have different views, particularly about the nature of the working relationship between the groups they represent. Each seems frustrated with what appears to them as lacking in the other. They interrupt one another, question one another's motives and experiences, and talk past rather than with one another. They are unable to provide useful feedback to one another in ways that allow for learning and change. They are caught pretty firmly in a relationship of blame rather than trust and respect.

The details of this scenario may be more or less familiar to some lay leaders and clergy, but its broad outlines—of a rabbi and board president who are unable to work together effectively on behalf of a shared agenda— are quite familiar to most of us. Too often we have rabbis or board presidents who merely tolerate one another, waiting until contracts or terms are finished and one or the other leaves his or her role. As bridges, they cannot fully support the weight of the work that must traverse their respective groups. To the extent that they are unable to repair their relationships, board presidents and rabbis create disturbance throughout the synagogue. They unwittingly create models for others to emulate. They make themselves available to be used by others who wish, for their own ends, to play off the two leaders against one another. They undermine one another, and like two rowers in a boat facing in opposing directions, paralyze the synagogue in its attempts to fulfill its mission.

Disturbance #5: Muddy Waters

Our case presents several instances of what we find endemic in synagogue life: a lack of clarity about who ought to do what, who is supervising whom, who has authority over whom, and who makes certain decisions. Such lack of clarity is disturbing to the individuals involved and to the system more generally. In the case study, the teaching assistants—the *madrichim*—are left adrift in the classrooms, not quite sure what they are supposed to do. It is not clear who, between the teachers and the youth group advisor, is supposed to supervise them, with each assuming, without checking for accuracy, that the other has responsibility. A similar lack of clarity marks the role of the executive director in the case. Does she have the authority to hold a meeting between the assistant rabbi and the director of education against the wishes of the senior rabbi? To whom does she report? How much authority does the senior rabbi have in relation to the executive director? The confusion about these questions leads to multiple interpretations, as the rabbi and executive director answer them in different ways that must certainly sow confusion within the staff itself.

The lack of clarity about tasks, roles, and authority often results in what we see in the case study: work does not get done in synagogues, as people assume that others are responsible or there is conflict over who has certain authority, as people assume that they have certain power. These two dynamics are the result of a certain vacuum, an empty space where there ought to be clearly prescribed and collectively understood information about who is doing what and with what authority. In that vacuum, people either move too far away from one another, shunning responsibility, or too close to one another, seeking authority. Both moves disturb the synagogue. Both moves distract people, forcing them to focus on issues of power and control rather than on the tasks that are critical to their roles and to the missions of their synagogues.

The question that must be posed in the face of this sort of disturbance is why it is allowed to remain. Confusion about who does what and who has what authority is usually readily apparent in synagogues, both to those who are at the center of the confusion and to those on the periphery. Why do people not make the effort to clarify the confusion, such that they do not have to resent one another or wage distracting struggles? The simplest answer, of course, is that achieving such clarity is not a simple process. People must work together to explore in some depth the boundaries around what they do and have potentially difficult conversations about authority and its limits. The more complicated answer is that it is often the case that people do not really wish to clarify that which is muddy; the ambiguity may serve them well—in terms of wielding influence in the synagogue—even as it disturbs a great many relationships within and between lay leaders and professional staff. Gaining clarity and transparency is often a matter of identifying those who thrive amid ambiguity and confusion.

Disturbance #6: Triangulation

An insidious type of disturbance comes from triangulation, in which people do not deal directly with one another but, instead, involve others in inappropriate ways. In synagogue life, this occurs when people, rather than confronting whatever issues they might have in the course of their work, rope in others as a way of putting the focus elsewhere. In our case, this occurred when Debbie, the vice president of youth, spoke with Richard, the staff director of education, and "recruited" him into her campaign against Sam, the youth group advisor, and Eric, the assistant rabbi. Debbie thus allowed herself to avoid direct engagement with Sam or Eric, while casting Richard into a triangle that led to a series of unfortunate skirmishes between him and Eric and between the executive director and the senior rabbi.

This dynamic creates various layers of disturbance. At its plainest, triangulation creates inappropriate distance between people who really ought to deal directly with one another. In its more sophisticated version, triangulation undermines relations between groups. In the case study, for example, the net result of Debbie's conversation with Richard was to transfer her issues with Sam and with Eric over to Richard who, for his own conscious or unconscious reasons, was a willing recipient. The issues that rightfully belonged to the board, which needed to struggle with its relation to the youth program, and to Debbie, who needed to work directly with the youth committee and the youth group advisor, were exported to the staff group, where they were imported into and then enacted in a confrontation between Eric and Richard. The struggle between the education and youth components of the synagogue was thus engaged, but in the wrong group, between the wrong people, and in the wrong way.

This sort of process occurs largely outside of people's conscious awareness. We are not always aware of when we triangulate others or when we ourselves are being triangulated. While our example focuses on the lay leaders exporting issues into the professional staff group, the opposite occurs just as often. In either case, people find themselves unwittingly filled up and acting out emotions and conflict that rightfully belong elsewhere. In synagogues, this occurs when the boundaries—around the board, a committee or task force, the clergy group, and/or the professional staff—are too loose. People inappropriately rope in others, trying to get them to take their sides, rather than maintaining their boundaries and working on the issues within the relationships and groups to which those issues belong. Triangles are notoriously unsteady, always inappropriate, with too many overlapping pairings and messy boundaries. They disturb relationships. They confuse things in synagogue life, where lay leaders and professional staff each need to work separately, undisturbed by the other, before they can effectively engage their work together.

Outrageous, Part 3

Rabbi Susan Klein placed calls to Debbie Scott (vice president of youth), Josh Singer (chair of the youth committee), Tamar Rosin (chair of the education committee), and Mel Sobel (board president) to schedule a meeting for the end of the week about the status of the youth program in the temple. At the meeting, Susan spoke about recent events—the events involving Sam Tarloff, the youth committee's involvement in not providing dinner, the argument between Richard and Eric about the *madrichim*, and her own conversation with Charlene. She said that she thought there was a larger issue that needed to be discussed that had contributed to each of these events: the lack of clarity about the place and meaning of the youth program in the temple. She talked about how each of those events signaled the need for a collective understanding about the purpose of the youth program and its function within the larger mission of the temple. Without that guiding sense, Susan said, it was not clear who was supposed to do what to support the youth group, how the youth program was related to education, and how it fit with other aspects of what the temple was trying to do. She ended by saying that it was up to this group of lay leaders to provide leadership in this area. Unless that occurred, there would continue to be squabbles and interpersonal difficulties.

The meeting did not go as well as Susan had hoped. The lay leaders nodded a fair amount during the conversation but did not add much in terms of what they were thinking. When Susan had finished speaking, they ignored much of what she had said and focused instead on the pizza event. They blamed Sam, the youth group advisor, for leaving the kids, and then began to go at his supervisor, Rabbi Stone. Susan found herself defending her staff. The lay leaders then began blaming one another for a host of accumulated slights and mishaps. Debbie and Josh each blamed the other for not being available for the youth group. Tamar said that she had given up on Josh as an effective chair of the youth committee and was waiting for a new chair to take over before she was ready to really try and integrate the education and youth agendas. Mel was quiet, until finally he said that this meeting was no longer productive and that he would need to figure out the next steps in making sure that the youth program received more support from both lay leaders and staff. The meeting adjourned.

Susan returned to her office frustrated with the lay leaders and their inability to focus on the larger issues. Mel arrived at her office several minutes later. He sat down heavily in a chair across from her desk and, sighing, told her that was a lousy meeting. She nodded, expecting him to share his frustration with the committee heads. Instead, he told her that he thought that she could have done a better job of managing the meeting. It was her meeting, he said, and thus her responsibility to keep people in line and get something done. Susan was stunned. Trying to remain calm, she told Mel that he was fully aware that she had limited power over the lay leaders, and her meeting or not, they were more likely to follow his lead because of his position as board president. Susan added that since the board was in the midst of evaluating her performance and making decisions about renewing her contract, it was even more difficult for her to wield authority with the lay leaders, simply because she felt more vulnerable with them. Mel nodded but was unconvinced, saying that he still believed it was Susan's responsibility to manage meetings that she had called. "Maybe managing is the operative word here, Rabbi," he added, rather ambiguously.

As Mel left Susan's office, he mentioned that the evaluation process was almost complete and that he would schedule a meeting soon to go over the results with her and with the evaluation task force that was just now completing its work. Susan was again surprised. She knew that the task force had been formed but had no idea that it was already finished with its work. She had expected that the evaluative process would include her in some fashion and would be an opportunity for herself and the board to look together at what had been accomplished during her tenure and identify what more could be done, both by herself and the lay leadership. She had also hoped the process would be seen as an opportunity to continue to improve what they were doing. Susan was frustrated to hear that the evaluation process was almost complete even though she had not had the chance for real dialogue with the lay leaders.

Susan's frustration blossomed into outright anger when she actually met the following week with Mel and Steven, the chair of the evaluation task force. Steven went through the report that the task force had put together. He reviewed the results of an informal survey taken of board members and members of the various synagogue committees, feedback from several senior staff members, data about synagogue membership growth, estimates of attendance at synagogue services and events, and the development of new programs. Susan was surprised by some of what she had heard—for example, that the board felt that membership was not growing because she was not developing enough new programs or delivering sermons that would create excitement and "buzz" in the community. She was upset by the assertion that some unnamed members of the congregation felt that she was not putting enough energy into the job. And she was infuriated when Steven told her that there were board members—again, unnamed—who felt that she spent too much time in pastoral care and not enough time being the kind of charismatic, dynamic spiritual leader who could motivate and direct her staff while helping the synagogue make a name for itself in the community.

Mel and Steven asked if she had any questions. Susan told them that she needed time to digest what she had heard and would get back to them shortly with her responses. Mel told her that she did not have much time, since the contract renewal process was gathering steam and the board would like to have her responses to the report as well as what changes she planned to make before they decided about the contract. He said that the contract decision would be partly influenced by her willingness to address the issues raised in the report. Susan was shaken by this but did her best not to show how she felt. She continued to be upset that there had been no room for dialogue with the board about their joint responsibility to solve some of the nagging problems of the congregation related to increasing membership and creating new and exciting programs. She left the meeting wondering whether it was even worth trying to remain at the synagogue. At the same time, she sensed that there might be some truth in what Steve had said about her relationship with her staff. Had she allowed each staff person too much freedom to set his or her own agenda? Had she trusted them too much to act like adults? Had they become the supportive team she wished they would be? Susan always hated "authority." But had she unwittingly allowed things to become too "loosey-goosey" and was now paying the price?

Several days later, Susan had lunch with Andrea Goffstein, a congregant who had served on the search committee that originally hired Susan and who had remained close with Susan even after leaving the board. Susan trusted Andrea and told her what had been happening. Andrea grimaced when she heard the story. She told Susan that something similar had happened with the previous senior rabbi whose contract had not been renewed because the board had felt that he had not been a significant presence in the larger community. The board had been excited about Susan, she said, because she had seemed so dynamic and engaging; the board felt that they finally had someone who could energize the entire community and lead them as they wished to be led. Susan said that ever since she had joined the synagogue, people had told her how powerful she was, how moving her sermons were, and how excited they were about her being there to lead a kind of renaissance in the community. She was flattered, of course, and tried hard her first few years to be dynamic and charismatic. Of late, however, she had been feeling that it was not her responsibility to save the synagogue, whose members consisted largely of an older generation, but to work with others to develop and implement long-term strategies. Andrea nodded her head, agreeing, but told Susan that while that made good sense, the congregants' hopes to be saved ran deep. Susan sighed, feeling tired and saddened.

Disturbance #7: (De)Valuation

In the third portion of our case, the ability of the senior rabbi to take a strong leadership role is compromised somewhat by the fact that, at the time, she is being both evaluated by the board and involved in a contracting process. She is less able to speak candidly about her experiences and her perceptions in the way that anyone would feel constrained by speaking truth to those who have the power to sanction them. This is not uncommon, of course: during any contracting process, the rabbi-as-employee assumes a larger place in the consciousness of both rabbis and lay leaders, and then gives way to rabbi-as-spiritual leader as contracts are settled. Even so, there is a problem if the rabbi-as-employee assumes too large a space in the rabbi-board relationship during the evaluation or contracting period; this complicates the transition into the rabbi-as-spiritual leader role for both the rabbi and the lay leaders. In the case study, the board president refers to the evaluation process at the end of a meeting where he has castigated the rabbi for her lack of leadership. In linking the two roles so clearly—rabbi-as-employee and rabbi-as-spiritual leader— he is implicitly sending a message about his inability or unwillingness to keep them separate. The message is, in fact, a warning, which the rabbi cannot help but receive.

The primary disturbance to the lay leader–rabbi relationship here is the way in which the evaluation process is handled. Indeed, the process depicted in the case study is more likely to lead to a devaluation rather than evaluation of the rabbi. The rabbi is more likely to feel ambushed than engaged in meaningful dialogue. The process is one-way: the lay leaders perform an evaluation *on* the rabbi rather than an evaluation *with* her. The distinction is crucial. The former allows only for a sharing of perceptions, the accuracy of which may be questionable given that they represent an unknown portion of the congregation with unknown motives. The latter allows for an examination of not simply the rabbi, but of his or her partnership with the lay leaders and its effectiveness in working toward the synagogue's mission. Ideally, lay leaders and rabbis take responsibility, separately and together, for what has worked well and not so well in the synagogue. Doing so creates the possibility of authentic partnerships whose members try and learn as much as they can about how they are working together and change accordingly. Otherwise, there is blame and recrimination and squandered opportunities for people to look together at their expectations and results.

The evaluation process further disturbs the lay leader–rabbi relationship when it is tightly linked to the length and terms of rabbinic contracts. It is difficult for people to take in useful feedback and learn about their performance when that feedback is linked to decisions about their employment. For this very reason, evaluative and developmental processes are usually separated in many organizations. Performance evaluations—assessments of what people have done, the skills that they have and those that they need to develop, and the nature of their collaborations with others—need to be kept separate from contractual decisions if people are to truly have the chance to absorb the developmental feedback. Otherwise, opportunities for real learning are driven out by concerns about one's future. In our case, the fact that the rabbi was surprised by some of what she heard is problematic, since it means that she was not being provided with helpful feedback during the year. The developmental process was folded into the evaluative process and thus rendered relatively insignificant.

Disturbance #8: Search and Destroy

The search process for a new rabbi is a road fraught with danger, both for the rabbi and the congregation, and needs to be traversed carefully. When the road has many signs, warning travelers of dangerous curves or particularly steep descents, people move more cautiously and make better decisions. Too often, there are not enough signs. Rabbis take jobs unaware that they are not the best fit for the congregation. Lay leaders choose rabbis based on various criteria that, while valid, do not take into account the nature of the fit with the culture and hopes of the congregation. In our case, the senior rabbi did not fit with the congregation's wishes for a dynamic, charismatic spiritual leader who would capture the attention not simply of the congregants, but of the wider community. This expectation is neither good nor bad; it is simply an expectation, which fits or does not fit with the skills and expectations of a particular rabbi. It so happens that in our case it did not fit. This disturbed the lay leader–rabbi relationship greatly.

The classic search process for a new rabbi goes something like this. A congregation decides to search for a new rabbi. They go through the appropriate steps in soliciting candidates, through the denominations, seminaries, and other contacts. They set up a committee to sort through applications, interview candidates, narrow down the list and arrange visits, and finally, make a recommendation to the board, which then approves a candidate or asks for further work. Contracts are developed and negotiated, and if all goes well, the new rabbi is welcomed and installed into his or her position. There are times, often enough, when this process works reasonably well. Rabbis and congregations that ought to find one another do so and commence an effective partnership in the way that singles who ought to marry find one another and commence an effective marriage. Yet is also the case that, just as people marry badly, rabbis and congregations who ought not to enter into a relationship do so anyway. This can happen for all sorts of reasons, but at their core, ill-fated matches reflect mismatched expectations. Rabbis and congregations simply have different expectations of what each will bring and contribute.

Such is life, of course, and people cannot always know how their choices will play out. But—and this is where the search process is disturbed and disturbing in a synagogue—people can make good-faith efforts to discover the fit between a rabbi and congregation during, not after, the search. When they do not, they engage in what we call, provocatively, search and destroy. As part of the search process, lay leaders must look closely at their synagogue's own history with rabbis. They must look at their real expectations for their rabbi. They must look at the culture of their congregation. And then they must speak honestly of what they find, with one another and with candidates in whom they are interested. They must mark the road, posting warning signs, pointing out where there is danger. To not do so is to set up rabbis, and the congregation more generally, for failure.

Disturbance #9: Seduction and Betrayal

Mismatched or hidden expectations also play a key role in another disturbance in the lay leader–rabbi relationship: the assumption that a newly engaged rabbi will solve a congregation's problems and lead congregants to the so-called promised land of congregational success. In our case, the rabbi was, unbeknownst to her, looked to as someone who would, with much charismatic leadership, engage congregants as they had never before been engaged. The congregation, she later discovers, had believed that they "finally had someone" to lead them as they wished to be led. Through her the congregation would emerge and "make a name for itself." Like Moses, she would stride forth, and with thundering sermons and the power of God, enlist new members and energize existing ones, building a congregation infused with heat and light. On a more practical level, she was to increase membership, raising the synagogue's profile and its resources. She was, it seems, to do this largely by herself, given that the board saw the membership issue as her responsibility and not theirs.

There is, in this process, a play of seduction and betrayal. A rabbi is seen as a synagogue's savior. He or she is seduced, with much flattery, into taking up that role. The congregants adopt a role of dependence, expecting the rabbi to take care of them, to do what they cannot do for themselves, and to save them from threatening forces—demographic trends, depleted resources, debilitating conflict. The rabbi is unable to do so fully; saving a congregation is an impossible task, for even as small wins accumulate, increasingly larger and more impossible ones are desired. Finally, the rabbi cannot be the savior, and the real promised land remains disconcertingly out of reach. The congregation feels betrayed by its rabbi who, seemingly, promised but could not deliver salvation.

The betrayal is more complicated, of course. Lay leaders betray their rabbis by seducing them into the savior role and then leaving them there, isolated and solely responsible. In our case, the board acted as if Rabbi Klein was by herself responsible for increasing membership and did little to help. Lay leaders then betray their rabbis doubly by blaming them for failing to deliver all that they had (not) promised. They distance themselves from the fallen rabbis whom they had helped prop up. The relationships between the lay leaders and their fallen rabbis are, of course, disturbed, sometimes fatally. It is difficult to recover from failures that are rooted in the irrational projection and reception of outsized hopes, which leads to the offering and accepting of the role of savior. While the Jewish story is replete with charismatic leaders, our model is one of long treks to our land of promise that depend on the Jewish people and their leaders each taking up their appropriate responsibility while walking alongside one another.

Voices of Calm

The nine disturbances that we discussed in this chapter are each quite powerful in their ability to derail useful, effective working relationships between lay leaders and rabbis. In the previous chapter, we described various ways to prevent such disturbances from occurring: creating useful structures and processes; clarifying tasks, roles, and boundaries; strengthening the board president–rabbi relationship. In this section, we briefly review a process for working with relationships that are, in spite of such measures, disturbed. The process requires people to become voices of calm, that is, to use their voices in the service of calming that which is disturbed in their relationships.

Reflection. Change requires reflection. People must step back from situations that trouble or disturb them and examine them from a variety of different angles. They must try and explain what they see in ways that make clear that they, too, are responsible for disturbances. Lay leaders must examine how they are partly responsible for conflicts that occur among staff professionals and vice versa. Professional staff and lay leaders alike must examine how, by their lack of trust in others or by going it alone, they may often drive those others to become less than trustworthy. People caught in various triangles must reflect on how they made themselves available to be used by others in such ways. Lay leaders must look at their own patterns, in how they search for and set up rabbis; and too, rabbis must look at their own willingness to be seduced into saviorlike roles that they cannot possibly fulfill. Everyone must try and trace conflict to its sources, rather than accept simple stories about people just not liking one another. Disturbances will not simply disappear without synagogue leaders, professional and lay alike, working hard to reflect on how they have helped to create disturbed relationships.

Engagement. Reflection creates the possibility of insight, and importantly, humility. When we come to a realization that we, and not just *they,* are responsible for disturbed relationships, we make it far more likely that we will engage with others with humility, respect, and openness. We must then engage in thoughtful ways. This may mean repairing relationships damaged by broken trust, misperceptions, and labels, all of which are difficult to move beyond. This requires difficult conversations and a great deal of patience and willingness to work with and not against others. We recommend several resources. In the book *Difficult Conversations,* the authors—Douglas Stone, Bruce Patton, and Sheila Heen—focus on the importance of shifting away from the stance of blame to that of learning and offer some useful ways to create learning conversations.[1]

Similarly, in *How the Way We Talk Can Change the Way We Work,* Robert Kegan and Lisa Lahey describe how people can move from blame and complaint to commitment and responsibility.[2] Such shifts are crucial if lay leaders and professional staff are to engage one another—provide useful feedback, explore lack of trust, admit perceptions, negotiate tasks, roles, and boundaries—and move toward meaningful change.

Adjustment. Engagement is useful to the extent that it produces changes that calm disturbances. Lay leaders and staff need to identify and agree upon useful adjustments. Some adjustments are immediately apparent. When there is a lack of shared ownership over a program, people need to articulate mutual expectations and goals. When there is a lack of clarity about who is doing what, with what authority, and in consultation with whom, there again need to be adjustments in shared understandings. People caught in triangles must extricate themselves by talking directly *with* rather than *about* others and encouraging others to do similarly. The evaluation process for rabbis must be separated from the developmental process. Search committees must be prepared to examine and share with potential candidates the histories of their congregations, especially in terms of lay leader–rabbi relationships. Lay leaders and rabbis must alter patterns by which the former are overly dependent on the latter, which is a sure sign of a savior play being staged and enacted. These and other such adjustments must be made if lay leader–staff relationships are to become, and remain, undisturbed.

These three steps—reflection, engagement, and adjustment—are simple enough to point out but often quite difficult for people to take. We often remain caught in familiar ways of thinking and acting, partly because we grow used to them and partly because they produce results that are (just) good enough. It takes some burst of energy, some catalyst, to get us to interrupt these familiar ways, even as we may know that they create and maintain disturbance in our relationships and our lives. The catalyst may be some urgent situation, some crisis that forces us to turn to one another for help. More often, the catalyst is simply a leader or two who decide that things must change and that the change must start with himself or herself. They reflect, and engage, and make useful adjustments. And they ask others to do so as well: they prod, cajole, pressure, humor, and in other ways press others to fix that which is broken. They get help from others when they need to—from inside or outside the synagogue. They stay the course. Throughout, they hold tightly to the mission of the synagogue and, like Moses, ask others to raise their sights and their ambitions for the people of Israel. We believe that anyone can provide such leadership. Moreover, we believe that for any of us not to step into such leadership when we identify a real disturbance among lay leaders and professional staff is to perpetuate its existence.

Notes

1. Douglas Stone, Bruce Patton, and Sheila Heen, *Difficult Conversations: How to Discuss What Matters Most* (New York: Penguin Books, 1999).
2. Robert Kegan and Lisa Lahey, *How the Way We Talk Can Change the Way We Work: Seven Languages for Transformation* (San Francisco: Jossey-Bass, 2001).

16

The Other Team:
Rabbis and Professionals

Moses said to Aaron, "What did this people do to you that
you have brought such great sin upon them?" And Aaron replied, "Let not my lord be so angry. You know this people,
how they are bent on evil. They said to me, 'Make us a god to
lead us forward for that man Moses, we do not know what
has happened to him.' So I said, 'Whoever has gold, take it
off!' They gave it to me, I hurled it into the fire, and out came
this calf!"
(Exodus 32:21-24)

Synagogues function effectively when there is a professional team whose
tasks involve helping to develop and implement visions on behalf of the
congregation. Professionals enable congregations to pursue their missions
by helping to create and make real the steps by which those missions are
accomplished. The rabbi is the head of the staff team, and as such, is
charged with setting goals, delegating tasks, and coaching, supporting,
and mentoring others to fulfill themselves and their professional aspira-
tions. Staff members are charged with supporting rabbinic visions, not
blindly, but in ways that help translate those visions into reality.

The relationship between rabbis and their staff is marked as well by
protection, as each side is inevitably placed in the middle of the other's
relationship with lay leaders and congregants. Each thus needs to protect
the other's domains and areas of decision making, resisting the pull to
undermine one another's authority. In doing so, they will (when each is
working to the best of their abilities) protect the health of the synagogue,
which is directly related to maintaining healthy boundaries between
its various groups and roles. In the classic example cited above of how
this balance can be violated, Aaron, forgetting the mission of the fledg-
ling Jewish people to be faithful to God, and abandoning Moses's directives, acquiesces to the people's wants. He fails to protect his "boss." By

allowing himself to be triangulated in this way—perhaps out of fear of the mob, the desire to be popular with the people, jealousy toward his younger brother, or because he partly wished for a "golden calf" himself—Aaron winds up serving no one's purpose. He brings disaster to the very people he thought to serve.

The Professional Team

We call all the people who earn their livelihood at the synagogue the "professional team." If someone is receiving a check each month for the work he or she does (i.e., not a volunteer who might work just as hard and give as much of himself or herself), we consider that person a professional, part of the team. Therefore, it is important that we look carefully at what we mean by "professional team," examining both aspects of the phrase.

Professionals are people who train for, take seriously, and follow certain codes of standards and behaviors. In the synagogue, this includes rabbis, cantors, executive directors, education directors, and others who take seriously a field, study its material, and bring it into the world of the synagogue. There is a certain healthy respect for the particular discipline, and for the people who practice it, that comes along with the notion of professionalism. For their part, professionals continue to earn that respect by their ongoing growth and learning in their respective fields. And of course they must act "professionally," utilizing a standard of behavior that brings dignity to themselves and their chosen field. Professionals are aware that what they do reflects on more than just themselves.

The notion of *team* implies a set of people working together on behalf of shared, collective goals and objectives. To be a team requires a level of interdependence, with individuals relying on and working closely with one another and taking seriously their identity as members of that team. Further, members place the collective goal of the team above their own personal goals. As is often said, "Much more can be accomplished when no one is concerned with who gets the credit."

Synagogues are more likely to have effectively functioning administrations when people—lay leaders, congregational members, clergy, and the administrators themselves—take seriously both the "professional" and the "team" aspects. When those dimensions are undermined through lack of respect, the playing off of team members against one another, and the like, it reduces the ability of the professionals to function effectively.

Effective Professional Teams

The following dimensions characterize effective professional teams.

Cooperation and a Unified Effort. The members of a team must understand that their goals are collective as well as individual and that, as in sports teams, they succeed or fail together even as they each take on different tasks and roles. This requires that their collective goals are clear and meaningful. We find in many synagogues these are often vague, even amorphous. Individuals may know what their tasks are and what their job description requires, but they have little or no sense of how this fits into a larger picture, or even if there is a larger picture. Collective goals are enunciated, they generate buy in, and they are reiterated from time to time by various members of the team.

A Sense of Accountability. The individuals on a team feel accountable to one another and not just to their supervisors for the quality of their work. This requires explicit norms and expectations about performance and standards, as well as confronting and supporting underperforming members. In some synagogues, these norms are expressed as rules or policies upheld by supervisors and others in authority. In other synagogues, they may be termed "communal agreements," norms created and upheld by the team itself in nonhierarchical ways. And in still other institutions, there may be a combination of the two methods, with something like time away (i.e., vacation, personal days, etc.) as a rule and something like interoffice communication expressed as a communal agreement.

Flexibility. While the rabbi is the head of the team, it is also the case that other members of the professional staff will need to assume leadership when they are the most appropriate people to lead a particular task. For example, the executive director may be called upon to take the lead on a financial project; or the director of education might be placed in charge of a community effort to create a high school. More generally, effective teams are flexible in how they go about their tasks and can call on any member of the team to provide leadership and guidance. On a minimal level, each member of the team ought to be responsible for the *d'var Torah*, or teaching lesson (often based on a Jewish text), with which the weekly team meetings begin. This announces to the entire staff as well as the lay leadership that team members are capable and respected for their knowledge, not just their particular skills. Such flexibility may also be demonstrated at board meetings where different members of the professional team are called upon to teach and present.

Open-Ended Discussion and Active Problem-Solving Meetings. Professional teams require the active engagement and input of members who focus on identifying and solving problems together, with the awareness that complex problems are solved only when people speak openly, evaluate many alternatives, and manage differences and conflict constructively. This requires ongoing, open communication in an atmosphere of trust. Team members need to know that what they share will be held in the strictest of confidence and will not negatively impact on their job security. They also need to know that their thoughts and opinions will be taken seriously, that team meetings are not merely an exercise.

Collaboration. Too often, what passes for team meetings is simply a series of announcements or delegation of work tasks. Real teams are marked by members working together as well as separately. Meetings are the place for people to have meaningful conversations, examining issues together on the way to thoughtful decisions.

Self-awareness. Effective teams evaluate their strengths and weaknesses as a team and develop methods to learn how to improve through performance feedback. This requires individual self-awareness and the team's ability to recognize where it has fallen short of its stated goals. When this is done in an atmosphere of "we are in this together" as opposed to blame, finger-pointing, protecting one's individual turf, or recrimination, teams can be most effective at midcourse evaluation and self-correction. Again, the goal has to be to fix or solve problems en route to accomplishing the agreed upon goal.

Celebration. Teams often work quite hard. But they also need to know how to play and celebrate together. Part of sustaining the long-term health of a team is that they take time to get to know one another beyond their work tasks and that they take time to celebrate both their accomplishments and their working together. This can be accomplished by taking some time at each team meeting to share "good and welfare." What *simchas* are we celebrating? What *nachas* is putting a smile on our

faces? What sorrows or *tzuris* are giving us concern? Teams need to celebrate members' birthdays and anniversaries. And they need to take credit
for their successes, celebrating effective programs and projects. Each team
member needs to be reminded of his or her contribution to the overall
well-being of the synagogue. This is not about "tooting our own horns."
It is about giving credit where credit is due and giving appropriate recognition. It is about building an atmosphere of appreciation and gratitude,
which fuels our sense of well-being and provides personal meaning. Such
"celebration" (which ought to take the form of an actual party from time
to time) is quite sustaining and will often be the elixir that will fortify
team members for the difficult tasks they undertake on behalf of God
and the Jewish people.

We believe that as a matter of course real teams or working groups offer
a great deal to a congregation but that they are also difficult to create and
sustain. Too often, professional synagogue "teams" are that in name only;
in fact, they are actually collections of individuals, located in the administration or staff group, whose work is not very well coordinated and
whose whole is not really greater than the sum of its parts. To transcend
that state, there needs to be clarity and transparency about whether (and
when) the professional staff is working as a group or as a team. That will
ease a great deal of confusion, uncertainty, and frustration: for a synagogue or a rabbi to call a collection of people a team and not enable them
to act like one can be very demoralizing.

Clarity

Professional teams function most effectively when there are shared understandings about the *tasks, roles, boundaries,* and *authority* of the team
itself, its subgroups, and individual members. Such clarity creates the foundation for professionals working together productively; the lack of clarity
creates uncertainty, frustration, wasted efforts, mixed signals, and covert
plays for power. And clarity needs to exist throughout the organization.

   The professional staff team needs clarity in relation to lay leadership (as discussed in previous chapters). It must be clearly articulated what
roles and tasks the staff group assumes in their partnership with lay leadership, the boundaries between the two, and where decision making
lies for various areas of synagogue functioning. Again, the primary function

of boards is policy making and financial stewardship. The primary function of staff is daily operations. In synagogues, of course, there is overlap, especially in committee work. Lay volunteers work hand in hand with staff to create and carry out the programs, educational and social, that animate the life of the synagogue. Though rabbis and cantors are the experts when it comes to liturgy, prayer, and ritual, lay leaders on ritual committees often have a lot to say about the religious life of the synagogue. Therefore, it is incumbent to be especially clear in all areas of overlapping concern and function. Or put more prosaically, who does get to decide what melody we use for the *Oseh Shalom?*

Subgroups need the same clarity. The clergy is one subgroup; the support staff of secretaries and assistants may be another; the educational department another. There needs to be clarity about the tasks, roles, boundaries and decision-making authority of each relative to other subgroups and to the staff more generally. Each subgroup will have its own task. Boundaries between subgroups will need to be permeable enough to allow for connection, impermeable enough to allow for separate identity and work. For example, the youth director will need to work with the head of the religious school when designing programs for teens. The sisterhood will want to coordinate with the program director when designing a new educational program for women. They might also want to check in with the head of the religious school. In healthy synagogues, all these subgroups feel comfortable in brainstorming together, in seeking out and consulting one another, and in sharing ideas, programs, and workloads, because clarity permeates the institution.

Individual staff members need clear definition as well of tasks, roles, boundaries, and authority in order to avoid confusion and frustration and to avoid redundancy. This can be understood in terms of job descriptions, hierarchy, and reporting relationships and/or supervisors (which ought to be documented on the synagogue's organizational chart). For example, does the assistant rabbi have the authority to create new programs? Can he or she start a Torah study group on Mondays and Thursdays to complement the one the senior rabbi leads on Shabbat? When the cantor is on vacation, can the religious school's song leader, an aspiring cantor herself, change the melodies of the service?

While these may seem to be minor things on the surface, they do not play out that way in the reality of congregational life. Communities, like families, can be complicated places. Therefore, roles must be clearly delineated. Such clarity needs to be transparent, such that staff and lay leaders alike easily understand what are the various roles and authority of individuals, subgroups, and the professional team itself. And when violations occur and toes get stepped on, as they inevitably will, there need to be the appropriate documents (e.g., job descriptions, organizational chart) and team spirit to resolve the problems.

Legacies

Arielle Kohn is Temple Tikvah's third rabbi in the last seven years. After the long and successful tenure of their now rabbi emeritus, Sydney Stall (who was preceded by the synagogue's founding rabbi, Sol Shank), Temple Tikvah seemingly made some "poor choices." Nevertheless, there was great excitement and a lot of hope when Rabbi Kohn was announced as their new rabbi. And that enthusiasm has continued throughout her first year. Rabbi Kohn has been feted and well received by veteran members as well as the younger families. Congregants have been impressed with her sermons and her special touch with the children. "This one is going to stay with us for a long, long time!" is the word on the Temple Tikvah "street."

For her part, Rabbi Kohn has felt a warm and heartfelt reception. After a five-year tenure as an assistant, then associate rabbi at a large synagogue, she is happy to have her "own shop" at a synagogue that is small enough for her to know everyone but large enough to do some very creative things. She is also happy to have enough staff so that she doesn't have to do it all alone. But that is just the problem. Coming to the end of her first year, she has some serious concerns about the staff that has been in place at the temple. But replacing them is going to be a problem, if not an outright war.

Throughout the interview process, and repeated often in her first year, Rabbi Kohn heard the message of her lay leadership loud and clear. "If not for Cantor Hertz's loving concern for us, and Terry Tabatchnik's firm and steady hand as executive director, who knows where we would be today. The congregation would have probably split. They kept us together. Thank God for the two of them!"

The problem is, Rabbi Kohn's experience is quite contrary. She finds Cantor Michelle Hertz to be devoid of anything that resembles a work ethic. She comes in late, leaves for long periods of time during the day in which no one knows where she is or what she is doing, and is not open to any suggestions as to the liturgical direction she wants for the congregation as part of her vision. But the cantor is truly popular with the congregants and is, when she wants to be, quite talented.

Terry Tabatchnik is another story. While he is competent and hardworking, he is unreceptive to any direction from Rabbi Kohn. At first the rabbi thought it might be a male-female thing; Terry is an older man of "that generation." But she is sure now that it has nothing to do with the fact that she is a woman. The root of the problem is the organizational structure. "Mr. T," as he is affectionately called by almost everyone (he wears some very obvious gold chains with his big *chai*), reports directly to the president of the congregation. Whenever Rabbi Kohn suggests an idea or wants him to do something that varies from the way things have always been done, his stock response is, "I will have to check with the president." And then he adds for emphasis, which is starting to drive her crazy, "You know, *she* is my boss."

At first Rabbi Kohn did not want to confront them. After all, she reasoned, "I am the new kid on the block. This congregation has gone through a lot of turmoil in the last few years. Let me earn their trust and that of the congregation as a whole, then I'll see if I can't get them to change their ways." But even now, almost one year into her tenure, the resistance has been great.

Rabbi Kohn has tried. She has spoken to the cantor on numerous occasions about working together, being part of a team. The cantor "yeses" her a lot but then does whatever she pleases. In one such conversation, Cantor Hertz said to her, "I understand what you want, but you see, this congregation has gone through a lot—two rabbis and an interim rabbi—and it needs me to keep a steady, even keel. I know them. I love them. That's what's best right now." As for the cantor's work ethic, every suggestion by Rabbi Kohn is met with what feels like excuses. "Oh, that day my son was sick at school." Or, "My voice teacher changed my lesson time, and you know she isn't available on my day off." Rabbi Kohn is frustrated to say the least.

In the past month, the rabbi began to make some overtures to the president and executive vice president of the shul. Their response was, "Yes, the cantor told us you have been putting some pressure on her. You know, she has been there for us in all the bad times. We owe her." And as for Rabbi Kohn's suggestions that they take a look at the organizational chart—so that she can be the direct supervisor of the executive director to make sure that he is carrying out her vision for the synagogue—the president simply said, "We'll think about it."

Rabbi Kohn was incensed that the cantor complained to the president about her efforts to get her to work, categorizing them as "pressure." She was even more incensed that some of the lay leaders seemed to be taking the cantor's side. And while she understood that working with the executive director directly was necessary while there was "rabbi turnover," she felt, and had said so during the interview process, that separate reporting to the lay leadership by herself and the executive director would undermine her efforts to create strong and coherent leadership. Their "we'll think about it," after a year in which she proved herself in every possible way, was demoralizing. What to do?

Our case study illustrates struggles about authority that can severely undermine professional staff teams in synagogues. The struggles stem from a lack of clear, and authorized, reporting relationships. Rabbi Kohn is boxed in by the synagogue's legacy of failed rabbis. The legacy lives on in the heightened influence of the cantor and the executive director, who because of their histories with the lay leaders, exist outside the appropriate authority structure among the staff. Both place their allegiance with the lay leaders, who protect them, and in doing so, unwittingly weaken the authority (and thus the effectiveness) of the rabbi. The team exists in name only; in reality, the team is split, with some members partnering with the lay leaders. The lay leaders allow this split to occur, knowingly or not, and thus maintain their own power at the expense of that of their rabbi. In all likelihood, this will weaken the rabbi's ability to be effective in her role and create the conditions for yet another failure.

The congregants and leaders like the new rabbi and say they believe in her, that "she is the one." We are sure they mean it. But our case would read very differently if the synagogue's lay leaders fully authorized her to do the job for which they had hired her. If that were the case, they would be quite clear with the cantor that she needed to meet the rabbi's performance expectations, and they would alter reporting relationships such that the rabbi supervised the executive director. This would require, of course, that the lay leaders themselves backed away and did not allow themselves to be pulled into relationships among staff members. As long as they intruded into those relationships, the staff would not form properly into a functioning team; team members would always have the exit—the safety valve—provided by the lay leaders, and thus not force themselves to confront, work with, and engage meaningfully with one another. And probably worst of all, the rabbi would never have the authority to lead.

The Role of the Rabbi

Our case highlights some of the complications inherent in the rabbi's role in the synagogue. It is said that the modern rabbi must wear many *kippot* in order to be effective. The professional team of the synagogue requires that the rabbi assume various roles that serve different leadership functions.

Team Leader. As team leader, the rabbi works with lay leaders to create the mission and then articulates a vision (a path by which a mission is accomplished) for team members and for the congregation more generally. In synagogues that already have a mission prior to the rabbi joining them, the first task of the rabbi is to fully understand and accept the mission as his or her own. Ideally, this is a task that began in the interview process. For example, let's say a certain congregation prides itself as a synagogue in which everyone knows everyone else and the rabbi knows everyone's name. Their rabbi articulates a vision of the synagogue as a family that provides and values various types of small group settings (in study, social gatherings, worship, social action) that allow for greater intimacy and depth. As team leader, the rabbi works to insure that other professional staff members understand and buy into that vision.

Bridge. As bridge (described in chapter 14), the rabbi serves as the primary link between professional staff and lay leadership, such that the work of the two groups remains integrated. In this role, the rabbi also serves to protect staff members in situations where lay leaders or congregants may triangulate them. In synagogues that have executive directors or chief operating officers, some of this task is shared, as the latter will most likely assume the role of supervisor with some of the staff. For example, while the rabbi will most likely supervise the other clergy and sometimes the director of education, the executive director might supervise all administrative staff. This will vary from synagogue to synagogue and will depend on job function, ability, and time.

Supervisor. The rabbi is also in a supervisory or managerial role, relative to some staff members, and therefore needs to fulfill the classic functions of that role: goal-setting, feedback and support, holding individuals accountable for their performance, coaching for improved performance, and managing relationships. Good supervisors also find ways to inspire their staff to dream their own dreams, matching them with the wider vision that has already been articulated. A rabbi who envisions adults and children learning together is both inspiration to and supported by an educational director who creates the *Bet Sefer Mishpacha*, an alternative religious school program that brings parents together with their children for Shabbat Torah study and worship.

Convener. As team leader, the rabbi is also called upon to convene the staff, to bring them together for a number of purposes: to share information and perspectives; to help them examine the various issues, struggles, and differences they have picked up from their work with congregants; to help depersonalize conflicts and create shared understanding of what they mean about the synagogue itself; and to encourage constructive dissent and creative problem solving. Again, in large synagogues, executive directors also serve in the capacity of convener. It is essential, therefore, that the senior rabbi and executive director work together to make sure there are no mixed messages or overlap in this regard. We will have more to say about this relationship later in the chapter.

In addition to managing multiple roles within the team, rabbis are called upon to manage multiple roles within the congregation more generally—as pastors and teachers for congregants, as partners with lay leaders, as leaders and supervisors with staff. Rabbis are best able to manage these roles when they can follow certain practices:

- Be clear and transparent about when they are operating from particular roles in relation to their staff members. It might not be a bad thing for a rabbi to verbally identify which *kippa* he or she is wearing in a particular situation, saying, "Let me put on my supervisory *kippa* for this conversation," or "I need to switch *kippot* right now." This reminds both the staff member and the rabbi of the multiple roles the rabbi is called upon to play and provides for clarity as to the specific conversation about to take place.
- Not be trapped in the role of rabbi—that is, as counselor—with staff members who need to seek their own rabbis in other settings. It is fine for rabbis to be available in crisis situations for their staff, of course, but not to remain in that role, given that it undermines if not obliterates the supervisory relationship. The counselor-to-staff role becomes particularly tricky when the staff person is also a congregant, which is often the case in synagogues. In fact, many synagogues offer free membership as a perk for staff. Again, identifying the *kippa* can help.
- Remain aware that they are in some respects caught in the middle between lay leaders and professional staff, which means that they do not have the ultimate authority in some aspects, cannot fully protect staff members, and need to bring together staff members and lay leaders in appropriate ways to work on issues directly. Rabbis must thus be clear with themselves and with others about the limits of their authority, while supporting others to assume their own.
- Resist inevitable pulls from staff members to assume complete control (to become the "father figure"). These pulls are inevitable, given that congregants project rabbis as ultimate authority figures and that staff cannot help but soak up and emulate this influence. Rabbis need to reinforce, over and again, the use of the team as an organizing principle of their practice, in words and in deeds; they must continuously pull for the competence of their staff members to emerge.

The Rabbi–Executive Director Partnership

In synagogues that have executive directors, the partnerships between them and the rabbis are crucial to the creation of effective professional teams. That partnership represents, symbolically and practically, the relationship between the religious/spiritual and the financial/temporal dimensions of the synagogue and can facilitate or undermine the effective integration of those dimensions. Ultimately, for Judaism these are all "religious matters" as the Torah makes no distinction between the *mitzvot*. How we observe the Sabbath and how we treat our workers both stem from God's commandments. Nevertheless, in our common understanding of these matters, we do make distinctions between religious function (worship, life-cycle moments, Torah study) and temporal or practical function (maintenance of the buildings, daily operations, finances) and depend on the rabbi and the executive director to integrate the two. Their partnership exists amid pulls from the congregation, lay leaders, staff, and even themselves to split the two dimensions and act as if they are separate from one another, partly because it is difficult to think about how the "religious" and the "business" aspects can actually inform one another in the synagogue. There are both structural as well as relational issues involved in this dynamic.

Structural Issues

The structural dimension is defined by whether the executive director reports to the lay leadership (the board or president), the rabbi, or to both simultaneously. Different congregations choose different options. There are costs and benefits to each. Each has certain implications for how the two aspects of the synagogue are integrated.

Executive director reports to lay leadership. In this structure, the rabbi is removed from concerns about the day-to-day operations, allowing him or her to do what he or she does best—teach, counsel, and lead congregants through their life-cycle moments of celebration and sorrow. This structure also keeps the rabbi's hands "clean" when staff does not get an anticipated raise or when a member is let go from a staff position. The potential downside of this structure is that the rabbi can become aloof or uninterested in the daily realities and problems that beset the congregation. Further, rabbis, who are called upon to be visionaries of Jewish life, can have that same vision undermined by those who are calling all the shots on budget, staff, and space allocations. The result can be that a "secular person" who may not have a deep Jewish education or background winds up making what are essentially "religious decisions" by saying, "We can have this creative worship service, but we do not have the budget to offer that educational program."

Executive director reports to the rabbi. In this structure, there exists the potential of greater clarity between the two. Since the executive director is working "for" the rabbi, so to speak, they understand each other's tasks and roles and can be more supportive of one another. In addition, each will have greater access to the other. The potential downside of this structure is that everything is "on the rabbi." The rabbi cannot pretend that certain areas of synagogue function, except for that which is clearly the role of the lay leaders, are "not in the job description." Financial problems and issues with staff can be very distracting and are not necessarily the rabbi's areas of expertise. There is the additional danger that the so-called squeaky wheel will garner too much of the rabbi's attention, and those areas that belong solely to the rabbi will get neglected. Synagogue leaders may also worry that if the two top professionals of the congregation are working in this structure, lay leaders can get shut out of their role and responsibility. In a worst case scenario, this could lead to unethical or even illegal behavior.

Executive director reports to rabbi and lay leaders. This structure, in theory, allows for a constant integration of religious and administrative dimensions, as rabbis and presidents work together to direct the executive director. In practice, however, the structure is problematic, if not impossible. The rabbi and president must be on the same page. Since the presidents in most congregations change every two years, it is difficult to imagine consistency in this regard. When the rabbi and the president disagree, the executive director gets mixed messages and does not know who the real boss is and whose dictates take precedence. For example, a rabbi insists that a specific program be created which the president believes is a waste of time and money. The president wants daily financial updates, and the rabbi has charged the executive director to create a new staff manual that is consuming all of his time. When one has two bosses, the priority list can become a slippery football with lots of dropped passes. Moreover, too much power may be ceded to an executive director who plays a rabbi and president off against one another.

While both positives and negatives are clearly involved in each structure, we do believe that an organizational structure in which the executive director reports directly to the senior rabbi has the best chance to create a healthy, effective synagogue, especially when each of them takes up his or her appropriate role. Ideally, an executive director is just that; he or she *directs* the vision of the synagogue toward fruition. Thus, the executive director is chief of operations, assuring smooth daily functioning so that the synagogue can both realize and live up to its mission as spelled out in the rabbi's vision. The executive director serves the lay leadership by providing them with accurate financial data and membership statistics; enforcing the policies they have created for the real world of synagogue life; and guiding them with their committees, structures, and leadership development. When the executive director is providing this service to the lay leadership, there is no need for a direct reporting relationship. And when this service is not being provided, or is haphazard and incomplete, the lay leadership can always seek out the rabbi, who does report to them, to fix the problem.

In large synagogues, we recommend a *management team* consisting of the senior rabbi, the executive director, the president, the executive vice president, and (perhaps) the treasurer. Such a team should meet weekly to discuss issues confronting the congregation and decide on strategies for dealing with them. This structure allows for both transparency and consensus between professionals and lay leaders. From time to time, depending on the issue, this management team can expand to include other professionals or lay leaders.

Relational Issues

Aside from reporting relationships, a key question is how easily rabbis and executive directors speak the language of the other in their conversations. The danger is that each gets trapped or locked into a certain role—trapped by projections—that limits their ability to collaborate. If the rabbi is seen only in terms of "religious" aspects, and the executive director only in terms of "business" aspects, and they are treated as distinct from one another, their ability to create a useful working relationship will be severely limited. Each needs to "own" aspects of the other such that together they are integrating the different dimensions of synagogues.

Rabbis thus have to be willing to compromise and let go of their "pet projects" and ideal notion of how and when things need to be done. It may not be practical to hold a certain worship service outdoors, because the custodians, already understaffed by the injury to one of their fellows, have to set up for a big wedding later that evening. Executive directors have to understand that while the synagogue must perform in an appropriate businesslike fashion, it is ultimately not a business and may from time to time have to make decisions based on individual or communal needs. "Is it good for the Jews?" is the question that needs to drive much of synagogue decision making. Rabbis and executive directors each must find ways to honor the other's perspective, training, and viewpoint and, in doing so, learn as much as they can from and with one another.

Teams, Stuck and Unstuck

Professional teams in synagogues can develop over time into highly effective performing units. With the appropriate leadership from both rabbis and executive directors, clergy and staff can develop relationships with one another that are trusting enough and safe enough to allow for ongoing learning—through constructive feedback, reflection on their work together, mutual support, and challenge. We highlight the importance of ongoing learning since, as Judaism teaches us, the world in which we live is still unredeemed and people are not perfect. As a result, no matter how great a synagogue we have created, professional teams inevitably run into difficulty and must be able to learn from their behaviors about their environments and the conditions that enable them to be most effective.

Healthy teams will confront issues, learn from them, and move on. They go from getting stuck in some fashion, to learning, to changing, and to performing effectively. They repeat over and again, like a wheel turning, moving, and progressing. These groups become learning systems. They tend to have productive ways to deal with differences in views and perspectives among members. They implicitly develop rules to deal with differences that allow members to learn and make necessary adjustments. Like the *Torah sh'b'al peh,* the oral Torah, useful unwritten rules include the following:

- Differences—among perspectives, beliefs, attitudes, and ideas—are allowed to surface and breathe and, if necessary, develop into conflicts. Members let differences exist and talk about them rather than rush to get away from them.
- Differences are embraced as opportunities for learning and creativity. Members view differences as the friend to the task, not the enemy. The lack of differences in opinions, ideas, and ap-

proaches is viewed with suspicion. Our rule of thumb is that when no differences emerge, either complacency or fear/distrust exists. In authoritative environments, members of the team see "no use" in discussing differences.

- Conflicts are framed around tasks, not individuals. Members look at conflicts in terms of what they say about the task rather than about the individuals who are raising issues. Members focus on dealing with difficult task-related issues rather than fixing someone's personality.

- Task-focused conflicts are based on a lot of data from which to evaluate various alternatives. Members move conversations from the abstract and the personal (and overly emotional) into the realm of facts.

- Members hang on to shared goals and interests rather than polarizing positions. They focus on shared interests and goals and thus move away from personalizing and positioning.

- Members examine their differences with respect, concern about process, and a sense of perspective as well as humor. This becomes more likely when members focus on both maintaining working relationships and performing high-quality work.

- Decision-making mechanisms do not demand consensus and are perceived as fair. Forced consensus does not work well; someone has to take responsibility for making a decision in a transparently fair process. On the other hand, teams need to leave room for honest consensus that emerges naturally.

Unhealthy teams avoid issues, stay stuck, and do not learn how to progress. They get stuck and then avoid the issues. They develop coping mechanisms that enable them to continue avoiding the issues and then underperform, which leaves them caught in a cycle, like a wheel stuck in mud, turning fruitlessly, digging itself deeper.

Often, when groups remain stuck, it is due to other unwritten rules by which they deal with differences in views and perspectives that disable productive work. These include, for example:

- Differences—and possible conflicts—are to be avoided, ignored, smoothed over, suppressed, laughed away, or in other ways made to disappear, as if they are simply too threatening for group members to deal with or as if the group is somehow too fragile to examine differences closely.

- Members act as if it is more important to "get along" than to productively engage differences and potential conflicts. The group substitutes one task (getting along) for another (performing highest-quality work).

- Differences are framed in terms of right/wrong thinking that shuts down creativity. Framing differences as either/or undercuts potential for differences to be avenues to new insights.

- Conflicts are framed in terms of people rather than in terms of the task-related issues they represent. Groups avoid dealing with task-related issues that raise anxiety by acting as if the issues are the people themselves. Team members gossip about rather than speak directly to one another.

- Conflicts are not traced to their originating sources. Conflicts are not always what they seem; what looks like a fight between two individuals is, often enough, a struggle in the team more generally about two different ways for that team to proceed. Team members take conflicts at face value rather than examining their underlying meanings.

- Conflicts get pushed outside the group. Groups sometimes export all their conflicts, finding enemies outside the group and acting as if all the conflict is with them—with other groups like "the board," or "the temple," or "the parents." While in the short run, this may have the effect of drawing members closer, in the long run it shuts down useful explorations of differences among team members.

These sorts of unproductive rules of dealing with conflict consistently lead to professional teams in synagogues becoming stuck in various patterns. Some patterns involve teams avoiding dealing with important issues directly. Staff members become too dependent on their rabbi, cantor, executive director, or one another in order to avoid fully engaging as a team, even though the results might lead to poor outcomes or repeated mistakes. Or they engage in passive-aggressive behaviors, such as withdrawal, absence, disengagement, politicking, or gossiping, rather than dealing with issues more directly. Other patterns involve fight/flight. Team members align against lay leaders/board and wage external struggles as a way to flee from the more difficult examining of the differences within their own teams/groups. Or teams split into various subgroups—based on roles, tenure, age, or perspective—that are at odds with one another and wage fights. Another pattern involves team members turning on one another. They scapegoat individuals in order to avoid learning about how the group as a whole did not perform effectively.

Getting unstuck from such patterns requires leadership and occasionally outside assistance from lay leaders or others skilled in working with groups. The process involves people recognizing that their teams are stuck and raising the issues in the group. People then need to develop a diagnosis that takes into account various factors, including leadership, clarity of tasks and roles, relations with lay leaders, and individual performance factors that are at play. Leaders need to use the mission as an anchor that helps keep members aligned and positive; they need to remain positive about signs of progress, by rewarding and reinforcing signs of movement. Finally, they need to make clear the new implicit rules—the "oral Torah"—and make them manifest to build in progress and make it part of how the professional team routinely functions.

Other Relationships

That rabbis and cantors do not get along, do not respect one another, is almost legendary in synagogue life. It is unfortunate. Yet it certainly does not have to be that way. While rabbis are the leaders of the synagogue, cantors are also clergy, as well as being the real experts when it comes to liturgy, prayer, and music. In an effectively functioning synagogue, the rabbi will set a vision that will include the prayer life of the community, but it will be the cantor who will create the canvas for what it will actually look like. For example, let's say the rabbi believes there ought to be lots of lay participation—a congregation in which congregants feel included and competent to participate, even lead. In such a synagogue, the cantor might train *shlichai tzibur* (prayer leaders) and *ba'alei korei* (Torah readers), teach during the service, and choose melodies that are easy for everyone to sing. If the rabbi is selecting the music each week, the congregation is in trouble. And if the cantor does not recognize that the rabbi is his or her "boss," there is similar trouble.

This same approach should hold true with the educator, youth director, program staff, assistant rabbi, and other team members. The rabbi sets the agenda but then must trust and empower each staff team member to carry it out, providing input and appropriate feedback. While the rabbi may be an expert in Talmud, it is the synagogue's director of education who is the curriculum expert. It will be his or her job to translate that expertise into learning.

Much has also been written about the unique relationship between the rabbi and the rabbi emeritus. Most of the movements have created guidelines for this relationship. Nevertheless, we have seen a great deal of failed transitions because of the difficulties involved in making this relationship work. When faced with such a transition, synagogues do well to create a transition team guided by someone who is not a part of the synagogue to help create and monitor absolute clarity of roles. Transitions, especially of a rabbi who has had a long career with a synagogue, are some of the trickier and more difficult moments in the life of a community. As we like to say, the new rabbi is only a successor if and when he or she succeeds. Everyone must be invested if this success will become a reality. The price of failure is way too high.

Teamwork Makes It Happen

One of the great mistakes we see in synagogue life is that it is overly dependent on individual talent. Congregations often delude themselves into thinking that if they can just get a few "superstars," their congregation will thrive or, worse, be able to compete with the other shuls in town. While we recognize that the "cult of the individual" does exist, we maintain that it is not that difficult to gather a talented group of individuals and have them create dynamic programs and educational opportunities for the membership. After all, there are a lot of smart, capable professionals within the Jewish community. The much more difficult task is to have these people working as a team with the lay leadership.

When they are able to do so, not only will the programmatic, learning, and worship opportunities sustain the congregants, but also the members of the team will help sustain one another. When this occurs, this spirit of caring for one another and working together is palpable, affecting all aspects of synagogue life, to the great benefit of congregants and staff alike.

17

POLITICS AND POWER

> And Pharaoh's courtiers said to him, "How long will this one
> be a snare to us? Let the people go so that they may worship
> their God. Are you not yet aware that Egypt is lost?"
> (Exodus 10:7)

Politics and power exist in synagogues as they do in any organization. This is not surprising to those who have spent any time trying to move synagogue projects or programs ahead, make changes happen, or serve as board members. Yet it is also quite surprising to those of us who see the word "political" as the antithesis of the idea of religion, feeling that the former has no place in the latter. We often hear from laypeople, "I refuse to get involved in my temple. I can't stand the politics!" This sentiment, we believe, is based on a misunderstanding of what politics is and is not. Politics is not a dirty word. And politics is not a dirty business, though it may seem that way sometimes when we look at our various governments and the way they operate. Politics is simply the way in which people sort through different agendas, options, and perspectives and try to get things done.

We take the stance in this chapter that there is such a thing as political reality that must be taken into account in our synagogues. Political reality refers to what will ultimately be acceptable to people and their long-term interests. Synagogues are filled with ambiguity; knowing what direction to take to energize congregants, attract and retain members, and create good clergy–lay leader working relationships is not always clear. Political realities help people sort through possible options. They separate what is possible from that which is less possible.

In the quote above, Pharaoh's men remind him of the political reality. The God of the Israelites has laid waste to Egypt, visiting plague after plague upon its people. The Egyptians are suffering. Their army is depleted and exhausted. Their economy is reeling. Pharaoh simply does not have the resources to continue. His people lack the strength and will to continue to fight what has become a hopeless battle. Such is the political reality. Pharaoh did not listen, of course. His army was swallowed, as much by the political reality that he refused to consider as by the Sea of Reeds itself.

The political realities of synagogues are not presented so starkly, of course, and they have quite a different flavor to them. There are no synagogue pharaohs (at least, we hope not), no supreme leaders who rule without consideration. Instead, we have various people—lay leaders, clergy, staff, and executive boards—who all have certain interests and agendas, certain beliefs about the wisest courses of action. Politics is one means by which those people sort out what will occur. People engage in politics—build coalitions, win over others, curry favor—in order to build momentum and power. People and ideas that attract enough synagogue resources to gain influence and constituents emerge as acceptable paths through ambiguity and uncertainty. Political behavior is thus the engine that propels the vetting of possible directions; those ultimately selected are, ideally, those that serve the most interests. Such are the methods or tactics involved in managing a government or state. This points to a relatively clear, transparent process by which people are represented, with checks and balances to aid decision-making processes about the direction of an institution and how resources are allocated within it.

Of course, we have presented the political process in its ideal state. Reality tells us that synagogue politics does not always work this way. Politics may also describe activities that are simply aimed at gaining power. These activities are often less transparent. They are subterranean. They lead to abuse rather than appropriate use of power. Such abuse occurs when people engage in corruption: they use the tools by which things get done in the service of their own ends or believe that their ends are those of the organization more generally. The abuse of power and politics causes a deflation of energy in the synagogue and undermines congregants' trust in their institution and that of religion more generally.

In this chapter, we focus on the use and abuse of politics and power in synagogue life and the ways in which healthy organizations enable the former and guard against the latter. The key issue that we will explore involves the nature of influence. The influence that some people wield might be directly proportional to that which they ought to wield, based on the roles they have in the synagogue and the people they represent in one fashion or another. Yet influence might be disproportional as well.

Individuals, because they rescue the synagogue from financial emergencies, or because of family history, or because they are able to stay in power seemingly "forever," might have more say in synagogue happenings than they ought. This is problematic. Governance structures may be undermined. People might grow cynical, feeling that they have little say or that the system is corrupt or unfair. Covert or shadow governance might become the norm. People become sorted into "in" and "out" groups. Healthy synagogues prevent such possibilities from taking hold.

The Fund

The president of Congregation Beth Emunah was conducting a second town hall meeting in as many weeks. Congregants were invited to organize and make presentations about the use of a youth activities fund. The fund was originally developed as a source of scholarships for youth who were unable to afford certain synagogue youth programs. The fund had minimal and, in some years, no use as the synagogue community grew wealthier and as the teens became increasingly focused on other activities. Donations to the fund had slowed to a trickle over the last several years. This captured the attention of several board members who happened to be leading an initiative to rehab a room in the building for the temple's youth group. They mentioned the relative inactivity of the fund to several parents of the teens who were leading the drive to create the youth room. The parents now wished to use this fund for the room, which would in effect eliminate the fund. They argued that nowadays the youth program was self-sustaining and that there were other sources for scholarships if someone could not attend certain events because of cost.

The parents brought their request to the president. He decided that, rather than simply have the board vote on the matter, he would use the issue as an opportunity to engage the synagogue community in a discussion about its agenda for the youth group more generally. He announced the town hall meetings as part of his weekly *Shabbos* message and again in the synagogue bulletin. He hoped that by asking people to put together presentations about the redirection and use of restricted funds different from its original purpose, there was a higher likelihood that the meetings would be marked by a certain degree of informed debate. He scheduled the meetings several months out to give people some time to organize their ideas and develop thoughtful presentations.

At the first town hall meeting, the parents of the teens who were leading the initiative to rehab the room and who had initially brought the issue before the board, made a presentation about the new room and how it would serve the youth group. They told the assembled group of thirty or so that times had changed since the creation of the youth activities fund and that while the fund had served a real purpose when it was created, it was no longer as necessary. They said that the synagogue was losing kids after their bar or bat mitzvah. If the teens could help design a space that they thought was "cool," the parents argued, it would keep them active longer.

The presentation was well received, particularly by the other parents of current and future teenagers in the congregation. A second group, smaller than the first, also made a presentation. They said that they represented people who had given to the fund over the years because they believed in the mission of the fund and purposely did not wish to give money to support what they called "bricks and mortar." They said that they feared that if the fund were used up, the kids who did need scholarships would not ask for them. There were several nods among those listening to the presentation and several follow-up questions. The president adjourned the first town hall meeting and said that another meeting would provide opportunity for more dialogue.

The day after the meeting, the president received a phone call from an older member of the congregation. She told him that she had just heard about the meeting and was disappointed not to have been there. She also said that she had been a close friend of the original donor, now deceased, whose substantial contribution had subsidized the fund. She was appalled, she said, on his behalf, that the synagogue that he had loved and supported so passionately would turn its back on his gift and destroy his vision. She told the president that she was beginning to circulate a petition to all of her old friends, whom she knew agreed with her, that would ask the board to halt the meetings and find another source of money for the new youth room. Before hanging up, she told the president that she was also trying to get in touch with the donor's children, who no longer lived in the community, so they too could protest what she called "this tragic turn of events." The president was taken off guard and could not respond adequately. The next day he arranged to meet with the woman and several others who agreed with her. They spoke for a long time. The president listened patiently and agreed with them that the donor's legacy ought to be preserved. He persuaded them to attend the second town hall meeting and present their points to others. They agreed not to circulate a petition.

In the days leading up to the second town hall meeting, the president heard of several instances of people lobbying their friends in the hopes that they would show up at the meeting and affirm desired positions. He hoped that the meeting would be manageable. It was. The rabbi weighed in, but only to clarify Jewish law on the issue of *tzedakah* and its use. People again made brief presentations in which they did their best to take into account the points that others had previously made. The president asked the assembled group to develop some proposals together that they could vote on. The vote would not be binding but would offer information to the board as the decision-making authority. The group developed several proposals—to use the fund entirely, not at all, or partially. The first votes were inconclusive. Then, with some compromise, the group moved toward agreement on the third option. Collectively, they decided to support the use of the majority of the fund for the new youth room but keep it open for future donations. They decided as well to name the new youth room in honor of the original donor of the fund, which pleased its supporters greatly.

This was a political process, but no one would call this "politics" with a negative connotation. People organized around an idea, created coalitions, made a decision, and voted, bringing the idea to fruition. It was a healthy process, and though sides were clearly drawn, it did both animate and bring the community together. People struggled, all wanting what they thought was best for the congregation. The president made the process as transparent as possible. He invited people to find others who agreed with them and to collect and present their ideas. He took people who felt left outside the process and brought them into it. He halted distracting processes, like the petition, which would have undermined the public vetting of ideas. He made explicit the fact that the board would make a decision but that he wanted that decision to be informed by the different perspectives of the community. And he created the space for people to fashion creative solutions.

Differences of opinion are inevitable in a congregation. Healthy organizations do not try to eliminate, ignore, minimize, or sweep these differences under the proverbial rug; rather, they utilize them as a way of redefining and clarifying the synagogue's mission and purpose. In this process there are always political realities that are in play. And there is power and authority that must always be considered. These are all part of getting things done in synagogues. The crucial issue is the extent to which politics and power are in the service of, rather than overwhelm the possibility of, healthy dialogue.

Politics in Perspective

We believe that synagogues are places of energy, creativity, excitement, and meaning when all the voices of their community members are represented. It is through diversity that new, creative ways of solving problems emerge. Unless we are confronted, more or less gently, with different perspectives or beliefs or ideas, our ways of seeing and acting remain basically unchanged. We become self-referential, lacking useful perspective from which to view our congregations and ourselves. We need to hear from as many people as possible. We need contradictions. We need questions that make us stop and consider. We need to be pushed to articulate and defend our ideas. All of this requires people who do not think alike to speak up and to be heard.

We know this intellectually. It is another matter entirely to actually seek out and embrace others who challenge and confront us and our beliefs, who pose real differences. Such differences are often unsettling. Competing perspectives, all with some validity, arouse a sense of contradiction, ambiguity, and uncertainty. Even as we move toward taking in the different voices of the synagogue community, we often move away from the noise and challenge and difficulty of it all. This is particularly true when the stakes are high. When issues matter a great deal and become invested with all sorts of emotions, people struggle with their twin impulses to attend carefully to different perspectives and to shut them out entirely. At such times, politics arise.

We can think of three general dimensions of synagogue life in which power and politics are often called into play. One dimension is when issues arise relating to a synagogue's mission or its survival as a viable institution. We have never heard of a congregation having any political rancor over whether or not to hold High Holy Day services. But there could be if the decision involved whether to have two separate "shifts" (i.e., an early and a late service) in the synagogue's sanctuary versus praying together as a community in a single service at a local hotel or auditorium. If the congregation's mission focused on creating an inclusive family-like community, this kind of decision could become highly politicized. And there could be rancor if the decision involved choosing from among different outreach programs to attract new members desperately needed for the synagogue to survive.

A second dimension is when current issues arise related to unresolved historical issues in a synagogue community. There are a fair number of such historical issues that, like underlying geological fault lines (or land mines) are always there and might well be triggered by seemingly incidental events. There are battles that were won and lost a long time ago but have not been forgotten, decisions made that turned out to have been ill-fated and not forgotten, relationships marked by betrayals, grudges held. Any issue might raise these histories, opening wounds and sending people forth into battle once again. The decisions that congregational leaders need to make as a matter of course—choosing melodies for the worship services, hiring or firing clergy, constructing a new building, creating a new social action program, crafting a new *siddur*, writing new bylaws that change power structures, making changes in dues structure—often represent not simply the present and future, but the past as well, and can be overwhelmed by it.

The third dimension in which power and politics are triggered is when larger societal issues get played out in our synagogues. Synagogues inevitably import and contain anxieties on behalf of the larger Jewish community: about the place and meaning of religion and God in modern life (religious practices), about the survival of Judaism in the context of demographic changes (intermarriage), about the success of children (education). The Jewish community struggles with these issues, often in the context of the synagogue. Congregations must engage with one another and make choices, and there are no easy answers. Political behavior in synagogues is often in reality the struggle between different ideologies, approaches, interests, and groups in the Jewish community more generally. These tensions are imported into our synagogues and waged just beneath the surface of overt battles for resources, influence, direction, and other vital elements of organizational life.

When such dimensions are activated in synagogues, much gets triggered: people get stirred up about issues and seek ways to control outcomes. They turn to political behaviors to try and manage situations about which they feel uncertain. They align with influential others to advance their projects and interests. They join with others in formal groups or informal coalitions. They seek to acquire, enhance, and use power and other resources to obtain their preferred outcomes. Such activities may be quite rational. They can define a process by which scarce resources are allocated to various synagogue programs and departments. Synagogue politics are thus distantly related to democratic politics. Both operate on the principle that the competing interests of various groups and constituencies will vie in various forums, out of which will emerge solutions that garner enough resources and power to influence the larger system. Both hold to the notion that the rightness of ideas about how best to achieve preferred outcomes shall emerge through a process by which proponents seek to persuade others, gaining champions and momentum.

Politics, then, is simply a way in which people attempt to influence others. Political behavior involves getting others to throw their energy, support, and resources behind certain initiatives. Good politicians are able to get others to believe that their interests are aligned with whatever initiatives the politicians are backing. They persuade people that their voices are heard and taken into account. They give others what they need in order to get them invested. They share credit. And good politicians act according to what they believe will work, what will pass muster; they understand and live within political realities, knowing that unless they have the support of the larger group, nothing much will happen.

There is an intricate story from the Torah that shows such political reality at work. In *parshat Terumah* and *Tetzaveh,* we read of the elaborate conceptualization of the tabernacle/*mishkan,* the portable sanctuary that would serve as the Jewish people's first place of worship. The description begins with the creation of the Ark of the Covenant, working its way outward, from the Holy of Holies to the outer courtyard, to the tent and its materials. The description is elaborate and complete, including measurements, numbers of pegs, and other arcane information. This description is then "interrupted" by Moses's return up Mount Sinai and the incident of the golden calf. Then, surprisingly, in a text that is known for its sparseness of detail, two more entire portions—*Vayakhel* and *Pekude*—seemingly repeat the entire description, again. What is going on?

Upon closer examination, we find that the latter two portions are not an identical repetition at all. They are mirror opposites, with some minor exceptions. While *parashat Terumah* begins with the inner sanctuary and works its way to the outer structure, *Vayakhel* begins with the outer and works its way to the inner. Since no words are wasted in the Torah, what we would like to suggest is that the first two portions represent the ideal and the latter two the real. In the ideal, we begin with what is most important, the Ark containing God's words to Moses. But in the real, the people wisely created the outer tent, which would protect the holy ritual items that would be contained within. What happened in the interim? Political reality. While Moses was away with God dreaming up the future relationship with the people of Israel, including, "You shall have no other gods beside Me," the people themselves were in a very different place—not yet ready for that level of commitment, or perhaps not yet ready for a belief in one God. They were not ready to accept the idealized tabernacle, which began with the Ark of the Covenant, representing the spiritual oneness of the people with God. The real tabernacle started with the outside tent walls, representing the physical and/or material world, the world of flesh and blood, the world in which the people dwelt. Reality had to temper the ideal so that the tabernacle could get built. And it did. In the end, the people wound up with a worship space, essentially the same as it was dreamt to be, but not exactly. That is politics at its best.

Politics Gone Awry

Synagogue leaders strive to create representative systems, beginning with boards and their various committees, that enable people's voices to be heard and registered. Yet widespread representation is difficult to achieve. Only some members strive to make their voices heard; as in national elections, only a certain percentage of people care to show up and vote. Those who do show up and care a great deal about certain issues may have outsized influence. Their voices may be loud or persistent. They fill the voids left by others. Certain portions of the congregation might thus be overrepresented at the expense of those that are underrepresented. This is, in part, simply the reality of synagogues. There is not a great deal that we can do about people who simply do not care enough to show up and speak, other than giving them continued opportunity to do so.

In some synagogues another, more insidious dynamic may be at work. People may have undue influence based not on the power of ideas and solutions, but on that of other dimensions—money, access to clergy, personal relations with board members, or having served on the board themselves—that enable them to serve their own interests rather than the interests of the congregation as a whole. In such ways, synagogue politics, often a useful tool by which leaders identify appropriate strategies and necessary changes, come to be viewed with skepticism.

We have seen this at play in synagogues. People create events and programs for friends without the use of committees. Committee chairs stay in place "for life." Board members appoint friends to head up areas of synagogue function or give them business with the temple without the benefit of multiple bids or open competition. Decisions are made behind the scenes in ways that do not allow for the open exploration of different possibilities. Individuals wield more influence than they ought simply because of their relationships with others. We believe that such acts point to the corruption of the representative process.

A synagogue's board of directors is the place where the dance of politics and corruption is most alluring. It is a fact of synagogue life that boards both attract and create friends to work together. Often enough, people serve on boards because someone they like or admire asked them to do so. Yet too often this plays out in ways that undermine the board. Members vote as blocs, voting with their friends or because someone told them how to vote rather than considering the issue. Members support or boycott events, programs, fund-raisers and other initiatives because their friends are doing so. Members give business to fellow congregants because they want to support them, and hope for good deals in return, without bidding out contracts or looking into other possibilities. In such ways, board members do not represent the best interests of the congregation as a whole. They are unable to set aside personal relationships. Yet this is exactly the religious obligation accepted when one chooses to serve on the synagogue's board.

When board members act to represent only part of a congregation, based on their own relationships, they step away from their roles as board members and stop working on behalf of the synagogue mission. This occurs as well when board members manipulate the timing of their decisions to serve their own interests. They may make decisions without deliberation or avoid making them at all. Rushing something through often indicates that there is very little real support for an issue. Or leaders cannot or will not create the appropriate mechanisms for an issue to have a thorough and fair hearing. This is particularly dangerous when an issue is made to belong to a single person or a small handful of people who want to impose their will on the synagogue community as a whole. Board members may also delay processes so often that decisions never seem to get made. There are times that tabling an issue or sending it back to committee is exactly the right thing to do to enable the community to think things through and deliberate on the appropriate course of action. Yet board members may also avoid making tough decisions or those that powerful members do not like. This is problematic for the integrity of the board as well as for the congregation it purportedly represents.

Finally, we must note that synagogues are not immune to politically motivated character assassinations. Members have been known to cast aspersions on others. Viewed through a political lens, such aspersions are designed to gain power by weakening the power of others. These are the dark arts. They include rumors—*lashon hara*. We wrote about this pernicious process in chapter 11 and simply wish to note here that *lashon hara* is meant, consciously or not, to weaken the power of others. Similarly, members may launch covert personal attacks. A congregant does not agree with the rabbi's position on Israel, and to weaken the rabbi's authority, questions his "Zionist credentials" or level of observance. Or congregants may attack family members, particularly of lay leaders and clergy, who are more vulnerable than the leaders themselves, but this wounds the leaders nevertheless. This, too, may be understood through a political lens as acts of strengthening one's own positions by weakening others'. The Talmud teaches us that there are two ways of elevating oneself. The first is to work on self-improvement through study, dedication to a cause, hard work, self-reflection, clarifying relationships, and the like. The other way is to push down the person next to whom you are standing. The first way is more difficult but is long lasting; the second way is quicker but harms the other and ultimately the self.

Ill Effects

It matters quite a bit that people may have more or less influence than they ought. Influence shapes how missions are framed and pursued, resources are allocated and used, programs are created and supported, and cultures are created and changed. Different synagogue groups—formal groups, like clergy and staff, and informal groups, like new members or single parents—may have different interests that are met, or not, based on how much influence their representatives might have. To the extent that covert behaviors and relationships gather influence and deposit it unfairly in some groups and not others, the synagogue as a whole is undermined. People begin to distrust the formal mechanisms by which ideas are developed and programs come to fruition. They become cynical, disillusioned with synagogue life or the entire Jewish enterprise. The cost to synagogue vitality and health is enormous.

It is an almost inevitable, yet unfortunate, dimension of organizational life that those in power tend to exert influence in ways that maintain their power. People appoint supporters to committees. They seek out like-minded others to serve as board members. They groom others to take their positions. With this as a backdrop, people who feel voiceless—unheard, without influence or representation—are limited to some particular options. They can assume the role of the engaged minority, raising objections and pressing for reasonable changes but ultimately falling into line with powerful others. They can create splits in the congregation by instigating other programs and events that run in parallel with those more formally sanctioned. They can gather together, lobby others, and create enough momentum to challenge boards in some fashion. They can become passive-aggressive or refuse to get involved and to offer useful ideas and energy. They can get overly political themselves, seeking access to some inner circle, turning toward some groups and away from others.

They can also act aggressively, and move toward splitting away. Moses did. One way to read the confrontation between Moses and Pharaoh is as a parable about the voiceless. Pharaoh had the influence. He wished to maintain the status quo. His community, he believed, was best served by maintaining slave labor. Moses, on the other hand, wished to create a new identity for his people marked by a shift in allegiance from Pharaoh to Adonai. Initially, Moses wished to gain Pharaoh's consent without confrontation. He asked Pharaoh to let his people go. Pharaoh refused. Turning a stick into a snake did not convince Pharaoh; after all, any magician could do that. Neither did the first plague. But with each successive plague, Moses's power grew. Pharaoh, however, remained locked within his own paradigm, within what the Torah describes as his "hardened heart." Pharaoh was unwilling or incapable of giving voice to the Israelites, of bringing them into the fold of the community. This cost him his life and, indeed, the life of his son, which in the Egyptian religion of the time meant his own immortality.

We believe there are lessons here. Synagogue leaders create the conditions for uprisings, or for withdrawals, when they give too little space for others to influence their destiny and that of the community more generally. Leaders create enemies rather than allies when they are invested in maintaining their own power. And leaders sow the seeds of their own destruction when they do not create ways to bring in others, give them fair hearings, and feel part of a larger community. If not, the community may come crashing down, in bits and pieces or, as in the Sea of Reeds, all at once. Pharaoh, of course, was a dictator, not a politician. His lack of political skill and his inability to understand political reality was his undoing. It distracted him from what ought to have been his overarching priority, his mission: the growth (rather than destruction) of Egypt.

In our list of actions that those without influence can take—become the engaged minority, create splits in the congregation, mount overt challenges to the board, withdraw, get overly political, or split away—only the first option is in the spirit of the healthy congregation. Those who take up the role of engaged minority offer a great service to the congregation in the challenges they offer and the ideas they help to shape. They become a vital part of the chorus of voices that mark the healthy congregation. Each of the other options we name creates damage. Each is, or ought to be, a last resort to which people finally and slowly turn, hopeless with the effort of trying to make their voices heard.

Open and Shut

We return to a note that we have sounded over and over in this book: the crucial importance of transparency. Political behavior is not simply tolerable, but necessary when a synagogue is faced with an array of choices and a sense of uncertainty. Such behavior must be transparent, however; it must be clear and public and beyond reproach. Politics is simply a process by which support is ascertained or created for certain paths to be taken through uncertainty and ambiguity that, ideally, enable the synagogue to stay true to its mission. Attention must be paid to political realities.

We offered a reasonable model of this in our case study, in which the board president created a public process for articulating and vetting ideas about what to do with a fund and an idea. The lessons from that case apply. The president was clear about the rules by which the decision would be made, namely, that the board would make the decision based on input from the community. An open process was created, enabling people to develop arguments and make presentations. The president sought out different constituencies and encouraged those who considered wielding influence outside the process to do so within the process instead. The board convened the meetings; members did their best to represent—to re-present, if you will—the different views alive within the congregation. A solution was developed that represented those different views. This was an overtly political process. It enabled a number of different people to see themselves represented in both the process and a solution. Not everyone was thrilled with the final result, but all felt heard and all felt represented. We believe that this is in itself a good outcome.

This is a good process partly because the relationships that move it along are *authorized* rather than unauthorized. By authorized, we mean that people wield influence in ways that are appropriate to their given roles. The president initiates and facilitates a process. Congregants prepare arguments, try to get others to join them, and make presentations.

Board members listen and then deliberate. Everyone is aware of these processes and what others are doing. The process is transparent. It helps people map and travel through their political landscapes.

Unauthorized relationships are far less public. They are shut, not open. They are political, in the distasteful sense of the word. Staff members work with lay leaders (and vice versa) with whom they do not have a reporting relationship, as when a teacher discusses a school problem with a board member without having discussed it with the school principal or a secretary fills the president in on what has been happening at the synagogue without the knowledge of the rabbi. The rabbi seeks the help of a powerful or wealthy congregant for a vote that the board of directors will take. Several wealthy congregants demand a policy change, ask for personal favors that contravene a policy, or move to fire clergy or other staff without going through the appropriate procedures that were, indeed, put in place to guard against exactly that sort of unauthorized process. Like mushrooms or secrets, such unauthorized relationships grow in the dark, away from public awareness. Inevitably, they erode the moral fabric of the synagogue. They leave members feeling betrayed, without quite knowing how or why, and less reluctant to engage in meaningful public processes.

We often hear from people "I'm very spiritual, but I do not like organized religion." Our usual flip response is, "Try a synagogue. Most of them are not that well organized!" But we get the point. The translation of spirituality—the desire to be close to God, to belong to a community of other seekers, to be fulfilled and filled up by one's Judaism—is too often undermined by the abuse of power, the misuse of the political system within the synagogue. In fact, we would venture to say that whenever there is abuse of power and politics, there is a deflation of energy in the enterprise, and there may also be a denigration of religion as well as trust in the institution of religion more generally. Taken to the extreme, this may very well lead to feelings of betrayal and violation about organized religion. Sadly, we see signs of this throughout the Jewish community. Such losses of people's faith and loyalty are difficult, if not impossible, to recover. They may very well be one of the underlying causes of the high rate of disaffiliation we see throughout the Jewish community. The Jewish people can ill afford it.

18

TRAUMA AND RECOVERY

May the Source of Strength, who blessed the ones before us,
help us find the courage to make our lives a blessing,
and let us say, Amen.
(From the mishebayrach prayer by Debbie Friedman)

Traumatic events occur not simply in the lives of individual congregants, but in the lives of congregations themselves. This notion has some precedent in our tradition. Korach questioned the integrity and authority of Moses, and the earth swallowed him and his followers. God struck down the worshipers of the golden calf, leaving the Israelites stunned and reeling. Moses died, leaving his people bereft just as they needed their courage to enter the promised land. Each of these cataclysmic events may be understood not simply in terms of what they meant for the individuals involved, but for the community more generally. Korach died, yes, as did a presumably somewhat frustrated Moses, as did those who gave in to their fear and doubt at the foot of Mount Sinai. They each suffered, yet their communities suffered as well. The Israelite people absorbed each trauma and were altered by it in ways large and small.

Synagogues of today house the modern Israelites, and we, too, as congregations may be deeply shaken. Events or ongoing patterns of behavior may leave us feeling wounded, violated, or betrayed. Unhappily, we see certain types of traumas in synagogue life with some regularity. There are boundary violations, in which a synagogue leader takes advantage of his or her position in ways that violate trust; for example, a rabbi has an affair with a congregant or other staff member, or a board member misuses temple funds or awards contracts to certain friends. There are failed leadership transitions, as with the succession of a long-standing senior rabbi when the previous senior (now emeritus) continues to involve himself or herself with leadership decisions or members continue to seek out "their" rabbi, and he or she colludes. There are firings of clergy or other key, perhaps beloved, staff. There is the abuse of children in school.

There are congregational splits or "breakaways" that tear apart congregations and force divided loyalties. There are rifts, often public, between rabbis and other leaders that cause dissension within the congregation.

Each of these types of events or patterns affects the congregation as well as the particular individuals involved. Trauma can be collective; it can be a property of the synagogue itself or of specific departments, not simply of individual members. Difficult moments in the life of a synagogue dramatically affect those closest in proximity, but the difficulty does not simply lodge within them. It radiates. Ripples reverberate throughout the congregation. The trauma becomes lodged within the congregation itself. If the congregation is able to process the trauma, members can figure out what it means and absorb both that knowledge and the emotions released by the trauma. If the congregation is unable to process the trauma, it seeps into the congregation itself. There it remains, disturbing the synagogue's functioning like bodily waste that cannot be flushed out of the human system. The synagogue is altered; it becomes "dis-eased."

In this chapter, we explore these dynamics more closely. We suggest that while healthy congregations can do much to ensure that issues are dealt with early and effectively, there is only so much that a congregation and its leaders can do to ward off trauma completely. People are human; they make mistakes. Their best intentions are not always enough to stop them from hurting others in traumatic ways. When traumas occur, however, there are relatively healthy and unhealthy ways to deal with them. Healthy processes bespeak resilience; unhealthy processes bespeak fragility. We will explain more about this throughout this chapter.

The earlier example of the rabbi who signed a discretionary fund check and was then accused of "pocketing the money" is again useful as an illustration of an even deeper unhealthy dynamic.

Broken Trust

"Can you explain what your signature is doing on the back of this check?"

That was not exactly the way Rabbi Asher Soforno anticipated starting his weekly meeting with his president; nevertheless, he looked up from the page of Talmud he had been studying that morning, and trying to appear calmer than he was feeling, replied, "And a *boker tov* to you, too, Joe. What on earth on you talking about?"

Joe Klein, the president of Agudath Achim, went on to say that he had received a phone call from Bill Schwartz, a former vice president of the shul, who had received a call from the writer of the check (who wanted to remain anonymous) saying that he was shocked and offended that the rabbi would "pocket the money he donated to the synagogue." Joe tried to assure Rabbi Soforno that he really did not believe anything unethical occurred but that it looked really bad that a check written to his discretionary fund wound up in his personal account. He needed an explanation.

Asher wanted to scream. Two years of working incredibly hard for this congregation and still there was this mistrust. He understood full well what had occurred before his tenure with A.A. (as it was called within the community). After a long and illustrious career, Rabbi Jacob Molino retired, to be succeeded by Stephen Miller, a "rising star" in the movement. It was a disaster. Rabbi Miller could do nothing right in the eyes of the congregants, and so after three years, his contract was not renewed, to the chagrin and anger of many young families who then left the synagogue to form a *havurah* with Rabbi Miller as their leader. Feeling great pressure, the search committee quickly formed and brought back one of Rabbi Molino's former assistants, Eric Stein, who had served A.A. well and had gone on to lead his own congregation to renowned success. A blip on the screen of A.A.'s magnificent history was erased, or so everyone thought. That is, until it was found out that Rabbi Stein was misusing his discretionary fund for personal reasons. To the shock of the entire community, he was fired, his contract bought out, and an agreement of silence worked out with the attorneys. As far as most members who were not on the board at the time knew, "things did not work out between A.A. and Rabbi Stein," but this public reason never made sense to the majority of the members. Though membership continued to decline, a strong group of lay leaders held A.A. together, and more than a year later, Asher Soforno accepted the position, knowing that his first job was to restore confidence and trust in the position of rabbi. Now in his third year at A.A., he thought he had succeeded. Until this morning.

"May I see the check?" Asher asked. "Of course," said Joe, "but just the back. The donor wants to remain anonymous." Asher looked at the cashed check with his signature, and though it had been cashed several months earlier, he instantly knew what had happened.

"Did you or Bill bother to check the number on the account? Don't answer. I know you didn't. Here is my discretionary account checkbook. Compare the numbers. You will find they are the same."

Joe Klein said he did not want to look, but Rabbi Soforno insisted. The numbers were identical. "Why did you sign the check, Asher? Why didn't you use your discretionary fund stamp?"

"At the end of last year, if you recall, I asked the board if I could switch my discretionary to my personal bank. First, it would be easier for me. Second, the shul's bank was charging us for each check. My bank was willing to give us free checking. You all agreed. This check was deposited before my new stamp was ready. I have been trying to acknowledge these gifts on a regular basis so that congregants feel their donations are appreciated and being used. I had to sign the check in order for it to be deposited."

Joe was clearly embarrassed. "I am sorry, Asher. You know this is not personal. I was just acting in my role as president. I have to protect the shul."

"I know, Joe. I know. But after two years of being here, and proving myself trustworthy, I thought you might have given me · the benefit of the doubt."

On the surface, this is a case of mistaken assumptions that get cleared up by one person going to another and receiving a logical explanation. Much lives beneath this surface, however. What lives on is the past history of violation that the congregation experienced in its relations with its most recent rabbi. That trauma left a wound in the congregation that left congregants longing for what was good in the past, both real and imagined, while mistrusting the future. Worse, it left the congregation unable to see the present for what it is and their current rabbi for whom he is. The wound blinded the congregation. It left the congregation stuck in the past, still trying to protect itself from a threat that was no longer there. What Rabbi Soforno found out that morning was that organizational traumas, like personal ones, can heal, but they heal very slowly. At the slightest provocation, the wound is likely to reopen, revealing all the pain that was there in the first place. Though he had done "everything right" since coming to Agudath Achim, the congregation's communal sense of betrayal hindered their ability to trust their new rabbi.

We can look a bit deeper and see a longer chain of events that led to the congregation's myopia and to Rabbi Soforno's distress. Agudath Achim was traumatized by the failed succession of their long-standing, beloved rabbi. After all, they had engaged in an extensive national search, "done their homework" on their candidates, and welcomed the chosen Rabbi Miller extensively through home-based coffees and a meaningful installation service in which their now rabbi emeritus even participated. However, when it was clear that the "new rabbi was just not going to work out," they tried to compensate for their failed rabbinic succession (and the guilt and discomfort they all felt) by moving quickly to engage another rabbi, who was different from the first successor—someone they already knew. Whether they said it aloud or not, they blamed Rabbi Miller for his failure to work out. Bringing in someone different was the solution. It had to be. But it was not.

In the congregation's collective mind, whether it was spoken or not, Rabbi Stein, already a familiar face, was going to rescue them. His arrival would heal the wound, still unacknowledged and unspoken of in the congregation, of the earlier failure. They would just move on. Those who wanted some kind of public forum to discuss keeping Rabbi Miller were largely ignored. The second search committee was a small group of hand-picked veterans who all loved A.A. and could be trusted. Rabbi Stein's return to the congregation was announced before this could be turned into a nasty, drawn-out conflict. The one hundred families that left the congregation were dismissed as people who were not really loyal anyway.

We are not saying that Rabbi Stein's misuse of his discretionary funds was excusable, or that the responsibility for such an act does not lie squarely on his shoulders. He did betray the community's trust. His was a boundary violation, perpetrated by him, the kind of act that deservedly results in termination of a contract. What we are saying, however, is that the congregational leadership's refusal to deal with the first trauma created a situation in which they silently colluded with Rabbi Stein to ignore his behavior for fear that they may have chosen inappropriately—for fear of a second failure. Why had no one ever audited his fund? Why did no one notice that he was undergoing financial problems? Why did no one question his lavish spending, even after his divorce?

The result for Agudath Achim was a silent decision on the part of the lay leadership—which modeled behavior for other staff as well—not to trust their rabbi, whoever he or she happened to be. Whether consciously or not, A.A. created and institutionalized structures that separated the rabbi from the power centers of the synagogue. The congregation's leaders and members were ready to pounce at the first sign of any misconduct, real or imagined, that they perceived. Their distrust can be understood as an outdated holdover from their earlier experience of being betrayed. Their watchfulness might even be understood as a once useful defense against not being taken advantage of. But, like an antibody that lives on in a human system after the passing of a virus, the distrust remained, lying in wait for an opportunity to emerge.

We can imagine several paths that the story of A.A. and its rabbi might follow. One path is the one that the congregation is already traveling. The congregation and its leaders can maintain its belief in the corruption of rabbis. They can hold themselves at some remove from their current rabbi, looking suspiciously for evidence to confirm that he is taking advantage of them. They can, finally, drive him away or create the conditions under which he will turn away from them in one fashion or another. This will confirm their belief that no rabbi is good enough to remain with them; perhaps, too, it will confirm their unconscious fears that they are not good enough to hold a rabbi. They are also left with some very familiar emotions: sadness and longing, anger and frustration, betrayal and mistrust. These emotions can remain under the surface for a very long time. They can continue to drive the unhealthy processes that led them to mistreat Rabbi Soforno and all those who would temporarily succeed him.

The other path, of course, is to excavate those emotions and that which created them initially and make the very real distinctions between the past and the present. This is the healthy—and often more difficult—

response to congregational trauma. There are, of course, certain barriers to such responses. We can understand a great deal about these barriers by exploring in more depth the unhealthy responses that we have seen and what gives rise to and maintains them in congregational life.

Unhealthy Responses to Congregational Trauma

Unhealthy responses to congregational trauma come in particular forms. First, people may deny that a difficult event—a leader caught giving contracts for synagogue services to friends, the rabbi having an affair with the cantor, the executive director stealing synagogue funds—ever happened. They may be simply pretending this is so, in the hope that the event does not occur again, or if it does, that it will not become widely known or lead to outcomes that are too bad. They may convince themselves that, indeed, the event did not really happen, which crosses over into the more insidious territory of denial. Or they may shrug it off, rationalizing that such things occur in all synagogues. Second, leaders may move quickly to get rid of a problem. This often means getting rid of individuals, such as the firing of a staff member who argued publicly with a powerful board member. Third, people may scapegoat individuals who become associated with a difficult event in the life of a congregation. For instance, the remaining members of a congregation that split apart—the "breakaway" congregation had wanted to remain a smaller worship community—blame their cantor for the split for not creating a more intimate atmosphere during services, to the point that she, too, is finally driven away. Fourth, congregants split into warring cliques, using weapons of gossip and rumor or the abuse of power to cause pain in a series of "we/they" clashes. Such conflicts may be waged as distractions. To the extent that people are angry at one another, they are less likely to focus on painful events in their synagogues, such as the dwindling number of new members or the debilitating illness of its longtime rabbi.

These strategies have a great deal in common. Each is a study in avoidance. In each, people avoid looking closely at events to see what they mean. When we deny that an event happened or pretend that it didn't, get rid of those who seem to be the "problem," scapegoat individuals, or pick fights with others, we do not allow ourselves to look at the events that gave rise to our reactions. We act without reflection. We avoid the opportunity to learn from and about difficult events in our congregations. This, of course, makes it just as likely that similar events will reoccur. Like an ill-equipped physician, we may have treated symptoms, but we have done nothing about inspecting the underlying "disease" in a congregation that triggered those symptoms. Indeed, by turning away from a more complete examination of the congregation, we turn a deaf ear toward synagogue members who through their behaviors may quite unwittingly be issuing calls to help fix the synagogue itself.

Avoidance is aided and abetted by people creating and telling simple stories about complicated events and dynamics. A rabbi fails. Rather than examining all that might have gone into that failure—a lack of support from lay leaders, a board president who disliked the rabbi, deep disagreements among congregants about the synagogue mission and vision that attracted the rabbi initially, and unresolved issues surrounding the abrupt retirement of the previous rabbi—the lay leaders tell themselves and others a simple story. The rabbi was not a good manager. Or the rabbi could not inspire the congregation. Or the rabbi had personal problems that kept him from working well with the board president. Such stories take a complex person and reduce him to a single concept. They take a complex set of relationships among lay leaders and clergy and staff and congregants, and reduce them to a single person's failure. The painful event—the hiring and firing of a rabbi—is reduced to a simple package, neatly wrapped and tied and placed on a darkened shelf. The congregation leaves it there as it moves into the search for a successor, a savior. The discarded rabbi is sacrificed, a casualty in the congregation's battle to avoid looking more carefully at itself.

The battle is also to avoid the painful emotions unleashed by traumatic episodes. A rabbi's failure triggers shame, anger, sadness, and loss. A lay leader's misappropriation of funds triggers rage and betrayal. A staff member's emotional breakdown triggers guilt and anxiety. A "breakaway" congregation triggers loss and abandonment. Such emotions are appropriate responses to difficult situations. Various parts of a congregation will contain certain of those emotions, given that it is difficult for individuals to hang on to all feelings at the same time. Board members may feel the most guilt about a rabbi's failure; older congregants may feel the most resentment; newer members may feel the most betrayed; staff members may feel the most sadness. These emotions get parceled out, as it were, to the various groups, just as in a marriage when it appears one parent is angry and the other sad about a slight to their child, even though both parents feel both things. When congregations avoid exploring these emotions, when they provide no forum to let people speak of their various experiences and reactions, people are stuck with the emotions. They remain lodged within, taking up space and preventing more complex ways of thinking and acting.

We are suggesting here that congregations have emotional lives of their own apart from those of their individual members. Congregations have collective emotional experiences. They can be collectively moved and uplifted by a sermon or a melody, inspired by the performance of a children's play, haunted by a Holocaust survivor's story told during the Yom Kippur service. And too, they can be collectively enraged by a leader stealing funds, pained by the sudden firing of a beloved staff member, guilty about driving away a new cantor by having elected a board president known for his inability to work effectively with clergy. Such emotions, positive and negative alike, course through a congregation, resting differently in different people and groups but residing in the whole itself.

In the aftermath of painful episodes, emotions require direct expression. They need to be honored, talked about in a way that shows they matter, until people understand what they mean. If there is no place for this, people bury their emotions. They disconnect them from the traumas that get forgotten or remembered in ways that may seem curiously dispassionate. But trauma-induced emotions cannot be buried deeply enough. Like toxic waste, they seep out. People unconsciously bootleg them into their current experiences, just as in our case study when the lay leaders instinctively mistrusted and felt betrayed by their current rabbi even before they knew the facts. These kinds of emotions are expressed at the slightest evocation of the earlier trauma, as if they are on tap waiting to be unleashed, which they are and will continue to be until the original traumas are excavated and worked with in their proper context. Until that happens, the emotions take up a great deal of space in people's internal lives. The emotions and the events that spawned them are outsized, not yet placed in proper perspective. They lay pooled beneath the surface of people's interactions and seep out everywhere.

Why does this occur? Simply put, people do not like to deal with painful emotions. We do not like the anxiety associated with digging into painful situations. We do not like telling stories that might implicate ourselves in situations that went badly and caused pain to others and ourselves. We would rather push painful events and feelings away, be done with them, make them disappear. We do this as individuals, and we do this collectively in congregations. It is in exactly this process that our congregations often become stuck. They are unable to develop as they might. They remain mired in unhealthy patterns of thought and behavior.

Stuckness

Ultimately, the enduring legacy of unhealthy responses to congregational trauma is what we call "stuckness." Congregations get stuck in various ways. They repeat some patterns over and again. We are reminded here of the time that we at Eitzah were called by the chair of a rabbinic search committee. The synagogue was looking for its fourth rabbi in ten years. New to the synagogue and new to the process, she intuitively sensed that something was wrong within the congregation itself; there was something they were not doing right. After hearing that these failed successions began after a long and illustrious career of their founding rabbi, we agreed with her conclusion and set forth an outline of what we would do to help the congregation move forward. Backed by the temple president, the search committee refused our plan, citing their history of "bad luck" in picking a new rabbi. That congregation is likely to continue to repeat its "bad luck" until some sort of intervention enables congregants to consider both their own culpability in enabling rabbis to fail and their underlying feelings of longing and anger that fuel such a destructive process.

Congregational stuckness may also occur in the form of paralysis. People are unable to make important decisions, move programs ahead, hire new staff, or make necessary changes for fear of somehow bringing up a painful past or bringing on another painful episode in the life of the congregation. A congregation that experienced a severe loss of members during the move to a new building years earlier, for example, somehow cannot bring itself to address questions about space that are becoming increasingly pressing as the congregation again grows. Or a congregation that experienced a very public falling out between its rabbi and cantor several years earlier is unable to move ahead on the decision about whether to bring in a new cantor, in spite of the growing need to prepare a large group of students for their bar and bat mitzvahs. In such cases, congregations are unable to move, frozen at the scenes of earlier crimes that they can neither fully address nor freely ignore. They are stuck in limbo.

Other signs of stuckness are worth noting. Congregations have too much conflict. People are always arguing. They make decisions based on whose voices are loudest. People take sides, passing petitions, taking votes when none are required. Decisions are always contentious. There is simply too much emotion attached to reasonably ordinary events. These congregations are stuck in cultures of distrust, fueled by a sense of anger and betrayal rooted in some painful experience in the life of the congregation, the details of which may or may not even be recalled by current members. Alternatively, congregations may have too little conflict. People withhold their ideas and energies. They do not explore differences in constructive ways. They give of themselves in limited ways and passively accept what their leadership decides. Congregants attach too little emotion to their experiences. These congregations, too, are stuck in cultures of passivity, fueled by a sense that congregant voices matter little in the life of the institution. This sense also has its roots in some earlier time, some event or series of events that left a residue of passivity and withdrawal.

When congregations are stuck in such ways, their natural evolutions are halted. Like people who have experienced real trauma at some point in their lives and, untreated, are condemned to remain developmentally frozen at those points, congregations, too, can remain developmentally stuck. They can spin their wheels or drive in circles, coming up against the same issues, failing to resolve them in ways that enable them to learn about themselves as congregations. With such insight, congregations can relegate the past to the past and let the present be different. When congregations are stuck, earlier traumatic episodes remain front and center in the institutions' lives, even as those episodes are denied, avoided, repressed, and seemingly forgotten.

Unacknowledged trauma means that people cannot fully mourn. Trauma brings loss: of basic trust, of attachments, of identity, of relationships. Loss must be grieved. Just as when we lose a loved one, explicit grieving allows us our full range of expressions in relation to that which we lost. We come to terms with that loss, placing it within some appropriate context, and can move on. At that point, the story becomes another memory, one without the capacity to cause so much pain so that congregants move from a collective identity as victims. When grief remains incomplete, the trauma continues to attract energy. People cannot move away from it: they are held there by a sense of incompleteness, of something unfinished. Unresolved or incomplete mourning traps people in the traumatic process. Congregations are unable or unwilling to let go of that which wounded them. They cannot move from that place to another.

Principles of Movement

Our congregations do not need to remain stuck. They can move on from painful episodes or patterns and create increasingly healthy, effective cultures. We describe three principles that can help congregations move in healthy ways when traumas have occurred. These principles are rooted in organizational psychology—in particular, the works of Ken Smith and David Berg, authors of *The Paradoxes of Group Life,* and one of us, Bill Kahn's *Holding Fast: The Creation of Resilient Caregiving Systems.*[1] These principles also parallel those that Judith Herman, in her book *Trauma and Recovery,* describes as vital to an individual's recovery from trauma.[2]

Move toward Anxiety

The first principle suggests the importance of people confronting difficult events and the anxiety associated with them. People need to tell the story of the trauma. They need to talk about what happened. This process, done well, has several components. First, leaders and members come together to construct a complex rather than simple narrative. Complex narratives allow for many people's experiences and perspectives to coexist. They also allow for many different people, rather than a single, simple scapegoat, to take appropriate responsibility for painful episodes. Second, the narratives contain both facts and emotions. Facts allow the story to emerge. Expressing emotions releases people from burdens they carry surrounding painful events. Third, narratives are told, over and again, until they become familiar and less powerful, until they assume an appropriate rather than outsized space in the emotional life of the congregation. Repeated enough, any story, regardless of how terrifying, becomes routine, even boring. It can then be *integrated into* rather than *dominate* people's lives.

When these conditions are met—complex narratives containing both facts and emotions are constructed, told, and retold—painful events in the life of a congregation assume proportionate rather than disproportionate places. People can have difficult conversations with one another and address issues that make them anxious. They can cut through what trauma researchers refer to as the "conspiracy of silence," a dynamic where "no talk" rules impede people from speaking of their trauma to others and cause them to redirect, shutdown, minimize, or neglect traumatic material. It is unhealthy for a synagogue to try and keep a painful event— the termination of a beloved staff member, the embezzlement of funds— secret. There is, of course, the importance of protecting people's privacy and reputations. And a congregation does not need to know all the specifics of a situation. Yet there must be a forum that enables public and honest conversations about what happened. People will talk anyway. It is best that they do so publicly and that there is an official response that is truly representative of what occurred. It is difficult to heal if no one knows what it is they are supposed to be healing from.

We understand that approaching difficult issues provokes anxiety. People would rather hope that a painful situation would resolve itself or go away. Hope, however, is not a useful strategy when it comes to dealing effectively with painful episodes in the life of a congregation. Openness and acknowledgment are; so too are public conversations that enable people to discharge what they are carrying. People wounded need to remove the bits of shrapnel embedded in them by explosions falling around them. There is often much collateral damage when traumatic moments occur in our synagogues. As much as it makes us anxious to inspect those moments as truthfully as we can, it is only by doing so that the damage is fixed and our congregations are healed.

Move toward One Another

The second principle suggests the importance of people coming together in the face of congregational trauma. This is intuitive and is embedded in our first principle as well, but it is more difficult than it sounds. The fallout of congregational trauma, often enough, is the fragmentation of the congregation itself. Inevitably, people take sides after a difficult event. Some people support and others blame an embattled lay leader forced to resign from a board after an impropriety. Some people are in favor and others are against supporting the new "breakaway" *havurah* that arises when the synagogue grows too large for some members. Some people defend and others attack the board president after she leads the board in making the difficult decision not to renew the contract of a cantor for financial reasons. People take sides on issues, and inevitably, against one another.

This fragmentation occurs along several dimensions. First, the story itself becomes fragmented. When people take sides, it makes it difficult for them to join together to tell complex stories about traumatic events. As long as people choose to be just for or against something or someone, they can never delve more deeply into events and issues. They simplify complex situations into win/lose, right/wrong, we/they. They find lightning rods—the embattled lay leader, the *havurah*, the board president— that attract their heat and energy, and thus never look more closely at what lies beneath them, the houses (the synagogues) that those rods protect. This means that different people in the congregation are holding on to different pieces of the story of what happened. Each believes that they know the whole story, like someone with a piece of a jigsaw puzzle who believes that piece is the whole picture. It is only when individuals move toward one another, each bearing his or her piece, and join together in a process of puzzle making that larger pictures of events emerge.

Second, the emotional fallout of painful events often becomes fragmented as well. People not only simplify the stories they tell about difficult events, but they simplify their emotional responses as well. A failed succession of a long-standing rabbi generates different emotions—sadness, frustration, anger, longing, hope, despair, guilt, shame. It is difficult for individuals to hang on to all of those emotions at the same time. In an unconscious process—what psychologists refer to as *projective identification*—people in a congregation select, on the basis of their own individual biases and tendencies, particular emotions to hang on to. Others select other emotions. All of the emotional reactions to a traumatic event exist, but they are parceled out to different members. This presents some difficulty, as individuals have emotional reactions to traumatic events that, like the different stories that they tell about those events, are not easily reconciled with one another. Often each person believes that his or her emotion is the only reasonable response to the event, discounting the experiences of others.

As long as a congregation maintains such fragmentation of stories and emotions, people will remain mired in trauma and its aftermath. Movement requires people to join together for insight, understanding, and support. The problem, however, is that trauma disrupts people's relations with others. When a congregation is traumatized, people's sense of basic trust is violated. The congregation fractures, and cannot, as a whole system, absorb the traumatic experience and integrate its different dimensions. This makes healing difficult. Groups have more capacity to bear and integrate traumatic experience than do individuals; as Jews, we know this from our experiences of sitting *shivah*. Unless congregations find ways to bring people together—in small groups, retreats, community town hall meetings, and the like—for the explicit purpose of helping people tell nuanced, complex stories about difficult events and open themselves up to the full range of emotional reactions to those events, the congregation cannot move from the place at which it was stuck.

Move toward Reparation

Our third principle focuses on reparation—the act or process of repairing, of making amends, of expiation. Ideally, synagogue leaders convene people, in various forums, in the aftermaths of painful institutional events. They help facilitate people's reflections on events—what happened, what those events mean, how people felt, and what ought to occur to repair that which has been damaged. In working through trauma, the role of the leader is as a trustworthy, secure base on whom others can rely. The leader listens to, absorbs, digests, and reacts respectfully to others' experiences. In so doing, he or she models a way for others to speak of their own experiences, listen carefully to one another, and join with others to make sense of difficult, complex, and painful events.

This process is complicated, however, by the fact that it is often synagogue leaders—board members, rabbis and cantors, and senior staff members—who are greatly impacted by traumatic episodes. They are closest to the major decisions such as hiring and firing, contract negotiations, financial improprieties, and program closings, whose outcomes have the potential to deeply disturb congregations. They are themselves likely to be lightning rods, attracting powerful projections and emotions. And they are likely to be filled up with various emotions, such as anger or guilt, that make it more difficult for them to help others look closely at and work through traumatic episodes. It will be more difficult for them to help excavate and bear witness to that which troubles the congregation, even as others look to them to do exactly that.

We see three general sorts of solutions to this problem. First, it is likely that at any point in time, not all synagogue leaders will be unable to help the congregation. While some, closest to the center of whatever storms have blown in, will be troubled and distracted, others who are less personally impacted are relatively available. For example, a successful movement by a disaffected parent group to get rid of the new director of education caused much pain in the staff, leaving the associate rabbi who supervised that person upset and reeling. However, there were other senior staff members and lay leaders who were less involved in that process who stepped in and began to help people tell their stories, share their emotions, examine their experiences, and make sense together of what occurred. The leaders of a congregation (including past presidents) are a leadership group, not simply a group of leaders; it is the group itself that bears the responsibility, and the capacity, to help a congregation move through and past difficult episodes. At any point in time, ideally, members of that group who are best able will step up to that responsibility.

Second, congregations have informal as well as formal leaders who can provide help. The ability to help people reflect on difficult events and come to some collective understanding is not limited simply to the professional staff or to elected lay leaders. People throughout the congregation may be able and willing to help. A relatively new synagogue member becomes increasingly aware of the tension among members of the finance committee that he recently joined. He asks the committee about the tension. With the skillful use of questions, he helps the group piece together the story of a financial impropriety by a former chair, something the committee had never spoken of openly with one another. Members were, finally, able to share their sense of anger and betrayal and their guilt and shame about what had occurred. They were able to begin to work together again with some sense of trust. The newer member led that process simply by authorizing himself to address tensions and ask questions. This sort of capacity exists throughout congregations and simply needs to be tapped and allowed to emerge.

Third, congregations can engage outsiders, such as consultants, organizational psychologists, and specialists in congregational life, to provide some help. Outsiders have the advantage of not being caught up in the history of events, emotions, and conflicts that often render synagogue leaders and members unable to create useful conversations and help one another move through difficult episodes. Consultants can provide perspectives that free people from the simplified ways in which we understand complex, difficult events. Like good therapists, they can help people work through traumatic moments in the life of a congregation. This involves creating safe places for synagogue staff, leaders, and congregants to look at what occurred, how they felt about it, and the ramifications. Good consultants help people put together jigsaw puzzles while helping them manage the anxiety of doing so without knowing quite what the picture is supposed to look like. Good consultants create ongoing relationships in which this work may occur, knowing that it is the congregations, not they themselves, who must be empowered to do much of that work on their own.

Each of these moves toward leadership is in the spirit of enabling collective reflection, insight, emotional expression, and relief—the primary ingredients of that which enables congregations to move toward reparation. We think of this as we think of the High Holy Days, the *Yamim Nora'im,* a time of penitence and prayer that begins with Rosh Hashanah and ends with Yom Kippur. The process of *t'shuvah*—literally, "turning," though often translated as "repentance"—requires Jews to take the steps necessary to repair that which is broken, in ourselves or with others, so as to enter the new year renewed. *T'shuvah* is, indeed, a returning. Our sages assure us that *t'shuvah,* real personal returning, results in divine forgiveness. By spending the month of Elul in introspection, searching our souls for our past mistakes, we prepare for the Days of Awe. For almost a thousand years this self-examination was done publicly in the synagogue. Jews stand and ritually go through the act of confessing mistakes and transgressions and openly ask for forgiveness.

We believe that this offers a useful template. Synagogue leaders can help congregations move toward *t'shuvah*. They can help their congregations return. They can help them move not simply toward divine forgiveness, but toward the forgiveness of themselves and of others for past wounds to their congregation as a whole. They can help them search their souls, not only privately, but also publicly. Our ancestors understood the power of self-examination done publicly. There is a cleansing that must be undergone to which people must be led. Without that cleansing, there can be no reparation. And without reparation, our congregations cannot return to wholeness.

Resilient Congregations

Traumatic moments occur in congregations. While healthy congregations can do much to prevent those moments by creating strong, clear, and vibrant relationships among and between professional staff, lay leaders, and congregants, they cannot guarantee that such moments will not occur. The question is how resilient any congregation is when those moments do occur. Healthy congregations bend but do not break in the face of difficult moments. They absorb the pain of traumatic episodes and, rather than becoming crippled by that pain, find ways to release it and understand its meanings. They repair themselves.

Congregations can repair themselves, however, only when people believe or imagine that repair is possible. Traumatic events may shake the foundations of such belief. People may be so wounded that they have misplaced hope. Synagogues, like families, are places where wounds can be deep. Families are the best places in the world to grow up and at times the most dangerous places; they have the potential to be filled with love and nurturing that allow us to become whole and find our ways in the world. But they can also be places of abuse and pain, diminishing and wounding us for life. In this regard, synagogues are a lot like families. They represent one of our greatest opportunities for Jewish growth and identity and at the same time can cause us untold pain and shame. The synagogue is the place to which we go to wrap ourselves in the *tallit* of our fathers and mothers, our grandfathers and grandmothers; it is the place to which we bring deep questions and yearnings and fears; it is the place to which we go when we need a deeper sense of home, of community, of belonging to a people; it is the primary place where we understand God to dwell. When we feel violated there, we feel the loss of these things. We can no longer trust the place that we most need to trust.

In resilient congregations, people strive together to restore that basic sense of trust. This process is aided by wise, caring leaders and people from throughout the congregation able to find enough courage to look squarely at difficult, painful events and help others do similarly. People having certain shared beliefs also aid the restoring of trust in the synagogue immeasurably. One belief is that people can best find shelter and strength in their relations with one another. Resilient congregations believe, and thus enact, the idea that resilience is created and found in the space between people, in the relationships they create and maintain. A second belief is in the importance of emotional expression. In resilient congregations, people tell one another when they are upset or saddened by a certain event; they express their joy to one another; they move toward rather than withdraw from or erect barriers against one another. A third belief is that congregational life is manageable, comprehensible, and meaningful, and that adversity can be overcome. In resilient congregations, people believe that they can survive and learn from whatever they discover in the course of examining and solving problems. The belief leads to the reality: members assume that they can handle adversity, make it manageable, and it becomes so.

Armed with these beliefs, congregations can approach painful events and work with them—what they were, what caused them, their repercussions—with grace and dignity. They can move into and through them without getting stuck in unhealthy patterns that create casualties, leave people wounded, and fracture the synagogue. They can find the courage necessary to do that which we, as Jews, are urged to do each year, *t'shuvah*. Our congregations deserve to be inscribed in the Book of Life. We have some power over this. Our congregations may be stuck, people preoccupied with past events that left emotional residues, relationships in disrepair, and convoluted organizational structures that hint at distrust. These things may be written but not sealed. We can repair them. We can tell our stories. We can speak of the emotions deposited within us. We can join together and figure out what we have done, all of us, as congregations, and what that meant for who we were and means for who we are to become. With the help of one another, our leaders, and God, the source of strength, who blessed the ones before us, we can find the courage to make our lives and our synagogues a blessing. And to this, let us say: Amen.

Notes

1. Ken Smith and David Berg, *Paradoxes of Group Life: Understanding Conflict, Paralysis, and Movement in Group Dynamics* (San Francisco: Jossey-Bass, 1987); William Kahn, *Holding Fast: The Struggle to Create Resilient Caregiving Organizations* (New York: Brunner-Routledge, 2005.

2. Judith Herman, *Trauma and Recovery: The Aftermath of Violence—from Domestic Abuse to Political Terror* (New York: Basic Books: 1992).

Afterword

Staying the Course

You alone have I singled out from all the families of the earth.
That is why I call you to account for your failures and iniquities.
(Amos 3:2)

The Israelites, singled out by God, allowing themselves to choose and be chosen, set out on a certain course. They were walking to the promised land, indeed, but more pointedly, they were journeying toward a certain relationship with God and with one another. It is a journey that Jews continue today. We move along the course first pointed out by our ancestors. We have many choices about how we get there—how we approach Torah, prayer, worship, and the repairing of the world. As the world around us changes, our choices shift as well. We do our best to stay the course, to continue the journey that began with the first, tentative steps toward freedom and responsibility. For many of us, that journey occurs within the context of the synagogue.

Throughout this book we have suggested the ways in which synagogues, and those who dwell within them, fall into unhealthy patterns of thought and action. These patterns exist; people and their institutions are mired in them more often than not. Indeed, we can imagine that God presumes no less. In calling for an accounting of our failures and iniquities, God presses us to look clearly at who we are and what we have done. He does so in a spirit of love, not punishment. God chose the Israelites. The Holy One wished for them—for us—success, not failure. Success can come only from looking closely at ourselves. It is only by accounting for our actions that we can learn about and from them and grow more effective. It is only by accounting for our synagogues that we can understand what we have created and how they can better serve those who work and worship within them.

We believe that there will always be obstacles to creating and maintaining vibrant, healthy synagogues. Communities change, leaders get lost or misplace their missions, lay leaders lose sight of their tasks and

roles, clergy get burned out or distracted, finances get shaky, politics overwhelm cooperation, staffing issues rise and swell, congregations suffer
loss. Such is the nature of synagogue life. There will always be tests of our
resolve and our abilities to remain healthy in our responses. It is not a
question of whether any particular synagogue will face such tests, but of
how we as synagogue leaders and members handle them. Do we struggle
well? Do we bend but not break under the weight of the obstacles? Does
our community split and fragment, or does it join together and hold
even as we differ and struggle?

Our concern here is with resilience. Resilient synagogues are those
whose members and leaders struggle well with the difficulties that inevitably arise as they change and grow. The life cycle of any system—an
individual, a marriage, a relationship, a group, an organization—requires
change and growth, plateaus and decline, ebbs and flows, peace and dissension. Synagogues are the same. As the demographics of the Jewish
people change, as the national and cultural communities in which they
live are shaped by events large and small, as new leaders replace old, the
purposes and meanings of synagogues will change for those who seek
them out. They will also remain much the same, rooted in the familiar
and comforting traditions of the Jewish people. The tension between the
pulls for change and those for stasis define the life cycle of the synagogue;
how their members and leaders engage that cycle defines their collective
health.

An/Other

Implicit throughout much of this book is our belief in the value of partnership—between Jews and God, of course, and between lay leaders,
clergy, staff, and congregants. All of these groups have roles to play in the
life of the synagogue; all are crucial. Just as crucial are the relations between these groups. It is the extent to which they assume responsibility,
separately and together, that most powerfully shapes the creation of a
synagogue community in which members, leaders, and staff want very
much to dwell.

Partnership is an idea that is easy to say and quite difficult to practice. Any number of things pose a threat to real partnership. Consider
this story. Right before the grand *vidui* (confessional) on Yom Kippur,

the rabbi jumps up from his seat, prostrates himself in front of the ark, and cries out, "*Ribbono Shel Olam,* Master of the universe, have mercy on this sinner for I am but dust and ashes, I am nothing before You." Moved by the rabbi's heartfelt outburst, the cantor kneels down next to him and cries out, "Holy One of the universe, *Ba'al haRachamim,* have compassion on this sinner for I am but dust and ashes; I am nothing before You." So moved by her two religious leaders, the president of the congregation jumps up from her seat, kneels next to the two of them, crying out, *"El Adon,* God on high, look down kindly on this sinner for I am but dust and ashes; I am nothing before You." Just then the cantor pokes the rabbi and whispers, "Look who thinks she is nothing!"

We like this story. It is not only funny but reveals something important about the difficulty of creating real partnership in synagogues. The problem is that people so often create barriers between themselves and others; they make them "other" in some important way. Partnership occurs when people expand the sense of the "we." They erase the lines that divide them from others and move closer; indeed, they move from "an/ other" to "another." When people in synagogues make this shift, they expand the boundaries of the "we." They release others from the boxes in which they had placed them—the categories and labels that had simplified and reduced them to something "other" than an ally in the synagogue community. The funny part of the story is how hard it is for people to remember that we are all equally "nothing" in our relations to God; and in that nothingness, we are all equally something in our relations with one another and our contributions to our synagogues.

As is apparent throughout this book, the notion of partnership between the lay leaders and clergy is particularly crucial because that is where much of the work in synagogues is located and performed. We have written much about the need for that partnership to be balanced in terms of shared responsibility for particular dimensions of leading the synagogue. The foundation for that balance is a real clarity about who does what, where authority and decision making are located, and what boundaries delineate how people work separately and together on behalf of the synagogue.

Achieving this balance may, for some synagogues, involve redressing imbalances. Lay leaders, for example, wield most of the influence in some synagogues. Such synagogues may have formed without rabbis, and

congregants grew used to making decisions and doing everything themselves. Or they may have had several difficult relationships with clergy
members that led to distrusting them. In such synagogues, creating a
reasonable balance means learning to include and trust rabbis and cantors, involve them in appropriate ways in decision making, and create
systems and processes that enable professional staff to do the work that
traditionally depended on particular congregants and their idiosyncratic
relationships. In other synagogues, the imbalance is the heavy influence
of clergy, with congregants and lay leaders dependent, particularly upon
rabbis, for direction and decisions. Such synagogues may have sprung up
around charismatic rabbis or simply evolved over time to a clergy-cen-
tered culture. A reasonable balance here involves clergy members involving lay leaders and congregants as much as possible; rabbis must act as if
congregants are perfectly competent to handle responsibility and work to
make it so.

Congregations are able to strike these kinds of balances—locating
some middle ground between lay- or clergy-led cultures—when their
leaders recognize the importance of doing so and help others become
mindful of how they lead and partner. Throughout this book we have
emphasized the singular importance of leaders. Rabbis and spiritual leaders, board presidents and executive officers, committee chairs and influential members can all offer leadership. Leadership can occur in different
forms, according to the ebb and flow of synagogue development. Leaders
can, like the patriarch Abraham, offer initial energy that propels the
congregation's journey toward some envisioned place. They can, like Isaac,
offer stable energy that keeps their synagogues securely moving along
productive paths. Or they can, like Rebekah or her son Jacob, provide
expansive energy that drives congregations to push the boundaries past
what they are into what they can become.

Leadership during any of these moments in the life of a congregation
depends on mindfulness about the nature of partnership. Indeed, leadership is not simply a matter of developing and implementing programs,
developing strategy, and supervising others. It is also a matter of helping
people engage one another usefully and productively. Effective leaders,
whether lay or clergy, help people expand their sense of who "we" are,
pointing to and reducing the barriers that people erect among themselves. More to the point, they help us all reflect on and make clear choices

about what kinds of cultures ought to exist in our synagogues. If we are not making such choices and doing so consciously, we are condemned to repeating our histories, over and again, whatever the consequences.

From Here to There

It has been five years since we first conceived of Eitzah. Since that time, we have traveled across the country working with more than a hundred rabbis and synagogue leaders. Time and again we have been impressed with the level of dedication, passion, and hard work that is poured into our nation's synagogues. Volunteers spend countless hours on behalf of their beloved shuls. Idealistic rabbis, cantors, educators, and synagogue professionals devote themselves to the Jewish future by educating and inspiring the Jewish present.

And it works in reverse as well. To paraphrase the great Zionist philosopher Ahad haAm, we are convinced that "more than the Jewish people have kept the synagogue, the synagogue has kept the Jewish people." The synagogue remains the primary portal of Jewish life. More Jews have some connection to the synagogue at some point in their lives than any other Jewish institution or experience. Now more than ever we believe in the necessity of the synagogue. It is in synagogues that Jews are nourished and fed religiously, spiritually, emotionally, and intellectually. It is in the synagogue that we journey toward the promised land and nurture the relationships with God and one another that sustain us on that journey. It is in the synagogue that we join our ancestors in the rituals through which we experience the seasons and cycles of our lives. It is in the synagogue, finally, that we are nourished and sustained as Jews.

At the same time, we are concerned that so few synagogues appear truly healthy. Rabbis and lay leaders are too often ill prepared for the reality of running the complex organization that is the modern synagogue. What makes matters worse is that they, as well as national organizations, are often in denial of this reality, setting aside little time and scant resources to improve or repair the situation. Rabbis are one of the few types of professionals who do not need to continue to learn and grow to recertify their credentials. This is especially shocking in a community that espouses lifelong learning. Though paid better than their Christian counterparts, many rabbis do not invest in themselves, their learning, their personal and spiritual growth, or their self-care. While they attend work-shops and meetings here and there, they have not focused in any system-atic way on strengthening themselves for a long and sustaining career.

We believe that the agenda for the future of synagogues is to develop capacity—of clergy, of lay leaders, and of synagogues as institutions that are productive and marked by collaboration. The notion of capacity is an important one. The word itself, derived from the Latin *capere,* means "to take, hold, and contain." The word has various common usages. It refers to our abilities to take in and "store" others, much like the volume capac-ity of batteries. It refers as well to productive output, the synagogue's capability to serve others. In the spirit of these meanings, we believe that our synagogues and their leaders need to expand their abilities to "take in" and serve others. The extent to which they are able to do so, in the face of changing demographics, cultural norms, and other larger institu-tional forces, will do much to influence the ongoing relevance of the synagogue to Jewish lives.

What does the idea of developing capacities mean in practice? To start, it means building the leadership capacities within synagogues and within communities. Clergy members need to learn many of the ideas we have offered in this book about the nature and practices of organiza-tional leadership, change, and growth. So, too, ought synagogue presi-dents to be certified in some fashion as a precursor for assuming their leadership roles. Synagogue leaders, clergy and lay alike, are not simply born; they may be created and nurtured through training programs that take seriously the idea that synagogues are complex organizations that require—indeed, that deserve—organizational as well as spiritual leader-ship. Creating leadership capacity is also a matter of training lay leaders more generally (executive committee members, board members, com-mittee chairs, and committee members), helping them understand the nature of their roles and the processes by which they exert leadership in the governance structure.

The congregation as a whole has capacities that can be developed as well. We do a disservice to synagogues if we suggest that their lay and professional leaders are wholly responsible for developing healthy con-gregations. Leadership cannot be understood apart from followership. Congregations that know how to follow their leaders—that is, support them with challenge, appreciation, involvement, and thoughtful participation—do much to create healthy communities. Such congregations, like leaders, are not simply born; these, too, are created, when influential members offer healthy models of working with leaders that others pick up and emulate. This does not have to be a hit-or-miss process. Congregants can learn, with a bit of training and a modest amount of dialogue among themselves and with their leaders, about how best to engage in the organizational life of their synagogues. They can create together a model for how to be involved, in ways that allow them to remain engaged while still authorizing their leaders to act on their behalf.

Capacity can be created in the Jewish community more generally, not just within particular synagogues. Much gets lost in the gaps that exist between synagogues and between synagogues and other Jewish institutions. That gap is marked, often enough, by competition, as our organizations rival one another in their attempts to "capture" Jews. They treat one another as enemies to be overcome and vanquished. The real "enemy," however, is disinterest and lack of affiliation. Large percentages of Jews are not identified as practicing their religion in significant ways. Synagogues and other Jewish institutions face real competition, not from one another, but from myriad other activities that beckon Jews. Synagogue leaders from across the denominations will have to work cooperatively to build better, more inclusive, and more inviting communities if they are to stave off the threats posed by these other activities and institutions. They will have to forgo the "go-it-alone" model that has so often dominated synagogue life, and replace it with a determinedly cooperative model. A cooperative ethos among synagogues, with other Jewish institutions, has the benefit of pooling resources and creating larger, more vibrant communities. It also allows us to create places where Jews can be nurtured by one another.

A Final Thought

Synagogues, like Jews, are themselves flawed and gifted, settled and restless, evolving and stuck. They are, in short, communities created by and for humans, who regularly fail and succeed in their efforts to fulfill their covenant with God. That we fail is not particularly interesting, nor is the profile of how we fail. What is interesting is what we *do* as synagogue leaders and members when our congregations are operating less effectively or suffering more than they might. Our hope is that people choose to move toward rather than away from that which troubles them. A Yiddish proverb says that if everyone were to put up their own *tzuris*— their own sorrows—and hang them like sheets on the clothesline, they would inevitably wind up taking back their own linens for themselves. It is an appealing proverb. It suggests to us that each synagogue, like each individual, has a unique set of issues that it must deal with in order to be healthy, and that its growth depends on engaging those issues. This is what we wish for synagogues and those who dwell within them: that we make the struggles of our synagogues our own; that we bring the problems back in; that we cherish the issues that mark our synagogues. For in doing so we come to know what they teach and offer about how to make a synagogue community healthy and holy.